The Kurdish Nationalist Movement

David Romano's book focuses on the Kurdish case to try and make sense of ethnic nationalist resurgence more generally. In a world rent by a growing number of such conflicts, the questions posed about why, how and when such challenges to the state are mounted are becoming increasingly urgent. Throughout, the author analyzes these questions through the lens of social movement theory, considering in particular politico-social structures, resource mobilization strategies, and cultural identity. His conclusions offer some thought-provoking insights into Kurdish nationalism, as well as into the strengths and weaknesses of various social movement theories. While the book offers a rigorous conceptual approach, the empirical material – the result of the author's first-hand experience in the region – makes it a compelling read. It will find a readership not only amongst students of the Middle East, but also amongst those interested in ethnic relations, minority rights, terrorism, state repression, social movement theories, and many other related issues.

DAVID ROMANO is Senior Fellow Researcher at the Inter-University Consortium for Arab and Middle East Studies (ICAMES), Montreal, Canada. His research focuses on nationalism and transnational social movements, especially in the Middle East.

D0879706

Cambridge Middle East Studies 22

Cambridge Middle East Studies has been established to publish books on the modern Middle East and North Africa. The aim of the series is to provide new and original interpretations of aspects of Middle Eastern societies and their histories. To achieve disciplinary diversity, books will be solicited from authors writing in a wide range of fields including history, sociology, anthropology, political science, and political economy. The emphasis will be on producing books offering an original approach along theoretical and empirical lines. The series is intended for students and academics, but the more accessible and wide-ranging studies will also appeal to the interested general reader.

A list of books in the series can be found after the index.

The Kurdish Nationalist Movement

Opportunity, Mobilization, and Identity

David Romano

*Inter-University Consortium for Arab and Middle East Studies,
Montreal, Canada*

CAMBRIDGE
UNIVERSITY PRESS

CAMBRIDGE UNIVERSITY PRESS
Cambridge, New York, Melbourne, Madrid, Cape Town, Singapore, São Paulo

CAMBRIDGE UNIVERSITY PRESS
The Edinburgh Building, Cambridge CB2 2RU, UK

Published in the United States of America by Cambridge University Press,
New York

www.cambridge.org
Information on this title: www.cambridge.org/9780521684262

First published 2006

Printed in the United Kingdom at the University Press, Cambridge

A catalogue record for this book is available from the British Library

ISBN-13 978-0-521-85041-4 hardback
ISBN-10 0-521-85041-X hardback
ISBN-13 978-0-521-68426-2 paperback
ISBN-10 0-521-68426-9 paperback

To my mother, naturally.

Contents

Acknowledgments

I would like to gratefully acknowledge the sources of financial support for my doctoral studies, which form the basis of this book: Quebec's *Fonds pour la Formation de Chercheurs et l'Aide à la Recherche*, the Canadian Department of National Defence *Security and Defense Forum Doctoral Scholarship*, and the University of Toronto's Department of Political Science and School of Graduate Studies.

Professor Richard Sandbrook supervised my doctoral studies with diligence, enthusiasm, and a congeniality that always made me look forward to my talks with him. One could not ask for more from a supervisor, and I hope other doctoral students will be as fortunate as I was in this respect. Professor Amir Hassanpour also assisted me in ways too numerous to mention (loaning me money for airfare to Teheran was just one of the many examples of his humanity and generosity). His considerable scholarship on the Kurds, nationalism, and language remain an inspiration to me. Additionally, Professor Paul Kingston provided enthusiastic support for my work, giving much needed suggestions for improving the dissertation. His sense of humor and cheerful disposition greatly added to the welcome I felt at the University of Toronto.

Earlier academic influences on me also deserve thanks, particularly professors Rex Brynen and Philip Oxhorn at McGill University. Rex first cultivated my interest in political science enough for me to pursue graduate studies in the subject, and Philip directed that interest towards the social movement theories that became so central to my research.

During the preparation of my doctoral thesis and its subsequent revision into a book, Hadi Elis frequently shared with me his considerable views on the Kurdish issue, as well as articles and other sources on the subject that he has collected over the years. Indeed, if any published source mentions the Kurds in English, Turkish, Kurdish, or even some other language, Hadi is likely to have a copy in his personal library. His help was invaluable and his friendship much appreciated. I am also very much indebted to the help given me by Nicole Leaver and Dominika Pawloska, my research assistants during 2003 when I taught political science at McGill University.

Members of the research team I led to Iraqi Kurdistan from October 2003 to May 2004 assisted me in ways too numerous to mention. Lucy Brown, Mike Boag, and Karim Khallayoun's company and friendship during those eight months have also become priceless, treasured memories. Right up until the final manuscript revisions in Montreal, Lucy continued to provide me with useful comments and help on the work.

Finally, I still feel the need to acknowledge the people this book is about, by including here the original dedication of my Ph.D. thesis: To all those of you who, acting only out of your sense of honor and goodness, were so kind and helpful to someone far from home and, occasionally, in serious difficulty. The hospitality shown to me during my fieldwork in Turkey, Iran, Iraq, Syria, and Kurdistan reminded me that whether we choose to call ourselves Turkish, Persian, Arab, Kurdish, Canadian, citizen, Muslim, Christian, Jewish, worker, owner, peasant, tribal member, man, woman, soldier, freedom fighter, or something else, in the end we are all human. I hope you will judge any shortcoming or errors in this work, for all of which I alone am responsible, forgivingly.

Acronyms and abbreviations

AK Partisi	Justice and Development Party [Turkey]
CPI	Communist Party of Iran
Congra-Gel	People's Democracy Congress [Turkey]
DEP	Democracy Party [Turkey]
Dev Genc	Revolutionary Youth [Turkey]
DISK	Confederation of Revolutionary Workers Unions [Turkey]
DP	Democratic Party [Turkey]
EU	European Union
HPG	People's Defence Forces [linked to PKK/Congra-Gel]
ICP	Iraqi Communist Party
IIADEP	People's Democracy Party [Turkey]
KADEK	Kurdish Freedom and Democracy Congress [Turkey]
KAZ	Kurdish Autonomous Zone [Iraq]
KDP	Kurdistan Democratic Party [Iraq]
KDPI	Kurdistan Democractic Party of Iran
KDPI-RL	Kurdistan Democratic Party of Iran Revolutionary Leadership [KDPI splinter]
KDPT	Kurdistan Democratic Party of Turkey
Komala	Kurdish Communist Party of Iran (pre-1946)
Komala	Revolutionary Organization of Toilers of Kurdistan [Iran – split from CPI in 2000]
Komalah	Kurdistan Organization of the Communist Party of Iran [Communist Party of Iran]
KRG	Kurdistan Regional Government [Iraq]
MGK	National Security Council [Turkey]
NGO	Non-Governmental Organization
OAPEC	Organization of Arab Petroleum Exporting Countries
OPEC	Organization of Petroleum Exporting Countries
PKK	Kurdistan Workers' Party [Turkey]
PSK	Socialist Party of Kurdistan [Turkey]
PUK	Patriotic Union of Kurdistan [Iraq]

RAF	Royal Air Force [UK]
RC	Rational Choice
RM	Resource Mobilization
RPP	Republican People's Party [Turkey]
TAL	Transitional Administrative Law [Iraq]
TKSP	Turkish Kurdistan Socialist Party [Turkey]
TSK	Kurdistan Socialist Movement [Turkey]
Tudeh	People's Party of Iran
TWP	Turkish Workers' Party [Turkey]
WPI	Worker-Communist Party of Iran

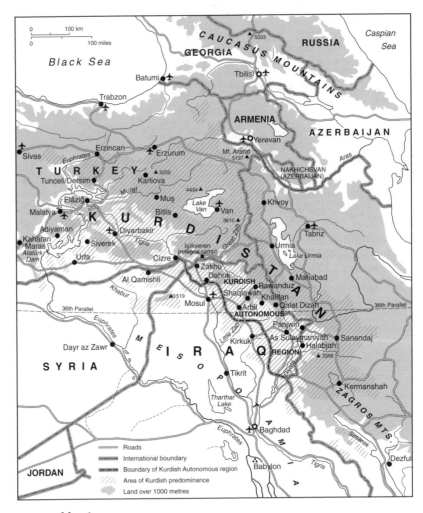

Map 1

1   Making sense of ethnic nationalist resurgence

Introduction

Throughout today's world, ethnic minorities are mobilizing along ethnic nationalist lines, demanding power and recognition as a group from the states in which they live. In some cases, they are demanding a state of their own, based on their group's status as a nation of its own. These challengers to the states in which they live are often brutally suppressed, yet mobilization often continues in the face of this repression. Why, despite the high risks involved and the often remote chances of success, have such movements continued to emerge?

Contextually specific accounts of ethnic nationalist resurgence typically lack much of a theoretical component. The historical details of specific cases are thought to present an "obvious" explanation for the conflict – "group 'X' was oppressed, dissatisfied, or simply in a position to wrench more power from the state, which it then tried to go about doing in the following way . . ." forms a common approach to the subject. The fact that we can probably find a vast array of injustices, grievances, and relative deprivation affecting ethnic minorities in every society on the planet, yet few ethnic minority groups mobilize for change, is left unexplained. Approaches that are more theoretical often focus so much on one element of the phenomenon (such as socio-political structures in society, movement strategies, or identity struggles) that the resulting account leaves out more than it explains.

The world certainly needs a better understanding of ethnic nationalist resurgence, given the shocking violence and high death toll that has occurred in places as far apart as Rwanda, the former Yugoslavia, East Timor, and, in the case examined here, Kurdistan. The study of politics and sociology includes many facets of human relations, but ethnic nationalist strife stands out as one of the most dramatic manifestations of the struggle for power that lies at the heart of political, and human, interaction. A better understanding of ethnic nationalist resurgence requires that one see both the individual trees as well as the forest. If we take the trees as specific cases of ethnic nationalist resurgence and strife, and the

1

forest as the broader generalizations and theoretical understandings of such phenomena, then we arrive at the spirit in which this study is undertaken. By rigorously applying general social movement theoretical frameworks to the Kurdish case, I hope to paint a clearer picture of the forest, while at the same time recognizing the rich detail of some of its trees. In this sense, the main contribution of this book is a theoretical one, although what is hopefully a compelling account that includes new details of the specifically Kurdish case, is also presented.

This study of Kurdish ethnic nationalism originally focused on how people are mobilized into ethnic nationalist organizations, given the often high risks and dubious prospects of success for many such movements. I initially expected that an analysis that clarifies the mobilization process could in turn explain the emergence of ethnic nationalist challenges to state authority. I found, however, that to discuss the mobilization process I needed to pay equal attention to the politico-structural context in which it was occurring. Although the analytical approaches that I planned to apply to Kurdish cases of nationalist mobilization (resource mobilization and rational choice theories) do pay some heed to the contemporary context in which actors exist, they are for the most part ahistorical, ignoring the less immediate context out of which actors emerge. Additionally, the rational actor and interest maximizing behavior upon which much of resource mobilization theory is predicated was unable to account for significant elements of the Kurdish case. In particular, the dynamic nature of people's identity, and hence an account of their grievances, interests, and goals, became a major issue rather than a given. Therefore, in addition to an account of the structural political context and mobilization methods of movements, identity politics emerged as the third essential component for a compelling explanation of the emergence and fortunes of Kurdish ethnic nationalist challenges to the state. The reciprocal effects of these three levels of analysis, structural political context, mobilization methods, and identity, proved to be an important part of a satisfying examination of the Kurdish issue. Moreover, I contend that the theoretical issues grappled with in this explanation are not limited to the Kurdish case. Not only the logic of analysis, but also the parcelling of an extremely complex phenomenon into cognitively manageable chunks, should be useful for anyone seeking to examine social movements in other contexts.

Why the Kurdish case?

Kurdistan, as its proponents call it, lies within and around the Zagros mountain range, and is currently divided between the borders of Turkey,

Iraq, Iran, and Syria. Kurds form roughly twenty-three percent of Turkey's population, twenty-three percent of Iraq's, and ten percent of Iran's population.[1] Kurdish is an Indo-European language related to Persian; the three major dialects spoken today (and not completely comprehensible to each other) are Kurmanji, Sorani, and Zaza. Seventy-five percent of Kurds speak Kurmanji and practice Shaffiite Sunni Islam, while the other twenty-five percent are divided between Shiite Muslims (fifteen percent) Alevi, Christian, Jewish, Yezidi, and Ahl-i-Haqq faiths.[2] A strong tribal element, a shared memory of a mountain pastoral-nomadic past, awareness of the homeland *Kurdistan* (roughly speaking, the mountainous region described above), and distinct social practices combine with language and history to form a Kurdish culture and ethnicity. This culture maintained its distinctiveness and integrity throughout the centuries.[3]

The Kurdish homeland's location at the meeting point of the Ottoman and Persian empires also meant that various Kurdish principalities (with varying degrees of attachment to the Ottomans and Persians) were used as a buffer and battleground between these empires. In the seventeenth century, Kurdish poet Ehmed-e Xani had already lamented the situation of the Kurds:

> I leave it to God's wisdom
> The Kurds in this world's state
> Why are they deprived of their rights?
> Why are they all doomed?
> See, from the Arabs to the Georgians
> Everything is Kurdish and, as with a citadel,
> The Turks and the Persians besiege them
> From four sides at once.
> And they both make the Kurdish people
> Into a target for Fate's arrow.[4]

Of course, Khani's nationalist view of the Kurds was at least three hundred years ahead of most of his countrymen. It was only around the time of World War One, as the break-up of the Ottoman Empire loomed on the horizon, that Kurdish nationalist movements emerged in significant form. For the purposes of this study, the contemporary division of

---

[1] David McDowall, *A Modern History of the Kurds* (London: I. B. Taurus, 1997), p. 3; and Martin van Bruinessen, *Agha, Shaikh and State* (London: Zed Books, Ltd., 1992), p. 15.
[2] Mehrdad Izady, *The Kurds: A Concise Handbook* (Washington DC: Taylor and Francis, 1992).
[3] Mordechai Nisan, *Minorities in the Middle East* (Jefferson, NC: McFarland, 1991), p. 28.
[4] Philip G. Kreyenbroek and Christine Allison, *Kurdish Culture and Identity* (London: Zed Books Ltd., 1996), p. 10.

the same ethnic group within three different states provides a rare comparative opportunity – the emergence of such Kurdish ethnic nationalist movements can be compared in three different structural contexts. More than twenty Kurdish revolts have broken out in the twentieth century. This provides us with a rich historical tapestry for the analysis of ethnic nationalist mobilization. To what extent these revolts were based on a politicized Kurdish ethnicity is one issue investigated here. Kurds in Iraq, Iran, and especially Turkey have traditionally had the option of assimilating into the dominant society, rather than pursuing their interests as Kurds. Many Kurdish elites did, in fact, choose this route. Explaining such choices strikes at the heart of the debate on the nature of ethnicity and the (re)emergence of ethnic nationalism.

The emergence of ethnic nationalist challenges to state authority in the Turkish, Iraqi, and Iranian cases is particularly puzzling. Especially in Turkey, discrimination against talented and motivated Kurdish individuals who assimilate to the dominant culture is minimal; Turkey's former President, Turgut Ozal, was half-Kurdish. Yet in all three states, political expressions of Kurdishness have been brutally suppressed. What accounts for continued Kurdish sub-national challenges, if the penalties for such challenges are so severe, and assimilation is an available, less dangerous option?[5] Given the awesome repressive capacity of these states, as well as some of the most vigilant imaginable policies opposing expressions of politicized Kurdish ethnicity, how were Kurdish opposition groups able to mobilize effective challenges? If we can satisfactorily explain the mobilization process in the Kurdish case, we might be able to explain it anywhere, particularly in contexts where sub-national challenges to the state are less dangerous.

Finally, the Kurdish nationalist movements themselves display fascinating differences. Today, we can compare the Turkish Kurdish PKK (Kurdistan Workers' Party) to the Iraqi Kurdish KDP (Kurdistan Democratic Party) and PUK (Patriotic Union of Kurdistan) as well as the Iranian Kurdish KDPI (Kurdistan Democratic Party of Iran) and Komala. The PKK, for instance, was a non-tribally based, avowedly Marxist-Leninist group, drawing much of its support from urban Kurds. Its leader, Abdullah Ocalan, was originally active in the Turkish political Left, but severed his connection with Turkish groups and

---

[5] For a Kurdish nationalist, the answer is simple: assimilating and forsaking one's identity is akin to suicide. Such an answer poses severe problems for many social scientists who favor a rational-choice approach and would attempt to explain such a choice in more utilitarian terms (e.g. the possible gains in improved status from a successful ethnic nationalist challenge make the risks worthwhile at times).

founded his own ethnically based Kurdistan Workers' Party.[6] The Iraqi KDP, on the other hand, has much more of a traditional tribal base (despite its urban origins), and is more conservative in its class and gender perspectives. It draws more of its support from rural Iraqi Kurds. The programs espoused by each movement differ considerably as well. Accounting for such differences sheds a great deal of light on theories of ethnic nationalism and social movements. New mechanisms and important variables in ethnic nationalist mobilization may also be uncovered.

On the nature of ethnicity

Kurdish nationalist challengers to the state belong to a subset of social movements known as ethnic nationalist movements. In order to understand what this means we must address the nature of ethnicity, a concept resistant to clear-cut definition. "Ethnicity" generally refers to a complex web of social and historical traits that combine to form someone's identity. Definitions currently in use generally highlight a group's emphasis on common origins and descent, as well as shared characteristics based on language, race, religion, territory, culture, values, or history.[7] These common origins and shared characteristics may be real or fictitious. These may be important to different degrees, or one or more may even be absent.[8]

David Brown describes the "traditional," or primordial, approach to understanding ethnicity as an assumption that groups sharing distinctive religious, linguistic, or racial characteristics will naturally arrive at a corresponding group consciousness, a consciousness that typically manifests itself in the nationalist desire for a state belonging to the group in question.[9] Works such as that of Geertz exemplify the primordial approach.[10] This view, however, fails to explain why some "objective" cultural groups fail to develop strong group consciousness, while others with more tenuously shared characteristics *do* emerge as fairly unified, ethnically conscious polities.[11] Scholars such as Smith and Stack respond

---

[6] McDowall, *A Modern History of the Kurds*, p. 418.

[7] Myron Weiner, "Peoples and States in a New Ethnic Order?" *Third World Quarterly*, Vol. 13, No. 4, (1992). Hutchinson and Smith provide the following definition of an *ethnie*: "[a] named population with myths of common ancestry, shared historical memories, one or more elements of common culture, a link with a homeland and a sense of solidarity among at least some of its members," *Ethnicity* (Oxford: Oxford University Press, 1996), p. 6.

[8] Crawford Young, *The Politics of Cultural Pluralism* (London: The University of Wisconsin Press, 1976), p. 11.

[9] David Brown, "Ethnic Revival: Perspectives on State and Society," *Third World Quarterly*, Vol. 11, No. 4 (1989), 5.

[10] Clifford Geertz, *The Interpretation of Cultures* (New York: Basic Books, 1973).   [11] Ibid.

by positing the existence of a latent primordial identity, which could be politically activated under the right stimulus.[12]

Instrumentalists such as Brass and Gurr, on the other hand, argue that ethnicity is an imagined identity, typically constructed by elites to further their instrumental goals.[13] Gurr and Harff state: "The main goals of a group are assumed to be material and political gains; cultural identity is invoked only as a means to attain those goals ... Political entrepreneurs capitalize on ... differences to establish ethnically based political movements aimed at increasing the economic and political well-being of their group or region."[14] Milton Esman adds the following:

Instrumentalists ... argue that ethnicity is not a historical given at all, but in fact a highly adaptive and malleable phenomenon. In response to changing conditions, the boundaries of an ethnic collectivity can expand or contract, individuals move in and out and even share membership in more than one community. The very content, symbols, and meaning of a particular collective identity can and do evolve. In effect, ethnicity is a dynamic, not fixed and immutable element of social and political relationships.[15]

Such an argument, however, may exaggerate the degree of flexibility of ethnic identities as well as understate the powerful emotional appeal of ethnicity.[16] In Donald Horowitz's memorable phrase, "The ethnic group is not just a trade union."[17]

The theoretical divide between instrumentalists and primordialists is often overstated, however. A view that takes the various components of ethnicity (language, culture, shared origins, religion) as the building blocks, or context, from which ethnic identification *may* be constructed, solves the problem. These building blocks limit the flexibility of the construction; although the ethnic kinship ties may be fictional, they cannot be pulled out of thin air.[18] Factors such as the state, the process of modernization, the manipulations of state and non-state elites, and

---

[12] Anthony Smith, *National Identity* (London: Penguin Books, 1991); John F. Stack (ed.), *The Primordial Challenge* (New York: Greenwood Press, 1986). Stack argues that such a latent primordial identity could nevertheless be dynamic in nature, as it experiences continual reinterpretation and adjusts to different circumstances, however.

[13] Paul Brass, *Ethnicity and Nationalism* (London: Sage Publications, 1991); Ted Robert Gurr and Barbara Harff, *Ethnic Conflict in World Politic* (Boulder: Westview Press, 1994).

[14] Gurr and Harff, *Ethnic Conflict*, p. 78.

[15] Milton J. Esman, *Ethnic Politics* (Ithaca: Cornell University Press, 1994), p. 10.

[16] Donald Horowitz, *Ethnic Groups in Conflict: Group Comparison and the Sources of Conflict* (Berkeley: University of California Press, 1985), p. 104.

[17] Ibid.

[18] Esman argues that "Efforts to 'construct' an ethnic identity from empty cultural materials usually fail, like the attempt in the 1960s to regenerate an 'Occitanian' identity in Southern France, for the label conveys no legitimate meaning to its intended constituents" (*Ethnic Politics*, p. 10).

the mobilization process itself determine the saliency of ethnic identification as a political factor.[19] If, as Ross and Cottrell contend, "Ethnicity is a particular type of collective identity which has at least the potential for being a basis of mobilization,"[20] then the literature on social movements can be profitably applied to cases of ethnic nationalist challenges to the state. Particularly if one views ethnicity as at least partially constructed (from fictional myths of origin, historical events interpreted in a nationalist light, and so on), the ethnic group and especially ethnic nationalist movements claiming to represent the group become ascriptive in nature. One can choose to be a member of the ethnic social movement or not.

Young and Esman in particular insist on the need to view ethnic identity as a dynamic variable, one that can ebb and flow in political importance. One of the tasks of an ethnic nationalist organization is to instill and maintain a strong sense of ethnic identity in all those who could conceivably fall within the ethnic group's defined category.[21] The organization's task does not end there: existing ethnic identities must then be politicized, that is, used as a basis for making claims or challenges towards the state. Hence, this study proposes a four-fold categorization of ethnic identity:

(1) those who lie structurally outside the ethnic group category (they can never identify with the ethnic group in question);
(2) those who may be within the ethnic category, but who do not identify themselves ethnically;
(3) those who consider themselves part of the ethnic group, but in a non-politicized way (they do not make claims on the state based on their ethnicity); and
(4) those whose ethnic identity is politicized.

Such a four-fold categorization is necessary in order to evaluate an ethnic nationalist movement's status amongst the populace (how many opponents, possible supporters, and active sympathizers it has available depends on

[19] Young, *Politics of Cultural Pluralism*; John F. Stack (ed.), *Ethnic Identities in a Transnational World* (Westport: Greenwood Press, 1981); Joseph Rothschild, *Ethnopolitics* (New York: Columbia University Press, 1981); Susan Olzak and Joane Nagel (eds.), *Competitive Ethnic Relations* (New York: Academic Press, Inc., 1986); Horowitz, *Ethnic Groups in Conflict*; Esman, *Ethnic Politics*.

[20] Jeffrey A. Ross, Phillip Rawkins, Ann B. Cottrell, and Robert St. Cry, *Mobilization of Collective Identity* (Lanham, MD: Rowman & Littlefield, 1980), p. x.

[21] Here I implicitly refer to the objective limits of constructed ethnic identities, which must be evaluated in a contextually sensitive manner. For instance, a Francophone Quebecer may move to Ontario as a child, forget French, and become an Anglophone Canadian. However, a fourth generation Chinese Malaysian cannot become a Malay by forgetting Chinese.

people's identity), as well as the values and motivations of different elements of the populace (since someone's goals cannot be known without first establishing their identity).

Ethnicity is one of several possible identifications and sources of motivation; other sources include occupation, ideology, class, region, and religion.[22] Yet, Esman convincingly adds, "Ethnicity is not, however, normally only one of several equal choices. The more politicized ethnicity becomes, the more it dominates other expressions of identity, eclipsing class, occupational, and ideological solidarities."[23] Hence if we can establish that a significant portion of the populace has developed a politicized ethnic identity, it would follow that this identity plays the central role in motivating their actions and forming their value preferences.

On social movements

Previous literature on both ethnic nationalist resurgence and social movements in general tended to derive its explanations from one of three broad levels of analysis: the state, its institutions, and their relationship with society (termed the "structural approach" here), the social movements and their mobilizational imperatives (referred to as "resource mobilization" and "rational choice" perspectives here), and finally, social psychology and identity. A few scholars such as Charles Tilly have important elements of all three approaches in their work, but one level of analysis dominates the others (in Tilly's case, the resource mobilization perspective), and the synthesized interplay of the variables is not clearly laid out.[24]

Structural approaches

Structural theorists agree with A. J. R. Groom's explanation of the structuralist approach in social sciences:

The starting point of structuralism is simple. An emphasis must be given to the whole since this has an impact greater than the sum of its parts and must therefore be taken into consideration in any empirical theory of behavior at whatever level. As Richard Little puts it, "Structuralists assume that human behaviour cannot be understood simply by examining individual motivation and intention because,

---

[22] Esman, *Ethnic Politics*, p. 15.   [23] Ibid.

[24] Charles Tilly, *From Mobilization to Revolution* (Reading: Addison-Wesley Publishing Company, 1978). Tilly's approach, for example, fails to consider identity as a dynamic variable, subject to influence by both social movements and structural changes in the state and society. As a result, people's identities, goals, and values are treated as a given.

Key variables RM theory[51] examines include resources internal and external to the movement (including the level of organization in the movement), the costs and benefits of participation in the movement, the availability of social networks for reaching and mobilizing support, and the state's capacities and weaknesses.[52] The approach views groups as rational strategic actors. When scholars examine "interests" and "strategic options" of ethnic collectivities, they operate from an RM-inspired theoretical framework.

Additionally, because they both focus on rational strategic action, RM theory is sometimes lumped together with rational choice (RC) theories of collective action.[53] The issue that usually unites these theories is Mancur Olson's free-rider problem: if the goods groups seek to attain are collective in nature (such as a better society or a cleaner environment), and one person's participation (or lack thereof) will have a negligible impact on the attainment of the goods, then rational individuals will free-ride off the efforts of others and not contribute to the collective project (particularly since collective goods such as a better society accrue to everyone, not only those who worked to attain them).[54] Hence RM and RC theorists devote considerable attention to showing how social movements (including ethnic nationalist groups) sometimes overcome this collective action problem. Selective incentives and disincentives, or a movement's ability to convince potential supporters that their contribution "makes a difference," form typical explanations around the problem.[55]

Samuel Popkin, for instance, shows how in Vietnam, "political entrepreneurs" made it individually rational for peasants to participate in the

---

[51] In the interests of brevity, I am painting this theory with a rather broad descriptive brush, one that is less sensitive to the variations of RM used by different scholars.

[52] RM theory does not ignore the structural variables (such as crisis within the state's ruling coalition) discussed earlier; rather, its emphasis is on the social movement acting within the structural context. The structural context is not the main focus, however, and the manner in which structural conditions affect the timing of movements' emergence and the form such movements take, is generally overlooked by RM theory.

[53] Taylor, *Rationality and Revolution*; Samuel L. Popkin, *The Rational Peasant* (Berkeley: University of California Press, 1979); James DeNardo, *Power in Numbers* (Princeton: Princeton University Press, 1985); Karl-Dieter Opp, *The Rationality of Political Protest* (Boulder: Westview Press, Inc., 1989).

[54] Mancur Olson, *The Logic of Collective Action* (Boston: Harvard University Press, 1965), p. 2.

[55] For a more complete discussion of the free-rider problem, see Olson, *Logic of Collective Action*; Klandermans, *Social Psychology of Protest*; Jean L. Cohen, "Strategy or Identity: New Theoretical Paradigms and Contemporary Social Movements," *Social Research* 52 (1985); and Craig Calhoun, "The Problem of Identity in Collective Action," in John Huber (ed.), *Macro-Micro Linkages in Sociology* (Newbury Park: Sage Publications Inc., 1991), pp. 51–75.

Communist (as well as other) collective movements, by initially helping them to overcome free-rider problems and collectively attain local goals – from these actions the entrepreneurs extracted a surplus of material and non-material resources, which they could then direct towards the larger goals of the revolution, in effect "building something from nothing."[56]

Applying an RM/RC analytical framework such as Oberschall and Popkin's to the Kurdish case provides some useful insights, in addition to testing it theoretically. The Kurdistan Workers' Party (PKK) in Turkey has, in fact, focused much of its efforts on organizing rural Kurds in pursuit of local interests. However, this approach only helps account for some aspects of the initial spread of a movement's appeal, mainly because explaining the commitment of "political entrepreneurs" (at the early, risky stages of a movement's growth), as well as the creation of a non-material "revolutionary surplus," requires one to step outside the logic of RC theory. Many social movements, and especially ethnic nationalist movements operating under a repressive regime, rely heavily on ideologically committed and "self-denying" cadres and members. RC assumptions cannot usually apply to such people; an analysis outside the RC framework is needed (more on this shortly).

Another major problem with RM and RC theories is that they take group and individual goals, values, and identities as given: "It is taken for granted that a collectivity or quasi-group ... with common latent interests, already exists and that the members of the collectivity are dissatisfied and have grievances."[57] Jean Cohen likewise observes the following about Tilly's approach: "He grants that there is as yet no convincing explanation of why an individual joins a collective action, or of what the connections are between individual and group interests. In what seems to be a self-critique, Tilly admits that the creation of solidarity and commonality of interests, which resource-mobilization theorists took for granted, is a pressing theoretical problem."[58] Thus even if a movement succeeds in organizing peasants to resist the local landlord, it is not then clear why the peasants will continue on with the movement to pursue larger less tangible goals (such as a separate state for their ethnic group), which are not of such immediate interest to them. If we posit that previous participation in local struggles created a sense of solidarity and a new communal identity,

---

[56] Popkin, *Rational Peasant*. Local interests which self-interested individuals could be organized around might include resisting exploitation by the landlords, work parties for building irrigation canals, etc. Such projects are not common goods, since only those participating in the movement directly benefit from the attainment of the goods in question. Hence free-riding is not a problem in such cases.

[57] Oberschall, *Social Conflict and Social Movements*, pp. 118–119.

[58] Cohen, "Strategy or Identity," 686.

then we have nonetheless stepped out of the realm of materialist rational choice theory, where actors are only self-interested, into that of identity and new social movement theory. Pursuing variants of RM theory that do not include RC assumptions also fails to resolve the issue – the identity and values of kinship groups, neighborhood collectives, social classes, and ethnic groups cannot be assumed *a priori*. Munck puts forth a similar point of view on the issue: "If rational choice theory, drawing upon the arsenal of game theory, had provided a fairly elegant way of explaining action in terms of a tight means–ends rationality, that is, the problems in getting from 'here' to 'there,' a theory of identity could illuminate the 'there' and why certain actors may want to get 'there.'"[59] Nor is Tilly's model of strategic interaction a solution to the problem – "An explanation of how *some* collective interests emerge in the mobilization process is not equivalent to an account of the formation of collective identities, ideologies, or solidarities. We are still not offered an analysis of the rewards of collective action from a nonstrategic point of view."[60]

Finally, Cohen adds that, "... for the collective actor to be able to calculate the costs and benefits of collective action and act strategically, his identity has to be established. The process of the creation of identity occurs through collective interaction itself, within and between groups."[61] It is with this problem and the dynamic nature of identity in mind that the aforementioned four-fold category of ethnic identity was introduced. The rational choice elements of RM theory can apply to materially motivated, self-interested individuals and to individuals and groups whose identity at a given time has been established. In order to get a better sense of what identities exist, however, and hence what values matter, we must turn to the third level of analysis employed in this study.

Social psychology and identity

New social movement theorists, eschewing RM theorists' discounting of ideology and identity, centered the focus of their analysis upon questions of culture and meaning.[62] When individuals or groups come to be motivated by strong ideologies or identities, a different logic of analysis must

---

[59] G. Munck, *Social Movements and Democracy in Latin America: Theoretical Debates and Comparative Perspectives* (Mimeo, 1991), p. 702.

[60] Cohen, "Strategy or Identity," 687.   [61] Ibid., 692.

[62] Alberto Melucci, "Getting Involved: Identity and Mobilization in Social Movements," *International Social Movement Research 1* (Greenwich: JAI Press, 1988), 329–348; Alain Touraine, *The Voice and the Eye: An Analysis of Social Movements* (New York: Cambridge University Press, 1981). New social movement theory also typically includes structural factors (described above) in conjunction with its attention to culture and identity.

then be used to explain their behavior.[63] Some individuals and communities may be possessed of a politicized ethnic identity even prior to the emergence of an ethnic nationalist movement – in which case such people would likely be a source of the movement's emergence in the first place. As discussed earlier, a rational choice theoretical approach accounts for some actors' behavior in the context of ethnic nationalist challenges to the state – for instance, those who do not have a strong ethnic identification, or those whose ethnicity is not politicized. Individuals close to an ethnic nationalist movement, however, may internalize new norms, values, and interests (to varying degrees) – in other words, their identity changes, at which point they may no longer fit into the self-interested utilitarian actor category of RC theory at all. For an ethnic nationalist movement to mount a significant state challenge, such a change in identity, values, and norms must be affected on a mass scale, however.

Craig Calhoun has in fact shown how identity can change in the course of collective action, radically altering the interests and cost–benefit calculus of participating individuals. The argument combines an RM perspective with an appreciation for the dynamism of identity, and hence merits a somewhat lengthy excerpt:

During spring 1989, Chinese student protestors went through a series of actions and experiences that shaped and reshaped the identities of many. They moved from small statements like marching to boycotts of classes, signing petitions, and hunger strikes. They made speeches – simply to each other as well as on television – that affirmed the primacy or even irreducible priority of certain values. They linked these values – freedom, national pride, and personal integrity or honor – to their positional identity, seeing them as particularly the responsibility of intellectuals. But their actions were more than a reflection of positional interests. Students joined the protest movement largely in blocks of classmates, so their primary immediate social network supported the process of redefinition of identity. Indeed, it seems that those more centrally placed in everyday social networks – such as class monitors and other leaders at school – were more active in the movement and felt more obligated to hold themselves to high standards of committed behavior.[64]

Calhoun goes on to argue that given the students' new identity, even the extremely risky and self-sacrificing actions the students took by the end of

---

[63] The reader may have noticed a levels of analysis problem when discussing individuals and the groups they form, and hence individual identities and goals versus group ones. Although this is not an issue I resolve satisfactorily, I attempt to show some sensitivity to the problem. Also, it should be possible to occasionally infer from observed events as well as secondary sources situations when individuals and their groups have become ideologically motivated.

[64] Craig Calhoun, "The Problem of Identity in Collective Action," in J. Huber (ed.), *Macro–Micro Linkages in Sociology* (Newbury Park: Sage Publications Inc., 1991), 69.

Beijing spring (such as standing in front of an advancing tank) can be seen as "rational":

> ... the condition of a rational action account of such behavior, paradoxically, is precisely not to see it literally as self-sacrificing but to see it as self-saving. That is, the rational choice to take extraordinary risk may depend on the social construction, in the midst of unusual collective action, of a personal identity that makes *not* taking a given risk more certain to imperil the self of the actor than taking it. This sort of calculation cannot be understood in terms of an approach to rational action that takes actors' identities as fixed attributes of individuals or one that analyses individual action solely in terms of interests derived from various external sources – such as class position. But it can be understood.[65]

Such "self-saving" behavior occupies a prominent place in the folk histories of many groups. For instance, in one story, a family of Jews resisting Roman rule 2,000 years ago chooses to be put to death rather than eat pork. In any case, it is clear that explaining the risks, sacrifices, and determination of many ethnic nationalist movement participants and sympathizers requires a consideration of non-material values and identity, which in most cases also corresponds more closely with people's own stated reasons for engaging in risky or costly behavior. Part of the difficulty in conducting such an analysis, however, is the amorphous and intangible nature of the subject in question. Identity and culture are not the ideal variables of social "science." Of course, this is no excuse for not wrestling with the issues.

Echoing similar concerns, Cohen points out that attempts to include considerations of "solidarity, collective identity, consciousness, or ideology" to the resource mobilization perspective bursts its theoretical framework.[66] This is the price we pay when the ugly reality of human behavior meets a beautiful theory. Nonetheless, this study accepts Cohen and Klandermans' arguments that a consideration of "values, norms, ideologies, projects, culture and identity in other than instrumental terms" must be used in conjunction with resource mobilization theory and an appreciation of the structural context in which movements arise and exist, although the resulting approach emerges as more of a framework of analysis than a theory in the traditional sense.[67] It is clear, moreover, that an identity and culture based theory cannot be relied upon in isolation. If we ignore questions of political structures and the means and strategies employed by organized groups, the remaining singular focus on

---

[65] Ibid.   [66] Cohen, "Strategy or Identity," 687.

[67] Ibid., p. 688; Bert Klandermans, Hanspeter Kriesi, and Sidney Tarrow (eds.), "From Structure to Action: Comparing Social Movement Research Across Cultures," *International Social Movement Research 1* (Greenwich: JAI Press, 1988).

culture risks explaining everything, and hence nothing. Such an approach would quickly risk losing sight of broad dynamics of human behavior and politics that may or may not generate certain kinds of culture and identity milieux in the first place.

Synthesis of the theoretical framework: opportunity structures, resource mobilization, and cultural framing

The discussion above highlighted the broad outlines of various theoretical approaches to the study of social movements. The problems inherent in each approach have, naturally, attracted the concern of social movement scholars. In their contribution to *Comparative Politics: Rationality, Culture, and Structure*, McAdam, Tarrow, and Tilly argue that it is time for a synthesis of theoretical approaches to understanding social movements and revolution.[68] They state that the study of contentious politics "includes all situations in which actors make collective claims on other actors, claims which, if realized would affect the actors' interests, when some government is somehow party to the claims."[69] In this sense, "wars, revolutions, rebellions, (most) social movements, industrial conflict, feuds, riots, banditry, shaming ceremonies, and many more forms of collective struggle" can and should be analyzed from a similar, and hence cumulative, analytical framework. They argue that in the past, "... specialists in different kinds of political contention have created sui generis models of their subject matter, often ignoring powerful analogies with neighboring phenomena. As a result, each group of practitioners has emphasized a different set of concepts, theoretical issues, and comparisons."[70] In the case of specialists of regions outside Western Europe and North America, they

have often borrowed the ideas and apparatus of social movement specialists but have not established a genuine dialogue with analysts of contemporary Western European and North American movements. Differences inherent in these settings have all too frequently been dealt with by culturalist proclamation – or by assuming the universality of certain models – rather than by parsing differences into variables that can be integrated into systematic comparisons with movements in various parts of the world. As a result, scholars of Western democratic and Third World movements frequently use different vocabularies, sometimes lapsing into

---

[68] "Toward an Integrated Perspective on Social Movements and Revolution," in Mark Irving Lichbach and Alan S. Zuckerman (eds.), *Comparative Politics: Rationality, Culture and Structure* (Cambridge: Cambridge University Press, 1997), pp. 142–173. One of the earliest major works specifying what such a synthesis might look like is Klandermans et al., "From Structure to Action."

[69] McAdam et al., " Toward an Integrated Perspective," 143.   [70] Ibid.

interpretative particularism and sometimes imagining they are theorizing broadly when their empirical bases exclude vast parts of the globe.[71]

McAdam, Tarrow, and Tilly refer to the three main theoretical paradigms used by scholars, and described in the previous section of this chapter, as *structure, mobilization,* and *culture.*[72] In another recent edited volume devoted to the need for a synthesis of these paradigms, McAdam, McCarthy, and Zald write that:

Increasingly one finds movement scholars from various countries and nominally representing different theoretical traditions emphasizing the importance of the same three broad sets of factors in analyzing the emergence and development of social movements/revolutions. These three factors are (1) the structure of political opportunities and constraints confronting the movement; (2) the forms of organization (informal as well as formal) available to insurgents; and (3) the collective processes of interpretation, attribution, and social construction that mediate between opportunity and action.[73]

They refer to these three factors as *political opportunities, mobilizing structures,* and *framing processes.* To avoid confusion and to better tie these factors to the theoretical paradigms from which each is derived, they are referred to in this study as (1) *opportunity structures*; (2) *resource mobilization*; and (3) *cultural framing.* I will now briefly describe these three factors as they will be employed in this study, including what aspects of ethnic nationalist resurgence they might be able to shed the most light on.

Opportunity structures

The concept of *opportunity structures* lends itself well to explaining the emergence, and in some cases the form, of insurgent social movements.[74] By looking at changes in available political opportunities, one could surmise where and when windows of opportunity open for challenger movements. Also, the kind of opportunities that arise can affect the form such emergent movements take: "In short, insurgents can be expected to mobilize in response to and in a manner consistent with the very specific changes that grant them more leverage."[75]

There is a risk, however, of including too many variables within the concept of opportunity structures (witness all the structural variables

---

[71] Ibid.   [72] Ibid., p. 158.
[73] Doug McAdam, John D. McCarthy, and Mayer N. Zald, *Comparative Perspectives on Social Movements: Political Opportunities, Mobilizing Structures, and Cultural Framings* (New York: Cambridge University Press, 1996), p. 2.
[74] Ibid., p. 10.   [75] Ibid.

listed at the outset of this chapter). For this reason, Doug McAdam attempts to differentiate opportunity structures from other facilitative conditions.[76] Some factors, such as the state of the economy, may act as antecedent variables affecting opportunity structures, but are not examined directly. An antecedent variable such as the economy gains importance to the extent that it impacts upon the political opportunity structures described below (such as when a state's fiscal crisis undermines its capacity to repress and to maintain elite support), sets the context for resource mobilization (when a movement or the government is able to offer supporters financial rewards during desperate economic times, for instance), or becomes central to the perceptions and understandings of the actors we are examining (for example, if the economic problems in a society can be blamed on government corruption or discrimination, thereby justifying an insurgent movement's challenge to the system). Including a consideration of variables such as the economy in this way should prove more successful than asking questions such as "Does economic inequality breed political conflict?" Mark Irving Lichbach, assessing the numerous studies that address precisely this question (economic inequality = conflict), came to the following conclusion: "Researchers should therefore take the bottom-line, stylized fact that results from this literature to be the following: economic inequality may either have positive, negative, or no impact on dissent."[77]

The factors that make up the opportunity structures level of analysis are:
(1) the relative openness or closure of the institutionalized political system
(2) the stability of that broad set of elite alignments that typically undergird a polity
(3) the presence of elite allies
(4) the state's capacity and propensity for repression

Although mindful of the need to keep the number of main variables to a manageable minimum, the case studies used in this study highlighted the absolute necessity of adding one more crucial factor to McAdam's four components of opportunity structures:
(5) international and foreign influences supportive of the state or its opponents[78]

---

[76] McAdam et al., "Toward an Integrated Perspective," p. 26.
[77] Mark Irving Lichbach, "An Evaluation of 'Does Economic Inequality Breed Political Conflict?' Studies," *World Politics* 12 (1989), 465.
[78] McAdam, in his introduction to the subject of opportunity structures, does acknowledge the possibility that the international political environment may be a factor that needs inclusion into the theoretical framework (McAdam et al., *Comparative Perspectives*, p. 39). He leaves the issue for future consideration, however.

The key issue involved in a consideration of opportunity structures is the degree to which each factor affects, facilitates, and constrains social movement challengers (Kurdish ethnic nationalist movements in our case).[79]

Resource mobilization

The resource mobilization level of analysis is described by McAdam, McCarthy, and Zald as "... those collective vehicles, informal as well as formal, through which people mobilize and engage in collective action."[80] The approach is particularly well suited to explaining how social movements emerge and mobilize to pursue their goals, and will be applied in this study in much the same form as the broader paradigm described earlier in this chapter.

Cultural framing

Borrowing from David Snow and various colleagues' work on the issue,[81] McAdam, McCarthy, and Zald define cultural framing as "... conscious strategic efforts by groups of people to fashion shared understandings of the world and of themselves that legitimate and motivate collective action."[82] Once again, this relatively narrow definition of the concept seeks to avoid the aforementioned tendency of using culture and social psychology variables to explain everything, and hence nothing. Analysis of cultural framing is further divided into the following five issues:

(1) the cultural tool kits available to would-be insurgents[83]
(2) the strategic framing efforts of movement groups
(3) the frame contests between the movement and other collective actors – principally the state, and countermovement groups

---

[79] For a justification of why these factors are deemed the most relevant for the opportunity structures level of analysis, and a more detailed discussion of the issue, see McAdam et al., *Comparative Perspectives*.

[80] McAdam et al., *Comparative Perspectives*, p. 3.

[81] D. Snow, B. Rochford, S. Worden, and R. Benford, "Frame Alignment Processes, Micromobilization, and Movement Participation," *American Sociological Review*, 51 (4): 464–481.

[82] McAdam et al., *Comparative Perspectives*, p. 6.

[83] What McAdam, McCarthy, and Zald mean (as I read their use of the term) by "cultural tool kit," can be broadly described as "ideational themes" and attitudes prevalent within a population. For instance, western societies have within their cultural tool kit an appreciation for individual human rights and freedoms – ideas that were drawn upon by social movements such as the civil rights movement in the 1960s and the pro-choice movement ("pro-choice" and "a woman's body is her own" are examples of framing an issue that taps into the cultural tool kit of western society).

(4) the structure and role of the media in mediating such contests

(5) the cultural impact of the movement in modifying the available tool kit

This level of analysis is particularly apt to answer the questions of why people and social movements seek the goals that they do, as well as how they go about conducting the struggle. The cultural framing approach attempts to apply an analysis in the spirit of the identity paradigm described in the previous section of this chapter.

The added purchase of a synthesized approach

By examining the mutual interplay of opportunity structures, mobilization strategies, and cultural framing, a more complete accounting of social movement challenges to the state, replete with new insights, may be possible. Divisions within a ruling body of elites, the removal of a state's capacity or willingness to repress, the presence of elite allies, and the opening of access points to the institutionalized political system (or its complete closure), form windows of opportunity for social movements. "No matter how momentous a change appears in retrospect, it only becomes an 'opportunity' when defined as such by a *group* of actors sufficiently well organized to act on this shared definition of the situation."[84] Whereas the old saying that "opportunities always look bigger when they are gone than when they are coming" may apply to our individual lives, it would seem that the situation is reversed in the social sciences. Scholars have a tendency of only identifying as opportunities those situations that were identified and successfully taken advantage of by social movements, discounting the possibility that many perfectly good political opportunities may be missed because no movement existed to take advantage of them, or because existing movements were disorganized or ideologically moot. Likewise, it is equally possible that well-organized movements capable of striking the "right" ideological and cultural chords within the population, successfully manage to precipitate structural changes within the state, creating opportunities for themselves (or others) where few or none existed before. Other possibilities include situations wherein system-critical framing of grievances has arisen amongst sections of the population, but their transfer to the wider masses and/or their translation into action depends on an organized movement.[85] Even more likely, however, is that in the absence of social movement organization, system-critical framings of grievances fail to emerge

---

[84] McAdam et al., *Comparative Perspectives*, p. 8.   [85] Ibid., p. 9.

at all: isolated individuals are more likely to attribute their problems to their own deficiencies or poorly elaborated views of the world.[86]

Ethnic nationalist movements, which seek to heighten ethnic identification within a target population and then in turn politicize ethnic identity in order to challenge the state, are a particularly promising subject of inquiry to illustrate such a process. States facing such challenges, of course, pursue the opposite strategy: they either try to assimilate an ethnic minority to the dominant *ethnie* (thereby removing those who are assimilated from the ethnic challenger movements' reach), or to encourage private (non-politicized) ethnic identities in tandem with civic citizenship and national belonging.[87] In both cases, the intent is to prevent large population groups from coming together, interacting, and forming a group ethnic consciousness, identifying group grievances and framing their grievances in opposition to the state or the dominant ethnic group that controls the state (or both), and finally organizing into movements that act to spread this process and eventually challenge the state to pursue identified group grievances and goals. Shifting opportunity structures in turn affect how successful such challenges can be, or how well the state can stop grievance framing and movement mobilization from developing in the first place.

In any case, only the synthesis of the three paradigms discussed here is capable of grappling with issues such as these. In short, the proposed analytical synthesis is not merely additive; rather, it places a good deal of attention on the *interaction* between the structural, strategic, and cultural levels of analysis.[88]

A heuristic application of the theoretical approach to the Kurdish case

This study shares McAdam, McCarthy, and Zald's concern of explaining the origins of social movements and revolutions as well as the extent and form of the movement over time.[89] By applying their framework of analysis to the Kurdish case, a preliminary step in assessing the utility of the approach to a wide variety of social movement phenomena is undertaken. Particularly because the Kurdish ethnic nationalist case is far removed from the Western European and North American context from which social movement scholars have typically theorized, a heuristic

---

[86] Ibid., p. 9.
[87] Both state strategies – assimilation and encouragement of strictly private ethnic identification – may simultaneously be pursued in some cases.
[88] McAdam et al., *Comparative Perspectives*, p. 8.   [89] Ibid., p. 7.

application of social movement theory to this case should prove to be both a novel and interesting project.

Although none of the three levels of analysis discussed here (opportunity structures, mobilization, and cultural framing) provides by itself a satisfactory account of social movement formation and challenge to the state, the preliminary task of applying them in isolation may prove useful. By examining a single phenomenon, Kurdish ethnic nationalist resurgence in Turkey, from each of these levels of analysis, we can get a better sense of the limitations of each and contribution each makes towards understanding our subject matter. For this reason, Chapters 2–4 examine Kurdish nationalist movements in Turkey from the opportunity structures, resource mobilization, and cultural framing perspectives, respectively. Following this "slicing" of an immensely complex issue into more cognitively manageable chunks, we assess what additional insights to the Kurdish case in Turkey are gained from an interactive, synthesized application of the three approaches. Finally, a tentative comparison (using the synthesis of levels of analysis) of Kurdish movements in Turkey, Iran, and Iraq is undertaken. Such a comparison allows us to assess the extent to which the theoretical approach used here is able to usefully account for similarities and differences in the emergence and fate of Kurdish challenges to the state in varying contexts. Conclusions based on such a synthesis may in turn help us assess policy implications for the region as well as the applicability of the theoretical approach used here to other cases.

This study focuses the bulk of its attention on Kurdish movements in Turkey for two reasons:

(1) Roughly fifty percent of the world Kurdish population originates from the Kurdish areas within present-day Turkey; and
(2) Turkey is a semi-democracy which has tried most actively to assimilate its Kurds, making it a very interesting case for the study of ethnic nationalist movements in the developing world.

Finally, a hermetic separation of opportunity structures, resource mobilization, and cultural framing, even for the theoretical exercise engaged in during the next three chapters, is not completely possible. Particularly for the chapter on resource mobilization, some attention to structural factors (such as the government's capacity and willingness to use force) are part and parcel of the RM approach itself. Likewise, issues related to identity and grievance framing cannot be discussed in total isolation from movements themselves and the structural context of the struggle. Nonetheless, the core emphasis and logic of each approach can be usefully pursued and compared in the following three chapters, followed by an explicit synthesis of the approaches.

2   Structural conditions and political opportunities

This chapter focuses on the usefulness of a structural analysis in explaining Kurdish ethnic-nationalist opposition to the state in Turkey. In particular, I probe the explanatory power of the following five variables:[1]

(1) the relative openness or closure of the institutionalized political system;
(2) the stability of that broad set of elite alignments that typically undergird a polity;
(3) the presence of elite allies;
(4) the state's capacity and propensity for repression; and
(5) international and foreign influences supportive of the state or its opponents.

The first four of these variables are those that constitute McAdam, McCarthy, and Zald's notion of *opportunity structures*.[2] The final variable (the international dimension) I judged simply too important to be left out. Understandably, there is a common tendency to include a long list of factors that constrain or encourage state opposition movements, but to make sense of such a complex phenomenon we must focus on a short list of variables and divide the subject into cognitively manageable chunks. The analysis presented here examines opportunity structures in different phases of Turkey's modern history, ending with the present.

---

[1] These variables coincide with important predominantly structural approaches to revolution, such as Goldstone's, which focuses on three factors: state resource failures, elite alienation and division, and popular mass mobilization potential. While "popular mass mobilization potential" is a variable addressed in the next two chapters of this study (under the resource mobilization and identity-framing levels of analysis), Goldstone's first two explanatory factors largely coincide with this chapter's variables of "state capacity and propensity for repression," "the presence of elite allies," and "the stability of that broad set of elite alignments that typically undergird a polity." Also, part of Goldstone's concept of state resource failures depends on the notion of state legitimacy, which is addressed in the chapter on "framing, identity, and grievance interpretation" of this study. Jack Goldstone, *Revolution and Rebellion in the Early Modern World* (Berkeley: University of California Press, 1991).

[2] Doug McAdam, John D. McCarthy, and Mayer N. Zald, *Comparative Perspectives on Social Movements: Political Opportunities, Mobilizing Structures, and Cultural Framings* (New York: Cambridge University Press, 1996).

Although there have been many outbreaks of subversive violence as well as specifically Kurdish rebellions in modern Turkey, there have been no cases of successful revolution or Kurdish revolts there. Hence it is not possible to even approach "proving" or "disproving" the importance of different approaches to the subject; rather, we can only hope to roughly evaluate the extent to which the opportunity structures concept contributes to a compelling explanation for the outbreak of ethnic nationalist rebellion in Turkey.

Additionally, the degree to which opportunity structures may allow for dissent and rebellion in a general sense, as opposed to only their effect on specifically Kurdish ethnic nationalist rebellion, will be considered here. Acknowledging the related but distinct nature of these phenomena is important, both for analysts as well as for participants: the Turkish government, for example, has claimed that there is no Kurdish problem in Turkey, but rather a socio-economic problem in its southeastern regions.[3] However, no one can dispute that, at the least, rebellion and dissent have marked these regions.

Missed opportunities: the dissolution of the Ottoman Empire and early years of the Turkish Republic (1918–1938)

Kurdish nationalists today view the waning days of the Ottoman Empire and early years of the Turkish Republic as the greatest opportunity for the creation of a Kurdish state ever to be missed. The First World War defeat of the Ottomans and the occupation of Istanbul and large parts of Turkey by Allied armies created a huge opening for Kurdish nationalists. State elites were severely divided in a contest between those who supported the Ottoman Sultanate and the nationalists, led by Kemal Ataturk, who wanted to found a modern Turkish republic. Kurdish elites, mainly tribal chiefs, nobles, and religious sheikhs, considered their options and in many cases openly pushed for a Kurdish state or autonomous region. The remnants of the Ottoman army, faced with Allied, Greek, and Armenian threats, was for the moment incapable of repressing potential Kurdish insurgencies. The Allied powers (particularly Britain) also openly declared their favorable inclination towards the creation of a Kurdish state.

Hence four of our five political opportunity variables (instability of governing elite alignments, the presence of elite allies, the state's

---

[3] "MGK advises government to take social, economic measures in Southeast," *Turkish Daily News*, December 24, 1997; also, "Dry up the swamp rather than fighting with the flies," *Hurriyet*, November 18, 1997 (in Turkish).

incapacity to repress, and a supportive international context) favored Kurdish challengers to the emergent Turkish state. Only one factor, the relative openness or closure of the institutionalized political system, played a less favorable role. In fact, as the following discussion will make clear, the *apparent* openness of the institutionalized political system forms the main explanation of why Kurdish groups by 1925 had completely failed to secure any of their interests *as Kurds*. A second major reason for Kurdish nationalist failure during this period relates to the ambiguous position of Kurdish elites at the time (and even today): of the many who were available as leaders and allies of Kurdish nationalism, many were more tribal or sectarian than nationalist, and therefore willing to be coopted by the Turkish state or to happily sit on their hands as their insurgent tribal rivals were crushed.[4]

The end of World War One and the armistice of 1918 left Turkey in a disastrous situation. The emerging Turkish republic was to be partitioned into spheres of Allied influence and Armenian, Kurdish, and Greek states. With Istanbul occupied by the Allies, the economy devastated from the war, and the Ottoman territory sliced into various chunks claimed by numerous outside forces, it seemed difficult to imagine more dire circumstances for Turkish leaders. The elites that had undergirded the Ottoman political system were severely divided between the Sultan's Ottoman camp in Istanbul and Mustafa Kemal Pasha's (Ataturk) nationalists in central Anatolia. The Sultan's camp reluctantly accepted all Allied dictates, culminating in the signing of the Treaty of Sèvres in 1920. For the Kurds, the most important element in the Treaty of Sèvres was Article 64:

---

[4] David McDowall provides the following analysis of the nature and meaning of tribal affiliations in Kurdistan:

Apart from the population on the plain and in the foothills, most Kurds belonged to nomadic or semi-nomadic tribes. Tribalism was frequently a mix between the ties of kinship and those of territory, being neither purely one nor the other. In the mountainous heartlands of Kurdistan the sense of tribe has always – until today – been strongest, but in the low-lying areas in the foothills and on the plain many Kurds lost their tribal identity ... Traditionally Kurdish tribal leaders have necessarily been guided in their politics by the conflicting balance of power among neighbouring tribes and with the more distant government of the region. Needless to say, central government often saw advantage in supporting an up-and-coming chief who might act as a counter-balance or "policeman" against neighbouring tribes which were unwilling to do the government's bidding. Many chiefs were quite willing to act on behalf of the government against a neighbour if properly rewarded. As recently as the 1950s, when asked by a British diplomat what he would do about a Kurdish tribe that was in revolt, the Iraqi Prime Minister Nuri al-Said replied, "Oh, it's quite simple, I shall send a bag of gold to a neighbouring chief."

"The Kurdish Question: A Historical Overview," in Philip G. Kreyenbroek and Stefan Sperl (eds.), *The Kurds: A Contemporary Overview* (London: Routledge, 1992), p. 12.

If within one year from the coming into force of the present Treaty the Kurdish peoples within the areas defined in Article 62[5] shall address themselves to the Council of the League of Nations in such a manner as to show that a majority of the population of these areas desires independence from Turkey, and if the Council then considers that these peoples are capable of such independence and recommends that it should be granted to them, Turkey hereby agrees to execute such a recommendation, and to renounce all rights and title over these areas ... If and when such renunciation takes place, no objection will be raised by the Principle Allied Powers to the voluntary adhesion to such an independent Kurdish State of the Kurds inhabiting that part of Kurdistan which has been hitherto included in the Mosul Vilayet.[6]

If there ever existed an auspicious political opportunity for Kurdish nationalists, it was embodied in the Treaty of Sèvres, forced upon the Sultan and his coterie of government elites and endorsed by the Allied powers. Ataturk's nationalist coalition, which rejected the Treaty, had its hands full in 1920 fighting Greek, Armenian, French, and pro-Sultan forces on all fronts.[7] Hence there existed little state capacity to repress Kurdish nationalists, should they have chosen this window of opportunity to make the Treaty of Sèvres' provisions for a Kurdish state a reality.

The Kuchgiri uprising

In fact, some Kurdish groups did try to take advantage of this opportunity. Only three months after the signing of the Treaty of Sèvres, the Istanbul-based Society for the Rise of Kurdistan and leaders of the Kuchgiri Kurdish tribe broke into revolt in the Dersim (Tunceli) region of eastern Turkey.[8] The rebels were no doubt attempting to take advantage of a clear opportunity, as implied in the following rendering of events:

In September of 1920 the position of the Kemalists had begun to look more fragile as the Armenians launched a major offensive in the east. A month later the Greeks mounted their offensive in the west. On 20 October the Kurds seized a large shipment of arms and, rather than returning it to the Kemalists, Alishan Beg [a Kuchgiri chief and a leader of the revolt] used this windfall to rally the Dersim tribes in rebellion.[9]

---

[5] Article 62 defined these areas as "the predominantly Kurdish areas lying east of the Euphrates, south of the boundary of Armenia as it may be hereafter determined, and north of the frontier of Turkey with Syria and Mesopotamia ..." Quoted in McDowall, *A Modern History of the Kurds*, p. 459.

[6] Ibid., pp. 459–460.

[7] Feroz Ahmad, *The Making of Modern Turkey* (London: Routledge, 1993), p. 50.

[8] Robert Olson, *The Emergence of Kurdish Nationalism and the Sheikh Said Rebellion, 1880–1925* (Austin: University of Texas Press, 1989), p. 28.

[9] McDowall, *A Modern History of the Kurds*, p. 185.

Robert Olson, the main English-language authority on the revolt, cites the following precipitating causes:

The main reason for the rebellion seems to have been that the Kurds wanted to use the stipulations of articles 62 and 64 of the Treaty of Sèvres to increase their autonomy within Anatolia. They wished to take advantage of the fledgling Kemalist government, which had only declared its National Pact (Misak-I Milli) one year before the rebellion. In Spring 1921, the Kemalists were locked in battle with the Greeks; as mentioned above, the Kurds wanted to take advantage of the situation. The Kurds were also in a good position to receive international support for their activities and even aid from the French, British, or Greeks.[10]

The rebels sent the following demands to Ataturk's government in Ankara:
(1) acceptance by Ankara of Kurdish autonomy as already agreed by Istanbul;
(2) the release of all Kurdish prisoners in Elaziz, Malatya, Sivas, and Erzinjan jails;
(3) the withdrawal of Turkish officials from areas with a Kurdish majority; and
(4) the withdrawal of all Turkish forces from the Kuchgiri region.[11]
Significantly, the demands were all Kurdish nationalist in nature, rather than religious, class, or otherwise based. The government in Ankara refrained from refusing the demands, since it was already fighting other forces on too many fronts. Instead, Ataturk played for time, sending representatives to negotiate with the rebels and even offering rebel leader Alishan Beg candidacy to the Ankara Assembly.[12]

The Kemalists were able to prevent the rebellion from spreading to other Kurdish tribes. The Kuchgiri Kurds were Alevi, a heterodox religion combining important aspects of Zoroastrian, Manichean, and Shiite Islamic beliefs. Alevis were often the target of persecution by larger and mainstream Sunni groups, and for the most part had not participated in the massacres and dispossession of the Armenians. Many Sunni Kurds had a history of "bad blood" with Alevi Kurds, and hence stood aside when they revolted. At the time, the greater concern of many Sunni Kurds involved the possible establishment of an Armenian state (especially on land claimed by Kurds) and the resulting likelihood of Armenian retribution towards Kurds implicated in the events of 1915 and before. In fact, Ataturk's first major congress to organize resistance against the Allies and Armenians attracted all of its Kurdish representatives from the Kurdish regions slated to fall within the borders of the proposed

---

[10] Olson, *The Emergence of Kurdish Nationalism*, p. 33.
[11] McDowall, *A Modern History of the Kurds*, p. 185. [12] Ibid., p. 186.

Armenian state.[13] Ataturk was thus able to paint the ongoing struggle as a contest between the infidel Western powers who supported the Christian Armenians and Greeks, and Muslim-Ottoman Turks and Kurds fighting to save the Sultan, Caliph, and homeland.[14] By framing the issue in this manner, the Kuchgiri rebels could be accused of treason to the Muslim homeland, seeing as they timed their revolt to coincide with the struggle against invading Armenian and Greek armies. Those who wished to prevent the establishment of an Armenian state and the subjugation of Muslim lands would support the Kemalists.[15]

Crucially, Ataturk at the time did not reveal what kind of state the Kemalists wished to establish (assuming he even knew himself before 1923). Instead, he allowed the Kurds to believe that joining the Kemalists meant fighting to save the Ottoman legacy (under which Kurds and Turks were equal as Muslims) and establishing a state based on Turkish-Kurdish brotherhood. In his own words: "As long as there are fine people with honour and respect, Turks and Kurds will continue to live together as brothers around the institution of the khilafa [Caliphate], and an unshakeable iron tower will be raised against internal and external enemies."[16] Pronouncements such as these, together with the offer of land and high government posts to Kurdish notables, made the institutionalized (or soon to be institutionalized) political system appear open to Kurds and Kurdish interests. Many cautious and reasonable Kurdish elites, unaware of Turkish secular, ethnic nationalist sentiments brewing in Ankara, therefore found it only logical at the time to support the Kemalists and pursue their interests from within the emerging system. Most Kurds ended up joining and making a vital contribution to the

---

[13] Kendal, "Kurdistan in Turkey," in Chaliand, ed., *People Without a Country* (London: Zed Press, 1980), p. 56.

[14] Olson, *The Emergence of Kurdish Nationalism*, ch. 2; and McDowall, *A Modern History of the Kurds*, ch. 9, are the source for much of the historical detail regarding this issue. By necessity, the account provided by me here is greatly simplified. Readers wishing to examine these events in depth should refer to the above works respectively.

[15] Ataturk explicitly used this argument on many occasions. Volume III of Mustafa Kemal's *Great Speech* contains letters to Kurdish leaders such as Sheikh Ziyaettin Efendi of Narsin (document 52, pp. 942–943, August 13, 1919). Robert Olson summarizes the letter:

Mustafa Kemal thanked the sheikh for his support in World War I and for his loyalty to the sultan and caliph, offering his heartfelt respect for this behavior. He stated, however, that it was now public knowledge that the same sultan and caliph wanted to make a gift of the eastern *vilayets* to the Armenians. The government in Istanbul was completely incapable of defending the country ... He asked the sheikh to give greetings from him to all of the patriots of the area. (*The Emergence of Kurdish Nationalism*, p. 37)

[16] *Sacak* no. 39, April 1987 quoting from the recorded speeches, instructions, and secret meeting records of the Grand National Assembly (in McDowall, *A Modern History of the Kurds*, p. 187).

Kemalist War of Independence against the Greeks, Armenians, and Allied powers. Although some Kurdish nationalist organizations insisted on putting the struggle for a Kurdish state ahead of protecting Muslim lands against the Allied, Armenian, and Greek threats, they were hamstrung by the more influential Kurdish chieftains, who had been won over to the Kemalist camp.[17]

Essentially, the illusion of an open institutionalized political system, combined with patronage from Ankara and tribal and religious divisions amongst the Kurds themselves, denied the Kurdish nationalists leaders of the Kuchgiri revolt the number of elite allies (along with their tribal or religious followers) necessary to succeed. By the spring of 1921, the Kemalists were able to divert enough troops from the other war fronts to crush the Kuchgiri, as the revolt was still limited to the Dersim region. Although the Kuchgiri Kurds and several Kurdish political organizations of the time had tried to frame their movement in broad, Kurdish nationalist terms, support from a broad section of Kurdistan never materialized.

The Treaty of Lausanne and the Sheikh Said revolt

If at the time of the Kuchgiri rebellion the emerging political system still appeared open to Kurds, by 1923 the true nature of the new government in Ankara became apparent. The Armenian and Greek threats had been dispelled, the War of Independence was won and the Kemalists now turned to the task of state building. With the destruction of Greek and Armenian forces and the Allies' unwillingness to fight Kemalist forces directly,[18] the Treaty of Sèvres was effectively dead. On November 1, 1922, the Kemalists abolished the Sultanate. On July 24, 1923 the Treaty of Lausanne replaced Sèvres. Ominously, it contained no mention

---

[17] Van Bruinessen provides the following illustrative account:

> Even apart from the confidence that Mustafa Kemal inspired, it is not surprising that many Kurdish chieftains turned to him: he had power that he might delegate to them, whereas the nationalist organizations did not. The latter might count on the Allies' goodwill and on the provisions of Sèvres, but most chieftains correctly perceived that the Allies were in the first place the Armenians' friends, not the Kurds'. Mustafa Kemal was the most likely person to protect Kurdish lands from Armenian claims. Thus, in November 1919, it happened that the Kurdish delegation at the Peace Conference saw its efforts to convey the demands for Kurdish independence crossed by a series of telegrams to the Peace Conference from Kurdish chieftains protesting that they did *not* want separation from the Turks. (*Agha, Shaikh and State* [London: Zed Books, Ltd., 1992], p. 279)

[18] Only the British were willing to fight over the vilayet of Mosul, due to its large oil deposits. For this reason Mosul was eventually included in the new British mandate of Iraq, and not Turkey.

whatsoever of the Kurds (or Armenians, for that matter).[19] In 1923, Turkey was declared a republic. Soon after, on March 3, 2004, the new Turkish Assembly in Ankara abolished the caliphate and, for good measure, all Kurdish schools, associations, publications, religious orders, and *madrasahs* (religious schools).[20] In addition to Turkish nationalism, secularism and populism became cornerstones of the new modernizing regime in Ankara. The new ideology sought to remove inequalities stemming from differences of class, religion, occupation, and ethnicity, and therefore socialist parties and trade unions were also added to the above-mentioned bans. The new regime even went so far as to deny the existence of non-Turkish Muslims in the country – decreeing that Kurds were in fact Turks.[21]

Suddenly the issues that had placed many Kurdish elites in the Kemalist camp were gone. Those Kurds who thought they had been fighting to save the sultanate, caliphate, and Ottoman-Muslim legacy were rudely awakened. Those who aspired to Kurdish autonomy or independence came face to face with a state that would deny the very existence of a Kurdish people, language, and culture. The newly institutionalized political system would only accept those who, in public, set aside their Kurdishness. Kurds had to become Turks. The new turn of events alienated most Kurdish elites, but unfortunately for Kurdish nationalists, internal divisions still foiled attempts at a unified Kurdish opposition. During the War of Independence, the Kemalists had also been careful to forbid the establishment of Kurdish organizations outside the army, thereby preventing the emergence of movements that could organize the Kurds once Turkish and Kurdish nationalist interests diverged. Although Kurdish elite allies were available to oppose the state in great numbers by 1924, one could not convince them to do so from the same camp. Part of the problem lay in the nature of Kurdish elites at the time – they were almost exclusively tribal leaders, religious

---

[19] The only indirect provision referring to Muslim minorities within Turkey such as the Kurds could be found in part of Article 39 of the Treaty:

> No restrictions shall be imposed on the free use by any Turkish national of any language in private intercourse, or in commerce, religion, in the press, or in publications of any kind or at public meetings. Notwithstanding the existence of the official language, adequate facilities shall be given to Turkish nationals of non-Turkish speech for the oral use of their own language before the courts.

For the complete text of the Treaty, see *The Treaties of Peace 1919–1923*, Vol. II (New York: Carnegie Endowment for International Peace, 1924).

[20] Kendal, "Kurdistan in Turkey," in Gerard Chaliand (ed.), *People Without a Country: The Kurds and Kurdistan* (London: Zed Press, 1980), p. 60.

[21] Ibid.

sheikhs, or large landowners.[22] There were few "modern" elites, meaning non-religious or tribally affiliated members of the bourgeoisie, intellectuals, or the professional classes. When tribal leaders took the helm of a revolt, members of traditionally competing tribes would likely either not participate or they would assist the government in putting down the revolt.[23] If the uprising were led by a religious figure, then Kurds belonging to other religious denominations or orders were unlikely to participate. Had Kurdish nationalist thought been a deeper part of average Kurds' identity at the time, two different possible scenarios might have occurred: first, the leaders of revolts might have been able to overcome sectarian divisions and rallied broader sections of the general population to the cause.[24] In such a scenario, sectarian difference could have been set aside until after independence was won. Second, the nature of the Kurdish leadership might have been different, with bourgeois, socialist, or urban radical democrats displacing the traditional feudal and tribal leadership.

In any case, by 1923 other factors also conspired to shrink the political opportunity structures available to rebellious Kurdish movements. The Turkish elites undergirding the government had by then stabilized and coalesced behind the Kemalists in Ankara, although Ataturk still faced some serious opposition from religious conservatives (due to his emphasis on secularism). Turkish opponents of Ataturk's government never came to the aid of Kurdish rebels, however, despite having been approached on several occasions.[25] The new Turkish Republic by 1923 was also much

---

[22] Traditional Kurdish elites are often referred to using the following terms: *agha, asiret beyi, shaikh,* and *sayyid.* Lale Yalcin-Heckman provides the following definitions of these titles:

> Briefly, *aga/agha* is a term with many meanings, but in relation to Eastern Turkey, it often means a rich landowner and a patron. *Asiret beyi* is simply the leader of a tribe (*asiret*). *Shaikh,* in the Eastern Turkish and Kurdish context, is a *tariqa* (religious brotherhood, sect) leader. *Shaikhs* have *murids* (followers) in the brotherhood. A *sayyid,* on the other hand, is someone who claims descent from the Prophet Muhammed's family, thus it is a hereditary title. ("Kurdish Tribal Organization," in Andrew Finkel and Nukhet Sirman [eds.], *Turkish State, Turkish Society* [London: Routledge, 1990], p. 290)

[23] John Bulloch and Harvey Morris, *No Friends but the Mountains* (London: Penguin Books Ltd., 1992), p. 77.

[24] In explaining the divisions amongst Kurdish elites at the time, the analysis used here unavoidably drifts into the realm of cultural framing and identity (issues addressed more directly in ch. 4). In effect, some aspects of a synthesis of theoretical approaches have thus already emerged in our argument.

[25] Van Bruinessen notes that at most, Turkish opponents of Ataturk such as Kazim Karabekir (commander of the Turkish Eighth army corps in Erzurum), dealt more leniently with Kurdish rebels than others (pp. 292–293). Their attitude towards the rebels never even reached the level of passive support, however. British observer Toynbee added that "it is noteworthy that the revolt [the 1925 Sheikh Said revolt] did not spread among the Turkish population of Erzurum, Trebizond, and Samsun, who were almost as backward and reactionary as their Kurdish neighbours, and who not long

better placed to use repressive force against internal threats, now that the external dangers had been overcome. Finally, the international context became unfavorable by the time of Lausanne, as is made clear by an examination of the 1925 Sheikh Said revolt and 1927–1930 Mount Ararat uprising. In contrast to international support that Arab nationalism received, the Kurds by 1923 were for the most part brushed aside,[26] while states they opposed proved more successful at securing foreign assistance.[27]

Azadi ('freedom' in Kurdish) was a clandestine Kurdish nationalist organization established in 1923, with the express aim of fomenting a revolt against Ankara.[28] Keenly aware of the need to overcome tribal divisions to mount a successful uprising, Azadi installed Sheikh Said, a charismatic Kurdish religious figure, as the leader of the planned revolt. In Kurdish society, sheikhs transcend tribal affiliations and were in fact traditionally relied upon to resolve and mediate conflicts between tribes. It was thus hoped that an uprising led by a charismatic sheikh and combining Kurdish nationalism with religious grievances against the Kemalists would create the broad appeal and momentum necessary for success. Sheikh Said was only partially successful in rallying competing tribes, however.[29] Also, his status as a Sunni Naqshibendi sheikh lost him support among some key Alevi tribes. The Khurmak and Lawlan Alevis, in light of many years of religious persecution at the hands of Sunnis, had no desire to see a rebellion led by an orthodox Sunni sheikh succeed. The Khurmak began fighting the Jibran, a rival tribe that, as soon as the uprising began, had aligned itself with Sheikh Said and the revolt, and the Khurmak and Lawlan were probably more effective against the rebels than the Turkish gendarmerie and army.[30]

Ankara well knew the plans of Azadi and Sheikh Said before the uprising broke out, and arrested many key leaders of Azadi prior to the revolt. When

---

afterwards ... rose on their own account ... against the Ankara government's westerniz-ing reforms" (A. J. Toynbee, *Survey of International Affairs 1925. Vol. 1 : The Islamic World Since the Peace Settlement* [Oxford: Oxford University Press, 1927], p. 508, n. 3, quoted in van Bruinessen, *Agha, Shaikh and State*, p. 293). For a discussion of elite interests and schisms in Turkey, see Ergun Ozbudun, *Social Change and Political Participation in Turkey* (Princeton, NJ: Princeton University Press, 1976).

[26] Hakan Ozoglu, "'Nationalism' and Kurdish Notables in the Late Ottoman – Early Republican Era," *International Journal of Middle East Studies*, 33 (2001), 405.

[27] As the Palestine case demonstrates, however, international support does not automati-cally translate into statehood – even in the portion of Palestine designated by the 1947 UN Partition Plan.

[28] For more information on Azadi and the Sheikh Said revolt in general, see van Bruinessen, *Agha, Shaikh and State*, ch. 5. I have relied primarily on van Bruinessen and Ihsan Nouri Pasha's memoirs – *La Révolte de l'Agri-dagh* (Geneva: Editions Kurdes, 1986) – for an account of the Sheikh Said and Mount Ararat uprisings.

[29] The majority of tribes supporting the revolt were Zaza-speaking Sunni tribes, although some important Kurmanji-speaking tribes, such as the Jibran, were also rallied.

[30] Van Bruinessen, *Agha, Shaikh and State*, p. 285.

circumstances forced Sheikh Said to take up arms before everything was ready, he managed to rally virtually all of the Zaza-speaking Sunni Kurdish tribes to the cause. Significantly, the members of these tribes were from the middle peasantry, a social stratum most easily mobilized in peasant or rural uprisings (as opposed to the poorest and severely oppressed peasants), along the lines of Eric Wolf's theory: "... in these tribes, nearly every man had his own piece of land and a few animals ... Secondly, the chieftains did not have economic power over the commoners, nor were they much richer. There were thus no conflicts of interest to make commoners refrain from participation at the demand of aghas."[31]

Thus in the absence of strong authoritarian elites pursuing their own sectarian interests or being co-opted by Ankara, nationalist elites such as Sheikh Said succeeded in rallying large numbers of supporters amongst the Zaza Sunni tribes. The revolt in fact achieved significant successes initially, including the capture of significant towns in large areas of eastern Anatolia.[32] The largest city in Turkish Kurdistan, Diyarbakir, was laid siege to and even penetrated at one point, but was never taken.

Ankara was initially slow in responding to the rebellion, mainly because its principal military forces in the area, the Seventh and Eighth army corps, had many Kurdish soldiers or commanders in political opposition to Ataturk (specifically Kazim Karabekir, commander of the Eighth corps), and were hence untrustworthy. In the early days of the revolt, the previously mentioned Khurmak and Lawlan tribes acted to prevent the spread of rebellion to northeastern parts of Turkish Kurdistan, assisting government garrisons in various areas while the Kemalists mobilized troops from the west.[33] Crucial to Ankara's counter-insurgency campaign, France allowed the transit of at least 35,000 Turkish troops through Syria, via the Baghdad railway.[34] When government troops finally arrived in force and began to push back the rebels, a brutal campaign of repression occurred:

Hundreds of villages were destroyed, thousands of innocent men, women and children killed. Special courts, established in accordance with the Law on the Reinforcement of Order, condemned many influential persons to death – including several who had no connection whatsoever with the revolt. On September 4, 1925, Shaikh Said and forty-seven other leading Kurds were hanged in Diyarbakir. Thousands of less influential Kurds were slaughtered without a trial. The population of entire districts were deported to the west. The role of shaikhs in the uprising

[31] Ibid., p. 293. Wolf, *Peasant Wars*.
[32] These included Darayeni, Hani, Lice, Chabaqchur, Maden, Chermik, Erghani, Menazgird, Bulanik, Varto, Elaziz, and Piran (van Bruinessen, *Agha, Shaikh and State*, pp. 286–289).
[33] Van Bruinessen, *Agha, Shaikh and State*, p. 290.   [34] Ibid.

was, moreover, the reason for a law ordering the closure of all *tekiyes* [religious orders], tombs and other places of pilgrimage (December 1925).[35]

Commenting on these tactics and the Law on the Reinforcement of Order, the British ambassador found it "difficult to imagine how the net of repression could have been thrown out more widely . . ."[36]

The British may have been taken aback by the severity with which the uprising was suppressed, but they should not have been dismayed. Despite the fact that a Kurdish uprising in Turkey helped them in their contest with the Kemalists over the vilayet of Mosul in northern Iraq, the British failed to provide the rebels with any assistance.[37] Little more than five years after Sèvres, the British were stating that "it forms no part of the policy of His Majesty's Government to encourage or accept any responsibility for the formation of any autonomous or independent Kurdish state."[38] France was also instrumental in aiding Ankara's military response.[39] The Soviet Union had likewise by 1921 signed a treaty of friendship with the Kemalists, and was in fact their main source of arms and financial aid by 1925.[40] Iran, although it may have wished to repay Turkey in similar coin for supporting Kurdish rebels fighting the Shah, also failed to substantially assist Sheikh Said's movement. In effect, Sheikh Said's rebels were left on their own, and their only source of arms were leftovers from the First World War and whatever could be captured from Turkish troops.

The lack of international support might not have been fatal, had it not been for the previously mentioned Achilles' heel of a fractious, disunited Kurdish society.[41] In fact, as long as most Kurds remained beholden and

---

[35] Ibid., pp. 290–291.

[36] FO 371/10867 Lindsay to Chamberlain, Istanbul, March 10, 1925 (cited in McDowall, *A Modern History of the Kurds*, p. 195).

[37] Van Bruinessen, *Agha, Shaikh and State*, p. 292.

[38] Statement made by the British ambassador to Iran, chastising his consul in Tabriz who was sympathetic towards some Kurdish nationalist projects (FO 371/10835 Loraine to Gilliat-Smith, Tehran, 7 October 1925, in McDowall, 1997, 199).

[39] Nouri Pasha, *La Révolte de l'Agri-dagh*, p. 42.   [40] Ibid.

[41] The Kurds' chances of securing genuine international support for Kurdish statehood would never again be as good as they were following the First World War. In the 1920s the international system was briefly willing to accept post-war re-arrangements of political boundaries and the creation of new states. This window of opportunity for nations seeking their own state was soon replaced by an overriding international norm of respecting state sovereignty and existing political boundaries. For instance, UN resolution 1514 states that "any attempt aimed at the partial or total disruption of the national unity and the territorial integrity of a country is incompatible with the purposes and principles of the Charter of the United Nations" (cited in Robert Jackson, *Quasi-states: Sovereignty, International Relations, and the Third World* [Cambridge: Cambridge University Press, 1990], p. 78). Hence, after the 1920s the Kurds faced a world of states that was at best uninterested in, and at worst implacably hostile towards, Kurdish nationalist attempts to found a Kurdish state.

subservient to tribal and religious elites, the chances of overcoming such divisions in the name of a larger Kurdish nationalism would remain slim. More progressive and intellectual Kurdish elites could be found in Istanbul and other metropolises, but their distance from Kurdistan meant that they lacked authority and contact with the Kurdish masses. Revolts would continue to occur as various elites decided to resist a centralizing, authoritarian modernizing government, but they would remain isolated from each other and hence ineffective. The Mount Ararat uprising which followed Sheikh Said's revolt, as well as dozens of others throughout Kurdistan, suffered from the same dynamic hampering Kurdish nationalists in 1925:

Outside the central area, where the revolt had a mass character, participation and non-participation or even opposition of tribes to the revolt were apparently determined to a large extent by the same kind of considerations that had for centuries determined tribal politics and policies *vis-à-vis* the state. The motivation of the commoners – be it religious or nationalist – played no part as yet worth mentioning. Chieftains joined or opposed according to what seemed the most advantageous thing to do and to what their rivals did; the commoners simply followed their chieftains.[42]

Perhaps indicative of Kurdish society's predominantly feudal make-up until at least the 1950s, the only significant elites available to spearhead rebellion against the state were tribal leaders, religious sheikhs, and large landowners.[43] Thus, when revolts of the day were directed against the central government by feudal leaders resentful of its abrogation of their power, non-tribal Kurdish peasants also showed little support for the rebels. These groups would instead later rise up against their own Kurdish landlords. As for the urban lumpen-proletariat, many of these were recent immigrants to the cities, retained their tribal affiliations, and were often sympathetic to the Kurdish revolts in which their tribes participated. In the Sheikh Said revolt, they were the ones who let the rebels laying siege to Diyarbakir into the city at night. Lacking elites to provide organization and arms, they did not actively participate in the early rebellions against the Turkish Republic.

In the ensuing years, apart from the Mount Ararat uprising (1927–1930) and finally the Dersim revolt (1938) many other rebellions broke out, but under political opportunity structures that remained largely unfavorable. The completely closed nature of the institutionalized political system in Ankara nonetheless encouraged the violent pursuit of Kurdish demands, given that no other options besides

---

[42] Van Bruinessen, *Agha, Shaikh and State*, p. 294.
[43] Peresh, "Introduction," in Nouri Pasha, *La Révolte de l'Agri-dagh*, p. 42.

submission existed.[44] The stability of elite alignments undergirding the Kemalist government increased, making the insurgents' task even more difficult. Elite allies amongst the Kurds existed, but the previously mentioned disunity prevailed. The Turkish state's capacity and propensity for repression increased, with whole regions of Turkish Kurdistan under martial law and facing destruction and deportations.[45] Finally, international support for the Kemalists increased, while aid to Kurdish nationalists remained, for the most part, ephemeral or nonexistent.[46]

Kurdish dissent in dormancy: 1938–1946

After the brutal post-1925 campaigns of suppression, and finally the crushing of the Dersim revolt in 1938, Kurdish opposition to Ankara appeared to be finished. Rebellious Kurdish elites had all been exiled, killed, or deported to western Turkey, while the remaining aghas, beys, and sheikhs were either co-opted or cowed into silence. The Kurdish masses as well had seen too much repression, bloodshed, and chaos, and resistance to the state seemed pointless. Only the closed nature of the Kemalist political system remained as an incentive to revolt; other political opportunity structures (particularly the state's readiness and ability to use repressive force) remained less than favorable. By 1938 the Kurds were referred to as "mountain Turks" in Turkey, and heavy repression in Kurdistan seemed to have successfully subdued the

---

[44] It became increasingly clear after the suppression of the Sheikh Said revolt that in addition to the Turkish political system being closed to Kurdish aspirations, Ankara also sought to completely erase Kurdish identity from within its borders. Tewfik Rustu, Turkey's Minister of Foreign Affairs, expressed the Kemalists' view to British diplomat Sir George Clark: comparing the Kurds to the American Indians, Rustu stated that they must be suppressed and assimilated until they disappear (FO 371/12255 Clerk to Chamberlain, Istanbul, 22 June 1927, in Nouri Pasha, *La Révolte de l'Agri-dagh*, p. 43 and also McDowall, *A Modern History of the Kurds*, p. 199).

[45] McDowall provides the following observation regarding the Turkish state's propensity and capacity for repression:

Shaykh Said's revolt marked the beginning of "implacable Kemalism". Systematic deportation and razing of villages, brutality and killing of innocents, martial law or special regimes in Kurdistan now became the commonplace experience of Kurds whenever they defied the state. The army, deployed in strength for the first time since Lausanne, now found control of Kurdistan to be its prime function and *raison d'être*. Only one out of 18 Turkish military engagements during the years 1924–38 occurred outside Kurdistan. After 1945, apart from the Korean war, 1949–52 and the invasion of Cyprus, 1974, the only Turkish army operations continued to be against the Kurds. (*A Modern History of the Kurds*, p. 198)

[46] During the Mount Ararat uprising, the rebels received some support from Kurds and Armenians in Iran, while Ankara received help from the Soviets and also coerced Tehran into eventually denying the rebels use of Iranian territory.

region. Ankara could proceed on its assimilationist projects aimed at eliminating Kurdish identity, in addition to hopefully bringing much needed economic development to the war-ravaged southeast.

What little economic development occurred in the southeast during this time, however, was to the benefit of large landholding elites.[47] Poor or landless peasants remained subject to their feudal landlords, or migrated to swell the ranks of the urban poor. Efforts to assimilate the Kurds to Turkish language and culture, although an integral part of state policy, met with only partial implementation and success, mainly due to government's weak record during this period of installing anything more than gendarmerie posts and tax collectors in the Kurdish regions.

By 1946, however, Ataturk's one-party (the Republican People's Party, or RPP) legacy faced severe challenges from within the governing elite.[48] The resulting move to a multi-party system along with increasing socio-economic development would eventually set in motion changes in the political opportunity structure for Kurdish nationalists.

The seeds of new opportunities: 1946–1980

In the pursuit of economic modernization, the Republican People's Party had begun pushing economic reforms that violated the tacit alliance it had with rural and urban notables. Partly as a counterweight to the increasingly disaffected notables, the RPP in 1946 began pursuing a land-reform agenda that would attract the support of small and landless peasants.[49] Elite opposition to land reform, along with foreign policy concerns that called for closer ties with the West, finally provided the necessary impetus for a move to a multi-party system. The RPP made further attempts to broaden its base of support to the masses, including repealing its ban on labor unions.[50] Nonetheless, the new center-right Democratic Party (DP) won a large majority in the 1950 general election and formed a new government.

[47] Binnaz Toprak, *Islam and Political Development in Turkey* (Leiden: E. J. Brill, 1981), p. 70.
[48] During the 1923–1946 period, the elite alignment undergirding the state consisted of an alliance between military-bureaucrats at the national level and small town and rural notables at the local level:

> The alliance joining central state elites and dominant classes was based on a tacit compromise: social elites would support the continued hegemony of the bureaucratic elite and its modernizing reforms of state and cultural institutions as long as these reforms did not threaten the existing social and economic structure. (David Waldner, *State Building and Late Development* [Ithaca: Cornell University Press, 1999], p. 55)

[49] Waldner, *State Building*, p. 59.   [50] Ibid.

The DP drew a crucial number of its votes from the rural, and particularly Kurdish, segments of the population.[51] Most importantly, the move to a multi-party electoral system created the need to appeal to, and mobilize, the population at large. The RPP, the DP, and later parties that entered the system, from this time onwards pursued a strategy of political clientelism. Local-level patrons were wooed to the parties and given additional resources to distribute to their clients; these "big men" would in return deliver the large blocs of votes of their followers.[52] Traditional Kurdish society was particularly attractive to the political parties in this sense, since provinces such as Diyarbakir boasted fewer than twenty large landlords who between them delivered the region's electorate to whomever they wished. In the election of 1954, 34 of Turkish Kurdistan's 40 seats went to the Democratic Party.[53]

The advent of electoral politics in Turkey also brought forth what would be an enduring division between state elites (the military and professional elites concerned with maintaining the Kemalist legacy of secularism, Turkish nationalism, populism, statism, and a western orientation), and the political elite, dependent on patronage as a political tool and intent on pursuing whatever policies would garner votes.[54] Although the Turkish masses' dissatisfaction with Kemalist secularism was immediately seized upon by the DP as an election issue, the political elite remained aware of the limits to challenging basic tenets of Kemalism. Breaking the taboo on openly addressing Kurdish demands would never be tolerated by the military and other state elites.

As it happens, the DP's limited politicization of religion ended up being one of the major factors that provoked a military coup in 1960.[55] There were, of course, several different additional factors that precipitated the 1960 coup. Perhaps ironically (given the nature of the later 1971 and

---

[51] Whereas scholars such as Waldner, McDowall, and Toprak stress that the DP was more effective than the RPP in gaining votes from rural areas, Dodd argues that "it was the Democrat Party's substantial urban, not rural, vote which was crucial for its victory" (C. H. Dodd, *The Crisis of Turkish Democracy* [Huntingdon: Eothen Press, 1990], p. 9). The confusion stems in part from the complicated, multi-level issues involved in the election, and the fact that both parties derived support from a multitude of sources. Nonetheless, it appears that the Kurdish vote went disproportionately to the DP, as a result of both bitterness over past repression while the RPP was at the helm, and large Kurdish landlords' preference for the more pro-private enterprise stance of the DP (Edwin J. Cohn, *Turkish Economic, Social, and Political Change* [New York: Praeger Publishers, 1970], p. 16).

[52] Toprak, *Islam and Political Development*, p. 72.

[53] McDowall, *A Modern History of the Kurds*, p. 398.

[54] Metin Heper and Fuat Keyman, "Double-Faced State," in Sylvia Kedourie, *Turkey Before and After Ataturk* (London: Frank Cass, 1999), p. 259.

[55] Toprak, *Islam and Political Development*, p. 88.

1980 coups, by which time the military seemed to have changed its mind on certain issues), the military was also concerned with the Democrat Party's increasing authoritarianism – by the late 1950s, the party had introduced legislation restricting freedom of the press, public meetings, and opposition political parties.[56] Hence the 1960 military coup and the new constitution resulting from it focused on protecting and promoting democracy. Upon taking over government, the military junta hung DP Prime Minister Adnan Menderes and two of his ministers, and then set about drafting new rules that would check the power of civilian politicians in Turkey.[57]

The constitution drawn up in 1960 introduced new checks and balances on government, new social rights (such as the right to strike and a minimum wage), and increased individual rights and freedoms.[58] Although the more liberal political context did not in effect apply to the Kurdish issue (anyone promoting a Kurdish nationalist agenda would find themselves suppressed just as quickly as before),[59] some opening occurred for the growth of civil society and leftist opposition movements. Not surprisingly, Kurds joined the new leftist movements in disproportionate numbers, and the experience they garnered in the Turkish Left would later help provide the foundations for the emergence of a non-traditional, Kurdish intellectual and revolutionary elite.

Besides the democratic opening of 1960, two additional factors acted to create a new, non-traditional Kurdish nationalist elite: economic modernization and its attendant rural–urban migration of the Kurdish population. By the 1950s, Kurdish large landowners (aghas) had been largely co-opted into the Turkish political system (the "big men" that could deliver large blocs of votes): "... the aghas ceased to be Kurdish in two vital senses: they quietly disowned their Kurdish origin, and they exploited their relationship with the peasantry not as a means to semi-independence from the center as in the old days, but in order to

---

[56] Dodd, *The Crisis of Turkish Democracy*, p. 10.
[57] Just one year before the coup, Prime Minister Menderes had been pushing for the hanging of forty-nine Kurdish students and intellectuals, who had been arrested for demonstrating in the wake of anti-Kurdish statements made by the mayor of Nigde, a small city in central Anatolia. In retrospect, he might have found it more prudent to advocate a climate of leniency towards "political crimes."
[58] Dodd, *The Crisis of Turkish Democracy*, p. 11.
[59] In case there was any question on this issue, President Gursel (who led the 1960 coup) stated in 1960 that if Kurdish unrest occurred in Turkey, "The army will not hesitate to bombard towns and villages: there will be such a bloodbath that they will be swallowed in their country" (*Dagens Nyheter*, November 11, 1960, quoted in I. S. Vanly, *Survey of the National Question of Turkish Kurdistan* [Europe: Hevra, Organization of the Revolutionary Kurds of Turkey in Europe, 1971], p. 41).

become more closely integrated members of the ruling Turkish establishment."[60] The aghas also successfully blocked any attempts at land reform in the Kurdish regions, and the majority of the Kurdish peasantry remained sharecroppers or the holders of very tiny plots of land. With the introduction of tractors and mechanized agriculture, however, ever increasing numbers of these peasants were pushed off the land and migrated to cities in the Kurdish regions, in western Turkey, or abroad.[61] Apart from economic changes, destruction of Kurdish villages (particularly in the 1930s and from 1980 to 1999) and the political insecurity in Turkey's southeast also contributed to rural–urban migration.[62]

At the same time that increasing numbers of Kurds settled in various cities, economic modernization produced new challenges and opportunities. Education, particularly university education, exposed a new generation of both wealthy and talented poor Kurds to ideas of nationalism, socialism, and the struggle of other peoples against state tyranny. In urban contexts, the strength of tribal affiliations often declined. Many educated young Kurds thrived in their new urban milieux, adopted a Turkish identity and advanced to the top echelons of society and government. Others, however, refused to assimilate (a precondition for advancement in Turkey) or did not achieve the level of success their ambition strived for. High unemployment levels left increasing numbers of educated Kurds, who were now aware of the wealth and possibilities around them thanks to modern media and communications,[63] frustrated and in search of options to better their plight. This stratum of the population would emerge in the 1960s and 1970s as the new elite leadership of many left-wing and Kurdish nationalist movements. Leftist groups such as DISK (the Confederation of Revolutionary Workers Unions), Dev Genc (the Federation of Revolutionary Youth), and the TWP (the Turkish Workers' Party), organized mass protests in both western and eastern Turkey, and the party cells in the Kurdish regions attached demands for Kurdish rights and an end to repression of Kurds to the calls for workers' empowerment and democracy. The demonstrations were not only the first significant acts of opposition to Ankara since the

---

[60] McDowall, *A Modern History of the Kurds*, p. 400.

[61] In 1948 Turkey had only 1,750 tractors. By 1954 there were 40,000 tractors in the country (ibid., p. 399). It was particularly the large Kurdish feudal agha farmers who could afford to buy the newly imported tractors, with the consequent dislocation of their tenants.

[62] McDowall notes that the population of the largest primarily Kurdish city in the southeast (Diyarbakir), grew from 30,000 in the 1930s to 65,000 in 1956, 140,000 in 1970 and 400,000 by 1990 (*A Modern History of the Kurds*, p. 401).

[63] Michiel Leesenberg, "The Kurds and the City," *The Journal of Kurdish Studies* 2 (1997), 57.

1930s, but also an indication of a new Kurdish elite's increasing importance:

It [the organization of large demonstrations] signaled the critical shift in social mobilization away from the aghas and semi-tribal peasantry, towards urban-based, modestly educated students and young professionals, including a growing number who were themselves the scions of agha families but who rejected the values they had inherited. These formed the basis of a bourgeois intellectual leadership, largely of mildly leftist inclination, for growing Kurdish national feeling.[64]

Although young Kurdish intellectuals in the 1950s and 1960s founded some Kurdish journals and nationalist groups, such as *Ileri Yurt* (Musa Anter's Kurdish-Turkish journal) and the KDPT (founded by Yusif Azizoglu), the journals and similar publications were closed down by government after a few issues, and the KDPT failed to achieve much importance.[65] Significant actions until the mid-1970s came almost exclusively from the Turkish far-left, in which Kurds disproportionately participated. Some groups, such as the TWP, were given the legal right to exist in 1961. As a legal party with affiliated trade unions and cultural clubs, the TWP could act as an organizing platform for opponents of the policies coming out of Ankara. Not surprisingly, a disproportionate number of these opponents of Ankara's policies that the TWP attracted were Kurds.

Initially, Kurdish nationalists participating in (and at times leading) the TWP found it difficult to convince the party to recognize the Kurdish issue. In 1970, at the Party's Fourth Congress, the first statement concerning Kurds was made: "There is a Kurdish people in the East of Turkey ... The fascist authorities representing the ruling classes have subjected the Kurdish people to a policy of assimilation and intimidation which has often become a bloody repression."[66] This led to the party's closure after Turkey's 1971 military coup.[67]

The 1971 coup came about as a result of growing polarization and strife between left-wing and right-wing groups, urban guerrilla actions by various subversive groups, and the open call for recognition of the

---

[64] McDowall, *A Modern History of the Kurds*, p. 408.
[65] McDowall attributes the KDPT's (Kurdistan Democratic Party of Turkey) failure to its conservative bent, akin to the KDP in Iraq upon which it was based. Unwilling to challenge the feudal class system in Kurdistan, and with most Kurdish landlords and traditional elites already co-opted by the state, the KDPT "had little to offer" for those seeking change (*A Modern History of the Kurds*, p. 406).
[66] From Kendal, "Kurdistan in Turkey," p. 29.
[67] The TWP was closed down on the justification that its members were "propagating communist propaganda and advocating autonomy for the Kurds" (Dodd, *The Crisis of Turkish Democracy*, 1990, p. 16).

"Kurdish problem" by groups such as the TWP. The politicians in Ankara appeared to have lost control of the situation:

By January 1971, Turkey seemed to be in a state of chaos. The universities had ceased to function. Students emulating Latin American urban guerrillas robbed banks and kidnaped US servicemen, and attacked American targets. The homes of university professors critical of the government were bombed by neo-fascist militants. Factories were on strike and more workdays were lost between 1 January and 12 March 1971 than during any prior year.[68]

Electoral politics, the more liberal 1960 constitution, and the resulting political freedoms seem to have allowed the left in Turkey to organize and grow. Uneven development and dislocations inherent in developing economies further nurtured leftists' radicalism.[69] This growth quickly surpassed the limits that the political system (or more accurately, the self-appointed military guardians of the system) would tolerate. Prevented from pursuing meaningful change from within the institutionalized system, leftist groups resorted to subversion and tactics outside "legally accepted channels," just as Kurdish groups had done in the 1920s and 1930s.[70] Rightist neo-fascist counter-movements also emerged to pursue their aims outside the system, with the advantage that state authorities often turned a blind eye to their activities. The political elite undergirding the government was divided regarding economic and related social policies, and while large industrialists were willing to accept strong labour unions and higher wages, small entrepreneurs were vociferous in their opposition to such concessions to the left. Kurdish nationalists quickly began to attach their moribund program to leftist movements taking advantage of these favorable political opportunity structures.

Favorable political opportunities for the left went no further than this. The movement lacked elite allies with much significant power or resources – trade unionists, professors, intellectuals, and some professionals (journalists, lawyers, doctors ...) made up the bulk of the left's elite. International support, beyond the inspirational example of Che Guevara, the Paris Commune, and other international events, was unavailable to leftist movements in the country. Many Marxist groups were bitterly disappointed when the Soviet Union did nothing to aid them

---

[68] Ahmad, *The Making of Modern Turkey*, p. 147.
[69] Dodd, *The Crisis of Turkish Democracy*, p. 13.
[70] Although many leading elements in the military actually had a great deal of sympathy for left-wing policies such as land reform and nationalization of industries, they could not, of course, abide actions conducted outside the institutionalized political system or more radical Marxist programs.

during the 1971 coup and crackdown.[71] Finally, the state proved in 1971, as it would again later in 1980, that it had the capacity and propensity to repress harshly those groups whose opposition went too far – in exercising a coup d'état and subsequent crackdown, the Turkish military affirmed that it was the ready and able guardian of the Kemalist system.

Upon taking power, the Turkish military declared martial law and acted to restrict many of the freedoms introduced in the 1961 Constitution, especially freedom of the press, universities' autonomy, and the right of some groups to unionize.[72] In addition to the Turkish Workers' Party, groups such as Dev Genc were also outlawed. Dissidents, particularly from the left, were arrested and imprisoned in large numbers. It was also at this time that the role of the National Security Council (the MGK, composed of top generals, the Prime Minister, and the President) was strengthened – the MGK from 1971 onwards became a body that provided unsolicited "suggestions" to the civilian government, which could only be ignored at the government's own peril.[73]

In 1973 new elections were held, and another era of multiple, polarized parties and shifting, short-term coalition governments lasted until 1980. During this period, the country had the dubious honor of being ruled by ten different government coalitions. Divisions between different political parties had already begun to seep into the civil bureaucracy and various government organizations in the 1960s, but between 1973 and 1980, politicization of the bureaucracy, trade unions, professional associations, and even the police force reached new heights:

The police were divided into rival associations, one left-wing and the other (smaller) right-wing, which only added to the chaos caused by new top appointments to the police when new governments took office. Similarly the school teachers were divided along right-wing and left-wing lines in their membership of two rival associations. Above all some of the confederations of Turkish trade unions . . . stood very close to political parties. DISK was the most important. It became scarcely distinguishable from a political body in organizing invariably violent May Day demonstrations . . . Less important, but still disruptive, were the two smaller trade union confederations, MISK (which supported the [far right] Nationalist Action Party) and MAKIS (in sympathy with the [Islamist] National Salvation Party).[74]

---

[71] McDowall, *A Modern History of the Kurds*, p. 410.
[72] Dodd, *The Crisis of Turkish Democracy*, p. 16.
[73] As recently as 1998, when for the first time ever Necmettin Erbakan's Islamist Welfare Party chose to disregard several "suggestions" made to it by the MGK, the military removed the government in a pseudo-coup and installed Mesut Yilmaz's Motherland Party in its place. By 2003, however, conditions attached to Turkey's possible accession to the European Union led to some curtailment of the MGK's power, and the replacement of some military members of the council with civilian equivalents.
[74] Dodd, *The Crisis of Turkish Democracy*, pp. 47–48.

Within the institutionalized system, urban Kurds tended to support Bulent Ecevit's left-leaning Republican People's Party (RPP), while the countryside, still largely in thrall of its aghas and sheikhs, tended to vote for Necmettin Erbakan's National Salvation Party (an Islamist party) or Suleyman Demirel's Justice Party (the heir to the Democratic Party of the 1950s).

Initially, Kurdish nationalists continued to seek the inclusion of a Kurdish program within both legal political parties and the radical Turkish leftist groups. They soon became frustrated with their lack of progress on the issue, however. Ecevit's RPP, while willing to recognize the need for special help in promoting economic and social development in the Kurdish regions, refused to even recognize that a Kurdish question in Turkey existed. The institutionalized political system remained resolutely closed vis-à-vis Kurdish aspirations: in 1979 Serefettin Elci, a Kurdish member of Parliament, stated, "There are Kurds in Turkey. I too am a Kurd," which unleashed a furore and seventeen-hour crisis meeting in the Turkish Cabinet.[75]

Radical leftist groups in particular began to fragment and multiply after 1973, with several Marxist-Leninist and Maoist groups emerging from the 1960s Dev Genc (Revolutionary Youth) alone. At the same time, right-wing parties in Parliament sought to create a climate of fear, and encouraged rightist violent vigilante groups such as the Grey Wolves, who attacked their leftist opponents in universities and on the street.[76] It was hoped that a public fearful of anarchy and fighting in the streets would turn to the right-wing law and order parties to restore calm, deposing Ecevit's RPP (which had won the 1973 election). The left responded readily to the bait, and until the military coup of 1980 a climate of political assassinations and street skirmishes prevailed, with various groups controlling entire streets and neighborhoods that a divided police force feared to enter. Conservative rough estimates of deaths that occurred from this political violence are as follows: 1975: 35, 1976: 90, 1977: 260, 1978: 800–1,000, 1979: 1,500, 1980: 3,500.[77]

Once again, disproportionate numbers of Kurds participated in the left-wing movements. The Turkish left was more accepting of Kurdish identity, and at the very least did not engage in vitriolic epithets towards Kurdish culture and language of the extreme Turkish right. Nonetheless, Turkish left-wing movements remained unwilling to recognize a separate

[75] Elci was sentenced to two years and four months of hard labor for this statement (McDowall, A Modern History of the Kurds, p. 413).
[76] Ahmad, The Making of Modern Turkey, ch. 8.
[77] Dodd, The Crisis of Turkish Democracy, p. 32.

or specifically Kurdish program to deal with the problems and aspirations of Kurdish nationalists. From their point of view, the hardships faced by Kurds in Turkey were the same as those faced by average Turks – class oppression, exploitation, and the lack of a genuine people's democracy. Much of the left in Turkey was also as Turkish nationalist as it was leftist, and the response to so-called separate Kurdish concerns was, "Yes to liberty and equality, no to separatism."[78]

Having gained experience in Turkish leftist movements, and judging the political opportunity structures to be finally ripe once again, many Kurdish nationalists broke away to found their own Kurdish left-wing organizations in the 1970s. While the Kurdistan Democratic Party of Turkey was founded in 1965, the 1970s witnessed a virtual explosion of new Kurdish nationalist organizations. The groups that emerged from Turkish left-wing movements include:[79] Bes Parcacilar (1976), Sivancilar (1972), DDKO – Revolutionary Eastern Culture Clubs (1969), DDKD – Revolutionary Democratic Culture Association (1975), TKSP – Turkish Kurdistan Socialist Party (1975), Kawa (1976), Denge Kawa (1977), Red Kawa (1978), Rizgari (1977), Ala Rizgari (1979), KUK – Kurdistan National Liberationists (1978), TEKOSIN (1978), YEKBUN (1979), TSK – Kurdistan Socialist Movement (1980), and the PKK – Kurdistan Workers' Party (1978). These movements, along with an even larger number of Turkish splinter organizations, all emerged in some form from the previously mentioned 1960s' Turkish Workers' Party, Dev Genc, and DISK labor unions.

From a perspective of political opportunity structures, the emergence in the 1970s of so many new leftist Kurdish nationalist groups is some-what puzzling. On the whole, the opportunity structures favoring such groups did not appear much better than in the years just before the 1971 coup. International support for these movements was no better in the 1970s than in the 1960s. Although the police in Turkey suffered from increasing political divisions in the 1970s, and such divisions may have given leftist movements some additional room for maneuver, state security forces (including the police, but particularly the army) could still be counted on to harshly repress any manifestations of Kurdish nationalism. Elite allies supporting Kurdish nationalists were no more available in the 1970s than in the 1960s. Although the elites supporting

---

[78] Sabri Cigerli, *Les Kurdes et leur histoire* (Paris and Montreal: L'Harmattan, 1999), p. 129.

[79] The following list is taken from Ismet G. Imset, *The PKK* (Ankara: Turkish Daily News Publications, 1992). In some cases, the year of founding is an approximation, given the difficulty in obtaining accurate data on some of these movements.

the Turkish state were even more deeply polarized by the 1970s, they still appeared as unified as ever when it came to opposing Kurdish particularism. The final remaining element of political opportunity structures to be considered, however, may provide some explanation: in the 1960s, the growing Kurdish urban, non-tribal elite may have held some hope for pursuing Kurdish nationalist aspirations from within the institutionalized system. The 1960 Constitution and the increased freedoms it provided, along with the growth of the Turkish left, may have encouraged them to pursue their agendas through these seemingly newly available channels. By the mid-1970s, however, such hopes would have appeared futile to even the most optimistic Kurdish nationalists. The 1971 coup and resulting constitutional amendments took back the gains of 1960 and made it more clear that pluralism in Turkey would not be permitted to challenge basic Kemalist principles, as they were interpreted by the military guardians of the state. Seeing that Turkish leftists remained recalcitrant when it came to addressing the Kurdish issue, and also witnessing the fragmenting of left-wing movements, many nationalist-minded Kurds came to the conclusion that the time was ripe to found their own specifically Kurdish movements.[80] Although their experience in the Turkish left would play a large role in the way the new Kurdish groups were organized and the ideology they would put forth, the goal of the movements would be freedom and socialism for Kurdistan, first and foremost.

Given opportunity structures that were less than auspicious, however, and excluding some sudden shift in one or more of the five opportunity structures considered here, one would have expected the Kurdish and Turkish left to eventually meet the same unhappy fate. This was largely what happened after the 1980 military coup, except for one very major exception: the Kurdistan Workers' Party (PKK), whose founder, Abdullah Ocalan, had been active in Dev Genc as a student in Ankara during the late 1960s and early 1970s. Nonetheless, before the 1980 coup, the large majority of political violence in Turkey was conducted by the Turkish left, Islamists, and right-wing groups in the cities, and not Kurdish nationalists. One estimate put the number of crimes committed by separatist movements between December 26, 1978 and

---

[80] In a book published in 1979, Chris Kutschera stated that: "Actuellement, la situation est loin d'être claire, les dirigeant kurdes en Turquie se demandant s'ils doivent militer au sein des partis existants, ou s'ils doivent créer un grand parti kurde de gauche clandestin" (*Le Mouvement national kurde* [Paris: Flammarion, 1979], p. 343). Abdullah Ocalan and a handful of other Kurdish leaders, of course, came to the decision that given the closed political system, the formation of a clandestine leftist Kurdish party was necessary.

September 11, 1980, at only two percent of the total, or roughly 590 actions.[81]

The majority of Turkish and Kurdish revolutionary groups in the 1970s decided to base their strategies on urban guerrilla warfare and high profile, demonstrative attacks on opponents or symbols of Western imperialism. Such a strategy may have been symptomatic of international trends of the day, but was also likely influenced by the weakness of these groups *vis-à-vis* the state and its rightist allies.[82] After officially founding the PKK in 1978, Ocalan and his colleagues left for the smaller towns and rural landscape of the Kurdish southeast. They had not finished laying the groundwork for a rural Kurdish insurgency when the leftist–rightist violence and government paralysis in urban western Turkey precipitated the 1980 military coup.

Kurdish nationalist resurgence: 1980–1992

The 1980 military coup brought with it a period of severe repression and martial law throughout the country. Chapter 3 discusses the state's crackdown during this period in detail; suffice it to say here that particularly in the cities, the Turkish state proved itself to be quite willing and able to use repressive force. The vast majority of insurgent groups were broken between 1980 and 1983, their members either killed, arrested, or forced out of the country:[83]

... the takeover, which meant for the Turkish people a limitation of freedoms, and a nationwide curfew – not to forget thousands of detentions and claims of widespread torture – was quite effective in the short-term in suppressing all armed activities ... All other activities of political origin, from mass demonstrations

---

[81] Not all observers agree with Imset and the Turkish government's figures regarding the minimal extent of Kurdish separatist activity at the time, however. McDowall states that:

It was important for Ankara on the one hand to warn of the danger of Kurdish separatism but on the other to deny the actual extent of it ... The International League of Human Rights had a very different story. It claimed no fewer than 81,000 Kurds had been detained between September 1980 and September 1982. This suggested the problem of Kurdish dissidence was much more widespread than the generals cared to admit. The fact that two thirds of the Turkish army was deployed in Kurdistan in order to guarantee its tranquillity was not advertised. (*A Modern History of the Kurds*, p. 414)

[82] Relatively small groups of insurgents, lacking significant resources and arms, can often conduct urban terrorism and "hit and run" operations much more easily than rural actions. Given that the majority of radical leftist organizations at the time were based on workers and students, most of whom reside in cities, this was doubly true for Turkey in the 1970s.

[83] For more information on state security measures at this time, see the section "The Turkish state response" in ch. 3 or Michael Gunter, "The Kurdish Problem in Turkey," *The Middle East Journal*, Vol. 42, No. 3, 1988.

to poster-placard hanging and distribution of leaflets, also declined immediately after the take-over: The number of injuries in armed clashes dropped by 95 percent, the number of incidents regarding illegal poster/placard hanging declined by 65 percent and the number of armed assaults declined by 85 percent in this period.[84]

Ocalan and his PKK leadership, along with some other insurgent groups, had sensed the coming 1980 coup and fled the country shortly before the military takeover. But while the leaders of many Marxist urban groups eventually found refuge in Europe or the Soviet Union, the PKK and a handful of other groups continued preparations for their insurgencies from neighboring Syria and Lebanon.[85] Modest foreign support for Ocalan's group at this time probably saved the young PKK from being crushed into oblivion during the post-coup security campaigns in Turkey. Syria was happy to provide the insurgents with refuge and allow them to organize on its territory and in Lebanon, hoping to cultivate a political lever in its dealings with Turkey.[86] By 1983, the PKK also moved into Iraqi and Iranian territory, having reached an agreement of cooperation with Masoud Barzani's Kurdistan Democratic Party in northern Iraq.[87]

In 1984 the PKK began Viet-Cong style guerrilla attacks on Turkish security forces, government personnel and facilities, and Kurdish feudal elites that supported Ankara. Although initially the group was largely ignored by Ankara, which viewed them as little more than a handful of rural bandits, the attacks grew progressively more daring and sensational. In 1984–1985, the government's response to mounting PKK activity was also hampered by disputes amongst the political and economic elite in Ankara:

By then, the "PKK threat" was common knowledge, though terrorist activities were still at a lower level and intelligence reports from the region were piling up in Ankara. But political priorities tended to impede strong action against these movements, which would one day become a serious threat for the stability of the semi-democratic Turkish regime ... there were too many political disputes and too many conflicting interests in Ankara's political corridors. Turkish politicians, who after years of military rule, were busy trying to resume control

---

[84] Imset, *The PKK*, p. 2.   [85] Ibid., p. 31.

[86] Syria was particularly worried about Turkey's ongoing project (the GAP project) to dam the Tigris and Euphrates rivers, which are located in the Kurdish regions and provide Syria with the bulk of its water. Supporting Kurdish separatists in the area could delay the project and provide Syria with additional bargaining power concerning how much water Ankara would allow to flow south. For more on this issue, see Gun Kut, "Burning Waters: the Hydropolitics of the Euphrates and Tigris," *New Perspectives on Turkey*, 9, Fall (1993), 8–9.

[87] For more information on foreign support of Kurdish insurgents in Turkey, see Michael M. Gunter, "Transnational Sources of Support for the Kurdish Insurgency in Turkey," *Conflict Quarterly*, Spring (1991). Gunter argues that while foreign support was important, it cannot be credibly viewed as the source or instigator of Kurdish unrest in Turkey.

of the country failed to notice the PKK, who were believed to have only a few hundred members.[88]

By the late 1980s the PKK had gained the full attention of Ankara and the population of all of Turkey.[89] Because Ocalan's militants were waging a classic guerrilla war campaign, the state's security forces had difficulty identifying militants and protecting all their isolated outposts, police stations, and village officials. Counter-insurgency actions affected many innocent civilians, which may have sent the PKK several new recruits for every militant who was killed or captured. Although the PKK's military "victories" never went beyond killing a few dozen security personnel at a time, usually during ambushes and raids, the media impact of such actions put into question the state's capacity to deal with the group and maintain its rule. Support for the Kurdistan Workers' Party snowballed, and by the late 1980s and early 1990s the PKK had acquired the characteristics of a mass uprising.[90] Syria continued to provide sanctuary and training facilities for the group, as well as some intelligence support.[91] Besides gaining the support of large numbers of Kurdish students, professionals, and various intellectuals, Ocalan's movement also managed to exploit tribal divisions in the southeast to gain the adherence of some Kurdish traditional elites.[92]

Can a focus on political opportunity structures account for the emergence of the PKK and mass Kurdish dissent during the 1980–1992 period? First of all, the theoretical approach in this chapter does seem suitable for explaining the *form* that Kurdish nationalist dissent took in the 1980s. With the 1980 coup, the institutionalized political system appeared more closed than ever to Kurdish nationalists. Martial law and a new constitution that focused on restricting freedoms and strengthening state control did not sit well with those who were critical of Kemalist policies. In 1983 Ankara officially banned the use of Kurdish in public, adding teeth to what was already the *de facto* policy since the

---

[88] Imset, *The PKK*, p. 38.
[89] For a detailed chronological account of PKK activities during this period, see Imset, *The PKK*.
[90] Chs. 4 and 5 discuss at greater length why the PKK is judged here to have successfully formed a mass movement.
[91] Imset states that in return for some support and use of their territory, a number of countries in the region also received intelligence from the PKK regarding Turkish (as well as KDP) troop deployments and dispositions (*The PKK*, p. 41). The Syrians did not wish to provide too much aid, however, for fear of Turkish military action against them.
[92] Ch. 3 describes this process in greater detail. Some Kurdish tribal leaders and aghas in competition with others who enjoyed more support from Ankara eventually decided to side with the PKK, which by the late 1980s was beginning to look like a credible counterweight to the Turkish state.

1930s. With mainstream political parties unwilling or unable to address the Kurdish issue in anything but repressive terms,[93] and with civil society crushed under the coup, the only form of dissent left was that which the PKK adopted: violent subversion and guerrilla war. Because Turkey had largely succeeded in co-opting tribal elites, more conservative Kurdish movements pursuing less radical policies were no longer an option the way they were in Iraqi Kurdistan (this will be discussed at greater length in the chapter on Iraqi Kurdistan).[94] With no one in government to bargain with, it should come as little surprise that a radical Marxist Kurdish nationalist movement of the dispossessed and marginalized emerged, a movement willing to use violence against the state, Kurdish "collaborators," and revolutionary competitors. The plethora of similarly extreme-left Kurdish movements that emerged in the 1970s also attests to the fact that the political structures of Turkey were conducive to the emergence of such a form of dissent.

The question of explaining the growth and successes of Kurdish nationalist resurgence from 1980 to 1992 remains. We have already seen that the closed nature of the political system in Turkey (closed *vis-à-vis* Kurdish political demands) encouraged the emergence of radical Kurdish movements acting from outside the state.[95] Multi-party democratic politics in Turkey created divisions in the ruling political elite

---

[93] Few leaders in Turkey could expect to go far by calling for a softer state policy towards the Kurdish issue. Nonetheless, some politicians such as Turgut Ozal and political parties such as the Social Democrats (SHP) and the New Turkey Party did at times advance more conciliatory policies towards the Kurds, such as linguistic freedom and the abolition of emergency rule in the southeast. Such occasional efforts never really succeeded in affecting state policy, however, and were counterbalanced by actions on the opposite side of the political spectrum, such as purging several Kurdish party members in the case of the SHP (McDowall, *A Modern History of the Kurds*, p. 428). Although consistency has not always been the hallmark of Turkish politicians trying to gain votes, the military continues to set the policy boundaries.

[94] Francis Fanon's observations may be as applicable here as they were to Algeria:

These traditional authorities who have been upheld by the occupying power view with disfavour the attempts made by the [revolutionary] elite to penetrate the country districts. They know very well that the ideas which are likely to be introduced by these influences coming from the towns call in question the very nature of unchanging, ever-lasting feudalism. Thus their enemy is not at all the occupying power with which they get along on the whole very well, but these people with modern ideas who mean to dislocate the aboriginal society, and who in doing so will take the bread out of their mouths. (*The Wretched of the Earth* [New York: Grove Press, 1963], p. 110)

[95] An open political system encourages social movements to stay within the system (or in many cases become a part of the system, moving out of the realm of social movement classification), and provides them with a chance to access resources and power, increasing their ability to achieve their goals. A closed political system, however, encourages illegal action outside the system while at the same time (by definition) denying the

although the polity tended to unify to oppose the threat of Kurdish particularism. When such divisions were seen to threaten the state's ability to protect itself against subversives, the military intervened. The only elite allies initially available to Kurdish nationalist subversives came from the political left, which further affected the character these movements would take. The strength of elites on the left in Turkey, however, was not very great. Financial resources, the power to influence government policy, and large organized networks of followers (such as those enjoyed by Kurdish tribal leaders) were sorely lacking. The organizational assets of union leaders and the influence of intellectuals and teachers can only partly counterbalance such deficiencies. The PKK only succeeded in attracting some Kurdish tribal leaders and aghas after they began to look like a credible alternative to the state, which begs the question of how the movement reached such a point in the first place.

During the 1980 coup, the PKK survived thanks to the refuge provided by Syria and other countries. Continuing support from outside Turkey has been important to the group but such importance should not be exaggerated – Syria and other supporters (Greece, Armenia, Iran, and Iraq have all been accused) had to be careful not to be too obvious with their support, lest they face a myriad of possible consequences.[96] In any case, Turkey's neighbors did not wish to provide so much support that Kurdish rebels would actually achieve any of their objectives – such an outcome would be a bad precedent affecting their own sizeable Kurdish minorities. Finally, one should remember that insurgent groups must have more going for them than even a great deal of foreign support, as the example of the Contras in Nicaragua should make clear. Moreover, if we consider international support for the Turkish state, the asymmetries in power between the PKK and Ankara become grossly evident. The United States alone has provided Turkey with infinitely more aid than any insurgent group could ever come close to attaining from foreign sources: until 1999, Turkey was the third largest recipient of US military aid, receiving $9 billion worth of arms and $6.5 billion in grants and loans for military goods since 1980:

In a campaign to root out local Kurdish support for the PKK, U.S.-supplied attack helicopters, jets, tanks, and armored personnel carriers have been used to destroy over 3,000 Kurdish villages. U.S.-origin small arms have been used in

excluded groups many of the means they need to grow and press their agenda. Hence a closed system may encourage the growth of larger numbers of violent or extremist groups, but these groups also have reduced chances of surviving.

[96] For more on the incentives and disincentives affecting international support of the PKK and other Kurdish groups, see Kemal Kirisci and Gareth M. Winrow, *The Kurdish Question and Turkey* (London: Frank Cass, 1997), ch. 6.

the extrajudicial killing of suspected PKK soldiers or sympathizers, and American-made utility helicopters have been used to transport soldiers on these missions. Turkey's renewed faith in the ability to win the war probably encourages the military to continue using indiscriminate and disproportionate force, though Turkish authorities have prevented U.S. officials and international human rights groups from monitoring their activities in the region.[97]

In terms of opportunity structures, therefore, the PKK does not seem to have had sufficiently favorable circumstances to develop into a mass movement: a closed institutionalized political system, some instability and division within Ankara's political elite, the presence of relatively weak elite allies, and limited international support. When the final variable, state repression, is factored in, the situation looks much less favorable.

Particularly after the 1980 military coup, the Turkish state appeared ready and willing to use repressive force against "subversives." Although between 1983 and 1985 the previously mentioned political maneuvering in Ankara (civilian rule was restored in 1983) impeded an early response to the PKK, the state did turn its full attention to the problem by 1985. The large majority of Turkey's armed forces were, and continue to be, deployed in the southeastern Kurdish regions of the country. In 1992, Turkey's army alone (not including police forces, village guards, or special counter-insurgency teams) numbered around 600,000 soldiers. The military in Turkey is also considered relatively professional and well disciplined, and its inventory includes modern armaments purchased from the United States, Israel, and European countries. The repression employed in the Kurdish regions included the destruction of thousands of villages and the forced evacuation of their occupants, mass arrests, torture, and all the curtailments of individual liberties that come with the maintenance of martial law. Given the high level of repression and the fact that the political opportunity structures discussed above were not overly positive, we are left with a somewhat unsatisfactory explanation for Kurdish nationalist resurgence and the PKK's rise. States in most developing countries typically suffer from opportunity structures that are at least as favorable towards opposition movements, yet uprisings as widespread and enduring as that of the PKK remain a rarity.[98] We will return to these explanatory shortcomings of the political opportunity structures perspective in the concluding section of this chapter, following an examination of the 1992–2003 era in Turkey.

---

[97] Tamar Gabelnick, "Turkey: Arms and Human Rights," *Foreign Policy in Focus*, 4: 16, 1999.
[98] McDowall, *A Modern History of the Kurds*, p. 429.

Political openings, cease-fires, closures, and the decline of the PKK: 1992–2004

Turgut Ozal, who served alternately as both Prime Minister and President of Turkey during the 1983–1993 period, broke several Kemalist taboos towards the end of his term in office. Before his death in 1993, he began to symbolize a genuine division within the Turkish elite towards the Kurdish issue, and his actions opened the possibility for dialogue between Ankara and Kurdish nationalists. Ozal, who was part Kurdish himself, seems to have concluded that some fundamental changes were necessary to bring Turkey's Kurdish citizens back into the fold. Towards the end of 1991, Ozal succeeded in repealing Law 2932, thereby permitting the public use of Kurdish, "except in broadcasts, publications and education"[99] or public spaces such as government institutions and political campaigns. Once again, however, this step towards a more liberal policy was accompanied by another step in the opposite direction, in the form of a new anti-terrorism law so broad that anyone could be arrested on the most flimsy of pretexts – the new law defined terrorism as "any kind of action ... with the aim of changing the characteristics of the Republic."[100]

In 1992 Ozal went so far as to advocate an amnesty for Kurdish guerrillas and dealing with the PKK through more formal negotiations within the institutionalized political system. The hardliners and the military in Ankara would not permit this, however. Nonetheless, the fact that Ozal was even able to propose such a scheme attested to his influence and relative autonomy from the military. He was held in high esteem by Kurds in Turkey, and he appeared to be the only Turkish politician able to counterbalance the role of the military and its National Security Council "advisory" body (the MGK).[101] In 1993, after some

---

[99] If one accepts the resource mobilization literature's argument that grievances and groups with an interest in opposing the state are ubiquitous, the notion that the extent of and the nature of the grievances of the Kurds in Turkey accounts for the PKK's success does not solve the issue either. Ch. 4 addresses this question further.

[100] The full text of anti-terror law is available in Helsinki Watch, "Turkey: New Restrictive Anti-terror Law," June 10, 1991.

[101] Even during Ozal's leadership, many Kurds felt that the Turkish political system was closed to any Kurdish demands. In a 1992 interview with Paul White (*Primitive Rebels or Revolutionary Modernizers? The Kurdish national movement in Turkey* [London: Zed Books, 2000], p. 161), PSK (Partiya Sosyalist a Kurdistan) leader Kemal Burkay stated that such continuing closure might force his organization to reconsider its current non-violent approach to the Kurdish issue:

> KB: You know, Turkish authorities, the Turkish government, make propaganda that it doesn't have any other choice, any other alternative. It must fight terror. But we show to public opinion of Turkey and to international [public opinion] that the

heavy losses on the battlefield, the PKK announced a unilateral cease-fire, which many people believed President Ozal had played a role in procuring.[102] The PKK's offer to Turkey included: "a declaration in favour of a negotiated solution and a willingness to allow Kurdish deputies, rather than the PKK, to negotiate with Ankara on behalf of Kurdish people; a commitment to the unity of Turkey and rejection of separatism and a commitment to the legal democratic process."[103]

One month later Ocalan's PKK renewed the cease-fire indefinitely, and accompanied this renewal with demands that even mainstream Turkish politicians might be able to accept: "We should be given our cultural freedoms and the right to broadcast in Kurdish. The village guard system should be abolished and the Emergency legislation lifted. The Turkish authorities should take the necessary measures to prevent unsolved murders and should recognize the political rights of Kurdish organization."[104]

Given that Ocalan had ceased to even mention autonomy, self-determination, or separation, and given many of Ozal's earlier pronounce-ments on the issue, President Ozal might well have accepted such demands and opened the way for a political solution to the Kurdish issue. On the other hand, it was Ozal who instituted the above-mentioned draconian anti-terror law, as well as the village guard system and the (1987) emergency rule of the predominantly Kurdish provinces.[105] Ozal seemed imaginative enough to employ policies consisting of both carrots and sticks. How he would have reacted to the PKK's offer must

Kurdish movement is not a terrorist movement. We are ready to solve the question by democratic means, and peaceful means. We are ready to discuss the problem. To [have] dialogue. But I am not optimistic that the Turkish state will change its policy in a short time. No, they are insisting on carrying on their policy by terror actions, and it's very dangerous. I am not optimistic, in the near future, that the Kurdish problem will be solved, because this new coalition government is preparing the terror means – more police force, more military force, for Kurdistan.

Then, maybe we also must change our policy. We also, our organization, also, because we can't stay on the side and look at what happens. If the Turkish government doesn't change its policy, then we also must, maybe, take part in the armed struggle, in the future.

PW: This is the change you mean, which might be necessary?

KB: Maybe, sure! If there isn't any alternative, to solve the question by peaceful means. If the door is shut, then there isn't any other alternative for us.

By March 1999, Burkay stated that the PSK had indeed now concluded that armed struggle was necessary (ibid.). By that time, however, the PSK no longer had a discern-able presence in Turkish Kurdistan, having been virtually overrun by the PKK.

[102] Kirisci and Winrow, *The Kurdish Question and Turkey*, p. 138.
[103] McDowall, *A Modern History of the Kurds*, p. 437.
[104] Ibid., quotation taken from *Turkey Briefing*, vol. 7, no. 2, Summer 1993.
[105] Michael Gunter, *The Kurds and the Future of Turkey* (New York: St. Martin's Press, 1997), p. 61.

remain speculation. He died of a heart attack the day after Ocalan's new cease-fire offer.[106]

The Turkish political leaders who followed in the wake of Ozal's death, such as Suleyman Demirel, Tansu Ciller, Mesut Yilmaz, Necmettin Erbakan, Bulent Ecevit, and Recep Erdogan, lacked either Ozal's independence, influence, imagination, or willingness to pursue anything but the military's solution to the PKK insurgency. The Turkish military, seeing the PKK cease-fire as a sign of weakness, continued its counter-insurgency operations. Guerrilla attacks resumed after 1993, including a handful of terrorist bombings of tourist resort towns in the western part of Turkey. In 1994, under Prime Minister Tansu Ciller, US$8 billion was spent on military operations in the southeast, at the same time that more moderate Kurdish representatives were banished from Ankara's National Assembly.[107] Unexplained murders and disappearances of journalists reporting on the Kurdish issue, as well as Kurdish political party officials and intellectuals, accompanied the official state repression.[108]

By 1995, Ankara's military efforts appeared to have achieved some degree of success, however. Turkish pressure on the Iraqi Kurdish KDP led to joint KDP–Turkish operations that severely damaged the PKK's bases of operations in northern Iraq. Turkish troops and special contra-guerrilla forces in the southeast had gained in experience and effectiveness by 1995. After that year, the PKK no longer enjoyed nightly control of large areas of the southeast and was forced to fall back on smaller hit-and-run guerrilla raids reminiscent of its early days in the 1980s.[109] Although every spring the Turkish army confidently predicted the crushing of the movement by the end of the summer, the smaller scale guerrilla war simmered on.

Perhaps the biggest setback for the PKK occurred in February 1999, when Turkish agents captured Ocalan in Kenya. In the fall of 1998, Turkey had massed troops on the Syrian border and threatened war with Syria if Damascus insisted on continuing to allow Ocalan to reside

---

[106] After Ozal's death, Ocalan stated that "a solution to the problem could have been reached had the late President Turgut Ozal lived," and that he had heard that Ozal intended "to put some radical changes on Turkey's agenda" (ibid., p. 79; Ocalan's statements taken from Imset, "PKK Leader Says Attacks Will Force 'Political Solution,'" *Turkish Daily News*, June 12, 1993, pp. 1–11). Later in the interview with the TDN, Ocalan even expressed the view that Ozal's death at this time was "suspicious" (ibid.).

[107] McDowall, *A Modern History of the Kurds*, p. 441.

[108] For more on this matter, including the state's use of death squads and the attribution of these squads' actions to PKK terrorists, see Lord Avebury, "Turkey's Kurdish Policy in the Nineties," *Democracy at Gunpoint: The Economist, Turkey Survey*, June 8–14, 1996.

[109] Gunter, *The Kurds and the Future of Turkey*, p. 84.

there. The Syrians eventually blinked and expelled Ocalan, who then went on an odyssey across many nations in search of a new refuge, until he was eventually captured in Africa. Ocalan was tried in Turkey and sentenced to death, but the Turkish authorities refrained from carrying out Ocalan's sentence. In October 2002, the death sentence was officially commuted to life imprisonment. This decision reflected the Turkish government's desire to avoid more international censure regarding human rights, as well as the elevation of yet another Kurdish martyr.

By forcing Syria to expel Ocalan and exerting pressure on Kurdish groups in Iraq to deny the PKK a base of operations there, Turkey was able to remove crucial elements of the PKK's international support. Although some PKK camps continue to exist in Syria, Iraq, and Iran, the organization's numbers and freedom of maneuver in these regions has been severely curtailed.[110] Since the end of the American-led war in Iraq (Operation Iraqi Freedom), the approximately 5000 PKK (renamed KADEK – the "Kurdish Freedom and Democracy Congress" – in the spring of 2002, and then renamed Congra-Gel – the "People's Congress" – in the fall of the same year) units remaining in northern Iraq face the looming specter of joint American, Turkish, and Iraqi Kurdish military action against them. Throughout 2004, they remained uneasily encamped and constrained in the very mountainous region just inside the Iraqi side of the Turkish–Iraqi border. Although the PKK and its more recent manifestations continues to derive support from the Kurdish

---

[110] During the author's most recent visits to the Kurdish regions of Iran, Syria, Turkey, and Iraq (summer 1999, fall 2000, and fall 2003), Kurdish residents and NGO workers stated to the author that although PKK camps still operated in both countries' border area with Turkey, these were limited in size and number. In the case of Iran, the Iranian government wishes its support of the PKK to remain low profile, for fear of attracting too much Turkish attention (nonetheless, in July of 1999 a major diplomatic incident occurred when Turkish commandos in hot pursuit of PKK militants crossed over the Iranian border and Turkish jets bombed territory just inside Iran). In northern Iraq, both ruling Kurdish parties (the KDP and PUK) remain dependent on Turkish goodwill for trade and access to the outside world, given the international embargo on Iraq and Baghdad's embargo on the Kurdish north before 2003, and the uncertain status of Iraq since American occupation in 2003. Until 2002, competition between the Iraqi Kurdish groups and PKK units in the area was high, with the result that PKK activities in the region faced harassment and occasional armed attacks from the KDP and PUK. The situation changed frequently, however, with incidences of PKK–PUK rapprochement and cooperation not too uncommon. Since 1993, the PKK–KDP confrontation has appeared more bitter and enduring, however. It also seems likely that the PKK had some relationship with Saddam Hussein's government in Baghdad, receiving support in return for the provision of information on the Iraqi Kurdish groups in the area (this last observation is very speculative, however, and based on the author's informal discussions with various people in the region).

diaspora community (particularly those in Europe) as well as Greece and Armenia, this can hardly substitute for the crucial bases of operations in Iraq and Syria, as well as the more substantial support Syria appeared to have been giving the movement. Likewise, NGO and European support for general Kurdish rights in Turkey are helpful to the PKK, but cannot save the movement from Turkish military operations. The PKK/Congra Gel also seems quite aware of its weakened military position – on September 1, 2003, its most recent cease-fire declaration ended, yet the resumption of the movement's attacks remained quite limited well into 2004. Acknowledging the difficult situation faced by his organization, one of Congra Gel's leaders recently insisted that Kurdish fighters would only engage in defensive actions when attacked by Turkish forces, and not initiate attacks.[111]

In fact, the increasing effectiveness of state security forces in Turkey's southeast (including frequent border incursions into northern Iraq) created a situation in which the state's capacity for repression proved difficult to overcome. The military in Turkey continues to make the most important state policy decisions, and the occasional division between military leaders and vote-seeking Turkish politicians has failed to change this fact.[112] Particularly after the death of Ozal, no Turkish politician appeared capable of challenging the military's approach to the Kurdish issue in the country. Hence, the system remained closed to Kurdish nationalist aspirations even after Ocalan's capture.

Especially since the late 1980s, the Turkish state has pursued a strategy of eliminating elite allies of the PKK. Prosecution for crimes of thought against the Turkish state were vigorously pursued: "Turkey's leaders have gotten so carried away that intellectual crimes have been regarded as among the most serious; people have rotted away in prisons, been killed and exiled for writing or speaking their minds. Over 200 people are serving sentences for crimes of thought; hundreds more are on trial. Among them are professors, journalists, writers and union leaders."[113] Kurdish sources obtained access to a Turkish Interior Ministry secret

---

[111] Author's interview with Congra-Gel Vice President Ramsey Kartal, April 26, 2004, Qandil Mountains, Iraq.

[112] After the death of Ozal, the only significant evidence of Turkish state elite division *vis-à-vis* the Kurdish issue appeared in a statement made by Ocalan during his trial on the island of Imrali. The prosecution asked Ocalan if it were true that the leader of an unnamed political party in Ankara warned him of an imminent Turkish attempt on his life at his home in Damascus (the bombing attempt failed on May 6, 1996). Ocalan replied that, "It would be normal for opposition parties to report something like that, because if the attempt had succeeded the party in power would gain points" (Istanbul *Hurriyet*, March 17, 1999, FBIS-WEU-1999-0325).

[113] Yasar Kemal, *The New York Times*, op-ed, May 6, 1995.

document that outlines the state's strategy in this regard.[114] Under the heading "Measures to be applied at specific times," the following is included: "In response to the PKK separatist terrorist organization's steering of men of thinking and art and other influential people who may impress the public at home and abroad to serve its aims: People who may be qualified as thinkers and are currently being used by the organization should be identified and their past histories and intelligence information relating to them be secured (January–March 1997) ... People the organization may use should be presented to the public at home and abroad in such a manner as to remove any influence they may have (January–May 1997)." Under the heading "Measures to be applied continuously," the state further outlined its desire to prevent the PKK from securing elite allies from left-wing or religious circles:

In response to the organization creating an environment of closer collaboration with extreme left-wing organizations, Yezidis, Alevis and radical Islamic groups, its setting into action of the institutions it has formed and its carrying out of direct action at home and abroad; With the aim of preventing extreme left-wing elements from uniting with the PKK in actions and thought, possible leaders in thought and action in this matter should be suitably enlightened, and those who cannot be directed should have their influence over the public rocked as professional degenerates. Measures should be taken to support those who are in the positions of being natural leaders of Alevi and Yezidi groups at home and who support the state, in such a manner as to increase their influence over these groups and to prevent exploitation of these groups by means of these people [text quoted as is].

The strategies quoted above were pursued parallel to policies of physically eliminating journalists, business people, and other elites thought to be supportive of the PKK.[115] In any case, the Turkish state appears to have succeeded in denying the PKK many of the elite allies that could have come to its aid in the face of defeats on the battlefield and the elimination of important sources of foreign support.

---

[114] "Secret T.C. Interior Ministry, Public Relations Office Chairmanship, Number: B050HID0000073/472 03/01/1997, Matter: Measures to be taken against PKK activities in 1997, Regarding: Prime Ministerial orders dated 12.11.1993, Signed: Dr. Meral Aksenir, Interior Minister State of Emerg. Comm. Chair." The author obtained the document from the KIC (Kurdistan Informatie Centrum, Nederland). ABC News carried the following report concerning the document: "Turkey's all-powerful military, an institution rarely held accountable for its actions, has admitted that it drew up a plan to discredit journalists, politicians and activists whom generals believed were sympathetic to Kurdish rebels" (http://www.abcnews.go.com/wire/World/ap20001108_592.html).

[115] For more on the issue of extra-judicial killings, death squads, and disappearances, see the previously cited sources on human rights in Turkey or Maryam Elahi, "Clinton, Ankara and Kurdish Human Rights," in Middle East Report, Number 189, July–August 1994; or "Democracy at Gunpoint," The Economist, Turkey Survey, June 8–14, 1996.

By the year 2000, many outside observers expressed the belief that the PKK was virtually finished.[116] Indeed, with its paramount leader in the hands of the Turkish state, the future of the PKK and Kurdish dissent in Turkey is unclear. Whether or not the PKK can survive the capture of its leader and the blows dealt to it remains to be seen. Without a favourable (from the PKK's perspective) change in political opportunity structures, the analysis pursued in this chapter would predict a fate akin to that of the Shining Path movement in Peru, after the capture of Abimael Guzman. While a closed political system in Turkey would continue to favor the formation of illegal, radical Kurdish groups, the remaining four opportunity structure variables continue to appear less than favorable regarding the possible success of such groups. Also, as later chapters will discuss, the institutionalized political system in Turkey seems to have recently opened somewhat, a trend which would remove the main factor encouraging the emergence of militant subversive Kurdish opposition movements in the country.

The opportunity structures approach: utility and limits

The analysis in this chapter attempted to explain Kurdish nationalist resurgence in Turkey from a political opportunity structures perspective. Although an attempt was made to limit the explanatory variables to the five components of opportunity structures described at the outset of the chapter, contextual detail occasionally led to the inclusion of other explanatory factors (such as widespread state repression causing more disgruntled Kurds to join the PKK). Such occasional lapses notwithstanding, the bulk of the analysis remained faithful to the theoretical perspective in question. Only in this way is it possible to evaluate the utility, limits, and compelling explanatory power of the opportunity structures perspective.

In the Turkish-Kurdish case, the perspective used here did seem to provide a very compelling way of explaining (and perhaps predicting) the broad nature of social movements that arise to challenge the state. When the institutionalized political system appeared more open, movements willing to operate legally within the system arose. Before the closing of the system in 1924, many Kurdish nationalists sought to be a part of and work from within Ankara's National Assembly. With the advent of the more liberal 1960 Constitution in Turkey, Kurdish nationalists (as well as many voters) supported and joined the legalized leftist movements. After

---

[116] For instance, see Michael Radu, "Is the PKK on the Ropes?" E-Notes, Foreign Policy Research Institute, September 28, 1999.

1960, several attempts were made to found legal political movements and parties supportive of Kurdish aspirations, such as Dev Genc, the TWP, DISK, and, later, DEP and HADEP. All of these openings of the system proved ephemeral, with Turkish-Kurdish brotherhood crushed in 1925, leftist movements outlawed in 1971, liberal freedoms further suppressed in 1980, and parties such as DEP and HADEP closed down by the military. The result of such closures in the system were the Kurdish uprisings in the early days of the Republic and the subversive, violent left-wing (Kurdish as well as non-Kurdish) movements that emerged in the 1970s, of which the PKK became the most successful and best known.

It is not only the relative openness or closure of the political system that had a compelling effect on the character of emergent Kurdish movements. The other variables may also play an important role.[117] Elites available to support Kurdish nationalist movements in the 1920s and 1930s tended to be aghas, tribal leaders, and religious sheikhs. Consequently, the movements that arose during this time period were conservative, melding religion, tribal politics, and Kurdish nationalism together, but not seeking to transform Kurdish society or modes of economic production. By the 1960s and 1970s, however, the majority of the old elites were either gone (killed, exiled, or reduced to insignificance and poverty) or co-opted by the state. In their place, leftist union leaders, intellectuals, media figures, and members of the professional classes emerged as the allies available to both leftist and Kurdish nationalist projects. Most of the Kurdish movements (such as the PKK) that arose at this time in turn espoused a socialist and revolutionary brand of Kurdish nationalism.

As for the stability or instability of elite alignments undergirding the state, some degree of influence on the form Kurdish nationalist movements took might be discerned. The 1925 Sheikh Said uprising sought to attract pro-Ottoman religious Turks upset with Kemalist secularism to their cause, and Sheikh Said stressed that they were fighting for the restoration of the Muslim Caliphate. This could just as easily be discussed as an attempt to gain elite allies, however. The religious aspect of the 1925 revolt is better explained by the rebels' need to have a respected sheikh unite competing tribes under the umbrella of religion, as well the need to appeal to Kurdish masses that at the time identified themselves more

---

[117] For the purpose of examining the form that movements take, it seems reasonable to omit a state's capacity and willingness to repress as a significant variable. Repression in this case becomes an aspect of closed political systems. Closed political systems that are unwilling or unable to repress would be expected to have a short lifespan.

along religious than Kurdish nationalist lines. The latter notion falls outside the opportunity structures theoretical perspective, however.[118]

Finally, the international variable may also affect the character of emergent social movements, although the evidence from the Turkish-Kurdish case appears scant. The KDPT (Kurdistan Democratic Party of Turkey) of the 1960s was formed with aid from its model, the Iraqi KDP, but the KDPT failed to achieve significance in Turkey. A country such as the Islamic Republic of Iran might also conceivably nurture Islamic Kurdish subversive movements in Turkey, although again, no such movement gained much significance. Likewise, subversive movements seeking to avoid unpleasant American attention might decide to tone down their Marxist-Leninist rhetoric (or, since September 11, 2001, their Islamist rhetoric).

Although other theoretical perspectives (particularly identity-based approaches) would explain social movement forms quite differently, the opportunity structures approach applied here to the Turkish-Kurdish case seems to have provided a satisfactorily compelling explanation for the forms such movements take. By examining the openness of a political system, available elite allies, and the nature of possible international support, one might also achieve some predictive ability regarding the forms future social movements may take. In both these senses, the case examined here seems to support McAdam, McCarthy, and Zald's contention that:

> ... social movements and revolutions are shaped by the broader set of political constraints and opportunities unique to the national context in which they are embedded ... Change in any of the four dimensions [with the addition of the international variable, five dimensions of opportunity structures – DR] may encourage mobilization, but the form the mobilization takes is very likely to be affected by the kind of opportunity presented ... In short, insurgents can be expected to mobilize in response to and in a manner consistent with the very specific changes that grant them more leverage.[119]

As Chapter 1 makes clear, I did not expect the opportunity structures approach to provide by itself a satisfactory explanation for the growth and fate, as opposed to the form, of ethnic nationalist movements. Although the period of 1918 to around 1930, discussed above, appeared to be a political opportunity "made in heaven" for Kurdish nationalists, their

---

[118] It may be more useful to view unstable ruling elite alignments as situations offering movements either elite allies, openings in the political system, or a lesser likelihood of state repression. As such, the variable would not be relied on directly to explain the emergent forms of social movements.

[119] McAdam et al., *Comparative Perspectives*, pp. 3–10.

challenge to the new Turkish Republic was completely smashed. The reasons for the uprisings' failure were both inter-related and contextual: first of all, the strategic and political genius of Kemal Ataturk success-fully divided the Kurdish rebels and postponed the larger showdown with Ankara, to a time when the state would be better prepared. A leader less skillful than Ataturk might well have failed to accomplish such a task. In this sense, a contextual factor (the presence of an unusually adept leader like Ataturk) hindered the Kurds' ability to take advantage of favorable political opportunities. Second, divisions amongst the Kurds not only denied them the advantage of a single, united uprising, but also prevented them from attracting international support. The League of Nations, and particularly France and Britain, would have been much more likely to support Kurdish nationalist aspirations had the Kurds been able to present some semblance of a united front seeking Kurdish self-determination.[120] By the same token, greater international interest in the establishment of a Kurdish state might have overcome the weakness of mediocre Kurdish leadership – Kurdish elites were probably no more divided and traditional in the 1920s than their Arab counterparts in Arabia. Also, Christian subjects of the Ottoman Empire, who were more successful than the Kurds at courting Western aid and creating a national consciousness, attained independence well before the First World War.[121] Nonetheless, most observers place a large amount of responsibility for the defeats of the 1920s and 1930s on the Kurdish groups themselves, who were not sufficiently organized to take advantage of the opportunities that presented themselves.[122] Such an observation highlights the need to combine an analysis of strategic resource mobiliza-tion with opportunity structures.

In examining the 1918–1938 period, the opportunity structures per-spective appears to have nonetheless served us well. One would not expect the perspective to deterministically indicate situations in which challenges to the state or revolution will be successful. Rather, the

---

[120] For more on the effect Kurdish disunity had on British and French policy appraisals for the region, see McDowall, *A Modern History of the Kurds*, ch. 7. Hakan Ozoglu adds that, "Great Britain was not convinced that Kurdish nationalism in the long run would help British interests in the region" ("'Nationalism' and Kurdish Notables in the Late Ottoman – Early Republican Era," *International Journal of Middle East Studies* 33 [2001], 383–409, p. 405).

[121] Ibid., p. 404.

[122] Observation like this one, from Peresh's introduction to Ihsan Nouri Pasha's *La Révolte de l'Agri-dagh*, are common: "Il faut l'admettre, les Kurdes n'etaient pas en état de saisir cette chance, de prendre en mains leur destin ... Malheureusement, ils le firent par ordre dispersé, sans stratégie d'ensemble, sans guère innover dans la tactique et les méthodes" (pp. 17–18).

approach seeks to highlight and understand windows of opportunity and danger, when such challenges are quite likely to erupt and succeed. In this sense, the early days of the Turkish Republic are accurately described as having been pregnant with Kurdish nationalist revolutionary possibilities. If the revolution was just barely aborted, due to contextual vagaries and astute leadership in Ankara, the theoretical framework that explains the timing and nature of the birthing process is not necessarily invalidated.

Roughly fifty year later, however, the growth and extent of the PKK challenge to Ankara (if not the emergence of the group in the 1970s) is more difficult to explain. As discussed above, the opportunity structures perspective would not have predicted much success for the PKK after the 1980 military coup in Turkey. That the PKK threat to Turkey appears to have receded by the year 2000 does not change the fact that the situation appeared much less certain in the early 1990s. If the PKK had never emerged, it seems possible that the 1980 coup would be credited with crushing Kurdish dissent, in addition to radical left-wing opposition movements. Social movement scholars would have then pointed to the quiet situation in Turkey as evidence of a context lacking political opportunity structures that favor social movement challengers. Hanspeter Kriesi's observation regarding structural approaches applied to the study of social movements seems to apply here:

European scholars studying new social movements often point to the structural developments that lie at the origin of these movements. They give causal explanations for the rise of these movements without much concern for the actual mobilizing strategies that the movements apply. In a way, the structural approaches of European scholars are still in the tradition of the "classic model" of conceptualizing collective behaviour and its emphasis on "structural conduciveness" ... These structural approaches cannot explain how structure is transformed into action.[123]

In order to arrive at a more satisfactory understanding of Kurdish nationalist resurgence in Turkey, we must therefore pursue an examination of the PKK's strategies, tactics, and resource mobilization. In many cases, the PKK also succeeded in effecting a change in the political opportunity structures within which it operated – such instances may become apparent in the next chapter, and will in any case be elaborated more clearly later on, when a synthesis of theories on social movements is discussed. In essence, where lack of organization and effective resource mobilization might explain Kurdish rebel failures of the 1920s (when

---

[123] In Bert Klandermans, Hanspeter Kriesi, and Sidney Tarrow (eds.), "From Structure to Action: Comparing Social Movement Research Across Cultures," *International Social Movement Research* 1 (Greenwich: JAI Press, 1988), 361.

opportunity structures were most favorable), the opposite kind of logic might be applied to the rise of the PKK: astute organization and resource mobilization can allow the mounting of a significant challenge to the state even when opportunity structures are not favorable.

The following chapter on resource mobilization will not resolve an additional problem inherent in the analysis undertaken so far. Identity, culture and the perceptions of the actors discussed here are generally taken for granted in the opportunity structures and resource mobilization approaches. Throughout this chapter, phrases such as "Kurdish nationalist aspirations" are used with virtually no question or explanation. The identity of elites and the masses should not be assumed *a priori*. For instance, in the case of the Kuchgiri revolt discussed at the outset of this chapter, the Kurdish nationalist appeals made by the revolt's leaders might have attracted mass support and broken the divisions of tribal or religious affiliation. Scholars such as McDowall attribute the main reason for the revolt's failure to the lack of Kurdish nationalist identification (politicized ethnicity) among the Kurdish masses of the 1920s: "The nationalist rhetoric employed by the Kuchgiri leaders had evinced no perceptible response from the Kurdish masses."[124] This is a question of grievance framing, which Chapter 4 will address.

[124] McDowall, *A Modern History of the Kurds*, pp. 184–186.

3   Resource mobilization and rational choices

At first glance, ethnic nationalist movements may seem amongst the least likely of social movement phenomena amenable to a rational choice (RC) analysis. We have a tendency to view ethnic nationalism as an expression of identity and the strong emotional values attached to identity. This chapter does not attempt to dispute the idea that powerful non-material values underpin ethnic identity and that these may act as strong behavioral motivators. If, however, we accept that identity is a dynamic phenomenon[1] and that ethnic nationalist movements often play a major role in fostering ethnic identification in the first place, then resource mobilization (RM) and rational choice analysis can provide some very useful insights.[2] If a given population lacks a strong sense of ethnic identity, or possesses a non-politicized ethnic identity,[3] then an ethnic nationalist movement may not be able to attract their support with ideological appeals centered around the ethnicity and non-material values of the ethnic group. Instead, the initial attempts to garner large-scale support may have to appeal to the material self-interest of the target population. Additionally, rational, material interest-based appeals, as well as strategic use of recruitment networks and other mobilizational vehicles, may serve as the crucial extra inducement to action for a population receptive to the politicized ethnic ideology of a movement but needing additional motivation.

---

[1] See, for instance, Milton J. Esman, *Ethnic Politics* (Ithaca: Cornell University Press, 1994) or Crawford Young, *The Politics of Cultural Pluralism* (London: The University of Wisconsin Press, 1976).

[2] The argument presented here is based on a loose application of the logic of the rational actor model, and does not attempt to attach mathematical game-model values to different goals and choices.

[3] As discussed in ch. 1, the politicized ethnic identity is one in which ethnicity is used to make claims upon the state, typically linguistic, minority, or special political rights (such as autonomy or secession) for the ethnic group in question. In contrast, people possessed of "private" ethnic identity might identify very strongly with their ethnic group, but at the some time regard the issue as a personal matter and not a relative basis from which to make claims upon the state.

As discussed earlier, RC theory derives from economics, and its basic premise is that rational actors will choose options that maximize their gain and minimize their risk, based on the information available to them. Gain is defined in material terms (wealth, power, security), and actors are assumed to desire as much gain as possible. Because non-material goods, such as a sense of belonging, culture, and identity, are difficult or impossible to put a value upon *vis-à-vis* material ones, the focus is placed on economic, material goods. A typical rational choice argument moves along these lines: unless individuals are given rational, self-interested reasons for supporting or joining a movement (or in our case, an ethnic nationalist project), the movement will fail to attract a mass following, reducing the movement's choices to either very small scale actions such as banditry and terrorist attacks, or failure. The argument is based on Mancur Olson's discussion of the "free-rider problem": "Unless there is coercion or some other special device to make individuals act in their common interest, rational, self-interested individuals will not act to achieve their common or group interests."[4] "Special devices" to make individuals act in their common interest typically revolve around selective incentives. In a situation where large numbers of people do not possess a politicized ethnic identity, however, the "common interest" may not even be felt, making selective incentives even more paramount to attracting support for an ethnic nationalist movement. Participation in "local" actions (by which I mean actions aimed at satisfying particular interests of small groups and individuals) of the movement may then eventually socialize people into the politicized identity of the ethnic nationalist movement.

In the case of ethnic nationalist organizations, the movements' resource mobilization challenges are manifold. Successful formation of "collective vehicles, informal as well as formal, through which people mobilize and engage in collective action"[5] requires that several imperatives be met:

(1) movements must offer to the people goals that matter to the people;
(2) they must convince people that their individual participation in movement activities is important and/or makes a difference in achieving the goals in question;
(3) they must convince people that most of their peers, or enough of their peers, are also going to participate in movement activities (and that hence the actions have a reasonable chance of success);

---

[4] Mancur Olson, *The Logic of Collective Action* (Boston: Harvard University Press, 1965), p. 2.
[5] Doug McAdam, John D. McCarthy, and Mayer N. Zald, *Comparative Perspectives on Social Movements: Political Opportunities, Mobilizing Structures and Cultural Framings* (New York: Cambridge University Press, 1996), p. 3.

(4) they need to, wherever possible, offer selective incentives to movement participants and selective disincentives or sanctions to non-participants or opponents of the movement (to deal with the free-rider problem);

(5) they must coordinate and organize the movement's activities so as to better achieve goals and build up movement resources from action to action;

(6) the movement must eventually be able to affect people's preferences so that they come to place value upon goals of the movement, should they differ from the masses' original values; and finally,

(7) the movement must present a credible image to the people, usually through an appealing ideology, vision of the future, *raison d'être*, and successful actions, so as to win the trust necessary for steps 2, 3, and 6.

This chapter will therefore put rational choice and resource mobilization[6] theory to a difficult test: it will attempt to explain the rise of the PKK in Turkey through their theoretical lenses. The case of the PKK intuitively appears least likely to fit into such theoretical perspectives for several reasons:

(1) the PKK emerged at a time when the Turkish armed forces could count themselves amongst the largest in the world, with modern weaponry and reasonably well-trained soldiers;

(2) the PKK did not emerge from groupings of tribal elites (as most previous Kurdish nationalist organizations did), and as a result lacked the start-up systems of patronage and resources with which to entice potential recruits and sympathizers; and

(3) opportunities within Turkey for Kurds willing to assimilate to Turkish culture and society are good.

Thus the challenge emerges of explaining the PKK's emergence and growth from a rational actor or resource mobilization perspective. Also, whereas structuralist approaches would look to Turkey's state, social, or economic characteristics as well as the international milieu to try to explain a Kurdish ethnic nationalist resurgence in Turkey, such approaches have great difficulty in accounting for the success, strength, and development of large opposition movements such as the PKK. One must remember that a plethora of Kurdish and revolutionary challengers

---

[6] In this analysis, RC and RM (resource mobilization) theories are treated as variants of the same rational actor logic explanation. "Although specific departures from some of the assumptions of the rational choice model are frequently made, the underlying premises of rational choice are evident in the language and overall research agenda of RM, its focus on incentives, obsession on free riding, distrust of emotionality, and excessive bureaucratic view of social movement organizations." (Aldon Morris and Carol M. Mueller [ed.], *Frontiers in Social Movement Theory* [New Haven: Yale University Press, 1992], p. 47)

to the Turkish state have existed in recent years, including: TSKP (Turkish Kurdish Socialist Party), KCP (Kurdistan Conservative Party), TKP/ML TIKKO (Turkish Communist Party and the Marxist-Leninist Turkish Worker and Peasant Army), Kizilordu (a breakaway faction of TKP/ML TIKKO), DHKP/C (Revolutionary People's Liberation Party/Front), Hizbullah (various different Hizbullah groups, such as the Menzil Grubu and Ilim Grubu), Musulman Kardes (Muslim Brotherhood), THKO (Turkish Revolutionary People's Army), MLM (Marxist-Leninist Maoist Party), PKK/RIZGARI (Kurdistan Freedom Party), KAWA (Kurdistan Proletarian Union), PIK (Kurdistan Islamic Union), and Raya Zazaistan (Path of Zazaistan), to name but a few from a long list.[7] Thus the question that should immediately come to the mind of any observer: why did Abdullah Ocalan's PKK emerge as a substantial challenger and threat to the Turkish state? This is, of course, precisely the kind of question that RC and RM theories try to answer.[8]

Sowing the seeds of ethnic nationalist challenge: the PKK's early years

Abdullah Ocalan began his political career as a student of political science in the University of Ankara. Originally from the Kurdish region of Urfa in Turkey's southeast, he was one of Turkey's many partially assimilated urban Kurds, who spoke Turkish better than Kurdish (many urban Kurds did not speak Kurdish at all). Although sympathetic to right-wing movements and even an admirer of Ataturk in his early days, Ocalan underwent an identity shift while studying political science at the University of Ankara. He became a member of Turkish leftist groups such as Devrimci Genc. He soon broke off from the Turkish Left as well, however, to found what would become the PKK. With six friends, he set off in 1975 for Turkey's southeastern Kurdish hinterland, or "Northern Kurdistan." They founded a specifically Kurdish leftist party, combining Marxism-Leninism with Kurdish national liberation. They also first focused on building a following in their home regions of Urfa, Elazig, Tunceli, Gaziantep, and Maras.[9]

From such modest beginnings, in less than twenty years Ocalan's group was able to field tens of thousands of armed guerrillas, establish

---

[7] This is a partial listing taken from "Terrorism and Youth," a 1999 May 24 report by Turkish intelligence branch director Mahmut Karaaslan.

[8] The argument which I will present here borrows stylistically from Popkin's analysis of the Communist rise in Vietnam, as presented in Michael Taylor's *Rationality and Revolution* (New York: Cambridge University Press, 1988).

[9] David McDowall, *A Modern History of the Kurds* (London: I. B. Taurus, 1997), p. 418.

camps and offices in dozens of countries, attract and withstand the full attention of the Turkish state (at least until the late 1990s), and gather a large degree of support from the Kurdish masses in Turkey. Undoubtedly, the strategies and tactics of the PKK account for its growth – otherwise the "PKK" acronym would be as internationally unknown as those of the myriad opposition groups in Turkey mentioned above. Early strategies and actions, during a movement's vulnerable youth, seem most important to understanding the PKK's emergence. Also, whereas Kurdish revolts that arose earlier in the history of the Turkish Republic were spearheaded by elites who already had authority and followings along tribal or religious lines, the PKK stands out as a movement that was built up from nothing. This fact further increases the need to explain the "how" of the movement's emergence, rather than just arguing that the socio-political or economic situation in Turkey at the time generated a Kurdish rebellion which happened to be more enduring than previous ones.

In attempting to explain the PKK's emergence along RC and RM theoretical lines, we immediately encounter our first obstacle: In 1975 Ocalan departed Ankara for the Kurdish southeast with six comrades,[10] and seven university students with little resources would definitely not be able to organize and attract the support of large numbers of people via appeals to their self-interest and selective incentives. Revolutionary and guerrilla movements elsewhere in the world typically required at least from fifty to a few hundred of what Popkin calls *political entrepreneurs*, that is, self-denying, ideologically motivated cadres who enlist mass support and kick-start the movement.[11] RC and RM theory need not, however, be required to explain the participation in a movement of every single individual; rather, the theories must be able to provide a convincing account for large scale, mass participation in a movement. It seems reasonable to assume that out of a population of a million people or

---

[10] One of the PKK's earliest formal meetings, at which it was decided to send out the cadres to begin work in Kurdish towns, was held in Ankara with a total participation of 25 people ("A Brief History of the Kurdistan's Workers' Party," 3, undated article distributed by the ERNK, PKK political wing).

[11] Fidel Castro and Che Guevara began the Cuban revolution with only eighty-two men, many of whom died ten days later after leaving Mexico, during the ambush of Alegria de Pio. The Cuban case was, however, an anomaly – other relatively successful guerrilla and revolutionary movements required a core starting group with at least a few hundred cadres. For a brief comparative survey of such cases, see Gerard Chaliand (ed.), *Guerrilla Strategies* (Berkeley: University of California Press, 1982); Robert Asprey, *War in the Shadows: the Guerrilla in History* (New York: William Morrow and Company, Inc., 1994); or Thomas Greene *Comparative Revolutionary Movements* (Englewood Cliffs, NJ: Prentice-Hall, 1974).

more, a group of several hundred individuals whose prime motivator is not self-interest and who are not as risk-averse as the general population, can be recruited to form the *political entrepreneur* base of a movement. The task then falls to this still small group to enlist the support of the masses.[12] That the PKK's leadership was ideologically and not materially motivated is clear – no intelligent rational individual would take up arms against a military as powerful as Turkey's just 'to get ahead' in material terms. The slim chances of success (witness the many failed uprisings discussed in Chapter 2 as well as the many subversive movements crushed by the state security apparatus) simply do not merit the risks. The fact that many PKK cadres committed suicide in prison rather than make a televised confession (central committee member Mazlum Dogan in 1982, for instance) simply flies in the face of official Turkish views regarding the movement, which paint the PKK as a group of self-seeking bandits, terrorists, and drug smugglers. Imprisoned PKK cadres typically chose to commit suicide by immolating themselves, and left written or oral testimonies explaining their resort to such an ultimate act of symbolism.

However, the ideological grievances and impetus for the cadres do not necessarily dictate the nature of the initial appeals made to their target population at large, but are instead the motivating factor for the core members of the group. After arriving in Turkey's southeastern Kurdish regions, Ocalan and his companions naturally first turned to their respective networks of friends and family to recruit the core PKK political entrepreneur group. To this group was also added students and youth frustrated with the status quo, people who could round out the core group of self-denying, dedicated cadres to a few hundred members. The PKK's political and diplomatic wing, the ERNK, provides the following account of the movement's early days, an account that bears striking similarities to those of movements as far away as the Viet Minh in Vietnam and the Shining Path in Peru:

The first activities were organized amongst the youths in schools since there was very little written propaganda material. The political ideas were spread by word of mouth. The work amongst the young students eventually had a big impact on the workers and peasants since, for the most part, the students came from villages or the poorer classes. It followed that influencing them, meant having an influence on their families . . .

---

[12] The case of the Shining Path rebel movement in Peru serves as a good example of this: using his position as a professor at the University of Ayacucho, Shining Path founder Abimael Guzman was able to gather around him a core group of a few hundred students, who then spread out in the countryside to begin living with peasantry and helping them with day to day problems (and in the process creating an organizational skeleton of a mass movement).

In 1977, in the premises of the union of architects and engineers, a general meeting was held in order to assess the work achieved which had been carried out with very modest means. 100 representatives from different professions took part in this meeting of representatives. Other left-wing organizations were also invited as observers thus it became clear how the group was developing into a political organization whose self-confidence and political support was growing. After this meeting the leading cadres were sent to other towns in Kurdistan ...[13]

One must remember that then (1977), the PKK had not yet begun armed confrontations with the Turkish state. Rather, it was building up its infrastructure along Maoist lines, educating its political entrepreneurs-to-be and sending them forth to live among the people and spread the message.[14] Vadim Makarenko describes the approach that the PKK cadres used in the villages: "They know the people entrusted to them: their needs, their problems, how many children they have, what their income is. Simple Kurdish families feed the guerrilla struggle with their manpower and their money."[15] The PKK's use of pre-existing networks such as the union of architects and engineers, as well as local schools, follows the RM process as described by Tilly and other RM theorists.[16]

The other subversive groups identified by Turkish Intelligence branch director Mahmut Karaaslan mentioned at the outset of this chapter engaged in a similar strategy, however, and they too accumulated core cadre groups of fifty to several hundred members. The pressing question thus remains: how did the PKK make the next step, from fringe subversive movement to mass movement challenging the Turkish state? What seems to differentiate the PKK from its local competitors is a strategy which could appeal to people who initially cared little for its Marxist-Leninist ideology or a politicized Kurdish ethnic nationalism.[17] Peasants had enough problems with local feudal landlords and tribal chiefs, as well as the general economic backwardness that afflicted all

---

[13] "A Brief History of the Kurdistan Workers' Party," 3.

[14] For a discussion of Maoist Revolutionary strategy, see Samuel B. Griffith (ed.), *Mao Tse Tung on Guerrilla Warfare* (Washington DC: Praeger Publishers, 1961) and Bernard B. Fall (ed.), *Ho Chi Minh on Revolution, Selected Writings, 1920–66* (Toronto: Signet Books, 1967).

[15] "The Non-Existent State and the Unknown War," *New Times*, November 1995, 53.

[16] Charles Tilly, *From Mobilization to Revolution* (Reading: Addison-Wesley Publishing Company, 1978).

[17] The argument that other people may not care about a politicized Kurdish ethnic ideology is not the same as saying that their Kurdish ethnic ideology holds no value for them, however. As discussed in ch. 1, people may identify themselves very much in ethnic terms, but at the same time not favor such ethnic identity as a basis from which make political claims upon the state (category number three – private ethnic identification). For the sake of argument, this chapter assumes that most people initially fall into this category.

residents of the Kurdish regions. The PKK, with only a few hundred cadres, was able to increase the Kurdish population's sympathy and support by coordinating actions that mattered to the local people, most important of which was opposition to the landlords and exploitative tribal chiefs.[18] Ismet G. Imset notes the following: "... the history of the PKK between when it was established in 1978 and 1980 is not truly indicative of its current or mid-1980s structure both in the form of its activities and its very limited membership at that time. *Most activities were locally supported peasant-based attacks on tribal chiefs* in the Urfa province and contained in that specific region."[19] Van Bruinessen adds that, "Although the PKK was occasionally allied with a 'patriotic' chieftain, tribal or landed elites never gained much influence in it, distinguishing the PKK from most other Kurdish organizations, whose leaderships usually included at least a few such persons. Much of the PKK's violence was directed against the haves in the name of the have-nots."[20]

Land distribution in the southeast of Turkey remains extremely uneven, and the PKK emerged on the scene at a time when "... 8 percent of farming families own over 50 percent of the land, while 80 percent of farming families are evenly balanced between those holding up to 5 hectares and those who own no land at all."[21] The scene was ripe for a movement which could emerge and offer poor Kurds a way out of their feudal subordination.[22] Kendal Nezan, writing in 1980 (before the PKK began armed activities), described occasional peasant actions already being spontaneously undertaken in the 1970s:

Here and there, peasants have occupied land belonging to the aghas (petty nobles) and demanded that it be redistributed; often they have not hesitated to confront the troops called in by the owner. This phenomenon is still at a very early stage, but each local success encourages the landless peasants. The conflict between peasants and landlords seems likely to spread quickly unless the Government introduces a land reform, as it has said it intends to do.[23]

---

[18] Samuel L. Popkin, "Political Entrepreneurs and Peasant Movements in Vietnam" in Michael Taylor, *Rationality and Revolution* (New York: Cambridge University Press, 1988), p. 61. He describes the same process in colonial Vietnam.

[19] Ismet G. Imset, "The PKK: Terrorists or Freedom Fighters?" *Democracy at Gunpoint; The Economist,* Turkey Survey, 8–14 June (1996), 26.

[20] Martin van Bruinessen, *Agha, Shaikh and State* (London: Zen Books Ltd., 1992), p. 42.

[21] McDowall, *A Modern History of the Kurds,* p. 243.

[22] Feudal modes of production and divergent class interests are in fact structural variables, as discussed in ch. 1. Although the structural approach of ch. 2 only touches upon these questions indirectly (as they affect the elites' relations to the government and its challengers), RM and RC theories address these variables by examining insurgent strategies to affect people's choices in such a context.

[23] Gerard Chaliand (ed.), *People Without a Country: the Kurds and Kurdistan* (London: Zed Press, 1980), p. 91.

The PKK correctly identified the explosive situation in the country-side and the peasants' mood. In consequence the group directed its 1978–1980 activities against Kurdish feudal landowners. The land-owners immediately lashed out at the fledgling organization, which only resulted in more PKK credibility *vis-à-vis* the peasantry:

... the feudal Kurdish landowners whose power was undermined with the growth of the organization [the PKK], tried to destroy it through brutal acts of violence. On May 19, 1978, Halil Cavus, a much loved leader of the Kurds, was murdered by a group of bandits hired by the landowners. This led to an intense war against the local landowners which gained a lot of support. Meetings attended by large audiences were held in Erzurum, Dersim, Elazig and Antep in which representatives from the surrounding regions and towns participated.[24]

An indicative example of the PKK's strategy at this time was their attempted assassination of Mehmet Celal Bucak, a local landlord who controlled twenty villages as well as the town of Siverek.[25] According to one resident of a Bucak-controlled village, the landlord would send his men to "burn our crops at night if we break the old patterns."[26] When their assassination of Bucak failed, the young PKK militants were not above resorting to more devious means of improving their position: "According to a dissident who then belonged to the PKK's central group, they did not shy away from provocations: he claims that the PKK, in order to get the support of a particular tribe, killed one of its members, making it seem as if he had been murdered by Bucak's outlaws. He accuses the PKK, or more precisely its leader Ocalan, of systemati-cally engaging in similar murderous provocations."[27] Thus with few resources at their disposal and only a few armed cadres, the PKK was able to manipulate local politics to its advantage. The PKK was also able to attract the attention and sympathy of the Kurdish peasantry by select-ively attacking certain hated Kurdish landowners, aghas and tribal chiefs:

Rather than assaulting the agha class as a whole, the PKK operated with fine calculation, exploiting blood feuds where these existed, helping to create them where they did not and, according to Western intelligence, becoming "involved in local politics by offering their services to local politicians and influential families in the Urfa region." As one close associate of Ocalan later remarked "whenever we managed to win one person from a family or tribe at that time [1978], the whole family or tribe came to our side."[28]

---

[24] "A Brief History of the Kurdistan Workers' Party," 4.
[25] McDowall, *A Modern History of the Kurds*, p. 419.   [26] Ibid., p. 419.
[27] Van Bruinessen, *Agha, Shaikh and State*, p. 42.
[28] McDowall, *A Modern History of the Kurds*, p. 419.

For self-interested Kurdish peasants, many of whom languished in serf-like conditions, it made sense not to inform on the PKK militants who challenged their landlords. The PKK's 1978 manifesto stated that the land of "feudal landlords" would be expropriated, while those of "patriotic landlords" would be untouched.[29] Other Kurdish nationalist groups in the region, such as Ala Rizgari, had tried to organize protests against landlords, but it was the PKK that successfully shattered past patterns of deference and obedience by shooting landlords.[30] In this way, Ocalan's group began to look like a new viable locus of authority in the area, and actively supporting the PKK could appear as a worthwhile possibility when weighed against the resultant risks.[31] When it came to supporting or joining in a PKK attack on the landlord, there was no free-rider problem – those peasants who helped the PKK would have their hated landlord weakened or removed, and would perhaps gain possession of their land and freedom from his predations. Those who did not aid the PKK could expect little change in the way of things, or at worst risk being left out if the PKK removed their landlord as a viable force and took control of the area. Once a peasant had sided with the PKK in an anti-landlord action, it became in their interest to see the PKK succeed on a more general level, lest the old conservative agha, tribal chief, and landlord class return and undo past gains, or worse, wreak vengeance on the peasants. Hence by pursuing their own self-interest and joining the PKK for small local actions, Kurdish peasants may have unwittingly changed the very nature of their interests and acquired a vested stake in the fate of the movement they "temporarily" allied with. Correspondingly, as the PKK mounted more successful actions, its credibility and the resources it could offer to its supporters (selective incentives) grew. By acting as mediators in local and tribal

---

[29] Ibid. He adds that "The (PKK's) founding Congress was allegedly held on the estate of one such 'patriotic' landlord. Within the year of its founding, the party was deeply involved in a tribal war between a 'collaborating' and a 'patriotic chieftain.'"

[30] Ibid.

[31] A PKK sympathizer from Mardin (southeastern Turkey, near the Iraqi and Syrian borders) described to me a crucial difference between the PKK and its local competitors, such as Ala Rizgari: in the early 1980s, the uneducated, poor peasants or townspeople would go to cadres of other "revolutionary" organizations and complain about a local official or gendarmes commander who abused them or enforced laws onto them too assiduously. The cadres would say, "Yes, let's discuss these. The officials are part of the government and class system that oppresses us, and we must unify against them." When they approached the representatives of the PKK about such a matter, however, the response was most often: "You have a problem with this official? O.K. He will be gone by next week" (author's interview, May 22, 2001, Toronto). Naturally, the latter kind of action-oriented response elicited a great deal of credibility within the local populace.

disputes,[32] as well as a force representing challenge to the status quo, the PKK further increased its standing and ability to carry out additional actions.

Ocalan and his original six comrades were effectively "creating something from nothing," their only original resources being "intangibles" such as education, the ability to organize, charisma, determination, a ruthless readiness to use violence when necessary, and the willingness to take great risks. By attacking and proving that the state could not protect the landlords, and later by staging guerrilla ambushes on state security forces (mid-1980s), the PKK pursued two of its main objectives: winning the sympathy of the Kurdish peasant class and demonstrating the limits of state control. Ocalan's movement could accomplish these tasks with remarkably few resources and little manpower during the initial stages of the PKK's growth.

By the late 1980s, reports of PKK units kidnapping village youth between the ages of sixteen and twenty emerged.[33] Such a strategy would make sense, since it would swell PKK ranks and relatives of the kidnapped youth would then have an interest in aiding the organization, for the welfare of those kidnapped. If the PKK could successfully kidnap youth from *village guard* areas (Kurdish villages armed by the state to fight the PKK), then they could be assured of somewhat less enthusiastic attacks by the village guards, who would fear targeting their own youth in the PKK. The military arm of the PKK (the ARGK) in fact likened such a policy to conscription for the guerrilla army, since Kurdish youth would otherwise be conscripted into the Turkish armed forces at the age of eighteen.[34] Once in PKK hands, the new recruits could be socialized into willing and motivated guerrilla combatants.

Another possible explanation exists for this phenomenon, however. As Imset explains, it would be in the interests of both the PKK and the

---

[32] Officials from Iraqi Kurdish parties (the KDP and PUK), when questioned on the issue, stated to this author that the PKK benefited from any instability or quarrel between other Kurdish groups, moving quickly to try and fill resulting power vacuums in the region (author's interviews conducted in Ankara on February 2, 1998 and March 20, 1999).

[33] Ismet G. Imset, *The PKK* (Ankara: Turkish Daily News Publications, 1992), p. 84.

[34] Imset writes that

According to the organization's 1989 *Compulsory Guerrilla System*, those Kurds living in the region who were approaching the age of 18 and who were bachelors, or those who were married but had not yet been recruited to the Turkish army, were to be forced to join the ARGK. If a family had only one son, he was not abducted. If there were two children in the family, the elder was abducted first and one child was left behind to take care of the family. Though the total number of abducted victims was never clearly spelled out by Turkish officials, it was evident that it was in the hundreds mainly in the border areas throughout 1989 and by the end of that year, more than 1,000 from the Hakkari province had reportedly joined the PKK ranks. (Ibid., p. 85)

Kurdish villagers to report the disappearance of village youth as PKK kidnappings.[35] Otherwise, the villages supplying recruits to the PKK would face government reprisals. Likewise, "kidnapped" youth who proved unsuited to the trials of guerrilla life could return to their villages (continuing to work for the PKK's political and support wing, the ERNK), telling the authorities that they had "escaped."[36] Although a lack of reliable information makes it difficult to ascertain the truth regarding kidnappings, the fact that around thirty percent of the PKK's recruits are women[37] may indicate that this latter explanation of the phenomenon is often the case: in traditional patriarchal Kurdish society, the honor of the kin group resides in large part in its women and their "purity." Tribal feuds and long-lasting enmities frequently revolved around raids in which one group's females were kidnapped by another. For this reason, a movement such as the PKK concerned with building a popular mass following would definitely prefer to kidnap male youth than female ones. Yet if nearly a third of the PKK's ranks are composed of women, the implication is that at least for women, joining the organization is more often voluntary. In fact, Kurdish women seeking to exit a system of strict patriarchal control might have viewed the PKK as one of their only avenues of escape. Finally, Kurdish males seeking to avoid service in the Turkish military might view the PKK as a preferable option.

The Turkish state response

Turkey's 1980 military coup further polarized the situation, however, and the army-led new government came down hard on all subversive and suspect groups. While the chaotic situation in Turkey that preceded the 1980 coup allowed the PKK and many other groups to take root, the 1980 coup marked a turning point and the beginning of difficult times for subversive social movements. In this light, we must examine the selective *dis*incentives that the PKK and the government aimed at the Kurdish population. Whereas selective incentives act like a carrot to induce self-interested individuals or groups to support or take part in various actions, selective disincentives are the stick that aims to punish those who oppose or refuse to support the movement (or government).[38]

---

[35] Ibid., pp. 86–88.

[36] Also, it is in the obvious interest of genuine dissenters and deserters from PKK ranks to tell state authorities that they were originally kidnapped into the movement.

[37] Shahrzad, Mojab (ed.), *Women of a Non-State Nation, the Kurds* (Costa Mesa: Mazda Publishers, 2001), p. 148.

[38] The argument presented here fails to maintain a strict levels of analysis separation of individuals and small groups or communities, mainly because selective incentives or

Sensing the looming military takeover and crackdown, Ocalan and the bulk of the PKK central command withdrew from Turkish territory and took refuge in Syria and Lebanon, from where they continued to direct the movement. The new military government in Ankara lashed out at all suspected subversives, including the young PKK: "By 1981, more than 2,000 alleged PKK members were in prison, while 447 were put on mass trial and accused of forming 'armed gangs' to 'annex' southeastern Turkey."[39] The Turkish security forces sought to demonstrate that membership in the PKK (or other subversive groups) incurred more costs than any rational person would want to bear. Despite its small size in the late 1970s, the PKK received the heaviest of the blows directed at Kurdish separatist organizations, having the largest number of militants arrested.[40] The PKK survived the coup period, growing several heads from the decapitation Ankara thought it had dealt the organization.

In retrospect, 1980 simply marked a reinvigoration of a militantly repressive state policy towards any perceived threats (but particularly communists and Kurdish nationalists) – a policy that had temporarily been put into question by the fractious infighting and lack of direction in Ankara's civilian government of the late 1970s. The Turkish military effectively killed off many of the PKK's competitors at this time, and remaining leftist and Kurdish separatist groups were either eventually assimilated into the PKK or thrown into armed, violent competition with the movement.

The selective disincentives applied by the government were also aimed at those who supported, sympathized with, or even simply refused to oppose subversives such as the PKK. The military junta that took control of Turkey in 1980 invoked martial law throughout the country, and most of the predominantly Kurdish provinces in 1987 were placed under "emergency rule" for the next decade.[41] The measures taken in 1980 included the following:

... all political parties ... were outlawed, and their leaders arrested; demonstrations banned; universities were prohibited from political activities; students associations, workers groups and intellectual communities were forced to close for their alleged Marxist functions; and Islamic political affiliations were banned and

---

disincentives can be applied to small groups such as village communities almost as effectively as to individuals. For more regarding such issues, see Mancur Olson's *The Logic of Collective Action* (Boston: Harvard University Press, 1965).

[39] Michael Gunter, "The Kurdish Problem in Turkey," *The Middle East Journal*, Vol. 42, No. 3 (1988), 395.

[40] McDowall, *A Modern History of the Kurds*, p. 420; Imset, *The PKK*, p. 29.

[41] Mark Muller, "Nationalism and the Rule of Law in Turkey," *Democracy at Gunpoint, The Economist, Turkey Survey*, June 8–14, 1996, 45.

their leaders tried. The extremists of both right and left along with Kurdish activists were either arrested or fled the country.[42]

Tens of thousands of people in Turkey were arrested, and a great many of those arrested faced interrogation and torture in prison cells and police stations throughout the country. In 1983 the government once again officially outlawed the Kurdish language in Turkey, continuing policies of changing Kurdish place-names to Turkish ones and forbidding parents to give their children Kurdish names. The coup generals also made fundamental changes to the constitution before relinquishing power in 1983, placing severe restrictions on individual freedoms and paving the way for easy prosecution of anyone even vaguely suspected of subversive activities. For instance, Article 14 of the new constitution stated that individuals who abuse their democratic freedoms "... with the aim of violating the indivisible integrity of the State with its territory and nation, of endangering the existence of the Turkish State and Republic ..." and "... who incite and provoke others to do the same shall be subject to punishments determined by law."[43] Articles of the Turkish penal code were updated in 1991 into the *Anti-Terror Law*, outlined crimes against the state in such general terms that almost anyone could be convicted of sedition. Article 8 of the *Anti-Terror Law* was the most commonly used provision to imprison intellectuals and other public figures the state disapproved of: "Written and oral propaganda and assemblies, meetings and demonstrations aimed at damaging the indivisible unity of the State of the Turkish Republic with its territory and nation are forbidden, regardless of method, intention, and ideas behind them."[44]

In 1986, a Turkish opposition party parliamentary fact-finding mission "... reported that all of eastern Turkey had become a sort of concentration camp where every citizen is being treated as a suspect and where oppression, torture and insult by the military are the rule rather than the exception."[45] McDowall adds the following observation:

---

[42] Hossein A. Shabazi, "Domestic and International Factors Precipitating Kurdish Ethnopolitical Conflict: A Comparative Analysis of Episodes of Rebellion in Iran, Iraq and Turkey," Ph.D. dissertation, University of Maryland, 1998, 203.

[43] Muller, "Nationalism and the Rule of Law in Turkey," 44.

[44] Ibid. Article 8 of the *Anti-Terror Law* was rescinded in 2003, as part of Turkey's European Union reform efforts. Despite this encouraging reform, however, remaining provisions elsewhere in the Constitution and Criminal Code continue to allow the state a fair amount of leeway in constraining free speech. For more on the issue, see Human Rights Watch, "Human Rights Overview: Turkey," January 2004, http://www.hrw.org/english/docs/2003/12/31/turkey7023.htm#2.

[45] Van Bruinessen, *Agha, Shaikh and State*, p. 46.

State oppression was most overwhelming and pervasive in the field of physical abuse and torture. Only pro-government villages were inexperienced in the routine of security sweeps in which hundreds were arbitrarily arrested and beaten to confess to assisting the PKK. Doubtless many had, either by conviction or intimidation, assisted the PKK with food, shelter or merely by looking the other way as they passed through ... Thus every Kurdish village learnt what the state meant by law and order.[46]

In some regions and towns considered hotbeds of dissent, the army deployed itself in overwhelming numbers, attempting to demonstrate the futility of opposing the state. The town of Tunceli (formerly Dersim in Kurdish), with a population of 19,000, had 55,000 soldiers deployed in it.[47] The government also began in the mid-1980s reimplementing the standard counterinsurgency practice of destroying and evacuating suspect villages in regions of guerrilla activity,[48] in order to punish supporters of the PKK and deny the insurgents help from the population: "The number of evacuated hamlets and villages, mainly along the border, reached 400 by the end of 1989, climbing inexorably during the next three years ... to exceed 2,000 villages destroyed by the end of 1994, with over 750,000 rendered homeless."[49] By 2003, the *New York Times* cited various human right organizations' estimate of roughly 4,000 Kurdish villages destroyed.[50] Whole mountainsides of the Kurdish countryside were also declared "forbidden military zones," and anything seen moving within these areas, whether civilian or not, was shot at.[51]

The Turkish state also appears to have been implicitly thinking along RM lines as it formulated elements of its response to the PKK. An Interior Ministry document outlined the following state strategy:

In response to the setting up of so-called front headquarters in so-called provinces defined by the organization and activities of the creation of institutions of logistics, education, finance, health, military branches, people's courts and the like,

---

[46] McDowall, *A Modern History of the Kurds*, p. 425.
[47] Shabazi, *Kurdish Ethnopolitical Conflict*, p. 205.   [48] Ibid., p. 426.
[49] For more information on forced displacement of Kurdish populations, human rights abuses, and the Anti-Terror Law, including eyewitness accounts, refer to: Amnesty International, *Turkey: Walls of Glass*, November 1992; Human Rights Watch Helsinki, *Turkey: Forced Displacement of Ethnic Kurds from Southeastern Turkey*, October 1994; James Ron, *Weapons Transfers and Violations of the Laws of War in Turkey*, Human Rights Watch, November 1995; Human Rights Watch Helsinki, *The Kurds of Turkey: Killings, Disappearances and Torture*, March 1993; U.S. Department of State, *Turkey Country Report on Human Rights Practices for 1996*, January, 1997; and Human Rights Watch Helsinki, *Turkey: New Restrictive Anti-Terror Law*, June 1991, among others.
[50] Dexter Filkins, "Kurds Are Finally Heard: Turkey Burned Our Villages," *New York Times*, October 24, 2003.
[51] James Ron, *Weapons Transfers and Violations of the Laws of War in Turkey*, Human Rights Watch, November 1995.

collaborators should be speedily exposed, persuasion should be applied to them, a spectacle should be made of them, and if necessary they should be penalized.[52]

Hence the bulk of the state response *vis-à-vis* the PKK and other subversive groups rested on repression – powerful selective disincentives to all those who would oppose the Kemalist regime. The Kurdish regions of Turkey were the most economically backward in the country, and little or no selective or group incentives were provided in the form of development funds or projects, official statements to the contrary notwithstanding.[53] But one very important selective incentive always remains in the background in Turkey: Kurds able and willing to assimilate to some degree and adopt the Turkish language, keeping their Kurdish identity in the private sphere, have little or no barriers to advancement in Turkey. Given the socio-political and economic situation in the southeast, however, Kurds adopting this strategy generally must leave their communities and migrate to western Turkey. Furthermore, once located in the western part of the country, they have no more guarantees of advancement than poor ethnic Turks, although they are largely spared the physical insecurities of their Kurdish brethren who remain in the guerrilla war zones. Essentially, assimilation may protect them from repression bluntly aimed at Kurdish nationalists, but not from the predations of the state and owners of capital, aimed at workers, peasantry, and intellectual dissidents.

When in 1985 Turkey introduced the village guard system, however, it brandished an interesting combination of selective incentives and disincentives which changed the nature of the conflict in the southeast. Pursuing a fairly common anti-guerrilla strategy (akin to Peru's strategy against its Shining Path guerrillas), the Turkish government began forming local armed Kurdish militias to combat the PKK. The intent was to have at least a half-dozen or so village guards in the smaller villages, with larger numbers for bigger communities. The selective incentives offered by the government to Kurds willing to enter the system were

---

[52] KIC, "Secret Interior Ministry . . .," 2.

[53] The government in Ankara periodically makes pronouncements about the need to improve the southeast's economy and attract investment there, in order to "Dry up the swamp rather than fighting with the flies" (Interview with Turkish Army General Staff, *Milliyet*, November 18, 1997). Apart from the Ataturk Dam Project (GAP), however, which should eventually greatly increase hydroelectric and agricultural output in the region, nothing significant has materialized. Even the GAP project, much like the Green Revolution in India, seems poised to mainly benefit the larger landowners who own most of the land and can afford the necessary investments to take advantage of the increased irrigation and new crop rotations afforded by the project.

significant; apart from being spared harassment by security forces, attractive financial carrots were offered:

With the government offering a high salary to would-be village guards, there was an immense interest in the system. Unemployment had been one of the main problems of the region for years and initially the project appeared to be an attractive offer to earn a good income and arm oneself ... In the first days of the practice, tens of people applied to become village guards, posing for newspapers and magazines with their machine guns, trekking the mountains alongside troops and hunting down PKK militants on the rugged border terrain. Today, Turkey has approximately 70,000 village guards and is paying each an attractive salary.[54]

In a region with an annual per capita income of around US$400, village guards were offered an extremely attractive monthly stipend of approximately $230.[55] Nor was the Turkish government above recruiting tribal groups it previously considered criminal and involved in smuggling or banditry.[56] Villages or tribes that entered the system could use their new authority and arms to increase their local standing:

... some drove Assyrian and Yazidi villagers from their land near Mardin, others did the same to Alevi villagers near Maras. The victims knew it would be foolish to take their case to court. The aghas also used their weapons to settle local scores. In 1992, for example, eight civilians traveling by minibus in Mardin province were stopped and shot. As intended it was assumed to be the work of the PKK, until an unusually painstaking prosecutor demonstrated the perpetrators were village guards.[57]

Hence the incentives for joining the village guard system were considerable, and of course the newly formed militia were also employed against the PKK and communities suspected of supporting them.

The selective disincentives for *not* joining the village guards, beyond the fact that neighboring or competing communities who did join advanced their relative power, were also powerful. Communities that refused to provide guardsmen were immediately suspected of pro-PKK leanings or active collaboration, and faced the considerable wrath of the Turkish security apparatus: "Turkish troops themselves started in 1991 to raid and torch villages where people refused to join the guards system and it is currently one of the main reasons for human rights abuses in the region."[58] An Amnesty International report presents several eye-witness accounts of such actions, and provides the following statement:

[54] Imset, "The PKK: Terrorists or Freedom Fighters?" 29.
[55] McDowall, *A Modern History of the Kurds*, p. 422.   [56] Ibid.   [57] Ibid.
[58] Imset, "The PKK: Terrorists or Freedom Fighters?" 29.

In southeast Turkey there were, during the summer and autumn of 1991, more than 50 alleged extrajudicial executions. In these killings, the victims, mostly villagers, were taken from their homes, often in rural areas and shot by groups of armed men, or possibly the same group, acting as a death squad. The victims were apparently singled out either because they were believed to be in contact with the PKK, or because they were active in the legal political opposition to the government's policies in the southeast. Nearly all were from villages which had refused to participate in the corps of government-appointed village guards.[59]

Multiple discussions held between this author and Kurds in the southeast of Turkey unearthed personal accounts exhibiting the same pattern of reprisals, all against villages refusing to join the village guards.[60]

In between the state and the PKK

The 1980 coup in Turkey and the resulting application of harsh repressive measures should have convinced any self-interested individual to avoid confronting the state. Later on, the village guard system acted as both a stick and a carrot to push the government's case even more forcefully. Yet in spite of all this, the PKK continued to organize (after a brief pause and retreat in 1980–1982) and grow in Turkey's Kurdish regions, eventually launching its guerrilla war against the state in 1984. Somehow, the fledgling PKK found a way to thrive in an environment that killed off many of its leftist, Kurdish, and revolutionary competitors. Can the PKK's survival be explained within a RC and RM framework? The argument must, of course, continue to follow along the lines presented at the outset of this chapter: in addition to the selective incentives it offered its target population (more of which will be discussed below), the PKK was able to brandish its own selective disincentives to match, or in some cases outdo, the threats put forth from Ankara.

Selective incentives and disincentives form part of the necessary elements of RC and RM mobilization mentioned at the outset of this chapter:

(1) goals that matter to the people;
(2) convincing people that their participation makes a difference;
(3) convincing people that enough of their peers are also participating;
(4) offering selective incentives and disincentives to affect people's behavior;
(5) coordinating and building up movement actions and resources;

---

[59] *Turkey: Walls of Glass*, November 1992, 9.
[60] Discussions were usually held during the one-year fieldwork in the region (1997–1998) as well as a subsequent trip in the summer of 1999.

(6) affecting people's values to bring them in line with the movement's goals; and finally,

(7) presenting a credible image to the people (via an ideology and successful actions).

When the bulk of the PKK's competitors (both groups operating legally within the system and illegal subversives) were eliminated in the post-1980 clampdown, the PKK was left standing as one of the only credible options for Kurds who did not want to side with the state. The repression of the early eighties targeted many Kurds who were likely innocent of subversive activity (as large scale repressions generally do), and these people may well have reasoned that if they were going to face repression in any case, they might as well support the one remaining movement that had a chance of displacing a state that had already labeled them as enemies. With legal opposition groups operating within the Turkish system already eliminated, the armed revolt the PKK launched in 1984 and 1985 gained added credibility. Indeed, once the PKK began its attacks against the Turkish state, each action brought it added credibility:

When in 1984 it raided two fortresses, the general image among the local people was one of petty affection. They were referred to as "the kids," or "the students." In a region torn by its own feudal conflicts and a history of banditry, the concept of having armed youngsters fighting was not too surprising. In 1987, as Ankara branded the outlaws as "a handful of bandits," local affection increased, describing them as "the resistance." Today, a whole population is talking of the "guerrillas" and in the words of several MPs, every family in the region now has a member with these guerrilla.[61]

With invaluable safe havens in Syria and northern Iraq to complement their forces within Turkey, PKK units began a typical guerrilla war campaign of ambushing army patrols, attacking isolated army and police posts, and sabotaging power stations or other elements of Turkey's economic infrastructure. Demonstrating that the Turkish state was not omnipotent, the PKK earned itself ever-increasing notoriety (and in the eyes of many Kurds, heroism), "claiming more than 50 separate actions from June through November 1985 in many different parts of Kurdistan that wiped out four army platoons and killed another 50 soldiers, over 10 policemen and more than 20 'traitors.'"[62] Although such actions could be carried out with a relatively small guerrilla force, their psychological impact was significant, presenting to the Kurdish people a credible image of the movement, showing them that significant numbers of Kurds

[61] Imset, "The PKK: Terrorists or Freedom Fighters?" 29.
[62] Van Bruinessen, *Agha, Shaikh and the State*, p. 44.

were participating in PKK opposition to the state, and that ordinary Kurdish people's actions could make a difference.

In the years prior to 1985, the PKK had acquired for itself several enemies, however. Its prior-mentioned policy of exploiting tribal feuds and attacking feudal landlords and elites had both its costs and benefits, attracting sympathy for the movement from some groups at the expense of other groups' hostility. When in 1985 Turkey introduced the village guard system, the PKK's actions became even more controversial. Given the myriad incentives for joining the village guards, the PKK reasoned that it had to demonstrate in no uncertain terms the heavy price of supporting the Turkish state. It therefore sought to apply its own heavy selective disincentives to a population in the midst of choosing between the rebels and the government.[63] To this end, the PKK tried to present itself as a force to be more feared than the state:

At the beginning of 1987 the PKK launched a ferocious assault on the [village guard] system. During the next two years it deliberately wiped out village guard and agha families, men, women and children, without compunction, in Mardin, Siirt and Hakkari provinces ... The PKK was able to demonstrate the inherent weakness of the village guard system. Most village guard contingents were only about half a dozen strong. Lacking telephone or radio, they were easy victims to surprise attacks.[64]

The gruesome murders of village guards and their entire families created a media frenzy in Turkey. But the constant media barrage of casualties of PKK attacks had the ironic effect of adding to the movement's notoriety and credibility as a force to be reckoned with. While Turks saw in the media images only evidence of the PKK's viciousness and indiscriminate barbarism ("the civilian victims were Kurds, their own kind!" being a common reaction), many Kurds in Turkey perceived a different story:[65]

As far as the local Kurds were concerned, they knew that PKK attacks were directed not at ordinary people but villagers with state connections, who agreed to collaborate against the Kurds although they themselves were Kurds ... All of those killed, including Kurdish infants and women, were related only to the village guards. The message was that any family who dealt with the state would be destroyed ... Thus news spread fast in the region of one village raid following another. The PKK managed to give the impression, with the indirect help of

---

[63] In a dialectic manner, an extremely repressive Turkish state engendered a mirror image of itself, in the form of a vicious and ruthless insurgent movement.

[64] McDowall, *A Modern History of the Kurds*, p. 423.

[65] In post-structuralist terms, the same text (PKK attacks on village guards and their families) produced multiple and different readings, depending on the audience (ethnic Turks or Kurds).

security officials, that it was strong and dangerous – and, unfortunately, often as vicious – as the state forces. In certain areas, fear of the PKK even replaced the age-old bogeyman of the Turkish gendarmerie.[66]

The PKK's tactics caused many observers in the late 1980s to hypothesize that the movement was losing whatever support it had achieved amongst the Kurdish populace. Certainly the PKK made itself many bitter enemies during this period. But because local Kurds were able to discern that the PKK's targets were solely state collaborators, pronouncements regarding the movement's fading popularity proved to be for the most part premature:

As ironic as it may sound, by determining the targets for such acts of terrorism in a selective way, the PKK was basically maintaining its effectiveness and gaining popular support – even if out of sheer fear at times. It was showing to the local Kurds what happened to "traitors" or state "collaborators." The message the PKK gave to the Kurdish people was clear. It was dangerous. It was determined. And, it was more effective than government troops. In short, it was simply in the peoples' best interest to give their support to this organization rather than to Turkey.[67]

From an RC and RM perspective, not responding to the village guard system with the kind of severe selective disincentives the PKK deployed would have amounted to suicide for the young movement. The organization's credibility, perceived chances of success, ability to function in the Kurdish countryside, and the image that a critical mass of Kurds were participating in the PKK, would all have been compromised. Although Ocalan's movement was never successful at completely eliminating the village guards, it did manage to keep the system on the defensive and largely ineffective at least until the late 1990s. The greatest misfortune fell upon those Kurds and Kurdish communities who wanted to stay neutral vis-à-vis the PKK–state conflict. With the creation of the village guard system, they were effectively caught in between the government and the guerrillas and forced to choose sides, lest they face attacks from both groups. Once they chose to join the village guards, they faced the PKK's wrath. If they chose to support the PKK or refused to join the village guards, they faced retribution from the Turkish military. In some cases, the PKK has even been suspected of extending itself logistically and conducting operations in areas around neutral villages, in order to provoke government repression there and induce such villages into choosing the insurgents' side. While the Turkish security forces refused to be

---

[66] Imset, "The PKK: Terrorists or Freedom Fighters?" 30.   [67] Ibid.

outdone when it came to selective disincentives,[68] the army's inability to channel repression very selectively – meaning only to those "who deserved it" (were actual active supporters of the PKK) – compared to the PKK's ability to identify and only target actively pro-state Kurds, meant that the PKK gained increasing popular support the longer the conflict continued. In the eyes of many people, the PKK began to look more credible because it was more discerning in its targets. This holds true even without considering the psychological argument (which is outside the RC framework) that people resent a state that represses innocents, tortures prisoners, and for its actions lacks a credo with which they can identify.[69]

The issue of credibility, however, goes beyond convincing people that, for instance, the PKK will make good on its threats to punish those who collaborate with the state. Possible supporters must be convinced of the movement's longer term goals, and that they will benefit from the movement's success.[70] It is in this light that the PKK's ideological pronouncements about creating a state where Kurds can thrive as Kurds (i.e. without having to learn how to function in the Turkish societal milieu and without having to change their culture, traditions, and general identity) in Kurdish (i.e. without having to gain fluency in Turkish) should be viewed. For those individuals of low socio-economic status and possessed of a feeling of powerlessness under the Turkish regime, such a vision holds undeniable appeal, giving them hope to advance themselves where little existed before. For some Kurdish elites who might feel that their current status in Turkey does not reflect their true worth or potential, the possibility of greater status and power in a Kurdish political entity would likewise be appealing. But in the grand tradition of revolutionary insurgencies, the PKK went further than simply talking about their vision – in regions they occasionally came to control or wield great influence in, the PKK established its own parallel government to challenge and displace Ankara: "The PKK, which was already strengthening, had then also the opportunity to establish local authority in various areas, filling the gap of state authority. Secret Kurdish schools started functioning in the darkness of the night. The number of court cases heard at Turkish civil courts

---

[68] McDowall, *A Modern History of the Kurds*, p. 425.

[69] A loyalist (to the state) Kurdish member of Parliament stated in 1987 that "When the military took over in 1980, the Kurds were happy. But then the military started getting worse than the terrorists, so now about 40 percent of the villagers in the border areas support the terrorists." Ibid., p. 425.

[70] As stated earlier, a long-term vision and ideology is even more important for instilling the necessary sense of purpose and sacrifice amongst the movement's cadres (political entrepreneurs), who in turn act as direct representatives of the group's credibility with the people.

declined rapidly as so-called PKK peoples' tribunals came to being. In several provinces the PKK even set up its local police and intelligence units."[71] Hence for Kurds lacking fluency in Turkish, unfamiliar with the mechanisms of the Turkish courts and state, lacking connections with the Turkish authorities, and therefore justifiably distrustful of their courts and police, strengthening of the PKK and fulfillment of its goals seemed to promise immediate benefits. Also, lest those with something to gain from a PKK ascension sit back and free-ride off the efforts of others who risk themselves and support the movement, the PKK stated in no uncertain terms that it would remember who supported the Kurdish struggle and offered a myriad of selective incentives in the form of economic help to poor villagers, protection from rivals,[72] medical aid, and other benefits.

Thus the economic backwardness of the Kurdish regions and the lack of prospects for many young Kurds worked very much in the PKK's favor, fueling its insurgency. Most of the PKK's active cadres in fact fell between the ages of eighteen and twenty-five, were poorly educated, worked as manual laborers, farmers, shepherds, or were unemployed.[73] With little to lose materially and little prospect of advancement within the Turkish status quo, such individuals and their families were the easiest to attract (and had the most to gain from the PKK's program). On the side of selective disincentives, the PKK ruthlessly executed dissenters and deserters from its ranks.[74]

That the PKK did attract large numbers of participants and support from the Kurdish population is one of the few certainties that emerges from the conflict in southeast Turkey. McDowall notes that, "The mayor of Nusaybin [a Kurdish-Arab town in eastern Turkey, on the Syrian border] caused a sensation (and lost his job) by telling the Reuters correspondent that about 95 percent of his townspeople were happy to support the PKK."[75] In addition to the statements of several Kurdish members of Turkey's parliament that "every family in the region now has

---

[71] Imset, "The PKK: Terrorists or Freedom Fighters?" 31.

[72] Many Kurdish individuals and families who lacked tribal affiliations or who belonged to weak tribes incapable of standing up to more powerful tribal rivals joined the PKK. Opponents would then steer clear of that person or family so as not to pick a fight with the PKK (author's interview with Faik Nerweyi, KDP Political Affairs representative, Ankara, August 17, 1997).

[73] Gunter, "The Kurdish Problem in Turkey," 395.

[74] A common accusation levied by the Turkish government, the PKK's practice of executing dissidents and deserters was confirmed during several of the author's interviews with former PKK militants who had escaped the organization (interviews conducted in Suleimaniya, northern Iraq during 2003 and 2004).

[75] McDowall, *A Modern History of the Kurds*, p. 427.

a member with the guerrillas,"[76] by the late 1980s Turkish sociologist Ismail Besikci was able to make the following observation: "When a village guard is killed, there aren't enough people willing to carry his body to the grave. No one goes to his house to offer their condolences. But the burial of a guerrilla attracts huge crowds. There is no end to those who visit the family to offer their condolences. Those who die in clashes are referred to as the 'martyrs.' "[77]

In a ground-breaking and controversial opinion poll of Turkish Kurds conducted by University of Ankara professor Dogu Ergil, the following question was asked: "Do you have a relative in the organization (PKK)?" The responses were as follows: 34.9% of respondents refused to reply to the question, and 34.8% had the courage to reply "yes."[78] If we assume that those who refused to reply did indeed have a relative in the PKK (hence their refusal to reply), the aggregate of "yes" answers is an amazing 69.7% of those surveyed. Such results correspond well with observations such as Imset's, who states that, "After 1989, the PKK strengthened rapidly in the region and faced almost no problems in finding new recruits, weapons or financial resources."[79] Some observers, however, cite the PKK's unheeded call to boycott local elections in 1995 as evidence of lack of support for the movement – in regions such as Diyarbakir and Hakkari (supposedly pro-PKK provinces), 72 percent and 82 percent of eligible voters cast valid ballots: "These results signaled two facts. First, PKK's instructions were not heeded, and people went to the ballot box. Second, by this behavior, the people of the region showed the state that they should no longer be suspected of being potential or actual PKK supporters."[80] Of course,

---

[76] Imset, "The PKK: Terrorists or Freedom Fighters?" 29.

[77] Ismail Besikci, *Kurdistan and Turkish Colonialism* (London: Kurdistan Solidarity Committee and Kurdistan Information Centre, 1991), p. 9.

[78] *Dogu Sorunu: Teshisler ve Tespitler, Ozel Arastirma Raporu*, 1995. Ergil's survey was conducted on a sample of 1500 Kurds, half of whom lived in Turkey's eastern (Kurdish) provinces and half of whom lived in recent migrant communities in the west of Turkey. The survey was conducted by selecting geographical districts and streets, and then using a quota sample system to select respondents. Due to the sensitive nature of the survey (respondents feared government repression), local representatives drawn from each community's chamber of commerce were used as "trusted intermediaries" to assure the respondents that their identities would remain confidential. In order to elicit a greater number of frank responses in a sensitive political climate, Professor Ergil's pollsters managed to dissuade local security personnel from accompanying them on their interviews, in part by concealing to the local authorities some aspects of the survey they planned to conduct (author's interview with Dogu Ergil, May 18, 1999, Ankara). Despite this, the survey faced serious criticism concerning its statistical methods and should be referred to with caution.

[79] Imset, "The PKK: Terrorists or Freedom Fighters?" 31.

[80] Nur Bilge Criss, "The Nature of PKK Terrorism in Turkey," *Studies in Conflict and Terrorism*, Vol. 18 (1995), 27.

another interpretation of this voting phenomenon is possible: Kurds in the region were acting rationally and strategically, trying to play both sides of the field. While often supporting the PKK, they also tried to "hedge their bets," pursue their interests within the system and acquire the fruits of political patronage, while at the same time hoping to dissuade security forces from continuing repressive operations in the area (by proving their electoral loyalty).

Once the PKK matured into a larger, more established movement, it could finance itself via contributions from Kurds in the region and abroad (a "revolutionary tax"), as well as with support from foreign state powers and involvement in the narcotics trade and smuggling.[81] Earlier sources of financing could have likely included robberies of banks and jewelry merchants, which was a favored tactic of urban leftist groups in the 1970s.[82] One must remember, however, that the PKK was not created by foreign state powers, and that groups such as that founded by Ocalan and a few associates must achieve a certain level of size, strength, and credibility before they can fund their activities via a takeover of the local narcotics trade or smuggling.[83] The PKK nucleus emerged from the university classrooms of Ankara, not rural elites and outlaws seeking to turn their criminal activities into a larger political movement.

---

[81] It is difficult, for obvious reasons, to establish the sources of the movement's financial resources. Observers such as Criss ("The Nature of PKK Terrorism") and Gunter ("The Kurdish Problem in Turkey") are quite definitive about the movement's involvement in the drug trade. Gunter provides the following observation: "The party financed itself through banditry and extortion. It is claimed that 'most of the Turkish heroin refining is carried out in rugged southeastern Turkey by Kurds' and that there exists 'a degree of overlap between the traffickers and Kurdish separatists in the region'" (395). Turkish sources further indicate that "the separatists have been particularly eager to trade drugs for weapons" (Mark Steinitz, "Insurgents, Terrorists and the Drug Trade," *The Washington Quarterly*, Fall [1985], 145).

[82] For an additional account of accusations against the PKK and its methods of financing, see The Turkish Democracy Foundation, "Fact Book on Turkey: Kurds and The PKK Terrorism," XXV, Ankara, May (1996). http://www.geocities.com/CapitolHill/8572/xxv.

[83] The vast majority of Kurds from Turkey's southeast that this author spoke to do not believe that the PKK has any involvement with the drug trade (although some argued that fringe elements of the organization might have such involvement). Instead, they pointed to village guards and state paramilitary special forces as the drug culprits. Whether this is more indicative of successful propaganda on the PKK's part than the truth is, of course, difficult to determine. A German court has, however, accused the highest levels of the Turkish government (and specifically Deputy Prime Minister Tansu Ciller) of involvement with and protection of heroin traffickers. The Turkish government vehemently denies the accusations ("Turkey Blasts German Court's Claim," *The Washington Post*, January 23 [1997], A24).

The RM and RC framework: strengths and inadequacies

This chapter sought to argue that by offering goals that mattered to the people, selective (dis)incentives, astute organization and coordination, and the establishment of credibility with the local Kurdish population through ideology, self-sacrifice, and demonstrative actions against Turkish security forces, the founders of the PKK were able to turn their movement into a mass-based, significant challenge to the Turkish state. That Ocalan and his comrades started out with almost no resources or pre-existing followings and networks at their disposal made an explanation of their successes all the more pressing.

For the purposes of testing the utility of RC and RM theoretical lenses, it is sufficient to end our examination of the rise of the PKK at the high-point in the organization's development (the early 1990s), given that our objective was to convincingly explain the emergence and development of such a movement. The RC/RM mode of analysis does appear to offer a compelling explanation for the emergence of the largest, most enduring Kurdish nationalist challenge ever to threaten Turkey. This is particularly salient in light of the analysis presented in Chapter 2 – an examination based on political opportunity structures would have led one to expect such a powerful challenge in the 1920–1930 period, but not in the 1980s and 1990s.

Several difficulties emerge in the explanation provided in this chapter. First of all, given the mortal risk faced by PKK cadres and supporters, can their choice to side with the insurgents be justified with the rational choice and resource mobilization arguments provided? How do we weigh material and economic values and goals *vis-à-vis* physical security and mortal risk? What of people's own stated reasons for joining or supporting ethnic nationalist movements such as the PKK? Typically the reasons given fall into the non-rational choice category of identity, full of the passions that common parlance associates with such movements and conflicts. Finally, if we accept that some people may attach greater value to goals such as "public recognition of my ethnic group (e.g. respect)" than material and economic goods, then rational choice theory finds itself in a difficult position. We must then establish what people's values are, which is in turn dependent on their identities. As argued in Chapter 1, it is difficult for RC and RM theories to show us how individuals and groups organize and achieve objective "X" without establishing what objective "X" is and why it holds importance for them.[84]

---

[84] The more strictly positivist manifestations of rational choice theories, wherein mathematical values are assigned to preference sets (for example), are not very applicable to the

Perhaps it would be helpful to bring the discussion back to the concrete case we have been using to illuminate RC and RM theory. We can formulate the question of explaining support for the PKK as the following problematic: after Turkey's 1980 coup, it still appears implausible that rational individuals would strongly side with the PKK rather than

(1) leave the region of conflict; or
(2) provide the minimum feasible level of support to their chosen camp (the PKK or the government) so as to lessen chances of incurring the other camp's retribution; or
(3) find ways to appear to both the insurgents and government as being on their side.

Many Kurds have, in fact, chosen to leave the southeastern conflict zone. It is estimated that more than 3 million people left the region in the last twenty years.[85] *Reuters* reports the following: "A mixture of economic hardship and separatist conflict in southeast Turkey swells the waves of Kurdish migrants currently lapping Europe's shores ... Turkey says they are economic migrants ... Human rights groups say harsh tactics against Kurdish separatists drive civilians abroad ... Employment [in the southeast] is scarce and average annual household incomes are around $3,500, compared with more than $11,000 in Istanbul."[86] One would assume that those Kurds choosing exit from the region pursued a rational choice strategy of maximizing material gains and minimizing risks and costs. For those remaining in the southeast, a variety of factors could account for their choice. Such factors could, of course, be rational choice value-maximizing considerations, or they could be psychological issues such as attachment to the land, family ties, and a belief in the Kurdish people's right to dwell in Kurdistan. According to recent figures available from the Turkish Demographic and Health Survey (TDHS), 70% of the Kurdish population in Turkey is still located in the east of the country.[87] If we add Kurds who have migrated abroad with the group that has moved to western Turkey, we can conclude that a little less than half of

vast complexity of ethnic nationalist mobilization. To begin with, the data at our disposal in conflict zones like southeastern Turkey (where it is difficult to ascertain who attacked which village, much less people's opinions and preference ordering) could not support such formal rational choice modelling. For this reason, a "looser" application of RC theory is employed.

[85] Ahmet Icduygu, David Romano, and Abrahim Sirkeci, "The Ethnic Question in the Environment of Insecurity: The Kurds in Turkey," *Ethnic and Racial Studies*, November (1999), 1003.

[86] *Turkish Daily News*, April 10, 1998.

[87] Icduygu et al., "The Ethnic Question in the Environment of Insecurity," 1002. This is also a good source for a more extensive discussion of the number of Kurds in Turkey based on TDHS data, the material conditions of Kurds *vis-à-vis* Turks in the country, and also material and non-material values for Kurds in Turkey.

Kurds in Turkey made the rational choice of exiting the untenable situation in the southeast. This still leaves over half the Kurdish population remaining in the conflict zone, and we must now try to explain their choice along RC (and not psychological, non-material) lines.

Many of those remaining in southeastern Turkey undoubtedly own land, livestock, businesses, and other fixed possessions that they prefer to maintain, reasoning that the risks of being caught somewhere between the PKK and the state are acceptable. Others may have employment in the region that makes the risks worthwhile. Finally, many may simply lack the financial means to move themselves and their family elsewhere, despite their desire to do so.

Another possible line of argument questions the level of accurate information available for rational decision-making in the region – perhaps people have been possessed of very inaccurate estimates regarding the risks posed by attachment to the PKK. The less perfect the information available to decision-makers, the less rational their decisions. This seems implausible, however, given the amount of Turkish media coverage of anti-PKK security operations and captured or killed PKK militants. Tales of state repression and torture are a mainstay of many conversations in the area, with many people claiming to have experienced such repression first-hand. It is therefore reasonably safe to assume that average Kurds in Turkey were quite aware of the risks involved for PKK members and sympathizers.

Results from Dogu Ergil's poll of Turkish Kurds provide interesting insights into Kurds' view of the conflict. When asked "[w]hich of its aims the organization [the PKK] cannot realize," a full 52% of the respondents refused to answer, while another 23.5% said they did not know.[88] Possibly, many of those who refused to answer believed that the PKK could accomplish a good deal, while those who said they "did not know" were indirectly acknowledging that they do not have good enough information to base their decisions on. When asked about the likelihood of success of the government's methods against the PKK, 9.8% refused to answer, and of those who answered, only 20.3% believed that the state was strong enough to crush the PKK, while 76.8% said that the government could not be successful against the PKK using the methods it has been pursuing so far.[89] Given such attitudes (that the PKK would not be defeated easily), it becomes less difficult to understand those Kurds who chose to ally themselves with the insurgents, even if we consider only rational choice, materialist impulses. Finally, when asked what goals the

---

[88] Dogu Ergil, "Suicide Terrorism in Turkey," *Civil Wars*, Vol. 3, No. 1 Spring (2000).
[89] Ibid.

PKK could in fact realize, 28.5% refused to answer, 14% answered "all of its goals," 11.2% said they did not know, 2.1% said they could destabilize the state and society, while the rest answered with a mix of items including cultural rights (2.3%), political and minority rights (4.1%), a Kurdish state (3.6%), a federal arrangement with Turkey (2.6%), more democracy in Turkey (1.6%), all its goals plus political rights (15.9%), all its goals plus political rights and a Kurdish state (2.4%), all its goals plus political rights and democracy (5.3%), and other unnamed goals (6.4%). These answers reveal a stunning amount of optimism and confidence in the PKK amongst the Kurds surveyed, further strengthening explanations of Kurdish support for the movement (even if we assume that those 11.2% who answered "do not know" believe that the PKK is unable to achieve anything). Thus, although we should assume that Kurds were aware of the risks associated with PKK subversive activities, the fair degree of optimism they displayed regarding the movement's future may have helped to offset the perceived risks when they decided where to place their support.

Regarding the possibility that Kurds in the region provided the minimum level of support to their chosen camp (the PKK or the state), or that they tried to appear to both parties as supporters, some evidence of such behavior exists. Village guards were accused on various occasions of having contact and arrangements with local PKK cells, in some cases even providing them with weapons.[90] Regrettably, it is impossible to know the extent of such behavior. Villages that aided PKK militants one day (refusing could have been dangerous) may also have informed on them to the army the next (once again, refusing could be dangerous). Many Kurds in the region continued to insist on their own neutrality, incurring risks *vis-à-vis* both the state and the rebels. Unfortunately, due to a lack of reliable data, even educated guesses regarding the prevalence of such choices are impossible.

At the outset of this chapter, it was posited that in every population of several million people, there must exist at least several thousand who do not act in a self-interested, rational manner. These individuals, typically in the 18–25 age group, are the prime recruits that form the core nucleus of young subversive movements (as well as state armies). If we take into account Kurdish extended family structures, we could assume that each such individual has a kin network of at least thirty people. A kin network by definition values the welfare of its members. The PKK over the years was probably able to recruit around 50,000 cadres, guerrilla fighters, and

---

[90] This author heard several accounts of such occurrences while in the region.

other active members (a number that still falls within our arbitrary parameters of less-rational individuals for a population of 10–20 million Kurds). If we assume each kin network to support its members who joined the PKK[91] (and hence support the PKK), we arrive at the surprising figure of 1,500,000 supporters – enough to sustain a mass movement. If we make a more conservative calculation, considering that many PKK recruits were siblings or otherwise related, and multiply thirty kin times 20,000 cadres, we still arrive at the impressive figure of 600,000 supporters.[92] If one will recall Dogu Ergil's aggregated figures ("refuse to answer" plus "yes") regarding respondents with a relative in the PKK (69.7%), the weight of such "automatic" kin support is probably much greater. Without more data on the subject,[93] however, this speculation must remain just an interesting hypothesis. Additionally, such an argument would fall outside the parameters of RC theory, since it depends on the recruitment of people motivated by non-material values. That people are not born as atomized individuals, but rather as part of a kin network and community, is a powerful detractor from rational choice theory.[94] Consideration of kin networks and village communities as mobilizing networks is, however, a part of resource mobilization theory.[95] Unfortunately, the political climate in states combating violent subversive movements typically does not permit a statistical investigation of the role of kin networks in mobilizing people.

[91] One should recall the statement cited earlier by one of Ocalan's close associates: "Whenever we managed to win one person from a family or tribe at that time [1978], the whole family or tribe came to our side" (Imset, "The PKK: Terrorists or Freedom Fighters?" 24, 18).

[92] Imset, basing his estimate on those of Turkish military officials, provides a figure of at least 400,000 active PKK supporters and sympathizers for 1994 in the southeast of Turkey. To this number he adds another estimated 500,000 Kurdish supporters throughout Europe (Imset, "The PKK: Terrorists or Freedom Fighters?" 15). Of course, these numbers are simply speculative.

[93] For instance, it would be interesting to see to what degree kin networks automatically support an individual who joins a dangerous group like the PKK, and to what degree families are divided, with some members in the state's camp and others with the rebels. Lale Yalcin-Heckmann argues that in Hakkari province (a very traditional Kurdish region in the far southeast of Turkey), kin support is in fact automatic: "One may not be a sympathizer of Hizbul Islam's [an insurgent Islamist movement] politics but one has to support a kin or affine who supports that political view," Lale Yalcin-Heckmann, *Tribe and Kinship Among the Kurds* (Frankfurt: Peter Lang, 1991), p. 38.

[94] For more on such a critique, see Myra Marx Ferree, "The Political Context of Rationality: Rational Choice Theory and Resource Mobilization," in Morris and Mueller (eds.), *Frontiers in Social Movement Theory* (New Haven: Yale University Press, 1992), or Kate Nash, *Contemporary Political Sociology: Globalization, Politics and Power* (Oxford: Blackwell Publishers Inc., 2000), ch. 3.

[95] It is on this issue in particular that some RM theories deviate from the RC foundations upon which they are generally based.

But perhaps the most damaging critique of RC and RM explanations comes from behavior and statements of Kurds themselves, at a time when the PKK's insurgency was in full swing:

In March that year [1990] the PKK offensive was eclipsed by the burgeoning civil resistance to the security forces. For the first time, families of PKK martyrs dared collect the corpses for burial from the authorities and arranged public funerals which rapidly became opportunities for mass protest. On 20 March 10,000 Kurds demonstrated in Cizre and security forces imposed a curfew on 11 towns in Mardin and Siirt provinces; a growing number of civilians were shot by the security forces.[96]

Besikci, observing the same phenomenon, makes the following observation:

Before the organized guerrilla movement and at its beginning, people were afraid to claim the bodies from the security forces. People were intimidated by oppression and frightened of torture. People would avoid being told "Since you are the father of that traitor, that anarchist, you too are guilty" and afraid of the likelihood of being subjected to all sorts of torture and other brutal measures that are difficult even to imagine. Families would therefore not enquire about their children or relatives. The corpses would remain in the wild ... The security forces would pick them up and throw them in a ditch. In fact the army and other security forces did not want the people to claim the dead bodies of their children at all. Thereby they would create the impression that "a handful of traitors" who had no connection with the people and whose dead bodies were not even wanted by their relatives were responsible for the clashes. "The outlaws don't enjoy the people's support. The people are on the government's side. No one claims their corpses either", was the propaganda.[97]

Spontaneous, mass demonstrations and families that eventually risked torture and death to claim the corpses of their kin speak of a different reality than that of self-interested, value-maximizing actors. In fact, the guerrilla war in southeast Turkey, as well as repression by security forces and the PKK, worked together to change people's identity and develop a politicized Kurdish ethnic nationalism. In 1990, Aliza Marcus of *Middle East Report* provided an account which may be indicative of the emotions and passions now unearthed:

For the people of Sirnak, a Kurdish town of 15,000 located at the foot of the Cudi Mountains in southeastern Turkey, the grave of 16-year-old Zayide is something of a shrine. A guerrilla fighter with the separatist Workers' Party of Kurdistan (PKK), Zayide was killed five years ago in a skirmish in Sirnak between the PKK and the Turkish army. Local myth has it that bulldozers trying to break the ground

---

[96] McDowall, *A Modern History of the Kurds*, p. 427.
[97] Ismail Besikci, *Kurdistan and Turkish Colonialism*, p. 9.

for her grave were mysteriously unable to do so in the spot ordered by government authorities. Zayide was buried instead in an empty lot on the outskirts of the town, and her grave is now surrounded by half a dozen smaller ones – parents believe it is good luck to bury their dead children nearby. Women hoping to become pregnant visit her grave side, leaving flowers and little mementos, beseeching her spirit to bless them with children.[98]

Stephen Kinzer of the *New York Times* added this account in 1999:

The Turkish government says that few Kurds support the idea of Kurdish nationalism and that nearly all are happy with the life Turkey offers them. But a four-day tour through Kurdish provinces of the southeast indicated that the opposite may be true. Throughout the region, Kurds appear more conscious of their identity than ever. It is difficult to find any who do not support the nationalist cause and even the armed rebellion that has been under way since 1984.[99]

The most plausible conclusion to be drawn from the contradictory accounts presented in this chapter is that people's identity is dynamic. Some people, at some times, may act as rational material-value maximizing individuals. Particularly in the early stages of an insurgency, appeals for [most?] people's support must be aimed at their own material interests. But as a conflict progresses, society polarizes and people become more politicized – i.e. their identity, and hence their values, change. In the case of Kurds in Turkey, as more Kurds began to adopt a politicized Kurdish identity (whether as a result of PKK propaganda or harsh treatment from government forces), psychological non-material values took a prominent place alongside the material concerns everyone has. Frustration towards the government and its refusal to recognize them as Kurds then motivated them to participate in mass demonstrations, at the risk of being shot or imprisoned. Others will continue to be motivated primarily by material self-interest values, and avoid risky behavior. Hence organizations like the PKK and the government fashion their strategies to appeal to both rational self-interested individuals as well as those with non-material values, recognizing that RC motivations hold true for some people some of the time, but not for everyone all of the time. Scholars seeking to explain social movement–state conflict must then likewise turn to both RC–RM explanations as well as theoretical lenses focusing on questions of identity and psychology, lest they capture only a very limited image of the elephantine reality they wish to analyze. The following chapter therefore applies a perspective based on identity and social psychology to explain Kurdish ethnic nationalist resurgence in Turkey.

---

[98] Aliza Marcus, "City in the War Zone," *Middle East Report*, March–April (1990), 16–18.
[99] Stephen Kinzer, *New York Times*, May 16, 1999.

4   Cultural framing

Having examined Kurdish nationalist challenges to the Turkish state from an "opportunity structures" as well as a "resource mobilization" perspective, we now consider the same issue from the perspective of social psychology and culture. As was the case in the previous two chapters, an attempt will be made to limit the bulk of our explanatory focus to this last theoretical perspective. Such a perspective should prove most useful for understanding "why" Kurdish ethnic nationalist dissent arose in Turkey, as well as the values, aims, and objectives of Kurds in the country. At the same time, important revelations concerning how Kurdish nationalist resurgence occurred and the prospects of this phenomenon should be made.

Many variants of cultural and social-psychological approaches could be applied to the Turkish-Kurdish case, and the intangible, amorphous nature of identity and culture makes the task doubly difficult. For the purpose of delimiting our task as well as furthering current research trends on social movements, the approach taken here applies the perspective adopted in McAdam, McCarthy, and Zald's *Comparative Perspectives on Social Movements*. "Framing" is defined along the same lines originally espoused by David Snow, as "conscious strategic efforts by groups of people to fashion shared understandings of the world and of themselves that legitimate and motivate collective action."[1] The analysis of cultural framing is therefore broken down into the following components:

(1) the cultural tool kits available to would-be insurgents;
(2) the strategic framing efforts of movement groups;

---

[1] For more on framing, cultural repertoires, and the application of an analysis of cognitive processes to social movements, see Doug McAdam, John D. McCarthy, and Mayer Zald (eds.), *Comparative Perspectives on Social Movements: Political Opportunities, Political Structures, and Cultural Framings* (New York: Cambridge University Press, 1996), chapter 11; David Snow, B. Rochford, S. Worden, and R. Benford, "Frame Alignment Processes, Micromobilization, and Movement Participation," *American Sociological Review*, 51: 4 (July 1986), 464–481.

(3) the frame contests between the movement and other collective actors – principally the state, and countermovement groups;

(4) the structure and role of the media in mediating such contests; and

(5) the cultural impact of the movement in modifying the available tool kit.

Hence, in the kind of analysis pursued here, the ideology of movements as well as the state is viewed as an example of highly elaborated frames. This view does not contradict more common understandings of ideology, such as the one presented by Nergis Canafe: "Ideologies are guides to political action. They furnish the individual with a sense of identity, purpose and a sense of belonging [Adams 1993, Meszaros 1989]. Ideologies are also bodies of knowledge, describing how the world is as well as prescribing what it should be."[2] At the same time that movements seek to instill their ideology in the target population, the state attempts to instill loyalty in the population by propagating its own official ideology. In this chapter, we consider ideology, along with culture, identity, and the media.

In Chapter 1, four possible categories of ethnic identification were introduced. These were:

(1) those who lie structurally outside the ethnic group category (they can never identify with the ethnic group in question);

(2) those who may be within the ethnic category, but who do not identify themselves ethnically;

(3) those who consider themselves part of the ethnic group, but in a non-politicized way (they do not make claims on the state based on their ethnicity); and

(4) those whose ethnic identity is politicized (ethnic difference is seen as a legitimate basis for making political demands, ranging from group cultural, linguistic, and educational rights, to autonomy and separatism – synonymous with ethnic nationalism here).

Ethnic nationalist movements (organizations grouping together people possessing a politicized ethnic identity) naturally seek to move potential ethnic group members (category #2) into category #3 (private ethnic identification) and finally, category #4 (politicized ethnicity). Politicized group members are in turn encouraged to act upon their convictions, by supporting or joining the movement and its state-challenging activities. Movements typically seek to accomplish such identity shifts and popular mobilization via cultural framing, as this chapter will show.

---

[2] Kenneth Christie, *Ethnic Conflict, Tribal Politics* (Surrey: Curzon Press, 1998), p. 5. Texts cited are Istvan Mészáros, *The Power of Ideology* (Hertfordshire: Harvester Wheatsheaf, 1989); E. M. Adams, *Religion and Cultural Freedom* (Philadelphia: Temple University Press, 1993).

Although the principal focus of this chapter centers around the PKK and its cultivation of Kurdish ethnic nationalist sentiment in Turkey, such a subject requires some minimum discussion of Kurdish history in the country.[3] Additionally, events precipitated by and affecting Kurds in neighboring countries have had a large impact on cultural frames for Kurds in Turkey, and must also be examined. Essentially, important historical events (such as the Kurdish uprisings of the 1920s and 1930s, as well as uprisings in the 1940s in Iran and the 1960s and 1970s in Iraq) had a major impact on the "cultural tool kits" (the first of our five analytical elements) from which movements fashion their system-critical frames.[4] Finally, we must arrive at some understanding of prevalent Kurdish identities before the 1960s in order to evaluate changes that may have occurred in more recent years.

Kurdish identities and cultural tool kits in Turkey

The concept of cultural tool kits centers around generalized attitudes and ideas within a given population. In this sense, cultural frames that have become prevalent within the population over time, and not through conscious strategic efforts of the organized groups we are examining, are included within the concept. People's identity plays an important role in determining the content of cultural tool kits, which include norms regarding desirable and acceptable behavior, tactics, values, and goals.

According to Martin van Bruinessen,

For the past few centuries at least, the Kurds have had a general awareness of being a separate people, distinct from Persians, Turks and Arabs as well as from the various Christian groups living in their midst. There was also, at least among the literate, a quite concrete idea of who were and who were not Kurds, and of where they lived. This awareness of identity and unity is surprising, given the many things that divided (and still divide) the Kurds. Language and religion are, to many Kurds, essential aspects of their identities, but neither do all Kurds adhere to the same religion, nor do they speak the same language.[5]

Hence Kurdish nationalist identity has always had to compete with other possible identities, such as tribal, religious, and class sources of identification. Assimilation to other ethnic groups (Arab, Turkish, or Persian) was also a possibility. As far back as the seventeenth century,

---

[3] Although important historical events in Turkey were discussed in ch. 2, additional analysis from a cultural, identity, and social-psychological point of view will be provided here.

[4] Ethnic differentiation and international events and trends are examples of other important contributors to the tool kits in question.

[5] Martin van Bruinessen, "Kurdish Society, Ethnicity, Nationalism and Refugee Problems," in Philip G. Kreyenbroek and Stefan Sperl (eds.), *The Kurds, A Contemporary Overview* (London: Routledge, 1992), p. 34.

however, some Kurdish elites displayed a politicized (nationalist) ethnicity.[6] Ehmed-e Xani, a Kurdish mullah and leading intellectual of the 1600s, was concerned with elevating the Kurdish language as one of the pillars upon which a Kurdish state could be built: "The two tasks, political (i.e., formation of a Kurdish state) and literary (i.e., writing and compiling in the native tongue) were considered by Khani to be two sides of the same coin. He did not view language cultivation as an end in itself. A prestigious literary language, together with a sovereign king, was the hallmark of a civilized and independent Kurdish nation."[7]

Nonetheless, a politicized ethnic identity does not appear to have predominated the identities of large parts of the Kurdish population until well into the twentieth century. Two of the possible reasons for this are the economic underdevelopment and the extremely rugged mountain terrain of Kurdistan, which has isolated Kurdish communities from each other as well as outsiders for generations. Such isolation bred multiple dialects of the Kurdish language, and also aided the maintenance of Kurdish communities and tribal groups with differing religions and cultural practices. Isolation thus had the dual effect of preserving Kurdish culture, ethnic distinctiveness, and private ethnic identification, while hampering a broader identification with, or striving for, a Kurdish nation-state.

As a result, some scholars such as Martin van Bruinessen and Paul White examine the difficulties in applying the term "Kurd" to, for instance, both Sunni Muslim Kurmanci-speakers (the largest religious and Kurdish dialectical group) and Alevi Dimili-speaking groups.[8] White relates the recent account of Kurdish guerrilla leader Seyfi Cengiz, who was trying to convince villagers in the Dersim region of Turkey that they were Kurds: They repeatedly told him, "We are Kirmanc. You are saying we are Kurdish.

---

[6] Although it is not within the scope of this work to explain why a Kurdish nationalist identity held sway over some Kurds as far back as the 1700s, the reader may wish to refer to works such as Donald Horowitz, *Ethnic Groups in Conflict* (Berkeley: University of California Press, 1985) or Crawford Young, *The Politics of Cultural Pluralism* (London: The University of Wisconsin Press, 1976) for more on the issue. For example, Horowitz states that "Since the individual 'sense of identity is the feeling of being a worthy person because he fits into a coherent and valued order of things,' ego identity depends heavily on affiliations. A threat to the value of those affiliations produces anxiety and defence" (Donald Horowitz, "Group Comparison and the Sources of Conflict," in *Ethnic Groups in Conflict* [Berkeley: University of California Press, 1985], p. 181).

[7] Amir Hassanpour, "The Pen and the Sword: Literacy, Education and Revolution in Kurdistan," in Peter Freebody and Anthony R. Welch, *Knowledge, Culture and Power: An International Perspective on Literacy as Policy and Practice* (London: Falmer Press, 1993), p. 42.

[8] Paul White, *Primitive Rebels or Revolutionary Modernizers? The Kurdish National Movement in Turkey* (London: Zed Books, 2000), ch. 3. To make matters even more complicated, Dimili speakers are divided into two additional sub-dialects, Zaza and Kirmanci (different from Kurmanci).

We are not Kurdish."[9] One must remember that identity is dynamic, however, and because the Kirmanc population were potential members of the
Kurdish *ethnie*, Kurdish nationalist activists sought to frame issues in such a
manner as to encourage identification with the Kurdish nation.[10]

The issue of linguistic, religious, and cultural divisions amongst the
Kurds is extremely political, of course. While opponents of Kurdish
nationalism seek to make so much out of these divisions that the existence
of a Kurdish people or nation is questioned, proponents attempt to stress
the overall unity of the Kurdish jigsaw puzzle:

In our times, the upsurge of nationalism among the Kurds is an important factor
behind rejections of the philologists' genealogies.[11] Nationalists in Kurdistan, as
elsewhere in the world, envision their people as a linguistically, culturally, ideologically and politically united entity. This nationalism emphasizes language as a
major indicator of Kurdishness (a Kurd is one who speaks Kurdish, according to
Haji Qadiri Koyi). It is well known that the idea of "one nation, one language" is
an ideological, clearly nationalist, position. Equally ideological is the rejection of
Kurdish linguistic unity when the speakers of Kurmanji, Sorani, Southern
Hewrami, and most of the Dimili identify themselves as Kurds. On the non-
academic front, a diverse group of journalists, army generals, parliamentarians,
judges, politicians and many others in Turkey, Iran, Iraq and Syria have declared
Kurdish a non-language.[12]

Although it is very difficult to determine to what extent politicized
ethnicity affects people's identity and motivations (relative to other sources
of identity), we can nonetheless hazard evaluations of the issue based on
historical events and the observations regarding these events. The first large
scale Kurdish revolts that included important nationalist references were
the Kuchgiri and Sheikh Said uprisings mentioned in Chapter 2. If, for
important segments of the population, a Kurdish nationalist identity had
predominated over other identities at the time, the rebellions would have
enjoyed much greater success. Instead, the Turkish government was able to
recruit large numbers of Kurds to help it suppress those in revolt. Although
it might be excessive to expect unity within diverse Kurdish groups, one

---

[9] White, *Primitive Rebels or Revolutionary Modernizers?*, p. 48, cites personal communication with Seyfi Cengiz, London, May 19, 1992.
[10] The context of the Kurdish case in Turkey is important here. Because the Kirmanc
   population do not identify themselves as ethnic Turks, and because their language and
   culture can be plausibly viewed as related to the dominant Kurdish dialects and culture,
   Kurdish nationalists could hope to bring them into the larger identification category of
   "Kurdish."
[11] Hassanpour refers here to Western philologists' genealogies that classified Gurani (also
   referred to as Hewrami) and its speakers as non-Kurdish.
[12] Amir Hassanpour, "The Identity of Hewrami Speakers: Reflections on the Theory and
   Ideology of Comparative Philology," Research Paper prepared at the Department of
   Near and Middle Eastern Civilizations, University of Toronto, undated, p. 6.

would at least expect Kurdish nationalists to refrain from aiding outsiders to suppress fellow Kurds in revolt, despite particularist tribal or religious differences. Evidence from the time, however, indicates that large numbers of both rival Kurdish elites and their followers enthusiastically participated in the suppression of the Kuchgiri and Sheikh Said revolts.

It was pointed out earlier that the demands made by the Kuchgiri rebels were Kurdish nationalist in nature, and not particular to Kuchgiri regional, tribal, or religious interests:

(1) acceptance by Ankara of Kurdish autonomy as already agreed by Istanbul;

(2) the release of all Kurdish prisoners in Elaziz, Malatya, Sivas, and Erzinjan jails;

(3) the withdrawal of Turkish officials from areas with a Kurdish majority; and

(4) the withdrawal of all Turkish forces from the Kuchgiri region.[13]

It is impossible to determine if the Kuchgiri leaders had framed their demands in broad nationalist terms simply to attract the support of other Kurds, rather than as a result of genuine Kurdish nationalist sentiment. Of greater importance is the fact that the support of other Kurdish groups did not materialize. As discussed in Chapter 2, Kemal Ataturk in 1920 was able to frame the ongoing struggle of the nascent Turkish state as a contest between the infidel Western powers, who supported the Christian Armenians and Greeks, and Muslim-Ottoman Turks and Kurds fighting to save the Sultan, Caliph and homeland. By framing the issue in this manner, the Kuchgiri rebels' appeal to Kurdish nationalism was countered by an appeal to the Kurds' Muslim identity. The majority of Kurds at the time in fact chose to heed Ataturk's appeal to their religious identity.[14] The Kuchgiri rebels, standing alone in their Kurdish nationalist uprising, were then crushed by a combination of Turkish and Kurdish forces.

---

[13] David McDowall, *A Modern History of the Kurds* (London: I. B. Taurus, 1997), p. 185.

[14] The Kuchgiri revolt received much direction from a Kurdish nationalist organization founded in Istanbul, the Kurdistan Taali Jamiyati (Society for the Elevation of Kurdistan). Van Bruinessen provides the following analysis on the revolt's failure:

The demands of these chieftains (no doubt inspired, if not dictated by the members of KTJ in their midst) went beyond narrow provincial or sectarian interests. Their Kurdistan included Sunnis and Alevis, Kurmanji- and Zaza-speakers. Support from other parts of Kurdistan was, however, not forthcoming, and Kemalist troops could suppress the movement without great trouble. One of the reasons for the failure was the lack of inter-regional coordination, due to bad communication and poor coordination. The uprising had not been centrally planned and there had been no previous contacts with influential persons in other parts of Kurdistan. Moreover, most Sunni Kurds saw it at the time as an Alevi uprising; they saw no reason to spontaneously support it (Martin van Bruinessen, *Agha, Shaikh and State* (London: Zed Books Ltd., 1992), p. 278).

By 1925, however, the framing opportunities for Kurdish challengers had improved. The Kemalists' abolition of the sultanate and caliphate, along with other now-evident secularizing reforms, allowed Kurdish nationalists to frame their opposition in both a Kurdish nationalist and a religious light. As discussed in Chapter 2, the inspirational and organizing force behind the 1925 uprising came from Azadi ("Freedom"), a Kurdish nationalist group founded in 1923 mainly by Kurdish military officers (who served in the Ottoman and then Turkish armies) and intellectuals. The Azadi leadership "had decided at its first congress, held probably . . . sometime in the late summer or fall of 1924, that it would be doubly advantageous to give the coming revolt . . . a religious appearance."[15] This was why Azadi chose Sheikh Said, both an ardent Kurdish nationalist and a deeply religious, influential Muslim leader, to lead the revolt. Hence, "While the Sheikh Said rebellion was a nationalist rebellion, the mobilization, propaganda, and symbols were those of a religious rebellion . . . For the average Kurd who participated in the rebellion, the religious and nationalist motivations were doubtless mixed. Most of the Kurds thought that the sheikhs who led the rebellion were religious and, more importantly, Kurds."[16] The Kurds within the new Turkish Republic's borders had all lived most of their lives under the Ottoman Empire, a multi-ethnic empire based on the Muslim religion. The discourse of the Ottoman empire was Islamic, and while non-Muslim groups were tolerated, all Muslim subjects were fairly equal.[17] Although many Kurds (particularly the elites) had been exposed to European-style nationalist ideas, it stands to reason that the most prevalent attitudes of the time (the cultural tool kit) centered around Islam and religious piety. It therefore made sense for Azadi to use the most readily available cultural tools and combine religion with their nationalist uprising.

Although the rebels' claim that the Kemalists were anti-religious was the most important framing tactic in their arsenal, other grievances against Ankara were also enunciated: "In the name of populism, the Kurdish language was forbidden in public places (1924); in the name of the abolition of feudalism, Kurdish aghas, but also intellectuals, were

---

[15] Robert Olson, *The Emergence of Kurdish Nationalism and the Sheikh Said Rebellion 1880–1925* (Austin: University of Texas Press, 1989), p. 28.

[16] Ibid.

[17] It is not my intention here to paint the Ottoman Empire as a completely benign regime. In many cases, Muslim and non-Muslim subjects were equal in their vulnerability to the predations of Ottoman magistrates, ministers, and officials intent on enriching themselves at the expense of those under their rule.

sent into exile to western Turkey. A new law (No. 1505) made it possible to expropriate the land of big Kurdish landlords and give it to Turkish-speakers who were to be settled in Kurdistan. Azadi's propagandists took up the grievances resulting from this, and found many willing ears."[18] The policy forbidding the use of the Kurdish language in public would have upset anyone with a private or politicized Kurdish identity. The policies of exile and Kurdish land appropriation would even alienate potential members of the Kurdish *ethnie* – if the state went ahead and decided on their behalf that they were indeed Kurds.

Despite several tactical mistakes, lack of foreign support, and coordination problems,[19] when Sheikh Said's rebellion broke out in 1925, it posed a significant challenge to Ankara. In the area of the revolt, Zaza-speaking Sunni Kurds rose *en masse*. The rebels made no attempt to recruit the non-tribal Kurdish peasantry, however, or to organize the urban lower class.[20] In any case, the peasantry at the time seems to have been more concerned with class issues – Sheikh Said's revolt promised them no relief from exploitative landlords, while Ankara had already announced its desire to curtail feudalism.[21] Urban notables fell into both camps, some supporting the rebels and others siding with Ankara. Finally, tribal support outside the Zaza Sunni areas was more mixed:

Outside the central area, where the revolt had a mass character, participation and non-participation or even opposition of tribes to the revolt were apparently determined to a large extent by the same kind of considerations that had for centuries determined tribal politics and policies vis-a-vis the state. The motivation of the commoners – be it religious or nationalist – played no part as yet worth mentioning. Chieftains joined or opposed according to what seemed the most advantageous thing to do and to what their rivals did; the commoners simply followed their chieftains. When chance turned against the rebels and they were on

---

[18] Van Bruinessen, *Agha, Shaikh and State*, p. 281.
[19] See van Bruinessen, *Agha, Shaikh and State*, ch. 5, for more detail regarding the revolt.
[20] Ibid., pp. 294–295.
[21] Van Bruinessen states that

> Contemporary reports from other, similar parts of Kurdistan, suggest that the subject peasantry, even if they had vague nationalist feelings, were more strongly motivated by resentment against landlords. Indeed, in the later Kurdish risings in Iraq, which were more widespread than Shaikh Said's revolt, the non-tribal peasants did not participate on any significant scale, but they did rise against the landlords several times. (Ibid., p. 292)

the losing side, several tribes that had remained neutral until then suddenly began to oppose them.[22]

If the Sirnak tribes (near the Iraqi border) and the Dersim Alevi tribes (who had launched the Kuchgiri rebellion just five years earlier) had participated in the uprising, the Turkish forces would probably have been defeated.[23] Olson points out that, "The lack of support of the Alevis greatly narrowed the area of operations for the rebels and correspondingly reduced the area that the Turks had to conquer, occupy, and pacify."[24]

Ironically, the strategy of framing the Sheikh Said revolt in both nationalist and religious garb denied the rebels crucial Alevi support at the same time that it unified and mobilized diverse groups of mainly Sunni and Zaza Kurds. One will recall from Chapter 2 that the Alevi Kurds, in light of many years of religious persecution at the hands of Sunni Kurds, had no desire to see a rebellion led by an orthodox Sunni sheikh succeed.[25] Religious divisions, in addition to the tribal politics mentioned above, prevailed over a larger sense of Kurdish nationalism, despite the manifest hostility towards Ankara of both Sunni and Alevi Kurdish groups. Twelve years later, Kirmanci Sunni and Zaza Kurds would return the favor by sitting on their hands while another major Alevi Kurdish revolt was crushed in Dersim (1937–1938). Ihsan Nouri's Mount Ararat uprising was crushed in 1930 largely due to a similar failure to overcome divisions within Kurdish society.

---

[22] Ibid. The exceedingly complex nature of different sources of identity and their motivational effect precludes a very extensive treatment of the subject here. For our purposes, the conclusion that "tribal considerations took precedence in determining people's actions" is sufficient. A more complex and sensitive kind of treatment of the issue can be found in sociological and anthropological works such as that of Lale Yalcin-Heckman, "Kurdish tribal organization and local political processes," in Andrew Finkel and Nukhet Sirman (eds.), *Turkish State, Turkish Society* (London: Routledge, 1990.). Regarding tribal identity, for example, Yalcin-Heckman writes the following: "A third aspect of tribal membership is the link it creates to local culture and history. It provides a local model of cultural meanings through which the individual places himself in a particular relationship to his social milieu ... [T]he peasant's representation of the state is part of the way of representing individual identity; similarly, tribal history and experiences are part of a tribesman's representation of himself as well as of the state. The tribal leader, kinsmen belonging to the same tribe and affines, are all part of an ideological and historical construct which provides frames of reference regarding modes of alliance, division, enmity and affinity." (Ibid., p. 304)

[23] Robert Olson, *The Emergence of Kurdish Nationalism*, pp. 97–98.   [24] Ibid.

[25] For the Alevis, given the historic oppression they faced from Sunni Kurdish tribes such as the Jibran, "An independent Kurdistan, under the authority of Sunni shaikhs, could only be to their disadvantage" (van Bruinessen, *Agha, Shaikh and State*, p. 294).

Such divisiveness has led scholars such as Joan Nagel to point out that "Nearly all Kurdish tribal uprisings against local governments from the late 1800s to 1975 were met with the combined resistance of the government in question and the rebels' traditional tribal enemies."[26] Although many Kurdish elites as well as average Kurds possessed important degrees of politicized ethnicity, more important numbers seem to have until recently lacked a very intense sense of Kurdish nationalism.[27] After visiting the area of the Sheikh Said revolt, the Turkish Minister of the Interior at the time concluded that while the local population was "strongly attached to its language and ethnicity," and while "the intellectuals were all Kurdish nationalists," Kurdish nationalism was still only an ideal amongst elites and was not "deep, all-embracing or dangerous."[28]

The average Kurds' "strong attachment to their language and ethnicity" but lack of Kurdish nationalist sentiment is the private ethnic identification referred to in this work. As mentioned earlier, states pursuing assimilationist programs such as Turkey's seek to remove such private ethnic identification and if possible replace it with Turkish ethnic identification. Kurdish nationalists would seek to politicize such private ethnic identity, whose existence is a prerequisite for a nationalist identity. That Kurdish culture and language (in all its variations) has a centuries-old history and continues to prove itself resilient to state onslaughts has left Kurdish nationalist movements an important base from which to build up.[29]

---

[26] Joan Nagel, "Conditions of Ethnic Separatism: The Kurds in Turkey, Iran and Iraq," *Ethnicity* 7: 3 (September 1980), 286.

[27] The following 1946 statement contained in a British Foreign Office report could be just as true of many elites in Turkish Kurdistan as the Iraqi Kurdish leaders it spoke of: "Their hostility to the 'Arab' government of Baghdad is fundamental and, in that sense, they may be regarded as champions of Kurdish nationalism; but it is a nationalism limited to achieving their personal ambitions rather than one inspired by a wider patriotism. Their primary aim is to be left alone to exercise their feudal tyranny over as many of their countrymen as they can contrive to control" (in John Bulloch and Harvey Morris, *No Friends but the Mountains* [London: Penguin Books Ltd., 1992], p. 97).

[28] Andrew Mango, "Turks and Kurds," *Middle Eastern Studies* (October 1994), 982.

[29] Kendal Nezan provides an anecdote indicative of the extent of Kurdish ethnic identification across even large distances, state borders, and long periods of separation:

Not very long ago, as I was attending a pan-Kurdish conference in Moscow in July 1990, I saw Kurdish shepherds and peasants who had come from Kirghizstan, from the Chinese borders, from Kazakhstan and Caucasia, and who were having discussions with Kurds from Turkey or Kurds from the Kurd Dagh region in Syria, on the Mediterranean coast. In spite of the total lack of contact, in spite of the huge distances that separated their homelands, these people were laughing at the same jokes and mentioning the same proverbs in the course of their conversation. They also shared a number of traditions of welcome and hospitality, and were moved by the same songs. Maybe being a Kurd means exactly that: to share, despite borders and geographical distances, the same basic cultural

Additionally, the large numbers of Kurdish uprisings that broke out in Turkey during the 1920s and 1930s, as well as uprisings in Iraq and Iran, would remain potent symbols for Kurdish nationalists later on. The collective memory of these events and the state repression that followed them would be powerful components of the cultural tool kits available to would-be insurgents. Kurdish attitudes romanticizing mountain rebels against the state, and approving of taking up arms to maintain one's freedom, were further cultivated from these events. An older Kurdish history full of tribal feuds, armed conflicts, banditry, raids on settled populations, and resistance to centralizing Ottoman and Persian empires, also promoted attitudes of martial pride, defiance, and rebellion.[30] As a result, a vast Kurdish literature (mainly in the form of poetry and songs) celebrates taking up arms for worthy causes of freedom and honor.

Consequently, one of the ironies of Kurdish nationalism (as well as many other nationalisms) is that the very repression states such as Turkey used to stamp it out ended up kindling the politicization of Kurdish ethnicity. People who may have had little awareness of their Kurdish ethnicity, or who viewed their ethnicity as a private matter, sometimes experienced a forced change of heart when the state persecuted them or razed their village because of their ethnic identity. The state treated its Kurdish-speaking citizens differently,[31] and because ethnic identity is always relative (the "we" of an ethnic group cannot exist without a "they"),[32] such differential treatment could only eventually lead to

identity forged by centuries of history. (quoted in Christine Allison and Philip Kreyenbroek [eds.], "Introduction," *Kurdish Culture and Identity* [London: Zed Books Ltd., 1996], p. 18)

[30] Throughout recorded history, many Kurds also served as professional soldiers in the armies of various rulers and empires. One of the most famous Kurds was Saladin, who retook Jerusalem from the Crusaders. Saladin, however, seemed to attach more importance to his Muslim religious identity than to his ethnic Kurdish one. In a time when European-style ethnic nationalism had yet to emerge, Saladin used his military victories to establish an Islamic kingdom rather than a Kurdish one.

[31] Supporters of Ankara's policy would deny, however, that the state treated Kurdish citizens differently. They would argue that all citizens are equal in Turkey, and that a Kurd can rise to the position of general or president if he or she wishes. Also, to Ankara's credit, the state for the most part carefully avoided stirring up hatred for the Kurdish minority (this may have been partly because they were pretending such a minority did not exist). From a Kurdish point of view, however, denying Kurds the right to give their children traditional Kurdish names or speak their mother tongue in public venues (among other things) amounts to differential treatment. The equality in question amounts to the equal right to assimilate to the Turkish *ethnie* and be good Turks.

[32] Sociologist Kate Nash adds this observation on the subject: "... in so far as individual identity requires recognition by others, it is in itself intrinsically social: by its very nature, identity cannot be constructed outside relationships which give it meaning" (Kate Nash, *Contemporary Political Sociology: Globalization, Politics and Power* [Oxford: Blackwell Publishers Inc., 2000], p. 29).

assimilation or politicization of Kurdish ethnic identity. Milton Esman's view on this issue comes to mind here: "Where the state has been created or captured by a particular ethnic community and operates as an agent of that community, that state becomes a party to ethnic conflicts."[33] Abbas Vali adds that,

the political specificity of Kurdish nationalism is also defined in part by the changing relationship of Kurdish identity to its "others." This relationship, which is already implicit in the dialectic of denial and resistance, is one of violence, of political exclusion and suppression of "difference." The perpetual suppression of Kurdish identity is the condition of the Kurds' "otherness" in these societies, their position as strangers in their own homes. That the Kurds remain unrepresentable is the fundamental cause of their obsession with their identity. This dialectics of violence defines not only the ethos of Kurdish national identity, but also the modality of its relationship with its others.[34]

In fact, some of the first major Kurdish unrest to occur in Turkey since 1938 happened in 1967, after a virulently Turkish nationalist magazine (*Otuken*) published two very anti-Kurdish articles. The first of these articles finished with, "When we tell the Kurds their home truths, they do not blush with shame, because they do not have the faces of human beings."[35] The second article, which led to demonstrations of tens of thousands of Kurds in different parts of the country, is worth quoting at length:

Let the Kurds go away from Turkey! But to where? To wherever they like! Let them go to Iran, to Pakistan, to India, to Barzani. Let them ask at [sic] the United Nations to find them a home in Africa. Let them go away before the Turkish nation gets angry. The Turkish race is very patient, but when we get angry we are like lions. Let the Kurds ask the Armenians about us!

You are only working for Kurdish nationalism. You will ask us to recognize your language, to have independent schools, a broadcasting program, and a press distinct from ours. You will continue secret meetings, where you speak of Barzani as your national hero, you will convey him arms through Turkey; you will read Kurdish poems to your children, and those of you who have attained the level of professorship will make contact with the Kurdish organizations in Europe . . . But the day when you will rise up to cut Turkey into pieces, you will see to what a hell we shall send you . . .[36]

[33] Milton J. Esman, *Ethnic Politics* (Ithaca: Cornell University Press, 1994), p. 217.

[34] Abbas Vali, "The Kurds and Their 'Others': Fragmented Identity and Fragmented Politics," *Comparative Studies of South Asia, Africa and the Middle East* 18: 2, (1998), 83–84. The reader should refer to Vali for a very high in-depth analysis of the dialectics of ethnic difference and the role that civil society, modernization, and repression had on Kurdish nationalism.

[35] White, *Primitive Rebels or Revolutionary Modernizers*, p. 132.   [36] Ibid., pp. 83–84.

Although the anonymous author of the article was never made public and no action was taken against the magazine, the Kurdish demonstrations provoked special commando "clearing operations" in the Kurdish regions. During these operations, Kurds were taken out of their homes, forced to line up, and beaten, all the while having racial slurs hurled at them.[37]

The repression of Kurds and their identity in Turkey as well as in neighboring countries, and the resentment it engendered, therefore became the pre-eminent item in the "cultural tool kits" of Kurdish nationalists. These nationalists would seek to inform all Kurds (and potential Kurds) of past and present injustices, framing the issue along the lines of, "look what the state does to us because of our ethnicity – because they repress us as a group, we must band together and seek redress as a group." Such logic lies at the heart of politicized ethnicity. According to Kurdish scholar Kendal Nezan, despite the destruction and massacres state repression inflicted on the Kurds, such conflicts "were able, by kindling the spirit of resistance, to forge a Kurdish national conscience and reinforce the ties which bind Kurds to their identity. The plight and the tragedy of the Kurdish people cemented a national consciousness which previously was to be found only among the elite."[38] Finally, Michael Ignatieff adds the following generalized observation to the subject: "Where ethnic minorities have been subjected to genuine tyranny, where language and culture have been genuinely suppressed, national revivals, even nationalist uprisings, are both inevitable and justified."[39]

When discussing the diffusion of Kurdish nationalist identity to larger segments of the general population, one cannot omit the impact of

---

[37] Chris Kutschera, *Le Movement national kurde* (Paris: Flammarion, 1979), pp. 341–342; and M. Kendal, "Kurdistan in Turkey," in Gerard Chaliand (ed.), *People Without a Country: The Kurds and Kurdistan* (London: Zed Press, 1980), p. 88.

[38] Allison and Kreyenbroek (eds.), *Kurdish Culture and Identity*, p. 14.

[39] Michael Ignatieff, *The Warrior's Honor: Ethnic War and the Modern Conscience* (Toronto: Viking Press, 1998), p. 59. One should not overstate the inevitability of resistance as a response to oppression, however. In some cases, such as the Iraqi government's genocide against the Kurds in 1988 (described in ch. 5) or the Syrian crushing of the Muslim Brotherhood in 1982 (in which roughly 20,000 people were killed), the most severe forms of repression can quell dissent. Although authoritarian leaders in Baghdad and Damascus felt capable of pursuing genocide or mass murder, states with pretensions to democratic rule such as Kemalist Turkey and Israel cannot go quite so far in today's international climate (two hundred years ago, however, states with democratic pretensions were quite able to pursue genocide against aboriginals in North America . . .). The choices for states such as Turkey and Israel, therefore, gravitate between a cycle of continued repression and resistance, compromise and accommodation, or the abandonment of democratic liberal principals and the pursuit of policies modeled upon a fascist discourse.

modernization. Modernization can be described as a general process in which increasing proportions of the population become urbanized, separated from agricultural and pastoral "traditional" lifestyles, exposed to new ideas, subject to increasing state intrusion into everyday life, inserted into state educational systems, and integrated into a market economy.[40] Modernization introduced changes that increased the size and dynamism of the Kurdish intelligentsia, as well as improving the education level of the general population and exposing them to the larger political arena of the region. By the 1950s, major changes in rural Kurdish feudal relations of production began to take place. This was in part due to immigration or deportations from rural Kurdish areas, as well as government land reforms.[41] Rural–urban migration increased, and the Kurdish working class and modern bourgeoisie began to grow. Migrant Kurdish laborers and immigrants settled in the metropolises of the Middle East – cities such as Ankara, Istanbul, Baghdad, Damascus, Tehran, and Isfahan. Larger numbers of Kurds entered the skilled artisan and professional workforce, swelling the numbers of Kurdish mechanics, printers, electricians, lawyers, doctors, and journalists. Increasing levels of education and participation in social, economic, political, and cultural life of the larger Middle Eastern milieu became available to the Kurdish populations.[42] These new urban-educated Kurds would gather in cities such as Ankara and Istanbul to form and elaborate a growing Kurdish politicized ethnicity.

In effect, as increasing numbers of Kurds came into contact with the nationalist ideologies of other groups, be they Turkish, Arab, Persian, or other, they began to re-examine their own identities.[43] In many cases, this self-reflection led to an increased sense of Kurdish nationalist identity,

---

[40] Modernization is an example of the antecedent structural variables discussed in ch. 1 – due to its importance in cultural change and the development of new framings, it is included in this chapter's analysis.

[41] Amir Hassanpour, "The Kurdish Experience," *The Middle East Report* 189 (July–August 1984), 4–5.

[42] Ibid.

[43] Mahmut Altunakar, a Kurdish MP in Ankara, relates the following experience of his youth: "Until I arrived in Kutahya I did not know I was Kurdish. We used to throw stones at those calling us Kurds in Diyarbakir. We came to Kutahya and they called us Kurds. They baited us with 'Where is your tail?' Going to school was an ordeal. Then we understood our villagers were right, we were Kurds" (McDowall, *A Modern History of the Kurds*, p. 403). PKK founder Abdullah Ocalan, for instance, originally was an admirer of Ataturk and viewed himself as Turkish. During his years as a political science student in Ankara, however, he claims to have "rediscovered" his Kurdishness and developed a politicized Kurdish ethnic identity. This process seems akin to that described in the works of Frantz Fanon, who underwent a profound identity change after going to study in the Parisian metropole.

mirroring the nationalism of other peoples around them.[44] Tribal, religious, or other identities may not have been completely forsaken, but insertion into a larger national and global milieu often encouraged the adoption of a larger ethnic identity that took precedence over other allegiances. In other cases, options included assimilation to the national Turkish identity, adoption of a pan-Islamic outlook, acceptance of Turkish civic identity co-mingled with a private Kurdish ethnic identity, or other variations and mixes of identities. More circumscribed tribal, village, or regional attachments probably declined as a result of modernization.[45]

The increasing access to news from outside the Kurds' immediate milieu that modernization provided had other indirect effects as well. For the thinking of Kurds in Turkey, events occurring in neighboring countries and internationally had an impact. In 1946, Iranian Kurds supported by the Soviet Union briefly succeeded in setting up a Kurdish state in part of Iranian Kurdistan – the Mahabad Republic. This event, combined with pre-twentieth-century instances of Kurdish feudal princes occasionally carving out principalities independent of the Ottoman or Persian empires, surely affected Kurdish attitudes in Turkey. The hoisting of the Kurdish flag over Mahabad on December 15, 1945, was an emotional moment for Kurdish nationalists, and to this day many Kurdish journals, periodicals, and newspapers carry photos of the event or references to it. Although the Mahabad Republic fell to Iranian troops a year later, the demonstration effect of its brief existence lingers on. The short-lived Republic's national anthem remains the anthem for all Kurdish nationalist parties to this day, and the anniversary of its founding is celebrated every year. There are no accounts of major demonstrations or agitation within Turkey's Kurdish community at the time of the Republic's fall in 1946, however (fear of the repercussions probably still outweighed other factors at the time). Nonetheless, by 1979 pan-Kurdish sentiment amongst some Kurds in

---

[44] The reader may wish to refer to Ernest Gellner, *Nations and Nationalism* (Oxford: Blackwell, 1983) for a deeper analysis of this process. Likewise, social psychology insights on the minimal basis of group differentiation and discrimination point to a human tendency to discriminate against "out groups," which in turn exacerbates divisions (see Henri Tajfel, "Intergroup Behaviour, Social Comparison and Social Change," Katz-Newcomb Lectures, University of Michigan, Ann Arbor, mimeo, 1974; Henri Tajfel, "Experiments in Intergroup Discrimination," *Scientific American* 223 [November 1970], 96–102; John C. Turner, "Social Comparison and Social Identity: Some Prospects for Intergroup Behaviour," *European Journal of Social Psychology* 5 [1975], 5–34; or Michael Billig, *Social Psychology and Intergroup Relations* [London: Academic Press, 1976]).

[45] Evidence to support these arguments about the impact of modernization is lacking. The statements made here are hypotheses.

Turkey was such that several thousand went to help Iranian Kurds fight the *pasdaran* troops of the new Islamic Republic.[46]

Events occurring in Iraqi Kurdistan had a more immediately discernible impact on the attitudes and identity of Kurds in Turkey, however. First of all, Kurdish uprisings against Baghdad erupted periodically since Iraq's founding after the First World War, and struck a responsive chord in the Kurds of neighboring countries. Moreover, negotiations between Iraqi Kurds and Baghdad produced several agreements, such as the Bazzaz Declaration of 1966 and the 1970 Accord, which recognized official Kurdish group rights and the principle of Kurdish autonomy.

By the 1960s, the aforementioned process of modernization had put Kurds in a better position to follow events in neighboring Iraq: "... the Kurds in Turkey had reports of the struggles and successes of their Iraqi brothers at this time: broadcasts in Kurdish reached them, as did cassettes with songs and stories in various dialects. All this had the effect of strengthening their sense of identity, and their pride in Kurdish."[47]

The agreements on Kurdish autonomy in Iraq, no matter how short-lived, were not achieved due to the openness or goodwill of Arab nationalists in Baghdad, but rather as a result of moments of state weakness *vis-à-vis* armed Kurdish opposition groups in the north of Iraq.[48] Again, the lesson would not be lost on Kurds in Turkey, who founded the Kurdistan Democratic Party of Turkey (based on the Iraqi and Syrian Kurds' KDP) in the 1960s, and in the 1970s began establishing several Kurdish organizations based on a guerrilla warfare strategy.[49]

Two additional events in Iraqi Kurdistan also had a major impact on Kurds in Turkey. The first was the genocidal *Anfal* campaigns of 1987–1988, in which Baghdad used chemical weapons on Kurdish

---

[46] For more on this episode, see McDowall, *A Modern History of the Kurds*, ch. 13.

[47] Kreyenbroek and Sperl (eds.), *The Kurds*, p. 75. Sabri Cigerli adds the following observation: "Ce dernier [Iraqi Kurdish leader Mustafa Barzani] vivait ses années les plus glorieuses. Sa radio qui diffusait dans les 'zones libres' habitées par les Kurdes irakiens était facilement capté dans les regions kurdes de Turquie. La presse turque parlait des réussites de Barzani, alors qu'elle ne faisait jamais référence aux Kurdes de Turquie" (Sabri Cigerli, *Les Kurdes et leur histoire* [Paris and Montreal: L'Harmattan, 1999], p. 132).

[48] For more on the issue, see McDowall, *A Modern History of the Kurds*, chs. 14–16.

[49] The implications of the 1970 autonomy agreement between Iraqi Kurds and Baghdad were not lost upon Ankara either. According to Kurdish scholar Kendal Nezan, immediately after the signing of the agreement in Iraq, "... Turkish commandos [already in the rural southeast on a general 'arms search'] redoubled their efforts to terrorize and intimidate the population of Kurdistan in Turkey, in order to discourage them from following the example given by the Kurds of Iraq" ("Kurdistan in Turkey," in Chaliand, *People Without a Country*, p. 88).

civilian populations and depopulated and massacred entire villages.[50] Besides highlighting once again the persecution they faced *as Kurds*, the genocide sent tens of thousands of Iraqi Kurdish refugees into Turkey, where they interacted and communicated with Turkish Kurds. Such contact strengthened feelings of Kurdish community and further politicized Kurdish ethnic identity. In 1991 following the first Gulf War, a second and even larger wave of Kurdish refugees arrived in southeastern Turkey, after the abortive Allied-inspired Kurdish and Shiite uprising against Saddam Hussein. The Kurdish Autonomous Zone and safe haven that was established in the wake of this event led to the creation of a *de facto* Kurdish state in northern Iraq, with the resultant demonstration effect and opportunities for uncensored Kurdish nationalist dialogue in the area.[51]

International events that appeared to come to a peak in the 1950s and 1960s, such as the Algerian independence struggle and other anti-colonial wars of liberation, civil rights protests, and leftist revolutionary movement activity in several countries, probably also affected the views of Kurds. Comparisons of their own situation with the plight and struggles of other peoples were difficult to avoid. Many Kurds, for instance, question why the Palestinian struggle for self-determination receives so much international support and acknowledgment, while the Kurdish population (which numbers roughly five times more than the Palestinians) is forgotten.[52] "If self-determination is the right of the Palestinians, why not us?" is a sentiment often heard in Kurdish circles. The example of world events such as the war in Vietnam, revolution in Cuba, and protests against discriminatory laws in the United States also helped to justify the appeal for a renewed Kurdish struggle in Turkey.

World events may have done more than provide ideological support to Kurdish grievances against Ankara, however. Ideas about *how* to challenge the state have a tendency to cross national borders. Joint student and labor activism and protests in places such as France and the United

---

[50] For more on the *Anfal* campaigns, see McDowall, *A Modern History of the Kurds*, ch. 17, or Khaled Salih, "Anfal: The Kurdish Genocide in Iraq," in *Digest of Middle East Studies* 4: 2 (Spring 1995) 24–39.

[51] The issue of uncensored Kurdish media emanating from northern Iraq since 1991 as well as elsewhere will be further addressed in the section on "state media, information monopolies, and insurgent media" of this chapter.

[52] A Jewish Kurd who had emigrated to Israel as a child related the following anecdote after his first return visit to the Kurdish town of his birth: "One of my hosts said he identified with Israel, 'especially after your defence minister apologized for using rubber bullets against Palestinians while Saddam bombarded us with gas and no Muslim country issued one word of condemnation' " (Mustafa Karadaghi, *Kurdistan Times* 3, [Fairfax: Kurdish Human Rights Watch, December 1993], 235).

States also emerged in similar urban form in Turkey, during the unrest of the 1960s and 1970s (described in Chapter 2). Tactics such as hunger strikes, self-immolation, and even suicide bombings may have also entered the Kurdish nationalist "action repertoire" from an awareness of similar strategies pursued in places as far off as India and Palestine.[53] Also, the example provided by Viet Cong and Latin American guerrillas defeating militarily superior foes could be easily absorbed by Kurds reading or listening to the news media in Turkey. As early as 1963, some young leaders of the Kurdistan Democratic Party in Iraq were familiar with the literature on guerrilla warfare in Latin America.[54] In any case, guerrilla war tactics appear to have a long tradition in Kurdish history and thinking, with the first recorded instance of such tactics going all the way back to 400 BCE, when the "Kardu" attacked Xenophon's retreating Ten Thousand.[55] If by chance observers in Turkey missed the implicit modern example set by such figures as Ho Chi Minh or Che Guevara, however, Kurdish nationalist movements would draw clearer parallels for their audience. One of the following sections of this chapter ("framing efforts of the PKK") will provide an example of the most important of such Kurdish nationalist framing efforts in Turkey.

Before proceeding, however, it may be useful to first summarize the issues raised above. A complex web of different identities (religious, tribal, national, linguistic, regional, and class) exists within the population we refer to as Kurdish. At different times and for different groups, many competing identities took precedence over a politicized Kurdish national identity. At the same time, a general sense of belonging to the Kurdish *ethnie* has existed for many hundreds of years within large segments of the population we are discussing. This private ethnic identification could serve as the necessary precursor and building block for a politicized Kurdish national identity. Particularly amongst the Kurdish urban elite, such a politicized ethnic identity often already superseded other identities

---

[53] Self-immolation and suicide bombings were described as "unKurdish" to the author in the course of some discussions with Kurds in Iraq, however (October 2000). This suggests two likely possibilities: the cultural tool kits of most Kurds do not contain attitudes supportive of these kinds of "martyrdom" tactics, or the common culture of Kurds in Iraq differs in this respect from that of Kurds in Turkey (these tactics were recently used by Kurds from Turkey in support of the PKK – for a more extensive analysis, see Dogu Ergil, "Suicide Terrorism in Turkey," *Civil Wars* 3: 1 [Spring 2000], 37–54).

[54] Author's interview with Amir Hassanpour, December 4, 2001.

[55] The "Kardu" referred to in accounts of the event are thought to be Kurds who lived in the Zagros mountains region that Xenophon retreated through (David McDowall, "The Kurdish Question: a Historical Review," in Kreyenbroek and Sperl [eds.], *The Kurds*, p. 10). I use the term "BCE" (before the common era) in preference to "BC."

by the time of the revolts of the 1920s and 1930s. Changes brought about as a result of modernization and urbanization facilitated the adoption of a more Kurdish nationalist identity among average Kurds. State repression of Kurds, international trends and events, the experience of Kurds in neighbouring countries, and contact with refugee Kurds from Iraq all had the effect of moving general Kurdish attitudes and thinking towards a more politicized ethnic identity. Innovations concerning means of opposing the state were also transmitted by the example of events occurring abroad. Finally, armed and particularly guerrilla-style opposition to an intrusive and repressive central government remained one of the oldest and accepted items within the Kurdish cultural tool kit.

Frame contests: the Turkish state and other social movements

Because the cultural frames promoted by the Turkish state set the context out of which the PKK emerged and sought to challenge the status quo, this subject will be addressed first. Also, state framing efforts were part of a broader assimilationist program; therefore the latter will also be discussed here in greater detail than previously.

At the same time that some Kurdish elites of the 1920s and 1930s attempted to carve out a Kurdish state, the leaders of the new Turkish Republic sought to assimilate the Kurdish population within their new state into a Turkish nation. One is reminded of Appadurai's (1990) observation that "the 'nation' and the 'state' are each other's projects."[56] From the point of view of Turkish state-builders, such inclusion had to be based on assimilation into the Turkish *ethnie*. The Kemalist elite had inherited a multi-ethnic, diverse population from the Ottoman Empire, and they determined that the only viable way to build a successful, durable nation-state was to forge a more homogenous population around the dominant Turkish ethnicity. Inspiration for Turkish state policy came from political and socio-philosophical works such as Ziya Gokalp's 1920 *The Principles of Turkism*, which advanced views such as the following:

since race has no relationship to social traits, neither can it have any with nationality, which is the sum total of social characteristics … [S]ocial solidarity rests on cultural unity, which is transmitted by means of education and therefore has no relationship with consanguinity … [A] nation is not a racial or ethnic or geographical or political or volitional group but one composed of individuals who share a

---

[56] Ali Mohammadi and Annabelle Sreberny-Mohammadi, *Small Media, Big Revolution* (Minneapolis: University of Minnesota Press, 1994), p. 10.

common language, religion, morality or aesthetics, that is to say, who have received the same education.[57]

The leaders of the new Turkish Republic were probably well aware that the population under their control did not share a common language, religion, morality, or aesthetics, but they could forge one out of the geographical unit that the War of Independence had left them. Hence everyone who found themselves within the new Turkish borders in 1923 became Turkish. Through a strong central government, a uniform education system, and the imposition of a single language (Turkish), the nation-state would be built along European lines.[58] Even though the official government rhetoric was one of civic nationalism (wherein a diverse population was united by Turkish citizenship, but retained their particularistic ethnic and linguistic attributes), in practice state-building was along ethnic nationalist lines. Leaders such as Ismet Inonu, Turkey's second president, made this abundantly clear when they stated that "only the Turkish nation is entitled to claim ethnic and national rights in this country. No other element has any such right."[59] Despite his own Kurdish ancestry, Inonu had apparently embraced Ziya Gokalp's notions of Turkism, which allowed him to advance to the highest post of the new republic.[60] One of Inonu's peers in the Ottoman establishment, Ihsan Nouri Pasha, had until 1925 followed a very similar career path (at the same time as Inonu), but in 1925 decided to embrace Kurdish identity.

---

[57] Ziya Gokalp, *The Principles of Turkism* (Ankara: Leiden, 1920), p. 12.

[58] The founders of the Turkish Republic were probably well aware of the fact that it was only during recent history that a majority of Frenchmen, Italians, and Germans shed their local languages and adopted "standard" French, Italian, and German, in the process creating a national culture and hence a nation. At the time of the French revolution, no more than half "the French" spoke French – Breton, Basques, Alsatian, Occitanian, Catalan, Corsican, and Fleming identities existed, whereas the state-builders came from the old Frankish kingdom based in Paris, the Loire Valley, and the north (Ian Spears, "States-within-states: An Introduction to Their Empirical Attributes," in Paul Kingston and Ian Spears [eds.], *States Within States* [New York: Palgrave Macmillan, 2004], p. 22). Even in the mid-nineteenth century, only roughly 3 percent of "Italians" spoke standard Italian (ibid.). For more on creating a nation within a state, see also Eugen Weber, *Peasants into Frenchmen* (Stanford: Stanford University Press, 1976).

[59] Jonathan C. Randal, *After Such Knowledge, What Forgiveness? My Encounters with Kurdistan* (Oxford: Westview Press, 1999), p. 260.

[60] Ismet Inonu's Kurdish background is not widely known or discussed. Besides Ihsan Nouri's memoires (Nouri Pasha, General Ihsan, *La Révolte de l'Agri-dagh* [Geneva: Editions Kurdes, 1986]), I know of only two other sources that mention it (in Turkish): Ahmet Kahraman, "Icte Teror, Dista da," *Ozgur Politika*, September 16, 2001 (http://www.ozgurpolitika.org/2001/10/16/hab41.html); and Turker Alkan, "Yatak Odasi Savaslari," *Radikal*, September 27, 2000. http://www.radikal.com.tr/2000/09/27/yazarlar/turalk.shtml.

Nouri ended up leading the Mount Ararat uprising against the new republic, and was pushed into exile in Iran in 1930.[61]

Although non-Muslim minorities could be allowed a few special rights as stipulated in the Treaty of Lausanne, the Kurds were deemed too large a threat to allow them such minority rights. As late as 1983, laws such as No. 2392, art. 3, stated that: "The native language of Turkish citizens is Turkish. It is forbidden: a) to use as a native language a language other than Turkish and to participate in any activity aiming to diffuse these languages."[62]

With the Armenians out of the picture, the Kurds did indeed form the largest minority in the new republic. Herein lay the central reason for the outlawing of the Kurdish language, Kurdish education, media, and public expressions of Kurdishness in general. Turkish state elites knew that bringing the Kurdish population into the Turkish ethnic fold would pose the greatest challenge, requiring a transformation of traditional socio-economic structures in the Kurdish regions as well as aggressive assimilationist policies.[63] In 1934, the state enacted one of many new policies to extinguish Kurdish identity in Turkey: "Law No. 2510 divided Turkey into three zones: (i) localities to be reserved for the habitation in compact form of persons possessing Turkish culture; (ii) regions to which populations of non-Turkish culture for assimilation into Turkish language and culture were to be moved; (iii) regions to be completely evacuated."[64] In this manner, all rural as well as urban areas where Turkish was not the mother tongue were to be evacuated, and the

---

[61] Cheriff Vanly speculates that had Nouri remained loyal to the Kemalists and, like Inonu, participated in the suppression of Kurdish rebels, he too could have risen to the highest offices of the Turkish Republic. Cheriff Vanly, "Introduction," in Nouri Pasha, General Ihasan, *La Révolte de l'Agri-dagh* (Geneva: Editions Kurdes, 1986), p. 3.

[62] Phillip Kreyenbroek, "On the Kurdish Language," in Kreyenbroek and Sperl (eds.), *The Kurds*, p. 75. It should be recalled from ch. 2 that Article 39 of the Treaty of Lausanne nonetheless stipulated that "No restrictions shall be imposed on the free use by any Turkish national of any language in private intercourse, in commerce, religion, in the press, or in publications of any kind or at public meetings ..." The justification for forbidding Kurdish sometimes given by Turkish officials then became that Kurdish is not a "real" language.

[63] For a detailed account of early assimilationist policies, mass deportations of Kurds, and post-rebellion "cleansing operations," see McDowall, *A Modern History of the Kurds*, ch. 9. In 1927, Turkey's foreign minister, Tawfiq Rushdi, expressed some of the more extreme state views: "... in their [Kurdish] case, their cultural level is so low, their mentality so backward, that they cannot be simply in the general Turkish body politic ... they will die out, economically unfitted for the struggle for life in competition with the more advanced and cultured Turks ... as many as can will emigrate into Persia and Iraq, while the rest will simply undergo the elimination of the unfit" (FO 271/12255, January 4, 1927; in McDowall, *A Modern History of the Kurds*, p. 200).

[64] Ibid., p. 207.

population dispersed within larger groupings of Turkish-speaking people.[65] Logistical difficulties in displacing and resettling over 3 million Kurds prevented these policies from being implemented. In any case by 1950 the introduction of electoral politics mitigated against such unpopular actions.

After crushing a long series of Kurdish revolts in 1938, it seemed that Ankara was succeeding with its assimilationist program. From 1938 until 1961, Kurdish nationalist activity in Turkey appeared largely dead or dormant. The Turkish education system (including training received during mandatory military service), media, and public discourse in general proceeded as if Kurds did not exist within the country. All things specifically Kurdish, be they language, cultural practices, names, history, or literature, were either excluded or taken over and determined to be actually Turkish in origin. Turkish academics produced studies that showed Kurdish to actually be a perverted dialect of Turkish rather than a distinct language, and even the term "Kurd" became taboo in public discourse.[66] Everyone within the state's borders was happy to be Turkish and equal on this basis; unlimited opportunity beckoned to all citizens. It was hoped that with a unified (and homogenous) population behind them, Turkey's leaders could build a prosperous, secular, and modern nation-state. Given the scarcely audible voice of Kurdish dissidence at the time, one might have been justified in believing that the state policy was succeeding. However, as Sreberny-Mohammadi and Mohammadi point out, "The outward appearance of submission is no proof of the inward acceptance of oppression."[67]

Events discussed earlier, however, such as modernization, Kurdish struggles in neighboring Iraq, and worldwide trends of leftist and anti-colonial agitation, probably made it impossible for the Turkish state to keep all of its Kurdish population quiet indefinitely. In any case, the new Turkish constitution of 1961 (discussed in Chapter 2) created an opening for freedom of expression. At the same time that reports of Iraqi Kurdish rebellion reached Turkish Kurds, Kurdish cultural and intellectual activity in Turkey had experienced a resurgence:

... in that year [1961] the new constitution allowed freedom of expression, of association and of the press. Kurdish affairs could once more be discussed, or at

---

[65] Ibid.

[66] For a more extensive discussion of the denial of the Kurdish reality in Turkey, see Jacqueline Sammali, *Etre Kurde, un délit?* (Paris: L'Harmattan, 1995), (particularly the introduction – "Le Déni Culturel") or McDowall, *A Modern History of the Kurds*, chs. 9, 19, and 20.

[67] Mohammadi and Sreberny-Mohammadi, *Small Media, Big Revolution*, p. 31.

least alluded to, in the media, and there appears to have been a surge of renewed interest among Kurds in their own cultural identity. Perhaps manuscripts came out of drawers where they had long been mouldering, and the years 1962–8 saw a number of publications in Kurmanji, such as the bilingual (Kurdish/Turkish) periodicals *Dicle-Firat* and *Deng* (Istanbul, 1962), a play (Anter, 1965), a Kurdish grammar book, a Kurdish–Turkish Dictionary, etc. Most of these were banned soon after they appeared, but some copies were usually available, and these were passed hand to hand. Clandestine literacy courses in Kurmanji were set up.[68]

The government responded by placing new bans on Kurdish language and publications, especially Kurdish language material brought into the country from abroad.[69] The official denial of Kurdish lasted until 1991 – by that time the conflict with the PKK had made it impossible to continue to ignore the Kurdish reality in the country. In 1991, portions of the official ban on public use of the Kurdish language were repealed by Turgut Ozal, and an effort was made to recognize that Kurds could possess a private Kurdish ethnic identity.

Ankara's response to the PKK insurgency in fact provides several excellent examples of state and counter-movement framing efforts. To both the domestic and international audiences, the Turkish state and pro-establishment groups sought to portray the PKK as a small band of terrorists who lacked popular support and were unrepresentative of Kurds in Turkey. While forced to concede that Kurds in the southeast were indeed disgruntled with Ankara, Turkish officials contended that the cause of disgruntlement was socio-economic in nature, and not one of competing nationalisms. Hence the solution to the problem lay in a combination of socio-economic development for the southeast and a strong military response to terrorism. Fundamental democratic reforms and recognition of Kurdish minority (or national) rights therefore remained off the agenda.

Examples of efforts to hammer in the terrorist appellation for the PKK can be found everywhere in Turkish state discourse and media, which never fail to add the "terrorist" adjective to any reference to the organization. Books such as *Bloodshed in Anatolia* (Istanbul: Editions Belge, 1992 – in Turkish, French, English, and German) are published, which lament the PKK's butchering of civilian populations, ascribe all such deaths solely to the PKK, and include gruesome photos of victims.[70] Series of

---

[68] Kreyenbroek, "On the Kurdish Language," in Kreyenbroek and Sperl (eds.), *The Kurds*, p. 74.

[69] Ibid.

[70] Some of the PKK's ardent critics had difficulty, however, accepting the fact that PKK guerrilla forces included many women, which evoked "... the image of Kurdish women

academic articles, such as those by Bilkent University (Ankara) professor Nure Bilge Criss, carry titles such as "The Nature of PKK Terrorism in Turkey" (1995) and "Terrorism and the Issue of International Cooperation" (2000). In addition to attacking the guerrillas' motives and tactics, such articles defend the state's reputation:

> Every murder in the region that might have been caused by blood feuds, honor, or plain personal vendetta was immediately attributed to the state. Struggle for regional leadership within the PKK ranks sometimes ended up in murder, which was again blamed on the state. And terrorist tactics were not above killing people who were loved and respected in the region – those who headed local Human Rights Associations, or even selected socialist party candidates as witnessed in 1994. But these murders remained unsolved, and fed conspiracy theories.[71]

Of course, "conspiracy theories" were fed by the fact that the state often failed to investigate any suspects in the mystery murders, and that human rights representatives are generally more of an irritant to governments waging counter-insurgency operations than to insurgents. Although the PKK has indeed been guilty of terror attacks (see below), the state also "regularly portrayed atrocities committed by the security forces and village guards as having been committed by the PKK."[72]

---

taking up arms against the masculine army of the Turkish state" (Shahrzad Mojab, "Introduction," in Shahrzad Mojab [ed.], *Women of a Non-State Nation: The Kurds* [Costa Mesa: Mazda Publishers, 2001], p. 4).

[71] Nur Bilge Criss, "The Nature of PKK Terrorism in Turkey," *Studies in Conflict and Terrorism* 18 (1995), 21.

[72] When pro-establishment observers do not blame the PKK for unsolved murders, they often point a figure at other shadowy, subversive groups, such as the Islamist Hizbullah. Lord Avebury makes the following observation on this issue:

> The suggestion is that while the arrests, tortures, judicial harassment, police raids and fines are all undoubtedly the work of the state, the violent attacks and murders are perpetrated by some other body which has no connection with the authorities. But common sense indicates that only the state has the motive and the opportunity not only to commit these crimes, but to enjoy absolute impunity. Nobody has ever been charged, let alone convicted, of any of the murders of journalists, though recently a few alleged members of "Hezbollah" have been arrested for other offenses. The then-Prime Minister, now President of Turkey, Suleyman Demirel, referring to the murdered writers of *Ozgur Gundem*, said: These people are not real journalists. They are militants in the guise of journalists. They are killing each other. (Lord Avebury, "Turkey's Kurdish Policy in the Nineties," in *Democracy at Gunpoint; The Economist, Turkey Survey*, [Parliamentary Human Rights Group, June 8–14, 1996], 4).

Regarding the assassination of political party representatives, the Turkish newspaper *Yeni Ulke* (March 22, 1992) published the transcript of a secretly recorded telephone conversation between the Silvan Gendarmerie commander and a sixteen-year-old Kurdish boy, whom he bribed and pressured to assassinate SHP (Social Democratic Populist Party) Board Member Mehmet Menge. A few days after being given a Kalashnikov rifle and hand grenades, the boy telephoned the commander, told him he

In any case, the state's refusal to permit free access to the Kurdish regions for journalists and independent observers makes it difficult to obtain any reliable information on the conflict.[73] People's reaction to grievance framing efforts of the state (as well as its opponents) are mediated by their pre-existing identity and frames of reference, with those already possessing a psychological attachment to the Kemalist state being the most likely to accept its version of the truth. Likewise, those already alienated from Ankara are most likely to receive any information emanating from the state or Turkish media with skepticism.

As discussed in Chapter 3, the PKK has in fact attacked many Kurdish villages and intentionally massacred entire families. Even though the victims were virtually all village guards and their families, the massacres gave the state some powerful propaganda images with which to paint the guerrillas as a "bunch of bloodthirsty bandits who had hit the mountains."[74] The PKK also attacked economic targets, state facilities, teachers, and schools, which it viewed as agents of Turkish colonialism and assimilation.[75] Bomb attacks have been staged in the west of Turkey,

had found the man, and asked how he should kill him. The commander replied, "Pull the fuse on the grenade and throw it at him. Shoot him in the head no more than three times. Do not worry, we have arranged everything. We'll say terrorists killed him. Your money is ready. I will make a big man of you." On the basis of the recording, a criminal investigation was launched, but two months later the commander in question was still on duty, having been transferred elsewhere in the country (Amnesty International, *Turkey: Walls of Glass* [November 1992], 13).

[73] Researchers attempting to determine exactly what is happening in the southeast have been forbidden by the Emergency Rule Governor to meet with witnesses to massacres and other atrocities (Avebury, "Turkey's Kurdish Policy in the Nineties," p. 10; and Human Rights Watch Helsinki, 6: 12 [1994], p. 21). In Michael Ignatieff's *Blood and Belonging: The Road to Nowhere*, Video Documentary, BBC Wales (1995), Ignatieff finds himself unable to gain interviews with average Kurds in Turkish Kurdistan because he is being followed by Turkish secret police, who appear more than recognizable as they "surreptitiously" follow him from afar wearing their suits, sunglasses, and earphones. When confronted by Ignatieff, they claim not to be following him at all, but rather keeping an eye on him for his own protection.

[74] Ismet G. Imset, *The PKK* (Ankara: Turkish Daily News Publications, 1992), p. 311.

[75] Imset states that

By the end of 1991, more than a thousand school buildings in the troubled region would be attacked as part of this campaign while those left untouched, in areas sympathetic to the guerrillas, would end up being occupied by military troops. Teachers would start to resign from public service after being appointed to the region while the state would gradually lose its interest in restoring educational services to the Southeast... In one attack, for instance, not more than five PKK militants entering the Demirkoyu village of Agri province in the summer of 1989, on a Saturday morning, first "executed" the village chieftain Barun Basut and then set fire on the local school. After the attack they even threw a grenade at the arriving local fire squad and wounded one person before running off. In another example the same day, terrorists entered the Dutlu hamlet of Hakkari, where they first burned down the house of a village guard and then set the school building on fire. (Ibid., p. 82)

especially against security force targets and tourist sites (the latter kind of attack intending to disrupt tourism, one of Turkey's main foreign exchange earning industries).[76] Naturally, the state has sought to focus attention on terrorist attacks in order to characterize the PKK as solely a terrorist organization rather than a national liberation movement willing to resort to terrorism. The distinction is important, since obviously one cannot be expected to negotiate with terrorists, whose primary motive is to sow terror and anarchy.[77]

The attacks and the Turkish media's publicizing of them increased the PKK's credibility as a force to be reckoned with, but also cost it a certain amount of sympathy amongst both the Kurdish population as well as Turks in the western part of the country.[78] The latter, although not part

---

[76] Human Rights Watch Helsinki 6: 12 (October 1994) provide the following details:

The PKK routinely commits such abuses as summary execution, hostage-taking, indiscriminate fire, and destruction of civilian property in an attempt to force the civilian population to comply with its wishes. From September 12, 1994 to October 12, 1994, for example, the PKK murdered fourteen teachers in southeastern Turkey. At its March 1994 Third National Conference, the PKK made the following declaration: "The struggle which the PKK carries out has left the stage of strategic defence . . . it is inevitable that we escalate our struggle in response to Turkey's declaration of all-out war. Consequently, all economic, political, military, social and cultural organizations, institutions, formations – and those who serve in them – have become targets. The entire country has become a battlefield." The PKK also promised to "liquidate" or "eliminate" political parties, "imperialist" cultural and educational institutions, legislative and representative bodies, and "all local collaborators and agents working for the Republic of Turkey in Kurdistan." In August 1993, the PKK reportedly reinstated its 1987 "Decree on Village Raids," which called for "mass destruction" for "non-revolutionary" villages, i.e. those with village guard, that do not support, "the national liberation struggle." The PKK also often kidnaps tourists travelling in the southeast and has also bombed tourist areas throughout Turkey. In 1993 it threatened to kill all Turkish journalists who continued working in southeastern Turkey, which effectively closed down all newspaper operations. For a time the only place one could purchase a newspaper was in a police station. (Ibid., p. 22)

For an analysis attempting to objectively determine the PKK's role in terrorism, kidnapping, extortion, and the drug trade, the reader should consult Paul White, *Primitive Rebels or Revolutionary Modernizers*, pp. 192–200.

[77] Nur Bilge Criss begins her article on "The Nature of PKK Terrorism in Turkey" with this statement: "Current history is characterized by dichotomous forces of integration and disintegration/anarchy" (Nur Bilge Criss, "The Nature of PKK Terrorism in Turkey," *Studies in Conflict and Terrorism* 18: 1 [1995], 17). The state represents integration, and the PKK represents terrorism and anarchy. Nonetheless, Criss does concede that reforms are needed in Turkey, mainly electoral reform, land reform, more efficient local administration, enhanced democratic rights (including "lifting the ban on naming places and individuals in Kurdish"), and perhaps added cultural freedoms and the teaching of Kurdish as a second language in Kurdish regions. These must also be accompanied by containment of terrorism and rejection of the PKK as a party for dialogue (ibid., 35).

[78] For an example of state publicized images of PKK massacres, the following official Turkish Internet site may be referred to: http://www.ohal.gov.tr/f_pkk.htm.

of the potential or existing Kurdish identity group, might nonetheless have been appealed to for sympathy and support, in the same way that parts of the American public sympathized with the north Vietnamese during the war in Vietnam.

Many less radical leftist and Kurdish groups in competition with the PKK have also sought to capitalize on terrorist framings of Ocalan's organization. Particularly Iraqi Kurdish groups such as the KDP (which faced PKK competition in its territory) and leftist groups (both Kurdish and Turkish) used the PKK's massacres of village guard families to attack its legitimacy.[79] This may have caused fewer Kurds to maintain a neutral attitude towards the group – one either despised the terrorists, or lionized the freedom fighters as the only group determined enough to fight Ankara by all means necessary.

Ankara has tolerated or encouraged other counter-movements to the PKK, however, such as neo-fascist Turkish defence organizations (the Grey Wolves) or groups such as the Mothers of Terror Victims and various professional associations. These groups further publicize the establishment view of the PKK. For instance, the Ankara's Journalists' Association provides the following statement: "All the people of our country and the whole world should know that the PKK terrorist organization has nothing to do with the 'Kurdish Identity.' Its leaders are in it for personal gain and have been hired by antidemocratic forces outside the country to upset peace and security in the region."[80] The placing in quotation marks of "Kurdish Identity" follows the official line that denies the reality of such a phenomenon, while at the same time attempting nonetheless to address the issue. Claiming that the PKK insurgency stems from outside agitators implies that the domestic situation and state policies towards the Kurds are not the source of the problem. In insurgencies anywhere in the world, from China in the 1940s to Nicaragua in the 1980s and Chechnya, Iran, and Iraq today, pro-government actors have attempted to frame the causes of the uprising as coming from outside sources. In addition to finding the source of the insurgency outside national borders, associations such as the Turkish Democracy Foundation attempt to highlight the PKK's link to unpopular ideologies and regimes:

---

[79] For instance, one of the PKK's main rivals in its early years, the Partiya Sosyalist a Kurdistan (PSK), argued until recently that armed struggle was premature: "For most of its existence it has denounced the armed struggle of the PKK as counter-revolutionary, terrorist and anarchist, which: 'instead of fighting the bourgeois system, directs an aggressive policy against the revolutionary movements of Turkey and of Kurdistan'" (White, *Primitive Rebels or Revolutionary Modernizers*, p. 157).

[80] "PKK Reality in Turkey and in the World," 3/5/98 http://www.access.ch/turkey/grupf/f642.1.

In line with Marxist-Leninist view, the PKK's leadership has adopted the ideology reigned in such Communist regimes as Soviet Union, Cambodia under the rule of Khmer Rouge and Cuba, all of which collapsed or in such a course [sic]. That ideology tends to penetrate each section of daily life by denying the existence of individual free will and private life and by comprising all values in the Party's leadership, Abdullah Ocalan ... [T]he PKK decided to cooperate with Revolutionary People's Liberation Party/Front (DHKP/C), one of the most disgusting Marxist terrorist organizations of Turkey.[81]

Additional statements of the Democracy Foundation include:

The terrorists have several main objectives in their mind when using the media for their own purposes. These objectives are combined to enable the terrorists to wage a propaganda war and in so doing strengthen and encourage their physical war. Therefore, giving license to MED TV which makes the propaganda of the PKK, a criminal and terrorist organization shall mean to back terrorism (xiii) ... It is public support which political parties get power from. And public will appear best in equal and democratic competition circumstances. Organizations that do not accept peaceful democratic competition conditions are not political parties. If their principal political means are violence, they are terrorist organizations or revolutionary groups to the extent of their purpose and support (xxiv).

The Turkish state brandishes more sophisticated forms of grievance framing in diplomatic, academic, and international milieux.[82] Referring to the Vienna Declaration of June 25, 1993, on peoples' right to self-determination, it is pointed out that the declaration makes a distinction between people under colonial rule or alien domination and those of different ethnic origin living in a democratic sovereign state. Since the majority of Kurds joined the Kemalists in fighting off invaders during Turkey's War of Independence (see Chapter 2), it is argued that Kurds have freely chosen to live within the Turkish Republic. Since the Republic has been an electoral democracy since 1945 (with brief exceptions following the coups of 1960, 1971, and 1980), the only form of legitimate action for Kurds in Turkey is from within this "open" electoral system. Hence, Kurds in Turkey are not compelled as a last resort to pursue armed rebellion against tyranny and oppression. Moreover, the point is moot since the Kurds are not a people, given that they are divided by different

---

[81] Turkish Democracy Foundation, "Fact Book on Turkey: Kurds and the PKK Terrorism," XXVII and XXVIII, Ankara (May 1996). Grammar unchanged from original passage.

[82] The following argument is taken from undated information notes from the Permanent Mission of Turkey in Geneva, and also corresponds well with informal discussions held between the author and Turkish academics at Bilkent University, Ankara, during the academic year of 1997–1998.

"Kurdish" languages and religions.[83] Rather, Kurds in Turkey are full citizens equal to all others. For these reasons, it is argued that the PKK is not a national liberation movement. Rather, it is a group of terrorists seeking to foment ethnic hatred and division where peaceful co-existence existed previously. In light of this, the Turkish state is justified in pursuing a military solution to a military problem.

Censorship undertaken on the grounds of national security has tried to ensure that the state's grievance framing remains the only interpretation of the world available to the Turkish public.[84] The dichotomous pull of an electoral democratic system and a military waging a counter-insurgency campaign created a fair amount of shifting grey area regarding what can be said and published, however. As a result, frames contradicting that of the state often reach the public, while their journalist or academic authors often reach prison.[85]

A Turkish Interior Ministry document also includes additional elements of state grievance framing and public relations strategy worth noting at length.[86]

3. In response to the organisation [the PKK] and its supporters using international institutions, non-governmental organisations, human rights organisations, news agencies, news and TV establishments, universities and internationally known people against Turkey;

[83] Additionally, the argument is often made that the various Kurdish languages are too "primitive" and poor in vocabulary to constitute languages of education or nationhood (Permanent Mission of Turkey, Geneva "Information Note," – undated secret document, although most likely a background note for the Mission's August 16, 1994 "Right of Reply by the Turkish Delegation," presented at the forty-sixth session of the Commission on Human Rights, Sub-Commission on Prevention of Discrimination and Protection of Minorities, Geneva).

[84] In addition to what has already been said above on this issue, the reader may refer to Amnesty International, *Turkey: Walls of Glass*, November 1992; and International Human Rights Law Group, "Criminalizing Parliamentary Speech in Turkey: Report of the Law Group Delegation to Turkey on the Detention of Parliamentarians and the Proceedings to Ban the Democracy Party (DEP)," (May 1994).

[85] Imset provides several examples of incarceration for "crimes of thought," including a recent case of "1,080 Turkish intellectuals who collectively defied the laws and issued a book containing banned articles. They are all now being prosecuted and may face up to three years in jail" (Ismet Imset, "The PKK: Terrorists or Freedom Fighters," in *Democracy at Gunpoint; The Economist, Turkey Survey* [Parliamentary Human Rights Group, June 8–14, 1996] 33). Also, Turkish sociologist Ismail Besikci, who is referred to several times in this chapter, faces up to 282 years of imprisonment for his various articles and books on the Kurds in Turkey (ibid., 33).

[86] Kurdistan Informatie Centrum Nederland, "Secret T.C. Interior Ministry, Public Relations Office Chairmanship," Number: B050HID0000073/472 03/01/1997, Matter: Measures to be taken against PKK activities in 1997, Regarding: Prime Ministerial orders dated 12.11.1993.

The special international enlightenment programmes should be applied, visits should be made to regional people who have suffered from terrorism in the presence of these individuals and institutions, faxes, letters, cards and photograph album campaigns [sic] should be organised.

Those suffering damages from terrorism should be made to apply to organisations like the Helsinki Watch Committee and International Human Rights with documentation and information, and protests should be made at the biased attitudes of these institutions.

Protest campaigns should be organised with the participation of various associations and institutions by reason of biased attitudes of the European Churches Association, press and publications organs, local and national governments and local administrations.

Programmes should be drawn up to discredit the book propounded abroad that the organisation has chosen the method of terrorism as there is not a democratic environment and that it is a political party, and this should be applied by means of the press, face to face meetings on television, enlightenment and information.

... 6. Parliamentarians, men of religion, representatives of the press and in particular members of NGOs like International Human Rights and Amnesty International who may come from abroad with the aim of collecting propaganda material should be steered appropriately and followed, and advantage should be taken of Diyarbakir Press Office to this end.

... 8. Administrative and legal measures should be taken against those attempting to propagate the Kurdish language, form institutions conducting research to make it a language of literacy and to start education and Kurdish literacy courses directed at front activities [sic].

... 10. In response to the efforts of the PKK to develop television and radio broadcasting along the lines of its aims:

Letter, fax and telegram campaigns should be organised and directed at foreign institutions and governments giving permission for broadcasting by nongovernmental institutions and individuals.

Information and documentation to the effect that MED TV[87] does not broadcast the music and entertainment for which it obtained the licence, but that the broadcasts are of political content and aimed at supporting a terrorist organisation, should be communicated to the countries granting broadcasting permission, and the initiatives to obstruct the broadcasts should be continued.

MED TV should be prevented from making programmes in Turkey.

Each malintentioned programme made by MED TV should be refuted to the international institutions thereafter, and this should be done through NGOs rather than directly.

Although many of the directives contained in this document aim at influencing international opinion, some are also focused on the domestic front. Particularly directive number eight, which advocates "administrative

---

[87] MED-TV was a Kurdish satellite television station based in Europe, which will be discussed at length below [DR].

and legal measures" against those attempting to propagate the Kurdish language, demonstrates an attempt to suppress Kurdish identity.

The final element of state framing efforts worth noting here involves the establishment of the village guard system. The intent of the program was to aid the authorities in combating the guerrillas, by arming local pro-state Kurdish groups. The extent to which a handful of isolated and vulnerable armed villagers in each community contributed to this effort is debatable. The program's impact in the realm of cultural framing, however, aided the state immensely. Authorities could point to the village guards and say, "You see, the PKK is not representative of Kurds in Turkey – here are ordinary Kurds arming themselves to defend their communities from the terrorists." When the PKK attacked the village guards, massacring them and their families, the movement's number of Kurdish victims began to quickly surpass the number of state officials killed. Authorities could then turn and proclaim, "These terrorists are not fighting for Kurdish rights! Most of their victims are their own kind!" As more of the Kurdish population itself then began to question the PKK's tactics, the movement suffered from greater divisions and a questionable image.

PKK framing efforts and the birth of KADEK

PKK framing efforts and ideology fused a modified Marxist-Leninist discourse with Kurdish nationalism and a focus on human rights abuses committed against Kurds. Depending on the audience, one or all three of these elements would be stressed. Poor rural and urban Kurds typically heard all three, although Marxist ideas were explained in a very crude, simplified manner.[88] Wealthy Kurdish elites were spared the Marxist discourse and instead appealed to with ideas of nationalism and continuing persecution of the Kurds. Students and intellectuals (both Kurdish and Turkish) also heard all three lines of thought, although the primary focus on a deeper Marxist analysis of the Kurds' plight in Turkey was evident. Finally, international audiences and NGOs were mainly targeted with the human rights discourse, while Kurdish nationalism became a variant of all peoples' right to self-determination. In this manner, an attempt was made to appeal for sympathy and support from outside the Kurdish group. Within the potential Kurdish group, people were first "educated" about their Kurdish ethnic identity, then encouraged to view

---

[88] Aliza Marcus provides the following observation: "Although the PKK's message of Marxist-Leninist revolution may not have spread much out of the mountains, its message of Kurdish freedom has. 'Socialism? What does that mean?' a Kurdish villager miles away [from a PKK camp she had visited] later asked me. 'All I know is that the PKK is fighting for our rights'" (Aliza Marcus, "City in the War Zone," *Middle East Report* [1994], 181).

this identity in a politicized way. Marx's class consciousness was fused with Kurdish national consciousness, with the result that traditional Kurdish social structures became a target of the PKK along with state structures of domination.

As mentioned in Chapter 3, the PKK's own history outlines the initial propaganda efforts that Ocalan and his colleagues made to attract followers: "The first activities were organized amongst the youths in schools since there was very little written propaganda material. The political ideas were spread by word of mouth. The work amongst the young students eventually had a big impact on the workers and peasants since, for the most part, the students came from villages or the poorer classes. It followed that influencing them, meant having an influence on their families."[89] Before 1984, the PKK pursued a strategy similar to that of Chinese and Vietnamese Communists. It sent its cadres to various communities throughout the Kurdish region, where they lived with the people and spread the group's vision of the world. As described in Chapter 3, the PKK avoided confrontations with the state during this period. Instead, it focused on developing a core group of indoctrinated, committed cadres, who would in turn also spread out and recruit the next level of militants and sympathizers.[90]

The PKK's first task was to counter decades of assimilationist policies pursued by Ankara. While such policies had only penetrated rural areas in

---

[89] "A Brief History of the Kurdistan Workers Party," undated ERNK document, courtesy of Toronto Kurdish Information Centre.

[90] It would be interesting to know if any of the PKK leadership had ever read Francis Fanon's 1963 *The Wretched of the Earth*. If they had, they might have found the following passage particularly interesting:

> They [the nationalist elite] fall back toward the countryside and the mountains, toward the peasant people. From the beginning, the peasantry closes in around them, and protects them from being pursued by the police. The militant nationalist who decides to throw in his lot with the country people instead of playing at hide-and-seek with the police in urban centers will lose nothing. The peasant's cloak will wrap him around with a gentleness and firmness that he never suspected. These men, who are in fact exiled to the backwoods, who are cut off from the urban background against which they had defined their ideas of the nation, and of the political fight, these men have in fact become "Maquisards." Since they are obliged to move about the whole time in order to escape from the police, often at night so as not to attract attention, they will have good reason to wander through their country and get to know it. The cafés are forgotten; so are the arguments about the next elections or the spitefulness of some policeman or other. Their ears hear the true voice of the country, and their eyes take in the great and infinite poverty of their people. They realize that precious time has been wasted in useless commentaries upon the colonial regime. They finally come to understand that the changeover will not be a reform, nor a bettering of things. They come to understand, with a sort of bewilderment that will from henceforth never quite leave them, that political action in the towns will always be powerless to modify or overthrow the colonial regime. (Francis Fanon, *The Wretched of the Earth* [New York: Grove Press, 1963], p. 126)

limited ways, many urban Kurds were already largely assimilated and no longer spoke much Kurdish (this in fact was true of many of the PKK's founding members). PKK cadres and thinkers thus took up the nation-building cause, promoting shared myths of common ancestry, territory, language, history, and past nationalist accomplishments:

They [the Kurds] are distinguished from their neighbours by their language, their homeland, the feeling to constitute but one people, the will to remain Kurds and the aspiration to live and to progress together under their own flag, in peace and cooperation with the neighbouring peoples. They speak an Indo-European language, alien to both Arabic and Turkish ... Kurdistan, the homeland in which they have been constituted across the ages as a people of their own, is a country geographically, as large as France, where they represent a majority of 90% of the population. Kurdistan is the backbone and the water shed [sic] of the area, with such large rivers as the upper Euphrates and the upper Tigris, green valleys, well cultivated plains, and a subsoil rich in natural resources, including oil.

... Our oppressors have described us, unjustly and successively, as a primitive mountain population refractory to civilization, lawless nomadic tribes without any national consciousness, highway robbers, eternal rebels, bloody landlords, red communists, and today as international terrorists. Contrary to historical facts, we are said to have never been organized into a state or states of our own. Our past has been so blurred, our present so full of struggle that it is often forgotten that we are a people of the Hurrians and the Medes, respectively the Kurds' first and second ancestors.[91]

By highlighting the oppression they suffered because of their Kurdish identity (as discussed at the outset of this chapter), the PKK sought to politicize Kurdish identity and mobilize Kurds to oppose the Turkish state. Tracing Kurdish national ancestry back to the Medes and Hurrians served to justify contemporary nationalist claims, since these groups ruled large independent kingdoms of their own. Hence, the PKK sought to build on national Kurdish myths of common ancestry and a past differentiated from that of other groups in the area, such as the Turks. Such a task is extremely important for any nationalist movement:

Such constructions of collective remembering not only (re-)create a past but perhaps more crucially (re-)create a collective identity that has a past. Opposition may consist of "refusing what we are," in Foucault's (1988) terms, and reconstituting a preferred collective identity that empowers actors. This is a shift from being subjects of/subject to a regime to becoming human subjects writing our own history. Competition over memory is also competition over how current collective identities should be conceived. Here Benjamin's (1970)

---

[91] Ismet Seriff Vanly, "Kurdistan, the Kurds and the Kurdish National Question: Historical Background and Perspective," paper prepared for the Preparatory Commission for Parliament of Kurdistan in Exile (1993), 1.

idea that revolution is a "tiger's leap into the past" becomes more complex; there is no single past, but rather competing definitions of how the past is to be read.[92]

In addition to focusing on Kurdish difference from others and resulting persecution (and later provoking additional persecution), the PKK invoked the example of other nations, arguing that the Kurds had the same rights to self-determination:

The Kurdish people do no longer accept to be the last colonized and the most oppressed people on the Earth. Whatever might be the price, they are decided to pursue their patriotic struggle to get rid of colonialism and racism, and to have a place of their own in the Sun. Their way is the path of democracy in the Near East. For the Kurds, it does not matter whether their colonizer is white or brown, Muslim or Christian. Theirs is the desire to live better, in a free and democratic Kurdistan, living in peace, cooperation and union with the neighbouring nations, just as the European nations are living united in one Europe, after the blood baths of two world wars.[93]

If one accepts Azar and Burton's contention that ethnic identity is a basic human need,[94] then such appeals could be expected to elicit a strong response from Kurds who had difficulties being Turkish.[95] Such difficulties could stem from lack of fluency in the Turkish language, lack of social mobility in Turkish society, or simply a pre-existing attachment to a Kurdish culture or language that was suppressed by Ankara. The majority of the PKK's recruits were in fact "the most marginal sections of Kurdish society: the ones who feel excluded from the country's social and economic development, victims of the rural transformation with frustrated expectations. The PKK offered them a simple and appropriate theory, and lots of opportunities for action, heroism and martyrdom."[96]

---

[92] Mohammadi and Sreberny-Mohammadi, *Small Media, Big Revolution*, p. 38.

[93] Vanly, "Kurdistan," p. 4.

[94] E. Azar and J. Burton (eds.), *International Conflict and Resolution: Theory and Practice* (Boulder: Lunner Rienner Publishers Inc., 1986), p. 146.

[95] Azar states that,

It is difficult to detect, to define and to measure a sense of insecurity and distributive injustice and other such deprivations. On the other hand, ethnic and communal cleavages and the political structures associated with them are more conspicuous. The fact that ethnic and communal cleavages as a source of protracted social conflicts are more obvious than others does not make ethnicity – used here to refer to identity groups that make up a polity – a special case. Ethnicity is an important case, though not a special one, because it draws our attention to a need that is fundamental. The study of ethnicity and the drive for ethnic identity enables us to understand the nature of conflicts generally. It is the denial of human needs, of which ethnic identity is merely one, that finally emerges as the source of conflict, be it domestic, communal, international or inter-state. (Ibid., 146)

[96] In an interview with Paul White (White, *Primitive Rebels or Revolutionary Modernizers*, p. 156), Abdullah Ocalan said the following regarding the PKK's members and supporters:

And in case any of its audience believed the state discourse concerning equality of all citizens in the country regardless of ethnic origins, the PKK and allied Kurdish nationalists provided many examples framing the contradiction between the state's words and actions. Among these, for example, was Turkey's attitude to the plight of Turkish minorities in countries such as Bulgaria, Greece, and Iraq: Ankara frequently protests against measures taken in these countries that circumscribe the use of the Turkish language, that attempt to assimilate the Turkish minority, and that infringe on Turkish human rights in various ways:

> The Turkish press and the authorities denounce priests and such like who are in favour of the Bulgarian government's policies and do not assert their Turkish ethnic identity, as "traitors." They call Thracian Turks who have become Greeks, "collaborators" and "traitors." The Turkish authorities and the press treat with favour those Kurds who deny their national identity and advocate the official state ideology, those who have been Turkified, who are objectively Kurds but subjectively Turks. There is no end to the praise bestowed upon them ... but this duplicity is becoming known to all and is being questioned.[97]

Kurdish nationalists point out that Bulgarian, Afghan, Thracian, and Iraqi Turks are vigorously defended, and when they come to Turkey as refugees they are warmly welcomed. When Saddam Hussein used chemical weapons on Iraqi Kurds, however, Ankara said nothing.[98] When Iraqi Kurdish refugees fleeing these attacks appeared at the Turkish

---

> AO: The working people are supporting the PKK: the peasants; the petty bourgeoisie; the bourgeois in the cities. The patriotic poor and the middle class are supporting the PKK.
>
> PW: But what is the one biggest group? You mentioned many different social groups. I think the main group, the biggest of all the social groups is the poor peasants. Is that true?
>
> AO: Well, yes, they are the main supporters of the struggle. Especially at the moment [mid-1992], they are the ones who support the struggle most. After the fifteenth of August, before the 1980s, when it was new, before it started, it was mostly young people in the cities, intellectuals, the urban middle class. (Abdullah Ocalan, personal communication, 2 July 1992, M. K. Akademisi, Bekaa Valley, Lebanon)

[97] Ismail Besikci, *Kurdistan and Turkish Colonialism* (London: Kurdistan Solidarity Committee and Kurdistan Information Centre, 1991), p. 7.

[98] Besikci gives the following comment on the issue:

> Let us remember the event in March 1988 Halabja, South Kurdistan. Over 5,000 Kurdish human beings, men, women and children, young and old were slaughtered by the racist and colonial Iraqi regime in a genocidal attack. Did it elicit any reaction from the Turkish state and government leaders? At the time of this President Evren of Turkey was participating in an Islamic summit conference meeting in Kuwait. Did he mention the massacre of the Kurds at the conference? Is this what being partners in fate, joy and grief means? To add insult to injury, Prime Minister Turgut Ozal visited Baghdad about two weeks after the event at the beginning of April as if he was congratulating the Iraqi

border, attempts were made to prevent them from entering and they were interned in camps:

> It can never be forgotten just how the Kurds who were compelled to run away from Saddam Hussein's chemical and biological weapons managed to reach Hakkari (Kurdish province on the Iraqi border – Tr.). They were kept at the border for a long time. Those who risked their lives to cross the border were handed over to Iraqi authorities who promptly executed them on the spot. Later on there was no shortage of headlines in the dailies "Those who came from Iraq are a heavy burden on the budget," "those who came from Iraq too have become a headache," ... "They should be sent back as soon as possible." These objections began as soon as the Kurds arrived. The Kurdish men, women, young and old were put behind barbed wire. A great deal of effort was expended in frustrating attempts to meet their basic needs. Helping them, being concerned about them was prohibited. Those from southern Kurdistan were treated like prisoners of war, like convicts. Soldiers were stationed outside the camp entrances. More measures with barbed wire were introduced. For days, weeks and months the Turkish authorities announced that a significant part of the burden the 40,000–50,000 Kurds from southern Kurdistan would impose on the budget would have to be paid for by the West. At every opportunity, they reminded the West of this. But when it comes to Bulgarian Turks, they say "Even if 2 million men of our race arrive here, we will accept them, Turkey is a big and rich country."[99]

Turkish officials would likely justify such a double standard by stating that Bulgarian or Iraqi Turks speak Turkey's official language, and hence do not require much assimilation into Turkish society. Kurds in the east of Turkey, however, speak the same Kirmanci dialect of Kurdish as most of the Kurdish refugees that arrived from Iraq, and view them as countrymen.[100] By framing and highlighting the double standard between Bulgarian Turks and Iraqi Kurds in this manner, Kurdish nationalists portrayed Ankara as solely the government of ethnic Turks.

As stated earlier, however, the PKK's ideology was leftist in addition to Kurdish nationalist. Thus the movement also sought to appeal to Kurds disaffected from their own traditional Kurdish social structures. True to Marxist doctrine, the PKK attacked religion as a veil of conservatism and ignorance, which helps keep Kurds in their backward and oppressed condition. As shown in Chapter 3, the PKK also tapped into a growing

---

colonialists. It is common knowledge just how the plight of, for example, the Palestinians is verbalised in tragic terms. Turkey did not show even one-thousandth of the concern it shows for the Palestinians for the Kurds in south Kurdistan. (Ibid., p. 5)

[99] Ibid., p. 6.

[100] The son of a tribal agha in Hakkari province told this author that in 1988 he was arrested and tortured for organizing food aid and community assistance to Iraqi Kurdish refugees at the border (personal communication, city of Van, June 6, 1999). The authorities claimed that while engaging in such activities, he was promoting Kurdish nationalism.

reservoir of resentment towards the Kurdish agha landlord class, and predicated the early phases of its struggle against this group. In PKK doctrine, all of Kurdistan is an internal colony of the capitalist classes of other nations, and the Kurdish comprador elite (Kurdistan's domestic feudal and bourgeoisie classes) collaborates in this exploitation of the Kurdish people: "Kurdistan's underdeveloped market offered a once-in-a-lifetime chance to the Turkish bourgeoisie to expand their economy. Road construction into the furthest corners of Kurdistan led to the acquisition by the Turks of Kurdistan's mineral and agricultural assets."[101]

When framing the issue to both new cadres and the masses, the obvious disparities between Turkey's Kurdish east and Turkish western regions were highlighted as a case of discrimination based on ethnic identity. The following text from Musa Anter (a Kurdish nationalist intellectual mysteriously murdered in 1992) is a particularly powerful example of such grievance framing: Anter begins his memoirs with a quotation from a famous Turkish author, Recaizade Ercument Ekrem Talu:

The Marmara region is the most civilized region of Turkey; Istanbul is the most beautiful city in the region of Marmara; the Bosphorus is the most pleasant part of Istanbul; Sariyer [on the Bosphorus] is the most agreeable district in Istanbul; Yeni Mahalle is the best neighbourhood in Sariyer; and the mansion of the Recaizade family is the most marvellous mansion in Yeni Mahalle ... it was in this mansion that I was born.

Musa Anter responds:

Kurdistan is the most backward region of Turkey; Mardin is the most backward province in Kurdistan; Nusaybin is the most distressed district in Mardin; Stelile [Akarsu in Turkish] is the poorest commune of Nusaybin; Zivinge [Eski Magara in Turkish] is the most backward village in Stetile; and, in accordance with the population register, it was in Cave No. 2 of the village that I was born.[102]

Musa Anter's framing of the Kurdish issue in Turkey fits well with Gurr's concept of relative deprivation[103] (1969): Kurds in the east, confronted with the wealth of Turks in the west, could be expected to feel frustrated with their relative lot and agitate for change. When the PKK told them that these disparities were not only a function of capitalist exploitation, but also of ethnic discrimination, the obvious course of action became to mobilize under a Kurdish socialist banner, i.e. the

---

[101] "Information about the Kurdistan Workers Party PKK: Kurdistan a history of oppression," ERNK undated document, p. 4.
[102] Andrew Mango, "Turks and Kurds," *Middle Eastern Studies* 30: 4 (October, 1994), 977.
[103] Ted Robert Gurr, *Why Men Rebel* (Princeton: Princeton University Press, 1969).

Kurdistan Workers' Party. Along the lines of Horowitz's theoretical perspective (1985), the simple existence of two different ethnic groups and the economic and power disparities between them, contained within it the seeds of conflict.[104] Such seeds, however, require nourishment in the form of grievance framing. An antecedent structural variable such as gross disparities in standards of living between groups only gains salience when it is perceived by the relevant actors. In effect, Gurr's notion of relative deprivation only exists when the deprived believe it exists (otherwise we may refer to simple deprivation), and movement activists often play a major role in fostering such perceptions. Ankara attempted to eliminate the seeds of group status-derived conflict by assimilating the weaker Kurdish group. For many Kurds, such an assimilationist program was the first salvo fired in the conflict.

In addition to the Kemalist regime, the Turkish left and most competing Kurdish organizations were also identified as enemies in the PKK's early days. While it opposed Turkish opposition movements because they would not recognize Kurdish nationalist aspirations, the PKK attacked competing Kurdish organizations even more harshly. Ocalan's group insisted that it can work only with "genuine Marxist-Leninists."[105] Essentially, the PKK sought to arouse anti-state, politicized Kurdish identities within the population, and then position itself as the only credible vehicle for such opposition. This necessitated eliminating local Turkish and Kurdish revolutionary parties, after which the state could be confronted from a more unified platform.[106] Attacks on those who should have normally been considered "progressive" comrades-in-arms were justified with accusations that the other groups were either chauvinist (the Turkish left) or bourgeois-reformist (and hence supporters of the state).

In short, the PKK "identified the enemies of the Kurdish people as the fascists (Grey Wolves and similar groups); agents of the state and those who supported them; the Turkish Left which subordinated the Kurdish question to the leftist revolution, Kurdish reformers who accepted the overall system, and finally, the exploitative Kurdish landlord class."[107] The PKK reminded its people who they were (Kurds, not Turks, Arabs, or Persians), who the enemy was and what unjust things had been done to

---

[104] For instance, Horowitz argues that "In the modern state ... the sources of ethnic conflict reside, above all, in the struggle for relative group worth" (Horowitz, "Group Comparison and the Sources of Conflict," in *Ethnic Groups in Conflict* [Berkeley: University of California Press, 1985], p. 143).

[105] White, *Primitive Rebels or Revolutionary Modernizers*, p. 148.

[106] For a more detailed discussion of the PKK's conflict with Turkish leftists and other Kurdish groups, see White, *Primitive Rebels or Revolutionary Modernizers*, pp. 147–158.

[107] McDowall, *A Modern History of the Kurds*, p. 419.

them by this enemy. Those who accepted this view of things came to see their own self-worth as individuals as being tied to the fate and status of their identity group. In the Kurdish case the PKK showed this group to be colonized and oppressed. Thomas Homer-Dixon argues that, "It is an interesting empirical truth that anger is always grounded in moral outrage. In turn, moral outrage is a function, in part, of the theory of the 'good' or justice held by the aggrieved party."[108] The moral outrage that the PKK both tapped into and fostered in Kurds, through its framing of grievances, garnered the support and mobilization that would eventually turn the organization into a mass movement.

The PKK also presented a vision of a better society, a Kurdish socialist state with equality, freedom, and democracy for all. Although such a state would eventually incorporate all of Kurdistan, it would begin with Turkish Kurdistan (or as they referred to it, Northern Kurdistan). As part of the journey to achieving this future good, the PKK sought to remold Kurds into a "new Kurdish personality," cleansed of the traditional mentality of a colonized people and fiercely loyal to the party, which was to be the embodiment of the re-awakened ethnic identity group.[109] "Political education," apart from the grievance frames described above, included for the PKK a focus on the "real" Kurdish personality. *Serxwebun*, a pro-PKK newspaper, described the new Kurdish personality:

The new person does not drink, does not gamble and never thinks about his personal pleasures and comfort and he won't womanize and the ones who (previously) indulged in these sort of activities will cut all these habits as sharply as a knife, once he or she is among the new persons. The new person's philosophy and morality, the way he sits, he stands up, his style, his ego, his attitude and his reactions (*tepki*) are uniquely his. The fundamentals of all these things are the rock solid love towards revolution, freedom, homeland and socialism. The application of scientific socialism to the reality of the homeland creates the new person.[110]

---

[108] Thomas F. Homer-Dixon, "They and We: An Empirical and Philosophical Study of a Theory of Social Conflict," Ph.D. Dissertation, Massachusetts Institute of Technology, 1989, p. 3.

[109] White describes the PKK's efforts along these lines as intense indoctrination, inspired from concepts of the

so-called "Socialist New Man" that have been utilized by many "Marxist-Leninist" movements in several countries ... In a nutshell, it is an attempt to impart the behaviour, morals and beliefs of what the Soviets called a "real Communist" to the non-Party people who make up the majority of the population, to enable them loyally to follow the Party unquestioningly. Despite its proponents' professed atheism, this project frequently takes on many of the features of a cloying religious devotion. The PKK has taken over this concept from Stalinism, and radically adapted it for its own purposes. (White, *Primitive Rebels or Revolutionary Modernizers?*, p. 139)

[110] Ibid., p. 141.

White adds that,

A ceaseless parade of obituaries for slain PKK fighters (referred to officially as "martyrs") appears in PKK publications, and youth especially are urged to copy these shining examples of patriots prepared to give their lives for Kurdistan and Baskan Apo [President Ocalan – DR], who always remains the peerless example to be emulated.

The organization's ability to remould its recruits' personas should not be underestimated. PKK members are expected to make a series of pledges, write regular reports on their own weaknesses and to submit to regular, frequent "criticism and self-criticism" sessions. Combined, these generally seem adequate as a means of ensuring adherence to the ideal personality type, not to mention an ideal means of social control. They also have the effect of keeping members perpetually active, by convincing them that, no matter how well they apply themselves, they can never do enough.[111]

It is in this manner that the PKK was able to create a high degree of selfless devotion in its followers, who often valued the organization, its goals, and the Kurdish identity group more highly than their own lives. Given the difficulties of the guerrilla war that the PKK would launch against the state in 1984, such "human resources" would be crucial to the movement's growth and success.

As outlined and discussed in Chapter 3, before 1984 the PKK movement limited itself to local politics and confrontations, aiding peasants to confront the regional feudal and "reactionary" classes. To gain wider credibility the PKK needed to take on the armed forces of the Turkish state. In Abdullah Ocalan's own words: "Before anything else, armed propaganda will attract the attention of the masses who have been lost in daily life and who have been brainwashed by imperialist media or become dependent on this or that establishment party, to the revolutionary movement. It will thus activate the pacified masses."[112]

In line with a long tradition of revolutionary guerrilla thinking, attacks and ambushes on Turkish security forces were meant to shatter the army's image of invincibility. "Armed propaganda's" initial and primary objective was psychological rather than military.[113] When the PKK launched its first attacks against Turkish security forces, it must have been obvious to both the guerrillas and the army that asymmetries in

---

[111] Ibid.   [112] Imset, "The PKK: Terrorists or Freedom Fighters," 28.

[113] For instance, the first official fighting force of the North Vietnamese was the "Viet-Nam Propaganda Unit for National Liberation," founded on December 22, 1944. Although meant to be the lead fighting force of the Vietnamese Communists, Ho Chi Minh says this of the unit: "The Viet-Nam Propaganda Unit of National Liberation shows by its name that greater importance should be attached to the political side than to the military side" (Ho Chi Minh, *Ho Chi Minh on Revolution: Selected Writings* [New York: Frederic A. Praeger Inc., 1967], p. 138).

power held out little hope for the guerrillas. The PKK sought to change this outlook. By attacking Turkish forces and provoking a repressive response from them, the PKK highlighted the fact that Ankara's rule relied on naked force. Moreover, the PKK sought to legitimate and motivate collective action against such rule by demonstrating the vulnerability of the state's forces. If a band of guerrillas could attack army columns and bases with impunity and then disappear, the PKK's chances of success might not be so bad after all. In this sense, the PKK was trying to promote the 'cognitive liberation' that McAdam, McCarthy, and Zald[114] argue is a necessary precursor to mobilization. Ocalan himself stated that "... there is the duty to elevate the people to the stage of being able to defend themselves and to *make them believe, before anything else, that they need to be defended.*"[115] In 1990, sociologist Ismail Besikci provided the following account of this psychological campaign:

About 20–30 years ago in Diyarbakir, Bitlis or similar cities when the subject of Kurdish national and democratic rights were mentioned, Kurdish villagers would say "Sir, we are all Muslims. We are brothers. It is not important to speak Kurdish either. The state does not want to give Kurds this right. And it won't either, because the Kurds are very weak and the state is very powerful. If we make demands we will be ruined, wiped out. Let the state fix our roads, build our schools and give us running water that is enough." And if you said, "Since the state doesn't want to give the Kurds their legitimate rights through peaceful means, then waging a struggle becomes necessary, because a human being's right to speak and write in his/her native language must be one of the most basic rights. And basic rights are worth fighting for," the villager's reaction would be much stronger: "Sir, a state is needed to wage a struggle against another state. We are a poor and ignorant people. The Turkish state on the other hand is big and powerful. It has a large army. It has jet fighters, tanks cannons and guns. It has everything like a police force, prisons, stations, schools, papers and radio network. What have we got? We have nothing. A struggle in such circumstances cannot last. It is better to sit tight ..." And if you pressed them further on the "Kurds' national and democratic rights," they would say, "Our cause is just, very just, but we have no power, no friends and no supporters."[116]

According to Besikci, "The guerrilla movement has initiated the process of destruction of this moral outlook and psychology of impotence."[117] Rand Corporation analyst Daniel Byman arrives at a similar conclusion as Besikci, but from a state-centric ideological perspective (as opposed to Besikci's social movement perspective):

[114] Doug McAdam and al. (eds.), *Comparative Perspectives on Social Movements*, p. 5.
[115] Imset, "The PKK: Terrorists or Freedom Fighters?" 26.
[116] Besikci, *Kurdistan and Turkish Colonialism*, pp. 8–9.   [117] Ibid.

Ethnic terrorists often seek to influence their own constituencies more than the country as a whole. Ethnic terrorists frequently seek to foster communal identity, in contrast to an identity proposed by the state. Ethnic terrorists often target potential intermediaries, who might otherwise compromise on identity issues. A secondary goal of the attacks is to create a climate of fear among a rival group's population ... Ethnic terrorism creates a difficult problem for the state: conventional countermeasures may engender broader support for an insurgency or a separatist movement even when they hamstring or defeat a specific terrorist group.[118]

Hence, in addition to destroying a Kurdish sense of impotence and fatalistic acceptance of their plight, the PKK's armed actions also benefited from the state crackdown that followed them. When state security forces razed or raided villages and towns to look for the guerrillas, when they imposed curfews and roadblocks throughout the region, or when they arrested people *en masse* to torture and question them in prison, Kurds were made to see in the starkest possible terms that this was not "their government." The bitterness thus engendered further swelled the ranks of the most radical movement, i.e. the PKK, since one could obviously not reason with or reform such a government. In this manner communal identity and solidarity in the face of repression were increased.[119]

One will also recall from Chapter 3 that the PKK's armed attacks increased the group's popularity, tapping into a pre-existing cultural tool kit that contained many historical examples of Kurdish guerrilla resistance:

When in 1984 it [the PKK] raided two fortresses, the general image among the local people was one of petty affection. They were referred to as "the kids," or "the students." In a region torn by its own feudal conflicts and a history of banditry, the concept of having armed youngsters fighting was not too surprising. In 1987, as Ankara branded the outlaws as "a handful of bandits," local affection increased, describing them as "the resistance." Today, a whole population is talking of the "guerrillas" and in the words of several MPs, every family in the region now has a member with these guerrilla.[120]

The PKK strategy was to display in undeniable terms the dedication and fearlessness of its fighters – every guerrilla casualty went a long way

---

[118] Daniel Byman, "The Logic of Ethnic Terrorism," *Conflict and Terrorism* 21: 2 (April–June 1998), 149.

[119] For this reason, it is also quite likely that the PKK at times attacked security forces near villages or towns that were unfriendly to the movement. The resulting security operations in those areas would then turn the villagers against the state. PKK cadres sent to propagandize and recruit in these areas after the "security operations" might then be received much more positively than before.

[120] Imset, "The PKK: Terrorists or Freedom Fighters?" 29.

towards showing the masses how determined the group was. This stood in stark contrast to some of the militants of other groups, who spoke a lot about revolution over cups of tea. In Ocalan's view, "The support of the Kurdish people is largely based on their keen observation of the collective and individual sacrifices for democracy and national identity that our members have made under the most difficult circumstances. The Kurdish people have been deceived many times in the past by pseudo-leaders. But when they are convinced of the sacrifices of the freedom fighters, they mobilize for them."[121] Besikci also stresses this point often: "To demonstrate this audacity and fearlessness of the movement let me quote a common example. We frequently hear on radio and TV: '... security forces in such and such a place came across a group of terrorists, informed them that they were surrounded and called on them to surrender. The terrorists responded by firing on security forces and armed clashes occurred.'"[122] Such media reports enhanced the romantic image of the outnumbered heroic Kurdish guerrilla, surrounded but still determined to fight. As mentioned earlier, such imagery has a long history in Kurdish culture. Turkish media in fact unintentionally contributed to the potent image of the PKK guerrilla, with a frenzy of coverage devoted to the attacks.

To further its image of a credible fighting force to be feared, the PKK at times may have encouraged exaggerated reports of its numbers. Imset cites the following statement by a Turkish military officer stationed near the Iraqi border: "One day a villager came to us and said the terrorists who came to their village were 176 people ... Then we questioned him. When we asked what they looked like, the villager said he could not see them because it was dark. When we asked him to count to 100, he could only count up to 11. Of course, it came out that the PKK had told him to tell us that they were 176 people while they were actually not more than 30."[123]

Despite the benefits of the Turkish media frenzy about them, the PKK nonetheless attempted to ban Turkish newspapers and journalists from the Kurdish regions.[124] At the time, the organization no doubt had the intention of stifling the Turkish media's framing efforts regarding the insurgency. Likewise, the PKK justified its attacks on school buildings and Turkish teachers on the grounds that these were the vehicles for the

[121] David Korn, "Interview with PKK Leader Abdullah Ocalan," (1995).
[122] Ismail Besikci, *Kurdistan and Turkish Colonialism* (London: Kurdistan Solidarity Committee and Kurdistan Information Centre, 1991), p. 8.
[123] Imset, *The PKK*, p. 58.
[124] Human Rights Watch, Helsinki, 6:12, October (1994), p. 22.

state's policy of cultural framing and assimilation, and that teachers posted to Kurdish regions served as government informants.

By around 1993, however, the PKK came to the conclusion that some of its actions were mistaken, and that the movement had to improve its image and reach out to more allies. The organization was aware of the fact that its Marxist-Leninist ideology held little appeal beyond its most active militants.[125] Additionally, the need to attract European support and avoid too much American attention, especially after the fall of the Soviet Union, led the PKK to stress its Kurdish nationalist and human rights grievance frames more than its socialist side.[126] Thus in 1995 the PKK removed the hammer and sickle from its flag. In any case, the movement's Marxist ideological attacks on religion had failed to strike a receptive chord in the Kurdish masses, for whom Islam was an important value.[127] Thus the movement began occasionally incorporating an Islamic discourse into its propaganda, if not its concrete platform.

The PKK leadership pursued other changes as well. In terms of policy, the organization made greater appeals to attract local allies. Since any serious contending Turkish or Kurdish organization had been eliminated by 1990, efforts were made at attracting the remnants of these groups and mending fences.[128] The PKK began adding greater emphasis to its view that Turkish workers and peasants were also exploited by the bourgeoisie-controlled Kemalist state. The state diverted their attention away from their true capitalist enemies onto minorities such as the Kurds, Armenians, and Greeks, as well as threats in neighboring countries. Because of this, the Turkish people in general were not the enemies of the Kurds, but rather potential allies against the state and its capitalist puppet masters. Just as the Turkish state had pursued assimilation of the Kurds while at the same time attempting to prevent racism towards them,[129] the PKK pursued Kurdish nationalist mobilization against

---

[125] Imset, "The PKK: Terrorists or Freedom Fighters?" 28.

[126] In 1995, at the organization's Fifth Congress, "PKK delegates voted to reject the concept of Soviet socialism and other dogmatic policies, emphasizing once again that it had to keep up with changes in world history ... In accordance with these changes, the PKK Party Regulation program was also completely re-written" (ibid., p. 36).

[127] In other words, secularism was not in the cultural tool kit of Kurdistan.

[128] After a March 20, 1993 meeting between Ocalan and PSK leader Kemal Burkay, a joint statement "calling for all 'Kurdish patriots' to work together" was issued (White, *Primitive Rebels or the Revolutionary Modernizers*, p. 169).

[129] Such an approach contains within it an inherent contradiction, however, since the assimilationist program implies a denigration of Kurdish ethnic characteristics, such as language and culture. A multi-culturalist approach, on the other hand, would include official changes to the state that recognize the characteristics of other ethnic groups and incorporates them to social and political structures, rather than only recognizing the features of the dominant founding ethnic group.

Ankara but not hatred of Turks unaffiliated with the state. Several important leaders of the PKK were in fact ethnic Turks, who had joined the group due to their socialist convictions.[130] The PKK's Fifth Congress addressed this issue:

It looked at the situation of Turkish people, who are poor and under disorganized leadership, making them the close and most strategic ally of the Kurdish people. It has been decided to make efforts, as much as possible, to develop a democratic and revolutionary movement of Turkey with a variety of approaches and to support the democratic and revolutionary popular forces of Turkey more than ever before ... Furthermore, we call on the Turkish people, who suffer the most, to see the truth not to support the genocidal war, not to be deceived by the propaganda and lies of the fascist, colonialist and ruling class. To comprehend and accept the national liberation struggle that is being out [sic] by our party, and to struggle and fight alongside the Kurdish people in solidarity against the fascist regime.[131]

Next, the PKK also realized that terrorist attacks on villagers, tourist sites, and Turkish targets in Europe were a mistake, "not only risking 'a reaction against the rebels from tolerant European countries,' but reinforcing the image of the PKK as a purely terrorist organization."[132] Apparently taking a page from Palestinian strategy guides, new efforts to gain international sympathy for a mass civilian uprising were made. In 1990, Kurdish village youth for the first time "started throwing stones at security forces."[133] If the parallel to the Palestinian *intifadah* (going on at the same time) was not already apparent enough, protesting Kurdish youth in towns such as Cizre also wrapped themselves in Palestinian-style head scarves.[134] Such conscious efforts to frame their struggle along lines similar to the Palestinians' met with little success, most likely because Turkey did not permit media access to the conflict zones the way Israel does. Public opinion as a result remained largely ignorant of these demonstrations.

Also in 1990, the PKK stated that it was halting "all centrally controlled activities which could harm civilians."[135] In response to questions

---

[130] Haki Karer, Kemal Pir, and Mustafa Karasu were all ethnic Turks and members of the PKK's Central Committee leadership.

[131] Central Committee of the Kurdistan Workers' Party, February (1995).

[132] Avebury, "Turkish National Policies in the Nineties," 7.

[133] White, *Primitive Rebels or Revolutionary Modernizers?* p. 164.

[134] Ibid., p. 164. In the terminology of social movements, the Kurds borrowed from the Palestinians' "action repertoire."

[135] Imset, "The PKK: Terrorists or Freedom Fighters?" 33. According to most of the human rights sources cited in this chapter, however, the PKK's record on this issue remained less than sterling after 1990. Imset states that by 1996, however, human rights

on the issue by Washington-based writer David Korn, Abdullah Ocalan stated:

The international press and media have been manufacturing unfair and grossly distorted views about our party. The USA plays a significant role in promoting these negative views. The chief of the CIA has referred to our party as a foremost international terrorist organization. Such a portrayal of the PKK obviously does not rely on facts but on deliberate distortions. The PKK has no other role but to promote the demands of the Kurds for their own national identity and national rights, as they today face genocide. How can our resistance against this genocide be mistaken for terrorism? The chief of the CIA should understand that we are the victims of terrorism. The Republic of Turkey is a well known perpetrator of genocide and of the destruction of cultures.[136]

Spearheaded by the PKK's political and diplomatic wing, the ERNK, a new focus on gaining legitimacy as a national liberation movement and shedding the terrorist image was undertaken. This effort was considered a greater threat by Ankara than that of the guerrillas fighting in the southeast, for it might result in the international community's "recognition of legitimate ethnic and self-determination demands of the Kurdish people."[137] As part of this effort, the PKK scaled down its original goals of Kurdish statehood to autonomy within Turkey, a federal state, or even just a formally multi-cultural state that guarantees Kurdish rights. The adoption of the new name of "KADEK" in April 2002, and then "Congra-Gel" ("People's Democracy Congress") in November 2003, was also indicative of the group's attempt to move itself out of the post-September 11 terrorist camp and into the category of human-rights and pro-democracy movements. This name change paralleled the new focus on attracting greater European and international support for the movement and its goals, as the PKK's fortunes on the battlefield began to wain after the mid-1990s. The discourse of Congra-Gel in turn presented a marked shift from that of the PKK, having dropped most of its Marxist-Leninist battlefield vocabulary and replaced it with more continuous, even incessant, references to democracy. Congra-Gel's vice-president, Ramsi Kartal, offered the following introductory statement describing the new organization:

groups had noted "a dramatic decline in attacks and activities directed at non-combatants," with some noteworthy lapses, such as a 1995 attack on Hamzali village where seventeen civilians were killed and for which the PKK admitted responsibility (ibid., 37). At his trial in 1999, Abdullah Ocalan argued that terrorist attacks committed after this change in PKK policy were directed by local commanders beyond his control: "I do not approve of these attacks ... I fought very hard to stop them, but I could not" (FBIS-WEU-1999-0325, from Istanbul *Hurriyet*, March 17, 1999).

[136] *Serxwebun*, April 1995.   [137] Imset, "The PKK: Terrorists or Freedom Fighters?" 37.

After 30 years of struggle and changes in the world, we also changed. As a result of the Kurdish freedom struggle we had to leave behind the struggle based on one class and nation. We have accepted Ocalan's defence writings for the Human Rights Court as a manifesto for us. The Manifesto aims for democratic civilization and an understanding of the history of human beings. We have a new organization: The Democratic Ecological Society. When we don't clash directly with the state but disagree with them, this leads to a more democratic approach. By doing this, the basic aim is to develop a democratic mentality in the society. In the Middle East there is a reality of religious/nationalist clashes. In this perspective, Congra-Gel tries to solve their problems within the Democratic Ecological Society in a democratic manner.[138]

By making a concerted, if somewhat clumsy, effort to adopt the new catchwords of the West ("democracy," "human rights," "ecological," "freedom," etc.), Congra-Gel hopes to present itself as a progressive force worthy of Western support and acceptance. Leaders of the organization also hope that this will take their party off the various post-9/11 lists of terrorist organizations – when Europe, the United States, Canada, Australia and others placed the PKK on their lists of terrorist groups, it signaled a major framing victory for the Turkish state.

As part of this more human-rights focused grievance framing, PKK–KADEK–Congra-Gel actions by the year 2000 came to consist more of peaceful protests demanding Kurdish language education and similar minority rights. Of course, such a grievance frame fits perfectly into the European Union's norms (cultural tool kit) and requirements regarding pluralism and minority rights. Because Turkey wishes to enter the EU, it has difficulty countering such demands and was forced to begin relaxing its bans on Kurdish language and education. Whether such a change in tactics reflected a genuine shift in goals and methods or the adoption of intermediate steps on the road to independent statehood is unclear, however.

As early as 1993, however, the PKK began announcing unilateral cease-fires, offers of cease-fires and negotiations, and proposed peace plans that respected Turkey's territorial integrity. In 1998, not long before his capture and incarceration in Turkey, Ocalan presented the following seven-point peace plan:

(1) the end of (Turkish) military operations against Kurdish villages;
(2) the return of forcibly displaced Kurdish refugees to their villages;
(3) the abolition of the "village guard system";
(4) autonomy for the Kurdish region within Turkey's existing borders;

---

[138] Author's interview, April 26, 2004, Qandil Mountains, Iraq.

(5) the granting to the Kurdish people of all democratic rights enjoyed by Turks;

(6) official recognition of Kurdish identity, language and culture; and

(7) freedom of religion and pluralism.

At the same time, Ocalan stated that "We want to do as the Basques (in Spain) and the IRA. We ask for greater autonomy and freedom, respect for our language and culture, and democracy like in the rest of Europe."[139] He also reiterated a pledge "to renounce terrorism and violence."[140] In fact, after being asked by his Syrian hosts to leave, Ocalan sought to bring the Kurdish case to The Hague. He accepted to be tried there by the International Court of Justice, in order to also bring international scrutiny upon Turkey's treatment of the Kurds. Semsi Kilic, a top-ranking ERNK representative, stated that:

The latest talks, the latest views of our leader was to transform the PKK, to transform the National Liberation Struggle in Kurdistan, in all its greatness, with all its power into a political movement. All of his efforts were in this direction. This last trip was going to be to Holland, he was going to the court at Hague and with a great trial, expose the Turkish State, expose the crimes of the Turkish State, even though he knew that this trip might very well be the last leg that concluded the international conspiracy. He had messages to Germany. He wanted the German government to stop its 15 year old criminalization policy toward our people. He wanted Europe to see that European efforts to label and prosecute the PKK as a terrorist group was at the bottom [of the violence] ... Our leader was ready for such a court, for such a judicial processes because he believed that with it, all truths would come out. He surely was ready for this.[141]

Of course, the trial that Ocalan received in Turkey did not proceed in a manner that would question the actions of the Turkish state. PKK efforts to frame their movement as a political, humanistic national liberation struggle do not seem to have met with great success outside the domestic and diaspora Kurdish communities. Such efforts continue, while armed actions inside Turkey have decreased to the point that Turkish generals are claiming success in the war.

Armed attacks are not the only way to advance one's objectives, however. In its attempt to change its image and garner international support, the PKK turned to the new battlefield of news media. New media

[139] Public Relations Office of the Center for Kurdish Political Studies, "Abdullah Ocalan proposes 7-point peace plan," (November 26–27,1998).

[140] Ibid.

[141] Undated ERNK document, "The following is a statement by Semsi Kilic, one of ERNK's European Representatives, which was delivered to MED-TV regarding the kidnapping of the PKK Chairman Abdullah Ocalan from Kenya," acquired from the Toronto Kurdish Community Cultural Center, Canada.

technologies outside the state's control turned out to be particularly helpful in this regard, and may have watered the seeds of enduring Kurdish disaffection in Turkey. Especially because of their lack of access to mainstream media in Turkey, Kurdish nationalists in general had to turn to alternative media outlets. This issue will now be addressed.

State media, information monopolies, and insurgent media

This particular category in McAdam, McCarthy, and Zald's social movement literature on cultural framing may be more useful in liberal democratic contexts where the media are more independent of the state. In places such as Saddam Hussein's Iraq, where the media acted as a mouthpiece of the state, their role is more usefully subsumed under the heading of "state framing efforts." Likewise, where underground media are completely controlled by an insurgent group, such media are part of that group's framing efforts rather a mediator of frame contests.

In the case of Turkey, the media often do criticize the state, but on issues relating to Kurds and Islam the media in Turkey have little leeway or freedom. When the occasional print article, television or radio broadcast did contradict state framings of the issue, the source of the contradiction was generally punished or closed down.[142] It should be recalled that the Turkish state until very recently forbade, through "anti-terror" articles of the 1982 Constitution, any actions that directly or indirectly, intentionally or unintentionally, sought to change "the characteristics of the Turkish Republic specified in the Constitution, its political, legal, social, secular and economic regime, to weaken the indivisible integrity of the State territory and nation ..."[143] Although efforts to meet European Union membership criteria during the last few years have led to changes in the Constitution and the anti-terror law, much progress still needs to be made. If the media fail to engage in self-censorship, the state can still employ a host of legal provisions to make sure that only cultural frames that it approves of consistently reach the public via the media. These provisions include:

---

[142] For instance, in May 1999 well known Turkish journalist Oral Calislar of the *Cumhuriyet* daily was jailed for conducting an interview with Abdullah Ocalan. Calislar stated that "This is like sentencing journalism itself, it's not even about freedom of expression but about a journalist doing his job" (Reuters, "Turkey sentences journalist over Ocalan interview," May 18, 1999).

[143] "The New Turkish 'Anti-Terrorism' Law," Article 1, *Information and Liaison Bulletin*, Kurdish Institute of Paris 74–75 (May–June 1991).

Penal Code Articles 312 (incitement to racial, ethnic, or religious enmity); 159 (insulting Parliament, the army, republic, or judiciary); 160 (insulting the Turkish Republic); 169 (aiding an illegal organization); the Law to Protect Ataturk; and over 150 articles of the Press Law (including a provision against commenting on ongoing trials). While prosecutors bring dozens of such cases to court each year, judges dismiss many charges brought under these laws. These cases constitute a form of harassment against writers, journalists, and political figures.[144]

In the powerful realm of television and radio, Turkey's Supreme Board of Radio and Television (RTUK) ensures that broadcasts conform to the limits set by the state. In addition to the forbidden acts described above, the RTUK could penalize broadcasters for offensive language, libel, obscenity, or, until very recently, broadcasting programs in Kurdish (the last item actually falls under the above heading of "separatist propaganda" and "incitement to racial and ethnic enmity" rather than "offensive language"). In 2000, "the Government provided RTUK closure figures of 62 television stations closed for 704 days, and 67 radio stations closed for 3,889 days."[145]

In short, the legal media in Turkey cannot be truly described as "mediating frame contests" *vis-à-vis* the Kurdish issue. Instead, such media is more often a vehicle of state framing efforts, including programs such as "Mehmetcik," which follows the daily lives of ordinary soldiers enduring harsh terrain and weather while combating Kurdish terrorists. The message is that the state, through average self-sacrificing patriots, fights night and day to protect the people. Other shows pursue similar framings, such as those produced by Erturk Yondem, one of which revolves around the remorseful confessions of repentant terrorists in prison. During the 1999 trial of Ocalan, mainstream media in Turkey displayed a shocking attachment to state grievance frames, ceaselessly running images of PKK-butchered women and children and never failing to attach the phrase "baby-killer" to Ocalan's name any time it was mentioned. Grieving families whose soldier sons were killed fighting the PKK were shown night and day on television. No grieving Kurdish mothers who had lost children in the PKK were shown, nor were victims of state repression ever even discussed.[146] The responsibility for roughly 30,000 deaths (this was the figure always referred to in the media at the time) since the PKK

---

[144] "Turkey: Country Reports on Human Rights Practices – 2000," US Department of State (February 2001), p. 22.

[145] Ibid., p. 23.

[146] On May 29, 1999, I happened across a Turkish friend on a street in Ankara who works for one of the major Turkish news networks. When I asked her about this lack of coverage of "the other side's" point of view, she expressed surprise, stating that as far as she knew, it had never occurred to anyone at her news station to provide any coverage of those who had suffered at the hands of state security forces.

insurgency began in 1984 was attributed solely to Ocalan, as if his organization had killed 30,000 people on its own and the state had killed no one. After the media had whipped up Turkish public opinion to such a frenzy, there would have been riots in the street had the court trying Ocalan sentenced him to anything other than death.[147] Another example of mainstream Turkish media's approach to the issue is described by Andrew Mango:

> In May 1994, Turkish ambassadors accredited to European countries and to the United States gathered in Ankara to discuss their country's response to accusations that it was oppressing its Kurdish citizens. After their meeting, they traveled east to study the situation on the spot. As they went for a walk in the town of Van, in the company of the regional governor in charge of provinces where a state of emergency had been declared, and also the regional director of general security, an unnamed private citizen was reported as saying to the Turkish ambassador in Germany, "Tell the Europeans to stop making distinctions between Kurds and Turks. There is no Kurdish-Turkish problem here. There is a problem of the Armenian [-supported] PKK. European backing has brought it on." The Istanbul daily *Milliyet* published this report under the headline "Europe Created the Problem."[148]

Occasionally, legally permitted programs unrelated to the Kurdish issue provide framings contradictory to that of the state. The film *Braveheart* reverberated strongly in Kurdish circles, with its depiction of Scottish resistance against a more powerful English colonizer (showing of the film was subsequently banned in the Kurdish parts of Turkey). Another example is the television series, *Belena*, which also had an unforeseen effect. The show was about the plight of the Turkish minority in Bulgaria, and the parallels to the Kurdish issue are described by Besikci:

> The "Belena" series shows that Bulgarian soldiers and police force frequently organised raids on Turkish villages. Raids on villages, mass searches are the events that take place, that are experienced every day in Kurdistan ... The Belena series emphasized that the Turks' properties were confiscated by the Bulgarians. Soldiers, special teams and village guards can confiscate the properties of the Kurds at will. It is frequently claimed that the Turks' names were replaced by Bulgarian names. Banning Kurdish names for the newly born, replacing the Kurdish names of villages with Turkish names are important dimensions of the Turkish state policy ... Kurdish people have understood the following fact too:

---

[147] For fear of creating a martyr as well as hurting their European Union candidacy, Turkish authorities never carried out the death sentence Ocalan received in July 1999. In November 2003, Turkey abolished the death penalty as part of its European reform efforts.

[148] Mango, "Turks and Kurds," 975.

When it comes to the Turks in Bulgaria, the Turkish statesmen and politicians, Turkish press, Turkish political parties, Turkish unions, the Turkish Bar Association etc. get closely involved. And when it comes to the Kurds they pretend to have never seen them, never heard of them.[149]

Finally, legally permitted Turkish films dealing with non-political issues, but set in the lesser-developed southeast of the country, indirectly affect the cultural framing contest between Kurdish nationalists and the state, as the difficult lives of Turkey's Kurdish citizens play themselves out on cinema and television screens. Since the mid-1990s, Turkish state regulatory bodies have allowed such films a little more leeway in how they address issues relating to the southeast.

Perhaps the most promising area of inquiry concerning the media's role in developing countries, however, centers around new communications technology, access to which can challenge the state's monopoly of information and ability to frame issues on a mass level. For the Kurds, access to such technology has provided an opportunity to engage in cultural framings aimed at the entire Kurdish population (including that of neighboring Iraq, Iran, Syria, and the diaspora in Europe) as well as international opinion.

Access to modern communications technology can take many forms. For instance, clandestine photographs or videos of state oppression help frame grievances in dramatic terms, serving to politicize, mobilize, and unite opposition movements. In a globalized world, such documented evidence of state repression is also used to garner support from others, such as populations and states friendly to the movement, human rights groups, international tribunals, and other NGOs. Most importantly, state monopolies on information and its distribution are broken. Like the Turkish media's *Bloodshed in Anatolia*, Kurdish and pro-PKK groups also published their own books and articles with accusations and photos of Turkish military atrocities committed on Kurds – one of the more well known of which depicts a photo of Turkish soldiers smilingly holding up the decapitated heads of Kurdish guerrillas.[150] Desktop publishing technology, scanners, the Internet, and faxes have all facilitated the reproduction and distribution of such photos. In Kurdish-controlled northern Iraq, videotapes documenting Iraqi torture and executions of Kurds were captured from Iraqi security buildings during the post-Gulf War

---

[149] Besikci, *Kurdistan and Turkish Colonialism*, pp. 10–11.
[150] This and other examples of Kurdish grievance framing can be viewed at the website of AKIN, the American Kurdish Information Network: http://kurdistan.org/Multimedia/index.html.

uprising.[151] One of the most popular video rentals there is *Saddam's Crimes*, and as one Kurdish shop owner explained, "Some people may sleep through *Rambo*, but if you ask them about any part of *Saddam's Crimes* they can recall every point in detail."[152] Such videos also reach Kurdish populations in Turkey, serving to highlight the fact that Kurds everywhere are persecuted for who they are. Captured local Iraqi television stations in the region have since 1991 been used by Iraqi Kurds to broadcast programs dealing with previously forbidden topics and to "acknowledge once-banned histories and heroes."[153] Such broadcasts reach nearby Kurdish communities in Turkey, providing them with the example of what Kurds can discuss when they are free of government censure. Using newly available and relatively inexpensive video camcorders, the PKK also produced videos of its raids on Turkish positions as well as other footage glorifying the guerrillas and the life they lead.

The Kurdish diaspora community in particular has taken full advantage of these new communications technologies to propagate a specifically Kurdish view of the world and important events. Desktop and electronic publishing have been wielded from Europe to counter restrictions on the Kurdish language and the cultural framings of states such as Turkey: ". . . Kurdish writers living in exile have made a key contribution to the development of a standardized written Kurmanci, as well as an extensive literature. Many Kurmanci texts originally published in Sweden and France, ranging from grammars and dictionaries to novels and journalistic work, have subsequently been republished in Turkey."[154] In addition to the older printing presses operated from outside the Kurdish arena of conflict, desktop publishing and other modern communications technology (described below) are now playing a big role in strengthening the Kurdish "imagined community." Although this is occurring more than one hundred years after Benedict Anderson's mass newspapers spread nationalist identification throughout Europe and the Americas, the rate of increase in Kurdish nationalist identification may be far greater than that of the cases Anderson examined.[155]

Pro-Kurdish newspapers such as *Ozgur Politika*, which is banned in Turkey, are also published in Europe and smuggled back to the Kurdish regions. Additionally, *Ozgur Politika* and other "subversive" texts are available in a new format, directly accessible from the Kurdish

---

[151] Marcus, "City in the War Zone," 21.   [152] Ibid.   [153] Ibid.
[154] Michiel Leezenberg, "The Kurds and the City," *The Journal of Kurdish Studies* 2 (1997), 62.
[155] I derive this hypothesis from the general rate at which flows of information and communication related to the Kurds and their language appears to be exponentially growing. As a facet of globalization, the pace of change and growth increases every year.

regions: the Internet. Before 1995, the number of Kurdish websites numbered under twenty, whereas in January of 2001 an *AltaVista* keyword search of "Kurd" done by the author drew 29,463 references; of the first one hundred, seventy-five referred to either news articles on the Kurds or Kurdish websites. The same search discovered 23,972 references to Web pages related to the Kurdish issue. Sites such as "kurd.com" and "kurdish.com" both contain hundreds of links to other Kurdish sites, with content available in English, French, German, Turkish, and the Kurdish dialects of Kurmanji, Sorani, and Zaza, among others.[156] According to the US State Department, "Internet use is growing and faces no government restrictions; in fact, some banned newspapers can be accessed freely on the Internet."[157]

E-mail has also begun to serve as an inexpensive, difficult to regulate, widely accessible medium for exchanging ideas, disseminating information, and organizing Kurdish projects globally.[158] The Internet thus provides a forum for discussions and arguments on "forbidden" subjects.[159] Internet and E-mail can sometimes be easier to access than older forms

---

[156] Kurdish groups such as the PKK–KADEK–Congra-Gel, PUK, KDP, KOMALA, and KDPI have all established numerous websites, in addition to the existing sites dealing with Kurdish culture, music, language, and history. In September 1997, the author discussed the existence of Kurdish Internet sites with a group of four Kurds working in an Ankara restaurant. All four had recently immigrated to Ankara from destroyed or impoverished villages in Turkey's Kurdish region, and only one of them had heard of the Internet at all. By connecting his laptop computer to the restaurant phone line, the author was able to connect to a server in Istanbul and proceeded to show the four a handful of Kurdish websites. All four Kurds were completely stunned that such sites could exist and remain beyond the reach of Turkish censors. One said, "I like this Internet. Do you need a computer to use the Internet?" When informed that a computer was indeed necessary, all four immediately began to discuss the prices of computers, the hardware necessary to use the Internet, and whether or not the author could return the following day to show them more sites. The discussion was accompanied by many worried glances towards the entrance of the restaurant.

[157] "Turkey: Country Reports on Human Rights Practices – 2000," February (2001).

[158] E-mail also serves as an inexpensive, difficult to safeguard and very useful source for government surveillance efforts.

[159] Conflicts fought in the domain of the Internet have sometimes gone to absurd lengths: in the wake of Abdullah Ocalan's capture, *Time Daily* ran an online poll asking "Should the United Nations support the creation of a Kurdish state?" The poll engendered a vociferous reaction:

TIME Daily writers were awash in form-letter hate [e-]mail with subject lines like "I am protesting you" and "demand for your apologize" – and the poll was under assault . . . The assault came from a Turkish university, and students were armed with a CPU to match TIME Daily's – the university's powerful server. The bots were identified and blocked by the IP and cookie-based defences, but they churned out so many voting attempts that defending against them overwhelmed TIME Daily's own server. ("When robots attack online polls: a report on ourselves," [February 26, 1999], http://members. xoom.com/ . . . h-university-protest.htm).

of communication such as print media, as exemplified by Arm The Spirit, a Canadian anti-imperialist organization that disseminates information about the Kurds and other issues:

A member of Arm The Spirit stated that the group started the KURD-L news list back in 1995 at a time when there were very few leftist or Kurdish groups active on the Internet, and that the interest shown in the list by Kurds and their supporters in countries all across the world has inspired them to continue their Kurdistan solidarity work. When publishing a printed magazine became too expensive for the group, the Internet provided a much cheaper means of reaching many people, even in places far away.[160]

Kurds in the diaspora and their supporters have thus found the Internet to be an inexpensive and extremely useful means of communicating and organizing amongst themselves, as well as informing others of the Kurdish issue. Political discussions held in cyberspace have become quite popular among Kurds. For the majority of Kurds still residing in Turkey and the rest of the Middle East, however, Internet resources are generally not as readily available. Discussions, news, and other information garnered from the Internet make their way back to Middle Eastern communities in indirect ways, such as by word of mouth or documents smuggled into the region.

Another form of communication originating from the diaspora Kurdish community has, however, had a dramatic impact on the "homeland" community: in 1994, by establishing MED-TV, a Kurdish satellite station based in London and Belgium, the Kurds became the world's first stateless "television nation."[161] The station's principal founder was a Kurd from Turkey, Hikmet Tabak:

Tabak fled his home on the Turkish/Armenian border in 1992. The UK granted him political asylum. He and 20 others launched MED-TV back in 1994 . . . They had just £5,000 in the bank. A poet, author and film maker, Tabak was one of the few with any experience of making programmes. None of the founders had any knowledge of how to run a satellite station; Kurdish TV journalists and directors are not that common. "But we saw our society slowly disappearing and knew we had to do something to stop this decline," he says. So they called British Telecom for advice . . .[162]

---

[160] "Kurdish Liberation on the Internet," February 3, 1998, akin@kurdish.org.
[161] Amir Hassanpour adds: "The launching of a daily satellite TV channel, MED-TV, by the Kurdish community in Europe is the first case of the access of stateless nations and minorities to transnational television" (Amir Hassanpour, "MED-TV, Britain, and the Turkish State: A Stateless Nation's Quest for Sovereignty in the Sky," paper presented at the Freie Universität Berlin, November 7 [1995]).
[162] Nick Ryan, "Television Nation," *Wired Magazine* (1997), 45.

MED-TV gave the Kurds a tool with which to counter the disproportionate power that states such as Turkey wield in the realm of
information:

The launching of the first Kurdish satellite television channel, MED-TV, opened
a new site of conflict between the Kurds and the Middle Eastern states that rule
over Kurdistan. After more than 30 years of military engagement between the
Kurdish people and the states of Iraq, Iran and Turkey, signals from the sky
changed the theater of war in favor of the Kurds. Transcending the international
borders which since 1918 have divided the land in which Kurds live, the channel
allowed the Kurds, for the first time in their history, to establish a powerful mode
of communication among themselves, and undermine the state-centered geo-
political order that has reduced them to the status of helpless minorities ...
[T]he Kurds feel that they have achieved sovereignty in the sky, i.e. a "great
historical leap" towards self-rule in their homeland.[163]

Ryan adds that "For the first time in their divided history, the Kurdish
people can now see their own lives, their own reality, reflected on television screens across the world. Iranian Kurds can speak to Turkish
Kurds in phone-ins, and Iraqi Kurds can see how fellow Kurds live in
Europe. For a few hours every night, the world's largest stateless nation
has a home."[164]

MED-TV, probably more than any other factor, served to promote
ethnic consciousness amongst Kurds today. MED-TV broadcasts
quickly became the most popular programs in the Kurdish world. Many
towns in southeastern Turkey have in turn seen a great proliferation of
visible satellite dishes on the roofs of buildings since 1995.[165] Local
residents in Diyarbakir (the largest predominantly Kurdish city, located
in southeastern Turkey) and throughout Kurdistan assured this author
that "everyone watches MED-TV; if they don't have a satellite dish, they
go to the home of someone who does or to a cafe that has it."[166] "Peasant

---

[163] Amir Hassanpour, "Satellite Footprints at National Borders: MED-TV and the
Extraterritoriality of Sovereignty," *Journal of Muslim Minority Affairs*, 18: 1 (April
1998), 53.

[164] Ryan, "Television Nation," 44–45.

[165] Personal observation of the author after several visits to the region in the summer of
1994, 1997–1998, and the summer of 1999.

[166] By 1998, the author's Turkish was fluent enough to pursue in-depth conversations with
Kurds in Turkish Kurdistan. In Iraqi, Iranian, and Syrian Kurdistan, conversations were
either held in English, French, or Turkish, or translated to one of these languages for the
author's benefit. Conversations were held with local children, shop owners, labourers,
farmers, shepherds, professionals, students, and members and officials of Kurdish
parties in Iraq (mainly the KDP and PUK). Visits to Iraqi Kurdistan were made in
July 1994 and September–October 2000, to Iranian Kurdistan in July 1999 and
September–October 2000, and to Syrian Kurdistan in June–July 1998. Every single
person with whom the author spoke who identified themselves as Kurdish, when asked

families in Kurdistan have even been known to sell cars and whole herds of goats to buy a satellite dish – often at considerable risk from local security forces."[167] The Turkish government itself estimated that around 90 percent of people in the Kurdish region of Turkey watch the channel: "It is watched even by 'village guards' hired by the government to fight PKK; also, the refugees of the war who relocate 'in shanties in western towns invest in satellite dishes to see it.' "[168]

Programming on MED-TV ran the gamut from a plethora of news and political programs to children's shows, music, drama, and documentaries, mostly in Kurmanji Kurdish, but also in Sorani, Turkish, Zaza, Persian, Aramaic, and Arabic. MED-TV not only defied Turkish law by broadcasting in Kurdish, it also challenged official government interpretations and framing of events and political issues, by providing its own differing news coverage and political discussion programs. These programs often addressed taboo subjects, such as Kurdish claims for self-determination. The impact of such a development should not be underestimated: "As an audiovisual medium, television is more effective than radio and print

about MED-TV, confirmed that it was the favorite television viewing of Kurds. This was in spite of the explosion of private cable television stations in Turkey offering a wide variety of programming. A PUK official in Turkey added that this also held true for those Kurds in Iraq, Iran, and Syria who could access the channel (interview with the author, March 5, 1999). Despite the fact that MED-TV was generally seen as being associated with the PKK, which was often at odds with the PUK, KDP, and others, the official conceded that it was his favorite channel as well.

[167] Ryan, "Television Nation," 46. Amir Hassanpour, "Satellite Footprints as National Borders: MED-TV and the Extraterritoriality of State Sovereignty," *Journal of Muslim Minority Affairs* 18: 1 (April, 1998), 53–72 provides details of the risks viewers face:

Throughout the Kurdish provinces, the police and the gendarmerie destroyed the receiving equipment. For instance, in Eruh (Batman), the army banned the sale of dishes and warned the public not to buy them ... When MED-TV announced the forthcoming broadcasting of the "Kurdistan parliament in exile" (April 12, 1995), the police raided coffee-houses which had satellite dishes, arrested the viewers and destroyed the receiving equipment. The Kurdish newspaper *Yeni Politika*, now banned in Turkey, published reports of the arrest and torture of viewers (see, for example, reports in *Yeni Politika* in May 1995, especially on May 11, 1995). "In spite of repression, one shop sold about 150 dishes a week. A Kurdish technician whose shop was raided by the police said that dish installers in Kurdish areas face repression. Fearing to speak on camera, he said that he installed 15 dishes every evening under the cover of darkness." ("Satellite Footprints as National Borders," p. 70)

Hassanpour takes his last quotation from *Beating the Censor, A Frontline* News report produced by Tony Smith and Tim Exton aired on Sweden's Channel 1, September 25, 1995). MED-TV itself has been raided by police at its Belgian, British, and German offices (no incriminating items were found) and some of its staff attacked by unknown assailants (Ryan, "Television Nation," 92).

[168] Amir Hassanpour, "Satellite Footprints as National Borders," 70 (quoted from *Turkish Daily News*, "Turkey said to be considering allowing Kurdish broadcasts," June 2, 1996).

media. Televisual images generally cross the social boundaries of illiteracy, language, regionalism, age, gender, and religion. Combining visuality with sound and language, both spoken and written, television is a powerful vehicle for creating national culture and identity."[169] MED-TV publicized declarations of the PKK, such as Ocalan's cease-fire offer in 1993 and subsequent years. It showed footage of the guerrillas in action, often romanticizing the scenes with inspirational music. During political discussions, representatives from Kurdish opposition groups all over the world came in and debated "national" issues, and viewers call in from even the most remote areas of Kurdistan to add their opinions to the show.[170] Hikmet Tabak insisted in 1997 that, "If we have a political program, we try and bring representatives from all sides, even if it's expensive."[171]

If the Turkish state had permitted the Kurds to have media in their own language, a station such as MED-TV could have emerged under the supervision and control of Turkey. As it happens, Kurdish intellectuals had no other option but to found their own independent media in Europe, with the advantage of a great deal more freedom of expression. The Turkish state was, in fact, very aware of MED-TV's role in promoting Kurdish nationalism, and sought to stifle the nascent station.[172] Satellite dishes were smashed by security forces in southeast Turkey and the owners were harassed. Several Turkish diplomatic initiatives also focused on trying to get the station's license revoked in Britain and Belgium; previous satellite providers such as France Telecom were successfully pressured not to renew MED-TV's license.[173] Turkey also pressured the private sector to not deal with MED-TV, with the result

---

[169] Ibid., 53.

[170] Many of the callers from rural areas were not used to the idea of speaking on live television or radio, leading to occasionally humorous situations when they used inappropriate language and strong expletives to reinforce their statements (Ryan, "Television Nation," 91).

[171] Ibid., 88.

[172] Amir Hassanpour stated that,

> ... it is clear that every second of MED-TV's broadcasting seriously undermines Turkish sovereign rule. The logo "MED-TV", which is always present in the upper left corner of the screen, is an assertion of Kurdishness (the Kurds are Medes not Turks). It also asserts Kurdish rights to statehood. The logo's colours of red, yellow and green are the colours of the Kurdish flag; moreover, the flag itself appears frequently in the programming, ranging from news and information to entertainment and culture. The daily menu begins with a grand orchestra performing the Kurdish national anthem, *Ey Requib* (O Enemy!). The ever presence of the Kurdish national flag and anthem means that MED-TV has the power to treat the Kurds not as an audience but as citizens of a Kurdish state. (Hassanpour, "Satellite Footprints at National Borders," 59)

[173] Ibid.

that many banks, legal firms, and other businesses refuse to do business with the Kurdish station, for fear of being denied Turkish contracts.[174]

On April 23, 1999 MED-TV's license was revoked by Britain's ITC – Independent Television Commission. The ITC finally accepted Turkish charges that MED-TV broadcasts were inciting Kurds in Turkey to violence, and gave the following explanation for the station's closure: "Whatever sympathy there may be in the United Kingdom for the Kurdish people, it is not in the public interest to have any broadcaster use the United Kingdom as a platform which incites people to violence."[175] By July 1999, a "new" Kurdish satellite station obtained a license in France. Named "MEDYA-TV," the station was generally perceived as the heir to MED-TV, run by many of the same people and confounding Turkey's efforts to silence an independent Kurdish media. The main production studio of MED-TV, located in Deenderleux (Belgium), simply became the main production studio of MEDYA-TV. Its corridors still hummed with the sounds of Turkish, Arabic, Persian, English, French, Flemish, and all the different Kurdish dialects, as the most pressing issues facing the Kurdish nation enjoyed lively debate.[176] Four years later, French authorities determined that MEDYA-TV was indeed the successor to MED-TV. In February 2004, the CSA (the French Licensing Authority) therefore closed MEDYA-TV down just as the British had closed MED-TV in 1999. By March 2004, another new Kurdish satellite station operating out of Denmark, ROJ-TV, sprang up. ROJ-TV operates from the same "Hotbird 6, 13 grade East" as its predecessor and offers a similar list of programming. Other satellite and regular television stations have now also begun running Kurdish language broadcasts, such as CTV, a British cultural television station that devotes several hours a day to Kurdish cultural programming on its satellite waves. Hence it seems that efforts to prevent Kurdish cultural framings have only multiplied their voices.

Although most observers felt that MED-TV/MEDYA-TV was pro-PKK, Turkish efforts to prove that the station was linked to, or a mouthpiece for the organization, have failed. One of MED-TV's founders, while admitting to the author that at times the station failed to meet western criteria of objectivity, insisted that MED-TV was nonetheless much more objective and open to differing viewpoints than Turkish or other Middle

[174] Amir Hassanpour, "Language Rights in the Emerging World Linguistic Order: The State, the Market and the Communication Technologies," *Language: A Right and a Resource* (Budapest: CEU Press, 1998), p. 233.

[175] "British Revoke Kurd TV License," AP, April 23 (1999).

[176] Author's visit to MEDYA-TV Deenderleux studio, July 12, 2002.

Eastern television networks.[177] Turkish government officials and pro-state individuals were often invited to take part in MED-TV talk shows, although only a few of the latter accepted the invitation. Also, he argued that the station was undergoing natural "growing pains" and improving its degree of objective professionalism daily.

Turkey's efforts to silence MED-TV did not end on the European diplomatic front, however. Maintaining that MED-TV was a "mouthpiece for the terrorist PKK," Turkey in 1997 began aiding the Iraqi KDP to launch its own "KTV" television, an "anti-PKK TV station." Ilnur Cevik, editor of the *Turkish Daily News*, was "one of the Turkish planners behind KTV":

The Barzani administration (KDP) made a decision on the television project two years ago. They realized that MED-TV was hurting them. Their goal was psychological. The KDP sees the PKK as a rival in its region. It sees the PKK as a serious threat. They were upset that the PKK entered northern Iraq and established a presence in three traditionally KDP areas. They were concerned that the PKK wants to become the leader of the Kurds in those areas and leapfrog ahead of them.[178]

Hence the Turkish government unofficially conceded that if it could not stop Kurdish satellite broadcasting, it may as well "fight fire with fire." Ankara therefore decided to try and promote Kurdish framings that competed with the pro-PKK Kurdish framings presented by MED-TV. Since the Iraqi Kurdish KDP was allied with Turkey, it could be used to present material that cast the Turkish state in a more positive light. MED-TV co-founder Hikmet Tabak, however, actually expressed pleasure with such a development, stating that "No matter what they [anti-MED-TV stations such as KTV] say, as long as it is in Kurdish, good. The Turks are breaking their own rules by allowing this."[179] His argument was that no matter what the actual message, the fact that the medium was in Kurdish added to the unsustainability of Ankara's ban on the language.

In any case, what seems clear is that Kurdish means of presenting their own framings of issues are increasing, largely due to communications

[177] Interview with Hikmet Tabak, August 27, 1999, Paris.
[178] *Arm the Spirit*, Feb. 22, 1999, translated from *Kurdistan-Rundbrief* #3/99, Feb. 10, 1999. KDP officials deny that KTV was established as an anti-PKK station, however. They state that the purpose of the station is simply to give a voice to Iraqi Kurdistan, its people, its reality, and its culture (author's interview with KDP Ankara representative Safeen Dizayee, June 11, 1999). Events also seem to vindicate the KDP's position on the issue, since KTV was still broadcasting at the time of this writing, while MED-TV, MEDYA-TV, and the PKK have all disappeared or morphed into new entities.
[179] Interview with Hikmet Tabak, August 27, 1999, Paris.

technology advances. Shortly after the author's interview with their Ankara representative, the PUK launched its own satellite television station, "Kurd-Sat," from Suleimaniya (Iraqi Kurdistan). In terms of cultural framing, "The good old days when smashing the printing press meant the end of radical agitation are long gone ... borders are leaky, smugglers adaptive, and popular interest and demand for media technologies generally high."[180] The communications technologies described above signal an increasing "deterritorialization of politics," wherein "Exiled political activists no longer wait for events to change so that they can return home, but instead propagandize to change conditions from outside their country ..."[181] The final section of this chapter will now address the cultural impact of the PKK as a social movement, although such an impact is part of, and impossible to disentangle from, the impact of media such as MED-TV.

The cultural impact of the PKK insurgency

If there is one thing that every observer of the conflict, be they Turkish generals, Kurdish peasants, or western academics, generally agree on, it is that the PKK succeeded in bringing the Kurdish issue back into the limelight of public discourse in Turkey. After the last rebellions of the

---

[180] Mohammadi and Sreberny-Mohammadi, *Small Media, Big Revolurtion*, p. 27. The reader should consult Mohammadi and Sreberny-Mohammadi *Small Media, Big Revolution*, for a very interesting account of new and old communications technologies' role in the Iranian revolution.

[181] Ibid., p. 29. I must stress again, however, that the extent to which Kurdish media are tied to various opposition movements opposing Turkey, and the degree to which "legal" media in Turkey are controlled by the state, puts into question the utility of a separate analytical category of "the media's structure and role in mediating frame contests." Both could be easily subsumed under the headings of state and insurgent framing efforts. This is particularly true if we remember that neither the state nor insurgent groups are monolithic entities.

Western media, although generally state-centric, may play a more ambiguous role that warrants such a category (unless, of course, you are a Marxist). The relative lack of attention that such media have given to the Kurdish issue (especially when compared to the Palestinian issue), however, means that apart from human rights questions such media are not an important vehicle of cultural framing for Kurds and Turks. If we consider the possibility that western media have largely ignored the Kurdish issue because most western states in which such media are based are hostile to Kurdish effort towards self-determination, however, then the role of the media has been to support states such as Turkey. Such a perspective might have some degree of merit, especially when one compares the amount of attention Iraqi Kurds received before the Gulf War to after Saddam Hussein became an enemy of the West. Likewise, recent European media attention on Turkish Kurds might well be linked to Turkey's European Union candidacy. A compelling examination of such questions, however, could easily fill the pages of another book.

1930s, even the word "Kurdish" had become taboo in the realm of public discourse. Although everyone knew that a Kurdish minority existed in the country, it was not to be openly spoken of.[182] Instead, their quiet assimilation was to be pursued until the job was finished and everyone was "happy to be a Turk." The PKK changed all that, by forcefully bringing the issue to the front and center of public attention. A people cannot be ignored when armed militants claiming to represent them stage attacks on representatives of the state.[183]

Hence, most people credit the PKK for forcing the government to repeal the official ban on the Kurdish language in 1991. Ankara's often repeated intent to improve the southeast's poor economic and social situation, which in the government's view breeds violence and terrorism, is also seen as stemming from the PKK's challenge. As stated earlier, the movement went a long way towards negating a Kurdish psychology of impotence, the colonized mentality that views the colonizer as invincible.[184] Once such a mentality is broken, it is impossible to go back to the way things were before. Even if the government succeeds in completely destroying the PKK's new KADEK, Congra-Gel, or other manifestations militarily, the example that a credible and forceful challenge to the state created in people's minds will remain, and another group may emerge to pick up where the PKK left off. Particularly in an era of global communication, PKK or other militants in Turkey may put down their guns but continue to broadcast cultural framings critical of the state from Europe or elsewhere. This is particularly true if Ankara fails to address the grievances that the PKK helped create and solidify in the Kurdish masses' minds during its insurgency.

In this sense, the PKK has altered the cultural tool kit of Kurds in Turkey. In addition to increasing the number of people who identified themselves as Kurds, and in many cases politicizing such an identity, the

---

[182] In private discourse, however, it is doubtful that anyone ever ceased speaking of the Kurds in Turkey, even during the "quiet" years of the 1940s and 1950s.

[183] It was Francis Fanon who wrote: "The native intellectual nevertheless sooner or later will realize that you do not show proof of your nation from its culture but that you substantiate its existence in the fight which the people wage against the forces of occupation" (Fanon, *The Wretched of the Earth*, p. 223).

[184] Jacqueline Sammali, summarizing the results of her interviews conducted in the Kurdish regions of Turkey, has also concluded that the PKK's fight with Ankara succeeded in removing average Kurds' sense of shame in their ethnic identity, restoring a sense of pride to being Kurdish (Jacqueline Sammali, *Etre Kurde, un délit?* p. 254). Kurds unhappy with Ankara began to take pride in the guerrilla actions, no longer viewing themselves as helpless victims. Others who did not consider themselves Kurdish, or who only identified themselves as Kurdish in a private sense, in some cases began to adopt a politicized Kurdish identity, now that they could take pride in an identity group resisting oppression.

PKK provided a vehicle for individuals to express their identity. Because most expressions of Kurdish identity in Turkey have been constrained for so long, joining the movement, supporting it, or simply participating in mass protests could function as a form of catharsis for a frustrated populace.[185] Many Kurds even came to identify so much with the larger Kurdish nation, or in Anderson's parlance the "imagined community," that they value the well-being and status of the group more than their own lives as individuals.[186] Given such changes in attitudes, Ankara's attempts at solving the problem solely through programs of socio-economic development would come too late. The PKK's insurgency has already changed the values and goals of too many Kurds – one need only think of Horowitz's observation that in situations of ethnic strife, symbols of ethnic inclusion and exclusion are more a source of conflict than economic competition.[187] This, of course, contradicts the conclusions that an analysis based on rational choice and resource mobilization would lead us to. In an analysis where people's motivations are assumed to revolve mainly around self-interest and economics, socio-economic palliatives might reasonably be expected to address their demands.

Can we reasonably assume, however, that the PKK insurgency (or perhaps related phenomena such as Kurdish media's coverage of the insurgency and Kurdish issues in general) has had a cultural impact, creating a situation wherein demands regarding the status of Kurds as a group are widely viewed as both legitimate and worth mobilizing for, even in the face of repression? Towards the end of chapter 3, McDowall and Besikci's observations of Kurdish "burgeoning civil resistance"[188] and spontaneous, mass shows of affection for the guerrilla movement[189] were discussed. Journalists such as Aliza Marcus or Stephen Kinzer observed as late as 1999 that "It is difficult to find any [Kurds in Turkey's south-east] who do not support the nationalist cause and even the armed

---

[185] For instance, Kendal Nezan states: "That silenced Kurdish populations and groups will seek to express themselves if given the chance seems obvious. In Iraq, after the Kurdish north was freed of Saddam Hussein's control in 1991, more than four Kurdish television channels and forty-two newspapers and magazines have sprung up, despite the embargo and the meagre resources available in the area." (Philip Kreyenbroek and Christine Allison [eds.], "Introduction," *Kurdish Culture and Identity*, p. 17)

[186] For an identity-based psychological analysis that compares militants' life in the PKK to membership in a cult, see Dogu Ergil, "Suicide Terrorism in Turkey."

[187] For an interesting and at times comical discussion of official Turkish attitudes denying that an ethnic problem exists in Turkey, see Zvi Barel, "Kurdish problem? What Kurdish problem?" *Ha'Aretz*, March 26, 1999. http://www.mnsi.net/~mergan95/26-3-99-5-stories.htm.

[188] McDowall, *A Modern History of the Kurds*, p. 427.

[189] Besikci, *Kurdistan and Turkish Colonialism*, p. 9.

rebellion that has been under way since 1984."[190] Nonetheless, some demonstrations and the observations of a handful of academics and journalists do not constitute solid evidence on the subject. Without reliable surveys on Kurdish public opinion and as long as explicitly Kurdish political parties are constrained from participating in Turkey's electoral system, we unfortunately have no way to make definitive conclusions on the issue.[191]

My own discussions with Kurds in Turkey, Iraq, Iran, and Syria, as well as mass Kurdish reactions to the 1999 arrest of Ocalan, lead me to believe

---

[190] Kinzer, "Nationalism is Mood in Turkey's Kurdish Enclaves," *New York Times* (May 16, 1999), S18. Kinzer also adds that:

> The growing support for Kurdish nationalism comes at a time when the rebel group known as the ... PKK, has suffered heavy losses, including the capture of its leader, Abdullah Ocalan. These reverses seem, if anything, to have emboldened ordinary people here, many of whom revere Ocalan as "our leader" – a vivid contrast to language used elsewhere in Turkey, where he is normally described as a terrorist and baby-killer ... The growth of nationalist sentiment here is evidently a product, at least in part, of Ocalan's rebellion. Even Kurds who expressed doubts about his tactics said he had awakened a new generation to a sense of common identity that their forefathers never felt. (Ibid.)

[191] HEP, DEP, HADEP, and DEHAP were political parties in Turkey that have been widely associated with, if not explicitly wedded to, a pro-Kurdish platform. The parties have faced a great deal of official and non-official harassment, facing periodic closure and censure. Villagers in Van province told this author in 1999 that before elections, the army often came into villages and warned the people of "unpleasant consequences" should HADEP be elected there (see also Belinda Parkes, "Hasan's trial," *New Statesmen and Society*, February 26, 1996, for another account of military coercion of villagers before, during, and after elections). HADEP was in the case of the 1999 municipal elections prevented from campaigning in many areas until the last minute. Nonetheless, the party elected mayors in 39 municipalities:

> Last month [April, 1999], voters in seven provincial capitals in the Kurdish region dealt the government a sharp blow by electing leaders of the Kurdish nationalist party as mayors. Here in Diyarbakir, the largest city in the region, the nationalist candidate won an astonishing 62 percent of the vote despite police harassment that included banning and attacking his rallies and arresting many who campaigned for him. "We won because we talked about identity, about the fact that there is a Kurdish population in this country that cannot be ignored," said the mayor, Feridun Celik ... Celik rejected government assertions that he and his party, People's Democracy, support separatism and terrorism. But a case to close the party is pending, based on the government's assertion that it maintains "organic links" with the guerrillas. After the recent elections, a senior prosecutor said he would seek to remove all People's Democracy mayors from office because their elections constituted "terrorist takeovers" of city halls ... Leaders of People's Democracy strenuously deny that their party is linked to the guerrillas. But many voters here agree with the government's assertion that it is. "Of course they are connected to our leader and his organization," said one shopkeeper. "That's why we voted for them." (Ibid.)

For more on HADEP's predecessor DEP, see "Election results," in "Democracy at Gunpoint," 22–23. The Turkish government closed down HADEP in March 2003.

that the PKK has made a strong cultural impact, however. This impact included Kurds outside Turkey, in the Kurdish regions of neighbouring states as well as the diaspora. This point is brought home by the speed and intensity with which Kurdish protests followed his capture: "When Ocalan was captured in Africa, he was put on a Turkish plane at 2 a.m. in Nairobi, Kenya. In less than two hours this event was broadcast in Europe, and protests began at 5 a.m."[192] With the aid of satellites, television cameras were able to broadcast events as they were happening. Telephones, fax, and Internet were able to pass the information on extremely rapidly to virtually all members of the Kurdish community worldwide.[193] Before time could even begin to calm their passions, Kurds feeling bitter and victimized organized and staged mass protests internationally and simultaneously. A Kurdish man arrested at a demonstration in front of the Israeli embassy in Montreal stated, "When I saw [on television] Apo [Abdullah Ocalan] captured, handcuffed and blindfolded by the Turks, I had to do something. He has done and sacrificed so much for us."[194] The man was also keen to point out that Kurds everywhere, and not just Kurds from Turkey or those who supported the PKK, demonstrated.

In fact, major Kurdish protests erupted in Iraqi and Iranian Kurdistan as well as in Turkey. In Iran, these demonstrations then turned against the Islamic regime: "While impossible for independent journalists to verify figures due to restricted access, it seems clear that major disturbances took place. That pro-Ocalan demonstrations erupted into protests against the Islamic regime points to both the transnational volatility of Kurdish issues and underlying dissatisfaction of Iranian Kurds with the regime."[195] The fact that many of the Kurds protesting in Western cities were from the non-Turkish parts of Kurdistan points to the importance that most Kurds worldwide attached to Ocalan as a symbol of Kurdish

---

[192] *RFE/RL* "Iraq Report," April 23, 1999.

[193] The author bases this observation on conversations held with the directors of Toronto's Kurdish Community Center, as well as Kurdish demonstrators in Toronto and Montreal. Demonstrators that the author spoke with had either heard of Ocalan's capture directly from MED-TV, or received a telephone call or e-mail from others who heard the news. They then proceeded to call family and friends in the community to organize immediate demonstrations in front of the Israeli and Greek consulates in Toronto and Montreal. Some demonstrators also added that they received telephone calls and e-mails from friends and family in Europe and the Middle East who told them they were doing the same things there.

[194] Discussion held on November 16, 2000, immediately after the man's appearance in court in Montreal. The author served as an expert witness at the trial, explaining the Kurdish issue to the court. The defendant was from the Kurdish region of Turkey and had had refugee status in Canada since 1997.

[195] WKI Press Release, March 3, 1999, www.clark.net/kurd/prIranViolence.html.

resistance. His capture was seen by Kurds everywhere, whether or not they supported the PKK's particular ideology, as yet another Kurdish humiliation and defeat.[196] Even the 1989 Iranian assassination of the well respected Kurdish leader Abd al Rahman Ghasemlou (Secretary General of the Kurdistan Democratic Party of Iran) did not elicit the same international Kurdish reaction as Ocalan's capture did. Although the difference in reactions may be due to a variety of factors, one cannot discount the possibility that Ocalan's PKK had created more enduring symbols of armed Kurdish resistance, and hence a more powerful cultural impact, than Ghasemlou and the KDPI had. The PKK was also more explicit in its ideology about the shared "nationhood" of all of Kurdistan than many of its Kurdish competitor movements, contributing to a larger Kurdish nationalism or, in McDowall's words, "pan-Kurdish" nationalism.[197]

From this chapter's analytical perspective, however, how can we then explain the relative quiet in Turkey after the initial furor over Ocalan's capture subsided? From his prison cell, Ocalan did make a call for all PKK militants to put down their arms and come down from the mountains. Certainly this has something to do with the observed change. But has Ankara defeated the Kurdish nationalist challenge? From the abovementioned discussion on the PKK's cultural impact, one would expect the answer to be "no." An awakening of and politicization of Kurdish identity in Turkey cannot be undone in the short term, if ever. Especially the Kurdish youth who came of age at the height of the PKK insurgency seem unlikely to ever assimilate to a Turkish *ethnie*. On the contrary, they could be expected to harbor radicalized views, derived from the conflict they witnessed around them as they grew up. Society in Turkey was increasingly polarized as a result of the PKK's insurgency. This chapter's perspective would lead us to conclude that although Turkey is presently enjoying a very significant reduction in armed attacks against the state, the relative calm may be short-lived.

Alternately, present and future salvos from Kurdish nationalists may well consist more of protests for minority rights and democracy than armed attacks. Moreover, Kurdish activity in the realm of publishing and media, in defiance of Turkish restrictions on the use of Kurdish in these venues, is more vigorous today than ever. Turkey's recent removal of the bans on Kurdish music and some forms of broadcasting may have

---

[196] Stephen Kinzer provided the following account: " 'My mother never had any particular sympathy for Ocalan or his organization,' said a businessman in his mid-30s. 'But when she saw the pictures of him in handcuffs, she cried.' " (Kinzer, "Nationalism is Mood in Turkey's Kurdish Enclaves.")

[197] McDowall, "The Kurdish Question: A Historical Review," in Kreyenbroek and Sperl (eds.), *A Contemporary Overview*, pp. 30–31.

convinced Kurdish nationalists that they can successfully seek change from within the system, even though they credit the PKK insurgency with the removal of the bans. Many Kurds (as well as Turks) in the country are in fact tired of the armed conflict the PKK launched in 1984. Since the 1980 military coup, Turkish generals and the political Right have used the "security threat" to Turkey as a justification to hold back further democratization in the country, particularly regarding Kurdish rights but also in other areas. Because armed struggle is only seen as legitimate when the system is closed to peaceful change,[198] people may want to give peaceful change a chance again. Now that Ankara is claiming victory over the PKK, Kurds as well as Turks may be sitting back and waiting to see if genuine democratic reforms will actually materialize. Such hopes are particularly salient in light of Turkey's European Union candidacy. As stated above, since 2001 the government in Turkey has begun introducing changes in its legislation, especially in order to please the European Community. If ascension to the EU also remains a plausible possibility, Kurds in Turkey could reasonably expect increasing protections and recognition of their identity as Kurds, which would in turn leave fewer Kurds feeling that recourse to arms was necessary or justified.

Notwithstanding EU reforms, however, Turkish state interest in addressing the core grievances of the Kurds still seems extremely limited. At the same time that changes were introduced to end the ban on "forbidden languages," for instance, a caveat was added which "stipulates that the right to use any language can be restricted in order to 'protect national security, public order and safety, the fundamental principles of the Republic, and the indivisible unity of the state and nation'."[199] It seems therefore that the government had no intention of letting Turkey's EU candidacy affect the core of its policy on the Kurds. When Turkish Chief of Staff General Kivrikoglu was asked about the EU-inspired constitutional amendments, he dismissed the notion that the changes would permit Kurdish-language broadcasts: "The Constitution is changing, but I believe this idea is blocked by provisions of the RTUK Law. The RTUK Law states that the broadcast language is Turkish. It would be wrong to think that Kurdish broadcasts would be permitted as long as these provisions exist. There is also a provision in article 42 of the Constitution."[200] This kind of attitude led an executive director of Human Rights Watch (Elizabeth Anderson, Europe and Central Asia Division) to state: "The

---

[198] This statement itself reflects a synthesis of opportunity structures and cultural framing.
[199] Ibid.
[200] Fikret Bila, "Warnings from General Kivrikoglu," *Milliyet*, October 3, 2001 www.kurdistanobserver.com.

Turkish parliament turned what could have been a defining moment of change into just another lost opportunity ... It was an opportunity to embrace European norms and Turkey missed it ... We are very disappointed."[201]

Further EU pressure eventually led to the legalization of broadcasts and education in Kurdish a year after General Kivrikoglu's statement. Although further pressure from the EU will likely cause the Turkish government to make additional adjustments to its legal code, the only real measure of such changes will involve a determination of whether or not they lead to changes in practice – if reasonable levels of Kurdish education and Kurdish language broadcasting become realities on the ground. It took a further two years after the 2002 legalization of Kurdish education and broadcasting to implement anything. As of Fall 2004, approximately four private Kurdish language classes had received permission to operate, and "Television stations will broadcast in Kurdish for two hours a week with Turkish subtitles, while radio stations will air Kurdish programmes for four hours a week and will have to run the same programme in Turkish immediately after."[202] Given the history of the Turkish Republic regarding these issues, this is nonetheless an extremely encouraging sign of change, albeit insufficient by itself to contradict the grievance framings (regarding ethnic oppression) of Kurdish nationalists.

The government of Tayip Recep Erdogan's Islamist AK Partisi, elected in November 2002, seems unlikely to move forward towards new policies on the Kurdish question any faster than the Kemalist establishment wishes, however. Already suspected of wishing to do away with the secular basis of the Kemalist state, Erdogan's party will most likely focus its efforts on avoiding a military coup, quietly promoting Islamic values, and using Turkey's European Union candidacy to lessen the military's say in politics. Although many of the AK Partisi's votes came from Kurds protesting the establishment parties and Kemalist norms, the Kurdish question is not a priority issue for the party, and certainly not an issue for which it will take great risks to change established policies. At the beginning of 2003, Erdogan's party went no further than offering a partial amnesty to PKK-KADEK fighters willing to turn themselves in. The amnesty applied only to rank and file members of the organization, and required them to admit their wrongdoing and provide intelligence

---

[201] AP, Ankara, "Turkish Parliament Passes Reforms, Education in Kurdish will remain banned," October 3, 2001, www.kurdistanobserver.com.

[202] "Kurds Unmoved By Turkish Preparations For State Broadcasts In Kurdish," AFP, May 28, 2004, article accessed at Kurdishmedia.com.

regarding the movement's remaining assets. The offer attracted little interest from Kurdish nationalists.

In the end, if Kurdish non-material grievances are not sufficiently addressed by Ankara, Turkey can expect a resurgence of Kurdish nationalist agitation and perhaps violence. In August 2001, a senior PKK commander appearing on MEDYA-TV warned that the rebels "would re-launch their armed campaign against Turkey if Ankara failed to address the grievances of its large Kurdish community."[203] Stressing Kurdish demands for greater cultural rights and dialogue, he stated that "We do not want war. (But) if the process (to resolve the dispute) runs into a bottleneck, we will try every means, including using arms . . . If we take up our weapons and restart the war, it would not be like the previous one, but more intense and destructive."[204]

On September 1, 2003, PKK-KADEK declared that its cease-fire with Turkey had ended, and that renewed guerrilla warfare was now an option. Small-scale clashes have erupted again in the southeast at the time of this writing. The identity and cultural framing perspective of this chapter suggests that Karayilan's threat could again attract the support of important segments of the Kurdish population, should Ankara fail to introduce significant changes in the short or medium term. The PKK's stance risks being vindicated if Kurdish nationalists are able to frame Ankara's stance in an intransigent light. Although pragmatism (and probably setbacks on the battlefield) seem to have moderated PKK demands from a separate Kurdish state to Kurdish cultural, linguistic, and minority rights within Turkey's existing borders, these appear to be the minimum demands for a Kurdish ethnicity that has become politicized. Nothing short of meeting these minimum demands will solve Turkey's Kurdish problem for the long term. This is perhaps the most significant conclusion stemming from the analysis employed here, and it is a conclusion that could not have been arrived at from the perspectives of the preceding two chapters, which treated identity as more of a given.

The Turkish state's ability to concede anything *vis-à-vis* Kurdish nationalist demands is constrained by the impact of its own framing efforts. State grievance framing efforts had their largest effect on the ethnic Turkish segment of the population, diminishing public appetite for any negotiations with or concessions to the "Kurdish terrorists." In this sense, the Turkish government's arousal of strong "anti-terrorist" sentiment within the population may limit the options that Ankara's leaders have

---

[203] AFP, Murat Karayilan, Ankara, "PKK threatens Turkey with renewed warfare," August 18, 2001, www.kurdistanobserver.com.
[204] Ibid.

in dealing with the PKK and the Kurdish problem in general. The extreme vilification of Kurdish nationalists, PKK or otherwise, seems to have been absorbed by large segments of the non-Kurdish population in Turkey. Without a public spirit of critical debate concerning the Kurds and some understanding of their point of view, Turkish society will be hard pressed to solve the fundamental problems of Kurdish alienation in the country. In this sense, the cultural impact of the state's framing efforts do not set the stage for a long-term resolution of the conflict. However, reform requirements for EU ascension may have emerged just in time to allow Turkish state leaders to extricate themselves from the box that their grievance framing had created. In the absence of EU demands and possible rewards, it seems likely that the state discourse and policy towards the Kurdish population in the country would not have shifted much. This would have been unfortunate, given that the perspective pursued in this chapter would make the following conclusion: as long as the state in Turkey continues to identify anyone who questions Kemalist principles (such as that of a unitary state based solely on Turkish identity) as a terrorist or supporter of terrorists, the possibilities for dialogue and conflict resolution are remote.[205]

Conclusion: the selective focus of cultural framing

Has the theoretical perspective employed here satisfactorily explained the emergence and growth of a Kurdish nationalist challenge to Ankara? This chapter examined the cultural background ("cultural tool kits") and identity of Kurds in Turkey, the state and insurgents' cultural framings, the use of media by both groups, and the contemporary cultural impact of PKK and state activities. The first factor demonstrated that at the very least, a private ethnic Kurdish identification existed amongst large numbers of the Kurds who found themselves within the new Turkish Republic in the 1920s. This seed had the potential to grow into politicized Kurdish consciousness amongst the masses, given the right conditions.

---

[205] Some hopeful signs to the contrary, however, include civil society initiatives in Turkey such as Dogu Ergil's TOSAV ("Toplum Sorunlari Arastirma Vakfi" – Foundation for Research on Societal Problems) foundation, which seeks to bring together Turks and Kurds in the country to discuss their worries, views, and basic needs, in an attempt to find common ground for a resolution of the conflict. For instance, TOSAV recently ran a series of radio programs entitled "Democracy, they say" ("Demokrasi diye diye") which aired viewpoints from both sides of the conflict. The result, unfortunately, was state censure of the program and confiscation of the written version of the show (a copy of which nevertheless evaded state capture and landed in the hands of this author after a recent visit to the foundation – Celal Inal, ed., *Demokrasi diye diye: "demokrasi radyosu" programlari*, Ankara: Toplum Sorunlari Arastirma Vakfi, undated).

Additionally, the "cultural tool kits" of Kurdish society included ample material that was conducive to armed opposition against the state. The Turkish state, aware of the multi-ethnic nature of its subject population, pursued cultural framings that would mold a unified Turkish nation within the state boundaries it had attained. The resulting Kemalist policies sought to crush Kurdish identity and assimilate the Kurds into the Turkish *ethnie*, whose primary identifying characteristic was the Turkish language. Kurdish nationalists, however, promoted an opposing vision and sought to mobilize Kurdish opposition to the state, based on politicized Kurdish ethnicity. Their cultural framings emphasized Kurdish nationhood (based on national markers such as language, cultural practice, a shared history, and a traditional homeland), repression directed at the Kurds because of their identity as Kurds, and the illegitimacy of the ruling state. Whereas state control of education and media gave Ankara an early advantage when it came to cultural framings, by the 1960s modernization, advances in communications technology, and world events (such as the Paris Commune and the war in Vietnam) began to shift some power into the hands of Kurdish insurgents. By the 1980s and 1990s, Kurdish nationalist framings enjoyed widespread dissemination through advanced technologies such as desktop publishing, radio, Internet, and satellite television, as well as from diaspora communities well plugged-in to such technology and free to pursue it. The cultural impact of the PKK's contest with the Turkish state polarized society in Turkey. While the bulk of the ethnic Turkish population remained implacably hostile to Kurdish nationalists (as opposed to largely incognizant of the Kurds in the 1950s), within the Kurdish population Kurdish nationalist sentiment experienced an awakening. This awakening of politicized ethnicity amongst the Kurds is unlikely to be undone by the Turkish state in today's context of easy communication and globalization.

Most of all, it appears that the perspective of this chapter has addressed the "why" of Kurdish nationalism in Turkey, by focusing on the ideology and views of the state and the PKK's challenge to it. Although an important revelation, this is of course not the whole story. Other Kurdish movements preceding and contemporary to the PKK, such as the PSK (Socialist Party of Kurdistan), pursued cultural framings and ideologies quite similar to the PKK's. Without the examination of mobilization strategies and material appeals undertaken in Chapter 3, we would remain unable to explain an essential element of the "how" of the PKK's rise. Skillful ideological appeals to potential supporters are only one element of this "how" explanation, and an insufficient one at that. It is quite likely that one could find significant grievances worthy of anti-state mobilization for every population group on the planet – but without a social movement able to conduct the right kind of mobilizing strategies, such as those discussed in Chapter 3, for example, groups consistently fail to act on these grievances. Likewise, the attention that Chapter 2 paid to the context in which such mobilization may or may not occur is the third crucial piece of the puzzle. Mobilization strategies and cultural framings are not undertaken in a vacuum, and it requires more than a cursory examination of the situation in which these are undertaken to understand them. The focus of Chapter 2 was particularly amenable to explaining the form and timing ("windows of opportunity") of movement emergence.

Can an additional level of understanding, explanation, and insight be gained through an interactive synthesis of the three perspectives, however? Employing the three modes of analysis sequentially, as I have done here, amounts to an additive approach. As was argued in Chapter 1, opportunity structures, mobilization strategies, and identity or cultural framing all interact dynamically. If this is the case, such a relationship must also be examined, in order to arrive at additional insights beyond those gained from the additive approach pursued thus far. The following chapter therefore attempts to evaluate the utility of a synthesized perspective.

5   Theoretical synthesis

"Men make their own history, but not under circumstances of their own choosing"   Karl Marx

Many of the sources on the Kurds consulted by this author made implicit use of a synthesis of the three theoretical approaches to understanding social movements examined in this study.[1] What concerns us here is whether or not an explicit synthesis of these theories contributes significantly to our understanding of the subject matter and the field of social science in general.

Consider this excellent example of a theoretical synthesis by Martin van Bruinessen. He argues, in essence:

A Sunni Zaza speaker is a Zaza, a Kurd, a Sunni Muslim and a citizen of Turkey. He also belongs to a specific social class and probably to a specific tribe, is an inhabitant of a specific village or valley, and may be a follower of a specific shaykh or an active member of a political organization. Each of these identities is appealed to at one time or another. At present, most Zaza define themselves first and foremost as Kurds, but their social and political behaviour is more often defined by narrower loyalties. In areas where there have been many Sunni–Alevi conflicts, people define themselves primarily as Sunni or Alevi rather than as Turk or Kurd. The emergence of Kurdish nationalism as a significant political force compelled many people to opt for an unambiguous ethnic identity. Many who had been partly or even entirely arabized or turkicized began to re-emphasize their Kurdish ethnic identity.[2]

---

[1] Nonetheless, most scholars of ethnic nationalism tend to rely on one or two of the theoretical perspectives examined here more than the other. Van Bruinessen's seminal *Agha, Shaikh and State* (London: Zed Books, Ltd., 1992), for example, places more analytic emphasis on opportunity structures and resource mobilization than grievance framing, although he of course does not omit questions of identity and social psychology.

[2] Van Bruinessen, "Kurdish Society, Ethnicity, Nationalism and Refugee Problems," in Philip G. Kreyenbroek and Stefan Sperl (eds.), *The Kurds: A Contemporary Overview* (London: Routledge, 1992), p. 48.

Hence, his claim is that people in Turkey have many different and possible identities, but the rise of the PKK as a significant challenger to the Turkish state brought a higher level, politicized Kurdish identity to the forefront of many people's consciousness. Had the PKK failed to engage in the kind of resource mobilization strategies that allowed it to expand and gain in strength, Kurdish nationalism would not have been viewed as a "significant political force" in contemporary Turkey. Only by mounting a significant challenge to the state, on the battlefield of rural Turkish Kurdistan, did the PKK attain the kind of credibility that made people view it as a significant political force. In essence, the two processes were mutually reinforcing and inter-dependent: by recruiting small numbers of people with a politicized ethnicity and willingness to mobilize in the 1970s and early 1980s, the movement was able to launch small-scale guerrilla warfare and local anti-landlord actions. The PKK could not have established itself in these early years, however, had there existed no seed of Kurdish ethnic identity for them to tap into (cultural tool kits). If their ideological appeals and grievance frames had initially fallen upon completely assimilated, deaf ears, there would be no Kurdish nationalist groups to speak of. By the mid-1980s, guerrilla successes, as well as resulting government repression, then propelled more people to mobilize and politicize their Kurdish identity, allowing for larger scale guerrilla actions, and so on until a mass movement emerged. This process was not a foregone conclusion – in the 1920s and 1930s in Turkey, Kurdish nationalism under the banner of traditional elites had been crushed, and the elites in question either eliminated or co-opted. After the destruction of the last Kurdish revolt in 1938, Kurdish nationalism as a significant political force in Turkey appeared to be either dead or in steady assimilation-induced decline.[3]

One of the insights provided by McAdam, McCarthy, and Zald is particularly applicable to this synthesis of framing and mobilization theories in the context of ethnic nationalism:

---

[3] Observers such as Imset feel that structural conditions in Turkey, particularly the closed nature of the system, are sufficient to account for the PKK's emergence: "I have argued for years and continue to do so, as did the head of Turkey's Gendarmerie Intelligence Organization who was assassinated before bringing his views to the public, that had it not been the PKK, there would definitely have been another organization fighting in the Turkish Southeast today" (Ismet Imset, "The PKK: Terrorists or Freedom Fighters?" in *Democracy at Gunpoint; The Economist, Turkey Survey* [Parliamentary Human Rights Group, June 8–14, 1996], 38). In light of the theoretical approach applied here, I do not agree with Imset's argument. Although another organization such as the PSK might have attempted to launch an armed struggle in the PKK's absence, without the resource mobilization strategies and effective grievance framing tactics described earlier, the war in Turkey's Kurdish regions would never have reached such proportions as to attract our attention.

... framing processes are held to be both more likely and of far greater consequence under conditions of strong rather than weak organization ... Even in the
unlikely event that system-critical framings were to emerge in the context of little
or no organization, the absence of any real mobilizing structure would almost
surely prevent their spread to the minimum number of people required to afford
a basis for collective action. More to the point, however, is the suspicion that
lacking organization these framings would never emerge in the first place ... This
suspicion rests, in part, on the supposition that what Ross (1977) calls the
"fundamental attribution error" – that is, the tendency of people to explain their
situation as a function of individual deficiencies rather than features of the
system – is more likely to occur under conditions of social isolation rather than
organization. Lacking the information and perspective that others afford, isolated
individuals would seem especially likely to explain their troubles on the basis of
personal rather than system attributions. Only "system attributions" afford the
necessary rationale for movement activity. For movement analysts, then, the key
question becomes, What social circumstances are productive of system critical
framing processes and the system attributions they yield? Following Ferree and
Miller (1977: 34) the answer would appear to be: "among homogenous people
who are in intense regular contact with each other." Their description speaks to
the essence of what we have called mobilizing structures.[4]

"Homogenous people in intense regular contact with each other" and
mobilizing on that basis are the essence of the ethnic nationalist project,
which is what makes a case such as ours particularly suitable for an
application of social movement theories.

In the case of the PKK, its various front groups, and other related
Kurdish organizations, effective resource mobilization helped reach and
bring together ever increasing numbers of people. After being convinced,
if necessary, of their belonging to the Kurdish nation, cultural framings
were presented that showed them that:
(1) their problems were not theirs alone, but rather shared by all Kurds;
(2) these problems resulted from a system perpetuated by foreign (non-
    Kurdish) colonizing and exploitative governments;
(3) the Kurdish nation should and could mobilize together to challenge
    the system; and
(4) the movement presently organized and bringing them this message
    was the most available, suitable, credible, and legitimate vehicle for
    such mobilization.
Kurdish groups in Turkey other than the PKK also attempted such system-
critical framings, but their failure to demonstrate as much organization
and action behind their words (rather than just revolutionary café talk)

---

[4] Doug McAdam, John D. McCarthy, and Mayer N. Zald, *Comparative Perspectives on Social
Movements: Political Opportunities, Mobilizing Structures, and Cultural Framings* (New York:
Cambridge University Press, 1996), p. 9.

denied them the perceived suitability, credibility, and legitimacy necessary to mobilize people and convince them to also risk their lives for the cause. Perhaps most importantly in the case of the PKK, the bulk of its early actions addressed the material goals of the local populace. Once the PKK brought people under its umbrella to participate in actions that mattered to them, the movement also took the opportunity to communicate its system-critical framings to the new participants. In essence, participation in any PKK-sponsored activity, whether this was an action against a local landlord or a cultural festival, allowed the movement to propagandize and affect people's identity towards Kurdish nationalism.

How do opportunity structures fit into such a synthesis, however? Opportunity structures in Turkey likewise both affected and were affected by challenger movements such as the PKK. In Chapter 2, I concluded that opportunity structures play an important role in determining the form that challenger movements take as well as the timing of their challenges. In the case of Turkey by the late 1970s, the closed nature of the political system and the elite allies available to would-be insurgents engendered the emergence of leftist revolutionary and armed challengers such as the PKK. Interaction with leftist elite allies in groups such as the Turkish Workers' Party during the 1970s profoundly affected the character of the movement and the ideological frames that the PKK would adopt upon its founding. Because the political system in Ankara was closed to any Kurdish demands, legal "moderate" Kurdish parties could not function. The closed nature of the system was also crucial to the legitimacy of the PKK, since people have a tendency to not accept cultural framings advocating armed revolt when more peaceful routes to political change exist. Aware of this, the PKK sought to clearly demonstrate to people that the system in Ankara was closed to even the most moderate Kurdish demands – in this sense, perception of a closed political system was as important as the fact in question. The Turkish political establishment was quite accommodating on this point, ignoring PKK cease-fire and negotiation offers and jailing Kurdish-origin MPs for daring to speak Kurdish in the National Assembly.[5] Insurgencies such as the PKK's, additionally, sometimes act to keep the political system closed, as politics retreats to the barracks.[6] In Turkey's case, however, there does not appear to be sufficient reason to believe that in the absence of the PKK's challenge, Kurdish demands would have ever been accepted into the official institutionalized system. Another possible

---

[5] The most famous of which is former Diyarbakir MP Leyla Zana, who is still in prison.
[6] The Muslim Brotherhood in Egypt comes to mind as a possible example of this phenomenon.

outcome is that an insurgent movement forces a closed system to open, after which the movement becomes an institutionalized part of politics.[7] When the PKK's challenge to the Turkish state coincided with Turkey's efforts to join the European Union, the resulting extra attention paid by the EU to human rights problems in Turkey led to even more pressure to open up the system. Hence the decline of the PKK after the mid-1990s could be explained by the simultaneous stick of an increasingly effective state counter-insurgency campaign and, more importantly, the carrot of a political establishment that began to open itself up to Kurdish group demands.[8] If the Turkish institutionalized political system continues to open itself up to Kurdish group demands, and allows legal, non-violent Kurdish parties to freely pursue their interests within the system, then groups like the PKK will be eclipsed by more moderate intra-systemic Kurdish movements.

The banning of parties such as HADEP, as well as the myriad practical hurdles placed in front of newly legalized Kurdish education and media in Turkey, leave room for worry, however. As was mentioned in Chapter 4, if Turkey retreats from current reforms and misses the opportunity to open its system to Kurdish demands, this could set the scene for renewed violence. Such violence could come from Congra-Gel, the PKK's successor, or a new more radical Kurdish movement. Unfortunately, the cultural frames pursued by Ankara over the years make it difficult for the Turkish populace to embrace Kurdish group demands into the institutionalized political system. The consequences of not doing so, however, may be enduring conflict in Turkey. If the PKK or a new Kurdish insurgent movement allies itself with Turkish leftist or Islamist opponents of Ankara, the Turkish government may face an even greater challenge than before.

Regarding other elements of opportunity structures – the stability of elite alignments undergirding Ankara's writ, the Turkish state's capacity and propensity for repression, and the influence of international actors and trends, the PKK appears to have timed its insurgency reasonably well. Although the 1960s and 1970s may have been the best time to launch its guerrilla war, the movement was not organized and ready to act at that time. In fact, no Kurdish group was sufficiently ready for rural

---

[7] A possible example of this phenomenon would be French Canadian resistance to English rule. British and later Canadian authorities eventually responded to Francophone demands by making the political system more inclusive and open to French Canadians.

[8] The Turkish state's counter-insurgency campaign also included the skillful application of more pressure on international supporters of the PKK, such Abdullah Ocalan's Syrian hosts, which further damaged the organization's position (Syria asked Ocalan to leave the country, after which he was captured and brought to trial in Turkey).

action then. Resource mobilization strategies and propaganda work amongst the rural Kurdish population took some years of preparation, and only by 1984 did the PKK have the organizational basis to:

(1) take advantage of government inattention in the southeast (Turkish politicians were busy with infighting and jockeying for position in the wake of the 1980 military coup);

(2) also take advantage of the Turkish army's unpreparedness to engage rural guerrillas, as opposed to the urban revolutionaries that it had grown used to suppressing; and

(3) avail itself of the assistance that neighboring states such as Syria, Iraq, and Iran would provide to any rebel group in Turkey that appeared capable of weakening Ankara.

Later on in the insurgency, when it became apparent that European countries, human rights NGOs, and international civil society in general might provide more enduring aid and pressure for change in Ankara than self-interested neighboring states,[9] the PKK moderated its demands and recast itself as a less radically violent movement. Although the international factor was no doubt not the only reason for such a change in strategy and cultural framing, it did play an important role.[10] The PKK can be credited, however, with drawing international attention to the situation of Kurds in Turkey, and thereby affecting one of the opportunity structure variables under which it operates: the availability of international support.[11]

A synthesis of all three approaches also comes into play regarding certain issues. In addition to being organized enough to take advantage

---

[9] Once again, Syria, Iran, and Iraq, although happy to weaken Turkey by playing "the Kurdish card," have no intention of allowing a Kurdish movement against Ankara to actually succeed in attaining a Kurdish state or Kurdish autonomy. As discussed in ch. 2, this results from the fear that such an example would foment more trouble among their own Kurdish minorities. The PKK is no doubt aware of these states' intention to supply it with just enough aid to keep the challenge to Ankara afloat, but not enough to achieve anything else. If Iraqi Kurds manage to consolidate their position in a post-Saddam Iraq, however, Turkish Kurds may be offered a more enduring and substantial level of support from their Iraqi brethren. For this reason, Turkish foreign policy seeks to limit and contain the advances of Iraqi Kurds to the south.

[10] Other elements that likely entered into the PKK's calculations included the best means to appeal to an even larger domestic constituency, difficulties the movement faced on the battlefield, and a genuine desire to negotiate an end to a conflict that was killing tens of thousands of people on both sides and displacing even more people.

[11] In a state-centric world, however, the Kurds face an uphill struggle when it comes to attracting international support. Although aid comes in many forms, the legitimating support and publicity that Kurds presently receive from NGOs and non-state actors, in addition to modest material support from some states, is unlikely to ever come close to matching the assistance their state opponents are able to rally. Chapter 6 also provides additional consideration of this issue.

of political opportunities, challenger movements must use their organization to help their constituents perceive the opportunities in question.[12] In the 1920s and 1930s, Kurdish nationalist organizations were not sufficiently organized to take advantage of auspicious opportunity structures.[13] Although they nonetheless attempted to mobilize for their objectives, the mobilization occurred at different times amongst different Kurdish groups, with the result that Ankara was able to defeat the various rebellions one at a time and one after another. Had Kurdish nationalist organization at the time effectively reached deeper into general Kurdish society (including many tribal elites, but also the non-tribal peasantry), they might have been able to

(1) affect the identity of the Kurdish masses so that politicized Kurdish ethnicity prevailed more often over regional, tribal, class, or religious identities;

(2) help the masses at large perceive the auspicious opportunity structures for Kurdish self-determination that lay before them between 1919 and 1938;

(3) organize a more unified, coordinated Kurdish mobilization to achieve these objectives, much like the Kemalists had organized a unified and coordinated resistance to Allied, Armenian, and Greek encroachments; and

(4) convince outside powers such as France and Britain that providing assistance to Kurdish nationalists would serve their own colonial interests, since the Kurds were a power to be reckoned with.

---

[12] Charles Kurzman, in "Structural Opportunity and Perceived Opportunity in Social-movement Theory: the Iranian Revolution of 1979," *American Sociological Review* 61: 1 (February 1996), 153–170, provides an interesting and novel spin on this issue: he argues that in the time leading up to the Iranian revolution, the Iranian public did not perceive the Shah's regime to be weak or unable to repress, yet they engaged in mass protests nonetheless. Kurzman's principal explanation for this was that the people (falsely) perceived the opposition movement to be stronger than the state after 1977. Chapters 4 and 5 show how the PKK in Turkey also attempted to portray itself as stronger than it really was, in order to encourage the same kind of mobilization based on people's faulty appraisal of the movement's chance of success. In the case of Iran, however, mass mobilization of all sectors of the population, rather than just one ethnic group, led to a situation in which both the Shah and significant portions of his armed forces were psychologically unwilling to massacre the large numbers of civilians necessary to restore order.

[13] PKK Leadership Council member Osman Ocalan (Abdullah Ocalan's brother) explicitly recognized this fact when he appeared on a political discussion program of MEDYA-TV: "Ocalan stated that Kurds who have been excluded during I World War because their unreadiness have then attained a certain level of organization and strength at every area, adding the following: 'Now everybody shows that the Kurds has gained strength. This time Kurds will not be sacrificed'" (cited as is, "There Can Be No Solution Without Kurds," *Ozgur Politika* [Oct. 17, 2001], www.kurdistanobserver.com).

Crawford Young, writing about ethnicity and politics in 1982, argued that "Most individuals ... have more than one cultural identity. Which has relevance will depend upon the situational context. So also will context determine the saliency and intensity of identities."[14] We might therefore add that in addition to the situational context, the existence of an organized movement that helps them view their context in a certain light is equally important for the saliency and intensity of identities. Hence the argument of some scholars, such as Melucci,[15] that the structural conditions forming opportunity structures are only important for collective action in so far as they are perceived by social movement actors and the population.[16]

Consideration of the tactics of challenger movements such as the PKK reveals an interesting interplay of political structures, framing, and mobilization. For instance, today's prevailing views on guerrilla warfare[17] hold that guerrilla war strategy actually depends less on the success of military operations than the psychological and catalyzing impact that attacks on the state have on the population (both the population that the guerrillas want to mobilize as well as the population that supports the state and provides it with military recruits). Imset captures this irony when he points out that, "Periods in which the PKK suffered its greatest losses, were also periods in which it received most of its recruits and drilled its popular grassroots for more support."[18] The goal is to expand the guerrilla movement indefinitely while simultaneously chipping away at the enemy's willingness to endure the costs of the conflict, and hence to eventually win the war despite losing the bulk of the battles. Such logic actually relates the mobilization and the identity-psychological level of analysis to what is perhaps the most crucial of opportunity structures: the state's capacity and willingness to use repression. No revolutionary movement can succeed as long as the government's armed forces are willing and able to fight – the modern state's armed force in most

---

[14] Crawford Young, "Patterns of Social Conflict: State, Class and Ethnicity," *Daedalus* 111: 2 (Spring 1982), 91.

[15] Bert Klandermans, Hanspeter Kriesi, and Sidney Tarrow (eds.), *From Structure to Action: Comparing Social Movement Research Across Cultures*, International Social Movement Research (London: Jai Press Inc., 1988), pp. 4, 361.

[16] Kate Nash, *Contemporary Political Sociology: Globalization, Politics, and Power* (Oxford: Blackwell Publishers, Inc., 2000), p. 139.

[17] See, for instance, Gerard Chaliand (ed.), *Guerrilla Strategies* (Berkeley: University of California Press, 1982), Robert Asprey, *War in the Shadows* (New York: William Morrow and Company, Inc., 1994), or Samuel B. Griffith, (ed.), *Mao Tse-Tung on Guerrilla Warfare* (Washington DC: Praeger Publishers, 1961) – particularly Griffith's introduction to the work.

[18] Ismet G. Imset, *The PKK* (Ankara: *Turkish Daily News Publications*, 1992), p. 82.

instances cannot be defeated by domestic insurgents, even in places like Batista's Cuba. If the armed forces begin to question the desirability of turning their arms upon the population when other options exist, however, revolutionaries can win the day. Such a change in the attitude of the armed forces can also be precipitated by the population from which they are drawn, should such a population begin to wonder if the goals for which it is fighting the guerrillas are worth the price being paid now and in the future. Thus, when the Shah of Iran, Samoza, or Batista's troops perceived a never-ending conflict and a population that was largely hostile towards its corrupt and authoritarian leader, their willingness to fight evaporated.

The Kurds' application of a strategy that worked in places such as Cuba, Iran, Nicaragua, and Vietnam, however, faces greater challenges in the Turkish context. Turks respect their army and view it as the guardian of a system that represents them (although they remain aware that democracy in Turkey has flaws). Turkey's status as a democracy and the state's ability to manipulate the cultural frames of Turks have maintained Ankara's legitimacy *vis-à-vis* the guerrillas. At the same time, domestic insurgencies predicated upon ethnic differences, rather than the attempt to forge a better society for everyone, do not seem to engender much of a search for non-violent options or a change in government. If the PKK had succeeded in convincing Turks in general that it was not seeking a separate Kurdish state, but rather a better society in Turkey that would be to everyone's benefit, the Turkish populace's appetite for continued conflict might have diminished. As it stands, in both the population's and the military's view, there exists a difference between killing separatist foreigners and citizens who want better government. When it comes to repressing foreign out-group members, the myriad ethnic conflicts around the world have already shown us how far such repression may go. Thus if Congra-Gel or other Kurdish challenger groups could successfully portray themselves simply as citizens demanding more democracy and recognition, the Turkish state's capacity to exclusively pursue a campaign of repression might well reach its limit. Since 1995, the PKK has, in fact, pursued such a strategy, but with little success *vis-à-vis* Turkish public opinion. To the ethnic Turkish population, state grievance framings were infinitely more successful than insurgent ones.

From Ankara's point of view, the dissolution of KADEK, like the end of its PKK predecessor in April of 2002, vindicated the state's military approach towards Kurdish nationalist agitation. The 1999 capture of Abdullah Ocalan and the "stick" of military force certainly played an important role in the PKK-KADEK's decline. In the language of this study, selective disincentives applied against Kurdish nationalist dissidents and those who might support them played a key role. Increasingly sophisticated Turkish counter-insurgency operations, along with the destruction of thousands of villages in Turkish Kurdistan, severely affected the PKK's ability to mobilize people and mount offensives.

Two other equally important factors explain the dissolution of the PKK and KADEK, however: the nascent opening and reform of the Turkish political system, and post-September 11 changes in the international scene. KADEK's own November 11 announcement highlights the organization's perception of both of these changes in political opportunity structures:

> There can be no doubt that the approach adopted by the KADEK had an encouraging impact on the political process that led to constitutional changes in Turkey, entailing the abolition of death penalty and the abrogation of the constitutional ban on the use of the Kurdish vernacular ... Noting that the policies of the regional states hinge on the refusal to acknowledge the Kurdish reality, and that these policies and the international support they can still rally constitute the foremost reason for the failure to achieve a settlement, the Kurdish movement nevertheless has to take steps on its own part to facilitate a resolution. The recent developments in the Middle East and the wider political conjuncture provide us with significant opportunities for democratisation and a resolution of the Kurdish conflict.[19]

KADEK officials thus cited openings in the political opportunity structures of the region as one justification for renouncing armed struggle and pursuing their goals by other means. Likewise, they acknowledged that the events of September 11 have changed the international context and grievance frames with which they can operate: "While deploring that the dominant regional states and some international forces pursued their long-standing efforts to eradicate the Kurdish freedom struggle against the backdrop of a clear misuse of the term 'terrorism', the KADEK is aware of its own responsibilities in resolving this situation."[20] In essence, KADEK militants were well aware that in the post-September 11 world, being associated with terrorism put them in a much more dangerous position than before. Because KADEK remained in the eyes of most observers a new variant of the PKK, and because the PKK engaged in terrorism during the 1980s and 1990s, the militants decided they needed

---

[19] "On the Dissolution of the KADEK," Press Release by KADEK – Kongra Azadî û Demokrasiya Kurdistan – Kurdistan Freedom and Democracy Congress – Congrès pour la Démocratie et la Liberté du Kurdistan, Kurdistanobserver.com (Nov. 11, 2003).
[20] Ibid.

to make a more complete break with the past. With reduced opportunities for armed struggle, and the simultaneous increase in avenues for peaceful change, the movement tried to undertake a strategic shift, more towards the human rights grievance framings and strategies that began to be emphasized by the PKK in the mid to late 1990s:

> The substantial democratic openings expressed in the organisation's program were only inadequately reflected in its inner structure; the personal continuity in the upper echelons fuelled spitefully dismissive notions that the KADEK is a mere continuation of the PKK. This, in turn, tainted international overtures and negatively affected the democratisation process envisaged ... It is on these grounds that the Congress for Democracy and Freedom in Kurdistan (KADEK) is being dissolved in order to make way for a new, more democratic organisational structure that allows for broader participation. This new structure shall be representative of the Kurdish people's interests, legitimate under international criteria, and conducive to the pursuit of democratic and lawful political articulation with a view on negotiating a peaceful settlement with the dominant nation states.[21]

Congra-Gel, the successor to PKK-KADEK, seems to have solved few, if any, of the framing and mobilization problems that bedeviled its predecessors, however. Congra-Gel is simply viewed by everyone in the region as the PKK's newest manifestation, just as KADEK was. Like its predecessors, it remains on American and European lists of terrorist organizations, and seems no likelier to get negotiations with Turkish authorities than the PKK was. Congra-Gel and its armed wing, the People's Defence Forces (HPG), has in turn resumed low-level guerrilla attacks within the Kurdish region of Turkey. History may be repeating itself, unfortunately.

It also remains unclear whether or not Turkey's European Union candidacy, combined with the decline of the PKK, will lead to a significant opening of the Turkish system *vis-à-vis* the Kurdish issue. The popular Turkish view holds that the 1999 capture of PKK leader Abdullah Ocalan, combined with the Turkish military's more effective counter-insurgency operations, effectively killed the PKK challenge to the Turkish state. With the movement's morale, credibility, and strength thus in question, mobilizing cadres, new recruits, and sympathizers proved more difficult, since such mobilization generally requires people to believe that they have a chance of success. For the Turkish state to truly take advantage of these new resource mobilization and grievance framing difficulties for Kurdish nationalists in Turkey, however, it should now continue opening up the political opportunity structure in the country to legitimate, legal, and non-violent attempts to pursue Kurdish group demands (at the same time that it defends itself

---

[21] Ibid.

from guerrilla attacks in the southeast). In this way, all the important variables in the three levels of analysis examined above would point towards the impossibility of a renewed militant, violent Kurdish challenge to the Turkish state.

As discussed earlier, however, it appears that many of the changes to the institutionalized Turkish political system remain for the time being more cosmetic than real. In an attempt to meet the requirements for European Union accession, Turkey has repealed some of its laws banning the Kurdish language in public space, for instance. While encouraging, such forward movement has been constrained by Turkish reliance on loopholes in the changes to the legal system to continue pursuing many of the same old policies. For instance, Turkish municipal governments continue to forbid Kurdish families from giving their children Kurdish names, under legal justifications that such practices are forbidden because the names in question contradict the culture of the Turkish state, or because they include letters that do not exist in the Turkish alphabet ("x" and "w," for instance, do not appear in Turkish, but do appear in many popular Kurdish names). Kurdish language education, although technically legal now, encounters so many restrictions that in practice little has changed in the Kurdish regions of Turkey.

If the political system does not open in a more substantial way, one should expect a Kurdish population with a significantly politicized ethnic identity (due to the years of PKK insurgency) to soon find new ways to challenge the state. An inventive Kurdish population that values its Kurdish identity will seek new grievance frames and mobilization strategies to pursue its goals, and if the system remains largely closed, then these tactics will take an illegal, extra-systemic form. Especially Kurdish youth who came of age during the PKK insurgency of the 1980s and 1990s, and are hence already somewhat radicalized compared to their elders, might be quicker to mobilize into armed Kurdish nationalist movements opposing the state.

We can take our heuristic application of the theoretical synthesis above further, however, by making a tentative comparison of the Kurdish case in Turkey to that of Iraq and Iran. By comparing the Kurdish situation in Turkey to that of Iraq and Iran, a better sense of the insights we have already arrived at, as well as additional points of analysis, should come to light. Although our treatment of the Kurdish case in Iraq and Iran (and Syria, for that matter) merits the same kind of detail as that which Turkey received, the examination and comparison engaged in here must unfortunately remain simplified, more brief, and tentative. Perhaps a more extensive comparison based on the theoretical framework elaborated here can be pursued in a later work.

6　Kurdish nationalist challenges to the Iraqi state

The creation of Iraq and early Kurdish revolts

Following the Treaty of Lausanne, Britain and the League of Nations in 1925 attached the Mosul Vilayet and the rest of today's Iraqi Kurdistan to the British-occupied Mesopotamian vilayets of Basra and Baghdad. Out of these holdings Iraq was created. The British installed Hashemite Emir Faysal, a prince from the Arabian peninsula, as King of the new Iraq, and Britain's mandate over Iraq was supposed to last twenty-five years.[1] Some Kurdish leaders who had been friendly towards Britain, in the hope that they would be helped to establish a Kurdish state in the area, were gravely disappointed. The opportunity structure of foreign support for their Kurdish nationalist aims was not as favorable as they had imagined. The British had decided that creating and controlling a single Iraq, including the Kurdish areas in question, would be the best way to exploit the oil fields around Kirkuk and Mosul, as well as to protect their colonial holdings elsewhere.

Sporadic Kurdish unrest and agitation against being included within the new Iraq had begun even before the Treaty of Sèvres.[2] Lacking sufficient troops to quell the unrest, as early as 1919 the British deployed the RAF to aerially bombard Kurdish rebels and civilian areas in

---

[1] Appointing a Sunni Muslim King from Arabia held some degree of irony, since even if we include the Sunni Muslim Kurds, the new state of Iraq included more Shiite Muslims (who lived mostly in the south) than Sunnis. The British hoped that Faysal's traditional and religious credentials, coming from a famous family descended from the Prophet, would help him consolidate his rule over the new Iraq.

[2] Kurdish unrest at the time had many different motives, among which Kurdish nationalism was only one. Ottoman and later Turkish agents, eager to prevent Britain from controlling the area, probably also played a role in fomenting unrest. One of the foremost grievances was the imposition of central government authority in a region where tribal and feudal leaders had long enjoyed significant degrees of autonomy under Ottoman rule. Different observers in different parts of the region could not agree, or pretended to not agree, on what the Kurdish population as a whole desired (see David McDowall, *A Modern History of the Kurds* [London: I. B. Taurus, 1997], ch. 8, for a wide array of British, Turkish, and League of Nations opinions on the issue).

rebellion, setting an enduring precedent for both the region and the world.[3] In order to assuage the restive Kurds, "a joint Anglo-Iraqi statement of intent regarding the Kurds" was agreed on in London and issued on December 20, 1922: "His Britannic Majesty's Government and the Government of Iraq recognize the right of the Kurds living within the boundaries of Iraq to set up a Kurdish Government within those boundaries and hope that the different Kurdish elements will, as soon as possible, arrive at an agreement between themselves as to the form which they wish that Government should take and the boundaries within which they wish it to extend and will send responsible delegates to Baghdad to discuss their economic and political relations with His Britannic Majesty's Government and the Government of Iraq."[4] Although this statement contradicted previous British promises to Iraqi King Faysal, High Commissioner Sir Percy Cox "privately assured Faysal that this declaration 'in no way implied separation politically or economically of Kurdistan from Iraq.'"[5] Britain's promise to the Kurds in fact bore some similarities to Ataturk's assurances of "Turkish-Kurdish brotherhood" discussed in Chapter 2 – it made the emerging political structure in the new Iraq appear open to Kurdish group demands, and contradicted Kurdish nationalist grievance framings that sought to portray the emerging state as suppressive of Kurdish aspirations. The intent and effect of the promise was to hamper the mobilization efforts and unity of Kurdish groups opposing the British and new Iraqi government. Once Kurdish groups in revolt were suppressed, the promises would be reneged upon, just as occurred in Turkey in the 1920s.

In any case, given Kurdish divisions at the time, the chances of "different Kurdish elements" arriving at an "agreement between themselves" were already quite poor. This was no doubt the intent with which the agreement's exact wording had been chosen. Economic interests, tribal, linguistic, regional, and religious differences all competed with Kurdish nationalist sentiment. Sheikh Mahmoud Barzinji, the leader of the most significant Kurdish rebellions in the area between 1919 and 1932, was

---

[3] For more on the RAF bombings and British policy in the area at this time, see McDowall, *A Modern History of the Kurds*, ch. 8; Ismet Chériff Vanly, *Le Kurdistan irakien: entité nationale* (Neuchatel: Les Editions de la Baconnière, 1970); or Ismet Chériff Vanly, "Kurdistan, the Kurds and the Kurdish National Question: Historical Background and Perspective," background paper prepared for the Preparatory Commission for Parliament of Kurdistan in Exile (1993).

[4] Cited in McDowall, *A Modern History of the Kurds*, p. 169.   [5] Ibid.

opposed by several other Kurdish elite rivals in the region.[6] As in Turkey at the time, no sufficiently organized Kurdish nationalist group existed to mobilize Kurds on the basis of such nationalism and in a manner that could supersede sectarian divisions. Had Kurdish leaders of the day been able to organize a more effective front, they could have forced a real change of policy in Britain, much as Ataturk's ability to rally forces to oppose the Treaty of Sèvres obliged the Allies to discard it. A more united and effective Kurdish front during this period of great change might have convinced Britain to create a Kurdish state in northern Iraq, in addition to the Arab ones to the south, in Jordan, and further afield. Essentially, although opportunity structures at the time (in the form of elite allies, international support, and the British/Arab capacity to repress) were rapidly turning sour for Iraqi Kurds, more effective resource mobilization strategies might have been able to alter the situation. A greater degree of Kurdish nationalist success at this stage in history would have in turn advanced Kurdish national consciousness in all of Kurdistan by several

---

[6] See Edgar O'Ballance, *The Kurdish Struggle: 1920–94* (London: MacMillan Press, Ltd., 1996), ch. 2; or McDowall, *A Modern History of the Kurds*, ch. 8, for more detail regarding Mahmoud Barzinji's uprisings. McDowall states that "It is tempting retrospectively to clothe Shaykh Mahmoud in the garb of modern nationalist ideas. But it is clear he had little in common with today's Kurdish leaders. Both the vocabulary and style are quite different. It is significant that Shaykh Mahmoud did not waste his time appealing to nationalist sentiment. He was a sayyid, and the language his constituency understood was the language of Islam. In 1919 he appealed for a *jihad*, not a national liberation struggle. Furthermore, his style was to use kin and tribal allies and his aim was the establishment of a personal fiefdom" (McDowall, *A Modern History of the Kurds*, p. 158). Nader Entessar, however, paints him as a nationalist – besides the proto-nationalist simple fear of outside control, Entessar states that, "The last major revolt by Shaikh Mahmoud against Iraqi and British authorities began after the British announced they would grant independence to Iraq in 1932. When it became clear that the treaty granting Iraq's independence did not contain guarantees for the rights of the country's minorities, Shaikh Mahmoud organized an offensive against Iraqi forces in the spring of 1931. Shaikh Mahmoud was defeated once again and could no longer muster any opposition to the Iraqi government. With hopes of creating an independent state of their own dashed, the Kurds initiated a series of minor revolts" (Nader Entessar, *Kurdish Ethnonationalism* [London: Lynne Rienner Publishers, Inc., 1992], p. 54). Although less so than his counterpart in Turkey (Sheikh Said, who led the 1925 uprising there), Mahmoud was probably both a Kurdish nationalist as well as a feudal tribal-religious leader. If he relied on tribal-kin networks to mobilize opposition, this was because these networks were the form of organization most readily available to him. Also, as with Sheikh Said's revolt, an Islamic framing of the revolt stood better chances of mobilizing Kurdish support that transcended tribal, regional, and linguistic divisions, especially since Islam was a long-accepted part of Kurdish cultural tool kits in the 1920s and 1930s while Kurdish nationalism was relatively new. Mahmoud's uprisings would have been successful, had it not been for British military assistance to Baghdad. Even with such assistance, it took several years, much politicking, and many insincere promises regarding future Kurdish autonomy for the British and Baghdad to quell the uprisings.

decades, further strengthening the movement in a kind of virtuous circle (virtuous from the point of view of Kurdish nationalists).

Sheikh Barzinji had been appointed governor of the Suleimaniya area of Iraqi Kurdistan by Ottoman authorities, and the British originally decided to retain him when they conquered the area. To their dismay, however, he used his existing political resources and networks, as well as his credentials as a religious (Naqshibendi) leader, tribal leader, and large landowner, to mobilize a revolt against British rule and incorporation of Kurdish areas into the new Iraq. Kurds in rival tribal areas did not rally to him, however, and the British managed to exile him. When in 1922 Turkish forces began to move south and attempt to take control of the area just north of Suleimaniya, however, the British called Barzinji back from exile in the hope of using him to counter the Turkish threat. Instead, Barzinji allied himself with Ataturk's forces and sought to again revolt against the British.[7] Barzinji hoped that with new elite allies in Turkey, he could manage better against the British RAF and nascent Iraqi army. His forces were not large enough for the task, however, and Turkish support not direct nor extensive enough to make up the difference. A history of Kurdish exploitation of and abuse of Assyrian Christian villagers in northern Iraq[8] also gave the British ready and willing local troops to help them quell Kurdish unrest in the region. The British defeated Barzinji and exiled him again.

By 1926, when control of the Kurdish regions seemed more assured, Baghdad and the British reneged on their promise of 1922: "... both His Majesty's Government and the Government of Iraq are fully absolved from any obligation to allow the setting up of a Kurdish Government by a complete failure of the Kurdish elements even to attempt, at the time this proclamation was made, to arrive at any agreement among themselves or put forward any definite proposals ..."[9] The only remaining assurances for the Kurds integrated into Iraq were stipulations made by the League of Nations, a Commission of which had advised that the Kurdish regions in question be attached to Iraq provided that: "The desire of the Kurds that the administrators, magistrates and teachers in their country be drawn from their own ranks, and adopt Kurdish as the official language in all their activities, will be taken into account."[10]

Under King Faysal, some meager efforts were made to respect this provision – limited education in Kurdish, publications in Kurdish, and

---

[7] O'Ballance, *Kurdish Struggle 1920–1994*, p. 20.
[8] Michael Gunter, *The Kurdish Predicament in Iraq* (New York: St. Martin's Press, 1999), p. 4.
[9] McDowall, *A Modern History of the Kurds*, p. 169.   [10] Vanly, "Kurdistan," p. 148.

minor Kurdish participation in government were all allowed. Education policy in the new Iraq, however, illustrated emerging state policy. Officials such as Said Husri, the first Director General of Iraq's ministry of education, promoted a pan-Arab educational policy that glorified Arab heroes and said virtually nothing of Kurds. Reeva Simon explains the ideology of the new Iraqi state: "Iraq's 'imagined community' was that of the Arabs, rather than Iraqis or Mesopotamians, Arabs whose identity and history were fashioned by Arab nationalist ideologues. These new elites, or 'priesthood,' teachers who taught from the textbooks commissioned and prescribed by the Ministry of Education in Baghdad, attempted to amalgamate the Sunni minority elite with the ethnic and religious minorities and the Shi'i majority via the glue of Arab nationalism in order to forge a pan-Arab identity for the Iraqis."[11]

The 1922 Anglo-Iraqi statement and the League of Nations provisions had, however, explicitly recognized the Kurds in Iraq and their claim to special rights *as a group*. In essence, politicized Kurdish ethnicity was officially accepted as one of the founding principals of the Iraqi state, unlike in Turkey. Thus in Iraq, the bulk of the Kurdish social movement project of encouraging Kurdish nationalist cultural framings was already accomplished from day one – Kurds did not have to be convinced that they should demand group rights from the state since these had already been promised by state authorities.[12] The result of this promise was enduring Kurdish nationalist attempts to see their rights fulfilled. Pan-Arabism and Arab nationalism of course held no appeal for the unassimilated Iraqi Kurds, since Kurds are not Arabs.[13] The fact that Iraq was a patently artificial colonial creation also critically hamstrung any state framings that attempted to encourage an alternate Iraqi national identity. If the Iraqi state had developed democratic institutions and

---

[11] Reeva S. Simon, "The imposition of Nationalism on a Non-Nation State: The Case of Iraq During the Interwar Period, 1921–1941," in James Jankowski and Israel Gershoni (eds.), *Rethinking Nationalism in the Arab Middle East* (New York: Columbia University Press, 1997), p. 88.

[12] In addition, the greater tolerance in Iraq for Kurdish publications, along with modernization trends in the 1950s and 1960s, permitted Kurdish nationalist sentiment to develop within urban Kurdish populations more quickly and solidly than in Turkey (A. Sherzad, "The Kurdish movement in Iraq: 1975–88," in Philip G. Kreyenbroek and Stefan Sperl [eds.], *The Kurds: A Contemporary Overview* [London: Routledge, 1992], p. 136).

[13] Arab nationalist ideology, as well as most definitions of "Arab" today, hold that those who speak Arabic as their mother tongue or primary language are Arabs, irrespective of religion or other identities. Although many Arabic-speaking Jews came to opt out of the Arab nationalist identity in favor of a Zionist (Jewish nationalist) one, many Arabic-speaking Christians such as Michel Aflaq, one of the founders of the Ba'ath Party, identified themselves as Arabs. Kurds in Iraq, however, overwhelmingly maintained Kurdish as their mother tongue, and hence fell out of the Arab identity group.

fulfilled most of its promises to the Kurds (e.g. an open political system), Kurdish nationalist identity might have eventually incorporated Iraqi civic identity and peacefully remained within Iraq's colonial borders. Unfortunately for Iraqi Sunni and Shiite Arabs as well as Kurds, years of conflict occurred instead.

Kurdish revolts followed the British announcement to end their mandate in 1930, as well as Iraq's accession to independence in 1932. As with all the Kurdish revolts in Iraq's history, many Kurdish soldiers in the Iraqi army defected to the side of the rebels. At the same time, many Kurdish tribes were recruited to fight their rebellious countrymen. In 1943 another major uprising, this time led by Mustafa Barzani, required British intervention to save an Iraqi army that had been overrun by Barzani's forces. When tribal rivals such as the Zibaris defected to the government's side, however, Barzani and his men were forced to retreat into Iranian Kurdistan. In Iran, they played a role in the establishment and defense of the short-lived Kurdish Republic (1945–1946).

Barzani and the Kurdistan Democratic Party of Iraq: tribalism weds nationalism

A tribal leader and large landowner, Mustafa Barzani soon became an enduring symbol of Kurdish nationalism. Kurdish nationalists in Iraq, although often leftist (many had joined the Iraqi Communist Party in Baghdad), urban, and critical of traditional Kurdish elites, decided that Kurdish nationalism's greatest chances for success in Iraq lay with Barzani and his tribal fighters. Barzani did not have to build up an armed movement from scratch, since he was already at the head of a considerable mobilizing network based on tribes, kinship, and, to a lesser extent, the religious followings of his brother Sheikh Ahmad Barzani. Thus they wedded their political organizations to Barzani in the newly formed Kurdistan Democratic Party, an alliance that in McDowall's view was "destined to dog the maturation of the Kurdish movement in Iraq well into the 1970s."[14] The alliance in question acted as a constraint on Kurdish nationalist development because of Barzani's status as an agha, a conservative tribal leader and large landowner, which would often hamper the allegiance of opposing tribes and non-tribal Kurdish peasants.[15]

[14] McDowall, *A Modern History of the Kurds*, p. 296.
[15] The KDP element of the alliance did manage to bring in Shiite Kurds, however, who had stayed aloof from Sheikh Barzinji's Sunni revolts of the 1920s and 1930s (van Bruinessen, in Kreyenbroek and Sperl [eds.], *The Kurds*, p. 52). This was in addition to some urban Kurds attracted to the intellectual nationalist element in the KDP.

Barzani's leadership would also soon end the Kurdish cooperation with ICP (Iraqi Communist Party) allies, who were a significant force throughout Iraq. Nonetheless, Barzani had proved that only he could organize and mobilize a respectable fighting force in the short term, in the form of his tribal fighters. Hence Kurdish nationalism in Iraq, because of the continuing availability of traditional Kurdish elite allies, never developed into the peasant-proletarian, leftist mass Kurdish movement epitomized by the PKK in Turkey:

> Virtually every Kurdish organization spoke in the name of all classes and even emphasized its identification with Kurdish peasants and workers, but most of the peasantry long remained aloof from the Kurdish movement. In the Iraqi Kurdish movement – in which, because of the long guerrilla war, the tribes came to play crucial parts again – virtually none of the non-tribal peasantry ever took part. They found that their interests were often better served by the central government, which offered land reform. The same, to some extent, was true of Iran under the Shah. Only in Turkey did the Kurdish movement, in the late 1970s, make significant inroads among the rural and urban poor. A part of the movement here, notably the Workers' Party of Kurdistan [the PKK], turned against the *aghawat* as a class (although at times cooperating with individual chieftains).[16]

With traditional elites such as Barzani gradually taking the helm of the Kurdish movement in Iraq, the government's land reform program for the north was effectively resisted. In the absence of traditional elite allies, one may assume that more Kurds would have continued participating in the Iraqi Communist Party, or that its offshoot Kurdish Communist Party would have been more seriously developed. In fact, closer ties with the ICP and a developing worker and peasant support base emerged between 1943 and 1958, when Mustafa Barzani was in exile in Iran and the Soviet Union and the KDP in Iraq was led by Ibrahim Ahmed.[17] Other urban-based, proletarian Kurdish nationalist organizations in Iraq such as *Komala-i Liwen, Komala Brayeti, Darkar, Shorish*, and *Rizgari Kurd* might have likewise become the focal point of Kurdish nationalism, had Barzani's readily available tribal resources not stood out as the quickest, most enticing resource. If Kurdish challenger movements such as these were built from the bottom up with more time and patience, some of the later intra-Kurdish fighting that characterized the movements in Iraq might have been avoided. This would have led to the eventual

---

[16] Martin van Bruinessen, "Kurdish society, ethnicity, nationalism and refugee problems," in Kreyenbroek and Sperl (eds.), *The Kurds*, p. 53.

[17] Gareth R. V. Stansfield, *Iraqi Kurdistan: Political Development and Emergent Democracy* (London: Routledge Curzon, 2003), pp. 66–67.

development of a stronger, more unified Kurdish nationalist movement in the country. As it happens, Barzani's tribal base led to competition between him and the elites of more urban Kurdish nationalist parties, the Iraqi Communist Party, and other tribal leaders.

In any case, although socialism was thrown out of the KDP that Barzani came to symbolize and lead, armed struggle did continue to characterize Barzani-led Kurdish nationalist challenges in the country. This was especially due to the continued closure of the political system in Baghdad and the weak Iraqi state's questionable ability to repress the Kurds.[18] Moments in Iraq's history when a change occurred in the apparent closure of the political system led without fail to negotiations and a lull in the fighting. In 1958, for instance, the Iraqi monarchy was overthrown by Abdul Karim Qasim, and a moment of hope appeared in the new revolutionary Iraq. Barzani was welcomed back from exile, and Qasim embraced the Kurds as an ally against pro-monarchy forces and other opponents within his regime. The extreme divisions amongst the elites undergirding Qasim's new government essentially propelled him into cooperation with Barzani and the Kurdish nationalists. Barzani declared to Qasim his "devotion to Arab–Kurdish co-operation"[19] and helped him suppress his non-Kurdish opponents in the country (Ba'thists, pan-Arabists, and Communists). For the first time an independent Iraqi constitution recognized Kurdish "national rights": "Iraqi society is based on complete co-operation between all its citizens, on respect for their rights and liberties. Arabs and Kurds are associates in this nation; the constitution guarantees their national rights within the Iraqi whole."[20]

The rapprochement did not last long, however. By 1960, Qasim began to fear that his Kurdish ally was growing too strong, and would soon be able to dictate policy to Baghdad. Qasim began backtracking on promises he made to Barzani, arming Barzani's tribal enemies, and basically trying to nurture counterweights to an ally he did not trust.[21] Baghdad also declared a new land reform at this time, which threatened the interests of Kurdish aghas and tribal elites. Barzani responded in 1961 by first attacking his Kurdish tribal rivals whom the government was arming, and then

---

[18] Barzani's credibility and military reputation in effect assisted Kurdish nationalist framings, which sought to highlight the Kurds' ability to defeat the Iraqi army.

[19] McDowall, *A Modern History of the Kurds*, p. 303.

[20] Cited in Vanly, "Kurdistan," p. 150.

[21] McDowall, *A Modern History of the Kurds*, p. 26. As in Turkish Kurdistan, the nature of tribal politics in the area meant that whenever a Kurdish nationalist movement led by one tribal grouping threatened to succeed, its traditional tribal opponents could usually be recruited by the government.

revolting against Baghdad.[22] Surprisingly, he received support and man-power from Assyrian Christians this time, who felt they were ignored and badly treated by the government in Baghdad.[23] Although Qasim's gov-ernment soon fell in the face of Kurdish revolts and intrigues within the capital, conflict between Barzani's Kurds and the Iraqi government endured. Between 1961 and 1969, four military campaigns were fought between Baghdad's often-changing government and the Kurds in the north.[24] Negotiations occurred each time the combatants had exhausted themselves, and at times, such as with an offer of autonomy called the Bazzaz Declaration in 1966, things looked as if they might be settled peacefully. Each time one of the parties felt itself to be considerably stronger than the other, however, compromise diminished and a return to the battlefield occurred. The longer the fighting endured, the less either side would be able to trust or deal amicably with the other at the negotiating table in future years. For instance, in 1966 at the battle of Hendrin, Kurdish irregulars spectacularly ambushed and defeated a much larger and better armed Iraqi army, losing fewer than twenty men and killing around 3,000 Iraqi soldiers; when his commanders brought him the news, Mustafa Barzani was angry: "Thirty or forty Iraqi dead . . . that's possible. But three thousand dead – now I can never speak to the Iraqi army."[25] The Iraqi government sued for peace, and the civilian prime minister, Abd al Rahman Bazzaz, offered the Kurds far-reaching autonomy, including a necessary provision for parliamentary democracy in all of Iraq (the Bazzaz Declaration), which they accepted. Bazzaz's offer seems to have been sincere, and it was Iraq's best chance for democracy and peace.[26] Iraq's army officers, however, were determined to avenge their crushing defeat of a few months back. Bazzaz, along with much of the Iraqi people's future, was forced to retire – and the cycle of

---

[22] O'Ballance, *Kurdish Struggle: 1920–94*, ch. 5. McDowall comments that traditional Kurdish elites such as Barzani were able to mobilize their followers at this time despite the fact that land reform was in the interest of average Kurds: "In striking testimony to the strength of tribal loyalties, their followers were insufficiently aware of the social and economic issues at stake to recognize that they were supporting the very class that exploited them, or that they stood to benefit from the land reform" (McDowall, *A Modern History of the Kurds*, p. 309). Another possibility is that "average" tribal Kurds were more interested in what they saw as part of the Kurdish nationalist project than were in land reform.

[23] O'Ballance, *Kurdish Struggle: 1920–94*, p. 47.   [24] Vanly, "Kurdistan," p. 153.

[25] Jonathan C. Randal, *After Such Knowledge, What Forgiveness? My Encounters with Kurdistan* (Oxford: Westview Press, 1999), p. 193. The figure of 3,000 Iraqi troops killed is enormous and may in fact be overstated – O'Ballance cites figures ranging from 1,000 to 2,000, which would still amount to very extensive losses *vis-à-vis* a guerrilla opponent (O'Ballance, *Kurdish Struggle: 1920–94*, p. 83).

[26] McDowall, *A Modern History of the Kurds*, p. 319.

conflict between Baghdad and the Kurds began anew. Throughout the 1960s, Barzani also continued to attack, and in a few cases destroy, the villages of his tribal rivals, attempting to assert his dominance and show them that they had more to fear from him than the government, unless of course they joined him. Although his tactics succeeded in converting many smaller tribes, larger ones such as the Baradostis, Herkis, and Surchis continued to side with the government.[27] Barzani's record of fighting Iranian government forces in 1946 (during which he beat a legendary fighting retreat from the Iraqi border to the Soviet Union, after the collapse of the Mahabad Republic) as well as his continuing contest with Baghdad, however, had by the 1960s made him the preeminent symbol of Kurdish nationalism. In Iraqi Kurdistan, he emerged as the practical leader of Kurdish nationalism as well, although his ascendance necessitated using force against and expelling several prominent political leaders of the KDP, such as Ibrahim Ahmad and Jalal Talibani, in order to assert his control over the organization.[28] Ahmad and Talibani responded by occasionally assisting Iraqi government forces against the Barzani Kurds in the coming years.

Weakening a dangerous Iraq: ephemeral international support of Kurdish rebels

The Arab nationalist Ba'th Party, which briefly held power in 1963 (deposing Qasim) and then continuously again after 1968, offered the Kurds in 1970 the most far-reaching autonomy agreement yet seen anywhere in Kurdistan. The military campaigns had gone badly for the Iraqi army, and Baghdad decided it needed more breathing space. Some of the more moderate elements in the divided regime had perhaps decided, as Abd al Rahman Bazzaz had before them, that for Iraq to become strong the country had to accommodate the Kurds and decisively bring them into the national fold. With the capacity of the Iraqi state to repress the Kurds still in question, Baghdad's ruling elites decided to offer a more open political system to the Kurds, in order to bring them into the fold. This apparent opening (as well as that of 1966) may be compared to Kemalist offers to the Kurds from 1919 to 1923 (Chapter 2), when Turkish forces were too weak and distracted to repress Kurdish insurgents. In any case, since the 1940s, Kurdish leaders (especially Barzani) had been repeatedly stating that they did not want to separate from Iraq, but rather aspired to Kurdish autonomy within Iraq's borders.

---

[27] O'Ballance, *Kurdish Struggle: 1920–94*, p. 52.   [28] Ibid., pp. 74–75.

If Baghdad's original intent, however, had been to simply buy itself time to prepare another campaign against the Kurds as the Kemalists had done, it is unlikely that the 1970 offer of autonomy would have been so extensive. Vice-President Saddam Hussein negotiated on behalf of Baghdad, and Mustafa Barzani negotiated for the Kurds. The agreement was hailed by both sides as a historic new page in Arab–Kurdish brotherhood within Iraq. The extent of autonomy offered to the Kurds also greatly worried Ankara, Tehran, and Damascus, who did not like the precedent that this would set for their own Kurdish minorities.[29]

The 1970 Agreement was never implemented, however. Its implementation encountered immediate difficulties when it came to determining the borders of the Kurdish region (Baghdad would never agree to sharing or relinquishing the oil-producing areas of Kirkuk and Mosul), and political power-sharing arrangements meant little when Iraq was ruled by a Ba'th Party dictatorship. What Baghdad apparently had in mind when it spoke of Kurdish participation in government, parliament, and other political bodies, was the Kurds' equal right to rubber stamp decisions taken by the Ba'th Party. Perhaps these difficulties could have been overcome. We will never know, however, since Iranian, CIA, and Mossad agents in contact with Barzani provided him with the weapons and the encouragement to forsake the agreement and its difficulties. The Shah of Iran wished to weaken Baghdad and had no desire to see the successful negotiation of Kurdish autonomy in Iraq, and the latter two also found it in their interests to foment problems for the revolutionary regime in Iraq. The opening in the Iraqi political system also did not appear sincere to the Kurds, and the offer of outside support allowed for Kurdish movement strategies of more violent confrontation with Baghdad. Assured of Iranian, US, and Israeli support, Barzani began raising his demands on Baghdad, while Baghdad began reneging on terms offered in 1970 and launching attempts to assassinate Barzani.[30]

---

[29] It was pointed out in ch. 4 that Turkey at this time sent commando teams into its own Kurdish regions, who searched Kurdish villages, rounded up inhabitants, and reminded them not to aspire to what Barzani's Kurds had just achieved (Gerard Chaliand [ed.], *People Without a Country: The Kurds and Kurdistan* [London: Zed Press, 1980], p. 88). For the details of the lengthy agreement, which included provisions for decentralization of political power to Kurdish regions, Kurdish local government, education and publishing in Kurdish, Kurdish civil society promotion, economic development of northern Iraq, official recognition of the Kurds as a founding partner to the Arabs of Iraq, and consociational arrangements for power-sharing in Baghdad, see Vanly, "Kurdistan," pp. 153–157.

[30] One of the more peculiar assassination attempts was the September 29, 1971 "case of the exploding mullahs." Jonathan Randal provides the following description, which is eerily similar to the methods used to assassinate Northern Alliance Afghan leader Massoud on September 9, 2001:

The Iraqi government's behavior could in turn be framed by Kurdish nationalists as evidence of the futility of dealing with Baghdad peacefully.

A 1972 Soviet–Iraqi "friendship and cooperation treaty" meant that at the same time that the Kurds were receiving arms from Iran, Israel, and the US, the Soviets were providing larger quantities of advanced and heavy weaponry to Baghdad. Both sides were preparing for war, as it became clear that the autonomy agreement would never see the light of day.

When heavy fighting finally broke out in 1974, Baghdad sent ". . . eight Army divisions (about 120,000 men) with 700–800 of the Iraqi Army's 900 tanks and some 20 battalions of mobile artillery; also the entire air force (11,000 men), equipped with several hundred planes including modern Tupolev-22 and Mig-23 bombers" against a force of roughly 50,000 Kurdish *peshmerga*[31] guerrillas. Soviet assistance and the huge income available from newly nationalized Iraqi petroleum companies[32] had greatly increased Iraqi military strength – from this day forward, the Kurds could no longer pose a challenge to Iraq's military without significant outside help. The Iraqi state's capacity and propensity for repression was now more solid than ever before. Part of the problem for the Kurds lay in the fact that in Iraq, unlike in Turkey, their strategy against the state was not truly based on guerrilla warfare. Baghdad could clearly identify the communities from which most of the Iraqi Kurdish tribal forces came, and defending the territory in which these communities lay was important to the rebels. Against a significantly more powerful foe such as the post-1972 Iraqi army, however, one cannot hold territory. Guerrilla warfare must instead rely on mobility, secrecy, and surprise, so as to avoid a direct confrontation with the enemy until a time is finally

A delegation of Shia and Sunni divines planning to visit Barzani was enlisted by the regime to sound out his views; some of them were prevailed upon to strap tape recorders to their bodies "to catch his every word," but unbeknownst to them the recorders were packed with explosives. The secret police figured correctly that Barzani's well-known respect for clerics would keep his guards from frisking the visitors. As soon as the meeting started, agents doubling as the delegation's drivers detonated the charges by activating switches in their vehicles. The clerics were sent to their maker, and bits of flesh remained stuck to the ceiling and walls for days. Barzani escaped shaken but otherwise unhurt, thanks to the fortuitous presence of a tea server, who shielded him and was killed in the blast. In the confusion Barzani's guards, thinking their leader was dead, slaughtered a number of the clerics and retainers who had survived the explosion. (Randal, *After Such Knowledge*, pp. 209–210)

[31] *Peshmerga* in Kurdish means "one who faces death," and is a term applied to Kurdish fighters (although not those serving in non-Kurdish armies).

[32] 1974 was also the year that the oil crisis began, as a result of the OAPEC (Organization of Arab Petroleum Exporting Countries) embargo on the West in the wake of the October Arab–Israeli war (which was later followed by OPEC's profit-driven restrictions on supply and consequent price increases). The resulting huge jump in oil prices swelled Baghdad's war chest.

reached when forces are more equal in strength. Only after 1975 would Iraqi Kurds revert to mainly this type of guerrilla warfare, after having recognized the mettle of the modernized Iraqi army.

By the end of 1974, Kurdish forces were eventually pushed back close to the Iranian, Turkish, and Syrian borders. A doctor from Save the Children Fund described the following encounter with a renowned Kurdish military commander during the 1974–1975 war: "We met him walking up the road towards Shillia, surrounded by a retinue of senior officers. A tall, thin man with a slight limp, aged about 60. Tears were pouring down his cheeks as he spoke to us of his despair. 'We had only ancient mortars and automatic rifles with little ammunition, insufficient to match the fire power of the Iraqi tanks and continued aerial bombardment from low-flying fighters.'"[33]

Additionally, the Kurdish nationalist side of the conflict continued to suffer from its internal divisions, with many tribes recruited to fight on Baghdad's side and the non-tribal peasantry and urban workers largely passive. Again, had a lack of available traditional elite allies back in the 1950s forced the Iraqi Kurdish nationalist movement to develop a more progressive program that mobilized the peasantry and urban classes, the challenge to Baghdad might have been much stronger. Many tribal forces would have likely still participated in the movement (with the resulting recruitment of opposing tribes by Baghdad), but in a manner more subservient to the political leadership. The combination of a mass Kurdish movement and patriotic tribal forces would have had greater chances of succeeding against Baghdad and tribal *jash* forces.[34] The incorporation of peasant and urban classes into the nationalist struggle would have also allowed for the pursuance of more effective guerrilla warfare tactics, rather than warfare dependent mainly on identifiable tribal groupings. If such a guerrilla struggle had in turn linked itself to leftist groups from the Sunni and Shiite Arab population (as a Kurdish movement not subservient to the ideology of conservative tribal elites would have been able to do), the challenge to the Ba'th party would have been greatly magnified. Again, the continuing availability and Kurdish nationalist reliance upon tribal elite allies precluded important kinds of resource mobilization strategies and cultural framings.

---

[33] David Nabarro, undated personal account of the Save the Children Fund Relief Expedition to Iraqi Kurdistan, cited in McDowall, *A Modern History of the Kurds*, p. 338.
[34] *Jash* is Kurdish for "little donkey," a term applied to those who "sell out" the nationalist cause and work for the state.

As it happens, the more traditional kind of warfare practiced by Barzani's fighters required the defense of bases, strategic areas, and supportive communities which Baghdad could clearly identify. By February 1975, the Iranian, American, and Israeli assistance had become critically important for hard-pressed Kurds who were face to face with the Iraqi army. Accepting this support from Iraq's enemies lost the Kurdish nationalist movement much of the sympathy some Iraqi Arab elites had for it, however. While they appreciated Barzani's insistence that he was fighting for autonomy rather than separation, no Iraqi Arab leader could accept Kurdish collaboration with Americans, Iranians, and Israelis.

Unfortunately for the Kurds, on March 6, 1975, the Shah of Iran and Saddam Hussein concluded the Algiers Agreement, wherein Iraq ceded to Iran a contested border demarcation in the Shatt al-Arab waterway, and Iran agreed to withdraw all support for Kurdish rebels in Iraq. This turn of events caught Barzani and his rebels completely by surprise. The Shah had not even bothered to give the Kurdish fighters "a few days notice so that they could get their women and children across the border before the time of killing began."[35] CIA and Mossad agents immediately heeded the Shah's demands and packed their bags and left the area, along with Iranian troops and support artillery. Supplies provided to the rebels were immediately cut off. Iran, the US, and Israel had all involved themselves with the Kurds in order to weaken the Arab nationalist regime in Baghdad, but neither Tehran nor Washington wished to see the Kurds successfully declare independence from Baghdad. In a PBS *Frontline* interview, James Akins (US attaché in Baghdad from 1963 to 1965 and then US Ambassador to Saudi Arabia) offered the following observation: "Kissinger was asked about the morality of a policy that encouraged the people to revolt against their central government in order to obtain a minor political gain for us – and then when we achieved other goals, we would betray the people and allow them to be slaughtered. And Kissinger replied that covert military activity is not to be confused with missionary work."[36] Two weeks after their betrayal and isolation, most of the Kurdish forces bitterly conceded defeat and either surrendered or fled. Hundreds of thousands of Kurdish refugees, including Barzani, evacuated to Iran, while others surrendered to the government in Iraq. His spirit broken, Mustafa Barzani died of cancer in an American

---

[35] *The Washington Star*, editorial (March 14, 1975).
[36] http://www.pbs.org/wgbh/pa ... tline/shows/saddam/interviews/akins.html.

hospital four years later (although he did live long enough to see the Shah deposed in the Iranian Revolution).[37]

After the defeat of 1975, smaller number of fighters continued the struggle via guerrilla warfare within Iraqi controlled territory. Relying on more traditional guerrilla warfare tactics, these bands hid by day and mounted occasional attacks at night. In June 1975, Barzani's old political rival Jalal Talabani, along with others whom Barzani had expelled from the KDP in the 1960s, formed the Patriotic Union of Kurdistan (PUK). Talabani's PUK rallied a disproportionate number of Sorani-speaking Kurds, tribes in opposition to Barzani, members of the Qadiri Sufi religious brotherhood, and people from the southeastern part of Iraqi Kurdistan. As such, the PUK became one of the poles in a bifurcated Iraqi Kurdistan – the opposite yet similar image of Barzani's KDP, which was disproportionately composed of Kurmanji-speaking Kurds, Barzani tribes and their allies, Naqshibendi Sufis, and people from the north-western part of Iraqi Kurdistan. Although Talibani and the founders of the PUK came from the more urban, intellectual, socialist, and political politburo of the old KDP, the PUK itself came in practice and behavior to resemble the KDP so much that average Kurds were often unable to specify a single policy or ideological difference between the two.[38] The KDP and PUK became the main contenders for the Kurdish nationalist mantle in Iraq. In subsequent years, both groups periodically negotiated with Baghdad. Each time one of them had a rapprochement with the government, the other would label that group *jash* and attempt to frame itself as the only true nationalist group.

Going back to 1975, however, it appears that Talabani had in effect used Barzani's abandonment of the armed struggle in 1975 as an opportunity to frame himself and the new PUK as the new torchbearers of Kurdish nationalism in Iraq.[39] Talabani's people began launching more

---

[37] For a detailed examination of how Barzani viewed the events leading up to the 1975 defeat, see David A. Korn, "The Last Years of Mustafa Barzani," *Middle East Quarterly* (June 1994). Although a brilliant military tactician, Barzani lacked political acumen. In 1978, he lamented: "How was I to know that the CIA isn't a part of this nation, that it is disliked so much by the Congress and the people of America?" (Korn, "Last Years of Mustafa Barzani," 26).

[38] Asking ardent backers of either the PUK or KDP what the policy and ideological differences between the two parties were quickly became one of my favorite pastimes during my 1994, 2000, and 2003–2004 visits to Iraqi Kurdistan. I have yet to receive an answer that goes beyond the contention that one party fights more valiantly for the Kurdish cause, while the other allies itself with the hated central government more frequently. Iraqi Kurds not too closely attached to either party, however, tended to ascribe the differences to the leaders' personalities, interests, and old tribal rivalries.

[39] David McDowall, "The Kurdish Question: A Historical Review," in Kreyenbroek and Sperl (eds.), *The Kurds*, p. 28.

sustained guerrilla attacks in 1976. Shortly afterwards, Barzani's sons likewise took up the torch and also renewed KDP guerrilla operations. Other smaller Kurdish groups, such as the Kurdistan Socialist Party, did the same. Even in such dire circumstances, however, the various Kurdish movements opposing Baghdad still allowed personal differences, tribal feuds, and ideological disagreements between themselves to distract them into internecine conflict, at the same time as they fought the Iraqi government. A complex and shifting tapestry of Kurdish infighting continued well into the 1980s, with Iran trading its support for Iraqi Kurdish help in fighting Iranian Kurds, while the KDP and PUK associated with myriad other opposition groups (both Kurdish and non-Kurdish, such as the ICP) and fought each other. Turkey even entered the area to ostensibly pursue its own Kurdish rebels, hitting KDP and PUK units in the process. It was a telling comment on pan-Kurdish solidarity in the area, and many ordinary Kurds loathed the politicking and opportunistic alliances of their leaders. In the meantime, having regained control of the north, Baghdad pursued policies of Arabization, particularly around the oil regions of Kirkuk and Mosul, forcing Kurds and Turkmen villagers into the south of the country and replacing them with ethnic Arabs.[40]

The path to genocide: The Iran–Iraq War and the *Anfal* campaigns

Saddam Hussein became Iraq's president in 1979. Now that he had suppressed Iraq's internal problem with the Kurds, Saddam sought to regain the territorial concessions he had made to Iran in 1975. Taking advantage of internal chaos following the 1979 Islamic revolution, Iraq launched a full-scale invasion against the new Islamic Republic in September of 1980.[41] During the eight years of bloody war that followed, Iraq enlisted Iranian Kurds to help it fight Tehran (mainly the KDPI), and Iran successfully mobilized Iraqi Kurds against Baghdad (both Massoud Barzani's KDP as well as the KDP breakaway faction from 1975, Jalal Talibani's PUK). The Iraqi Kurds could not pass up the

---

[40] For a detailed account of this policy during the 1970s, based on an official visit to the region, see Vanly, "Kurdistan," ch. 5.

[41] Baghdad's justification for the invasion was that Iran was fomenting Shiite unrest in Iraq. Following the revolution in Iran, there were in fact demonstrations against the Iraqi Ba'th government amongst Iraqi Shiites, who constitute at least 55 percent of Iraq's population (Entessar, *Kurdish Ethnonationalism*, p. 128). Eminent Iraqi Shiite spiritual leader Ayatollah Mohammad Baqer al-Sadr declared in 1979 and 1980 that Sunnis, Shiites, and Kurds should unite to overthrow the rulers of Iraq, whom he called "bloody murderers" and "despots" (ibid.). He was executed in April of 1980.

opportunity to recoup their losses of 1975, even if this meant risking Saddam's wrath for assisting Iranian forces. In effect, they were hoping to take advantage of the new political opportunities of foreign assistance (the new Islamic Republic of Iran) and the uncertain capacity of the Iraqi state to repress them while it was at war with its neighbor. Baghdad in turn framed the Kurds' cooperation with Iran as high treason in Iraq's most critical hour, even worse than past cooperation with the CIA and Mossad. Such framings were a dangerous omen, more comparable to Ottoman reaction to the Armenians' assistance of Russia than Turkey's relations with its Kurds.

In the latter years of the war, it began to seem as if Iran might defeat Iraq. Western aid poured into Iraq in order to prevent it from succumbing to the "fundamentalist threat." Turkey even launched several military attacks against Iraqi Kurdish positions in the north, for it too feared the success of the joint Kurdish–Iranian forces.[42] In the final stages of the war, and even before an exhausted Iran agreed to UN Security Council Resolution 598 for a cease-fire on July 18, 1988, Baghdad began wreaking its vengeance on the Kurdish population. Probably the first Iraqi Kurdish village that Baghdad attacked with poison gas was Shaikh Wisan, in April 1987.[43] The most famous of these reprisals was the March 16 attack on the town of Halabja. Halabja was in Iranian hands at the time – Kurdish forces from the area had helped Iran capture it the day before, and the civilian population of the town was viewed by Baghdad as disloyal since well before then. Roughly 5,000 civilians were killed in Halabja alone, when Iraqi war planes dropped mustard gas and other chemical compounds on the town: "Dead bodies – human and animal – littered the streets, huddled in doorways, slumped over the steering wheels of their cars. Survivors stumbled around, laughing hysterically, before collapsing ... Those who had been directly exposed to the gas found that their symptoms worsened as the night wore on. Many children died along the way and were abandoned where they fell."[44] Iran brought in photographers to record the grisly scene in Halabja the next day. Some of these photos reached the entire world; a particular powerful image showed a Kurdish man by the doorstep of a home, his body slumped over the child he was trying to protect. Nonetheless, the reaction from political leaders around the world was muted (with the exception of Iran),

---

[42] Entessar, *Kurdish Ethnonationalism*, pp. 132–137. Such a fear stemmed from both the possibility of Iraqi Kurdish independence in the war's aftermath, as well as the power that Iran would gain if it seized Iraq's oil producing areas.

[43] Kanan Makiya, "The Anfal: Uncovering an Iraqi Campaign to Exterminate the Kurds," *Harper's Magazine* (May 1992), 53, 58.

[44] Human Rights Watch, *Genocide in Iraq* (1993), 106.

while Iraq denied responsibility and instead accused Iran of the deed. Meanwhile, Baghdad continued to attack other Kurdish towns and villages with poison gas.

The gassing of villages such as Halabja was only incidental to a more organized, sinister, and less visible campaign begun in January of 1988, however. Saddam named the campaign "al-Anfal,"[45] and appointed his cousin Ali Hassan al-Majid to pursue "a large-scale Iraqi government campaign, carefully planned and executed, to exterminate a sizable portion of Iraq's Kurdish minority."[46] Saddam's attempt at genocide consisted of eight "Anfal operations":

A typical Anfal operation is perhaps best described by the regime itself. A letter printed on presidential stationary and marked SECRET AND PERSONAL tells of "2,532 people and 1,869 families" being "captured" during a "heroic Anfal operation" and sent to a "camp," the location of which is not disclosed. As to the fate of those captured and imprisoned, I quote here from an audiotape of the proceedings of a meeting of senior army, Baath Party, and secret police officers held on January 26, 1989, in the city of Kirkuk. The tape, which I listened to while I was in Iraq, records Ali Hassan al-Majid talking in crude Tikriti slang – he, like Saddam, is from the town of Tikrit – about the Kurds who wound up at forts like that of Qoratu: "[T]aking care of them means burying them with bulldozers. That's what taking care of them means ... These people gave themselves up. Does that mean I am going to leave them alive? Where shall I put these people, so many of them? So I began to distribute them across the provinces. And from there I had bulldozers going backward and forward."[47]

In a book entitled *Modernity and the Holocaust* (1989), Zygmunt Bauman provides us with a warning: "When the modernist dream is embraced by an absolute power able to monopolize modern vehicles of rational action, and when that power attains freedom from effective social control, genocide follows."[48] Saddam's Ba'th Party dreamt of a powerful, modern, Arab nationalist Iraq that would take a leading role in the Middle East, but the Kurds kept hindering such ambitions. Arab nationalist framings cast the Kurds as the dupes of foreign powers, intent on forever undermining the country's future. By the 1980s, however, Baghdad was able to build a modern and very efficient bureaucracy within the Ba'th party framework. Iraq was also awash in weapons happily supplied by the West and the USSR, in return for Iraqi oil, money, and strategic

---

[45] *Al-Anfal* refers to the eight *sura* of the Quran, which spell out the rules by which spoils may be claimed by the victors of a battle.
[46] Makiya, "The Anfal," 53.   [47] Ibid., 58.
[48] Cited in Khaled Salih. "Anfal: The Kurdish Genocide in Iraq," *Digest of Middle East Studies* 4: 2 (Spring 1995), 36. [Note: Khaled Salih was the pseudonym of Kanan Makiya, and this citation refers to an earlier version of his article, "The Anfal."]

advantage – i.e., their own "national interests."[49] Saddam's absolute rule in the "Republic of Fear" formed the last ingredient in Bauman's recipe for genocide. By the late 1980s, the state in Iraq therefore displayed a capacity and propensity for repression not seen since the time of National Socialism in Germany or Stalinism in the USSR. The results of a situation wherein Iraqi society, in all its diversity, could not check the power of the Iraqi state, are also described by McDowall:

We shall never know the exact number of those who perished in the Anfal operations, but they probably accounted for 150,000–200,000 lives. In a few cases villagers and *peshmergas* were shot without distinction on the spot. The vast majority of people, however, were sent to Topzawa, a large army base south-west of Kirkuk which housed a transient population of approximately 5,000. It was here that the registration and segregation took place with a brutality reminiscent of Nazi death camps. Teenage and adult males were lined up rank after rank, and stripped of everything but their clothes, and interrogated. Beatings were routine. "We saw them taking off the men's shirts and beating them," one old man recalled. "They were handcuffed in pairs, and they took away their shoes. This was going on from 8.00 am until noon." After two or three days at Topzawa, all these males were loaded onto closed trucks. They were not seen again.

Through the testimonies of six survivors we know the end of the road for the men of the Anfal. Taken to the execution grounds of Ramadi, Hatra and elsewhere, they were tied up in long lines alongside deep trenches, and shot. When the trenches were full, they were covered in.[50]

---

[49] Perhaps one of the more famous quotes regarding the American view of Saddam's unsavory nature was that provided by National Security Council advisor Geoffrey Kemp: "We knew he was an S.O.B., but he was our S.O.B." Quoted in Judith Miller and Laurie Mylroie, *Saddam Hussein and the Crisis in the Gulf* (New York: Times Books, 1990), p. 143.

[50] McDowall, *A Modern History of the Kurds*, p. 359. There are a great many gruesome accounts such as this one. The reader may wish to consult any of the following in addition to the sources quoted from here: Dlawer Ala'adeen, *Death Clouds: Saddam Hussein's Chemical War against the Kurds* (Kurdish Scientific and Medical Association, London, 1991); Samir al Khalil, *Republic of Fear: the Politics of Modern Iraq* (Los Angeles: University of California Press, 1989); Joost Hiltermann, *Bureaucracy of Repression: The Iraqi Government in its own Words* (Human Rights Watch, 1994); and various other Human Rights Watch and Amnesty International Country Reports on Iraq. The Iraqi regime itself unintentionally admitted to 100,000 victims in 1991: "When, much later, in the spring of 1991 the Kurds and the Iraqi government initiated a series of eventually sterile negotiations, somehow Massoud Barzani and the other Kurdish negotiators managed to control their emotions and deal with a notably nervous Majid as one of the government representatives. The Kurds told him that according to their calculations 182,000 Kurds had disappeared and were presumed dead, most of them in an unprecedented series of 1988 search-and-destroy operations known as al Anfal and directed principally against civilians. Majid jumped up in a rage and shouted, 'What is this exaggerated figure of 182,000? It couldn't have been more than 100,000.'" (Randal, *After Such Knowledge*, p. 214)

A PUK *peshmerga* at the time stated to the author that during Anfal 3, villages in his area of operation in the Garmyan region were surrounded by Iraqi forces on March 9, 1988. The *peshmerga* units defended the area for six days, but then had to fall back in the face of superior firepower. He and his men watched the Anfal operations from afar, aware of what was being done but completely helpless to stop it. The sense of demoralization amongst the *peshmerga* was beyond words.[51] Kurdish resistance effectively collapsed, as *peshmerga* who still had families went to collect them and fled for the borders. Hundreds of thousands of refugees fled towards Iran and Turkey, bringing with them gruesome scars from chemical bombs and accounts of the Anfal attacks. "By July 45,000 out of 75,000 square kilometers of Kurdistan had been cleared of Kurds."[52]

What happened to the Kurds in 1988 is one of the most powerful examples of the vulnerability of nations who lack a state of their own in a state-centric world. In the case of the Kurds, this is doubly true, since they have no dependable international allies to press their case on their behalf. The community of states took no action in the face of this genocide, despite the clear evidence before them, other than issuing a UN Security Council Resolution – UNSCR 620, condemning the use of chemical weapons in general and calling for "proper and effective measures" when such use occurred.[53] Although the US Senate voted a little later to impose sanctions on Iraq, the Reagan administration stopped the motion and one month later approved $1 billion in credit guarantees for Baghdad.[54] Turkey blocked UN teams from going to examine Iraqi Kurdish refugees on its territory.[55] Britain contradicted its own initial position by doubling its export credits to Iraq, soon after its Foreign Secretary had stated that "We have been at the forefront of anxiety and grave concern about these [CW] allegations."[56] Kuwait accused the media of fabricating lies to discredit Iraq (this was before Saddam expressed his attachment to Iraq's "19th province" in 1991), and

---

[51] Personal interview with Jalal Juhar, Head of Kirkuk Committee for Displaced Persons, September 28, 2000, Suleimaniya, Iraqi Kurdistan.

[52] McDowall, *A Modern History of the Kurds*, p. 360.   [53] Ibid., p. 362.

[54] Entessar, *Kurdish Ethnonationalism*, p. 139.

[55] Turkey did allow a two-person UNHCR team in during the month of September, many weeks after the chemical attacks had occurred. The team, after receiving some reports from Turkish medical authorities and quickly examining some of the refugees, stated that there was no evidence to substantiate the refugees' claims. Turkey's Foreign Ministry then announced that no additional teams would be allowed in the area to investigate the chemical weapons charge (*Tercuman* [September 15, 1988]; also cited in Entessar, *Kurdish Ethnonationalism*, p. 140). If evidence had been found, of course, Turkey would have been expected to join a sanctions regime against Iraq, from whom it received substantial amounts of oil and trade.

[56] McDowall, *A Modern History of the Kurds*, p. 363.

Baghdad "issued a statement charging that the real purpose of the anti-Iraq vote [in the US Senate] was to divert world attention from the Palestinian uprising in the occupied territories in Israel."[57] The Iraqi state's framing of the issue was that it never happened. Perhaps most odious of all, however, was the following kind of argument, which summarized most states' reasons for ignoring the Iraqi genocide: "Unappreciated for its historic victory over Iran, offended by America's unfounded charges of genocide and our close collaboration with Israel, Iraq is turning elsewhere. On Baghdad's busy streets, US cars will likely remain scarce, and US firms will be screened out as Iraq buys the tools, supplies, and training its development requires. Still worse, the United States will retain few avenues of influence in an important capital."[58]

Were it not for an unexpected turn of events in 1991, Saddam's genocide might have emerged as an example of the ability of extreme

---

[57] Entessar, *Kurdish Ethnonationalism*, p. 139. Hence the political right, obsessed with winning business contracts and selling weapons to the Iraqi "bulwark against fundamentalist Iran," was not the only group to ignore the Ba'th's genocide. Because of Iraq's anti-Israeli stance, many pro-Palestinian as well as leftist voices also failed to extend their concern for human rights to Saddam's Kurdish victims. As late as 1991, Edward Said was still trying to cast doubt on Iraq's guilt: "The claim that Iraq gassed its own citizens has often been repeated. At best, this is uncertain. There is at least one War College report, done while Iraq was a US ally, that claims that the gassing of the Kurds in Halabja was done by Iran. Few people mention such reports in the media today" (Edward Said, *London Review of Books* [March 7, 1991]; quoted in Salih, "Anfal," 27). For an in-depth analysis of such selective vision regarding human rights abuses on the part of some intellectuals, see Kanan Makiya, *Cruelty and Silence* [New York: W.W. Norton and Company, 1993]. Likewise, the *Washington Report on Middle East Affairs* published an article by Paul Findley entitled "The US Stake in Good Relations With Baghdad" (December, 1988), 15. In this article, Findley argued that instead of condemning Iraq for "unsubstantiated charges of the use of chemical weapons," the Americans should send the country that fought off Iran "a grateful salute from Washington to Baghdad." Findley added that,

On a week long visit recently to Iraq, I found Iraqi officials deeply distressed and offended at the charges. Iraq denies using chemical warfare but admits driving out of the country rebellious Kurds of several tribes who had collaborated with Iran throughout much of the eight-year war ... The anti-Iraq flap, to a great degree, is an offshoot of the Arab–Israeli conflict. Much of it is inspired by pro-Israel activists who have a vested interest in painting Iraq in the most offensive hues possible ... Most of the data on which Washington bases its charges of chemical warfare come from Israeli intelligence, information that is ambiguous to say the least ... Voting to cut off trade with a country that has suffered so much in a common cause is excessive, to say the least. It will hardly improve our ability to influence Iraqi behavior in the future. It should be noted that several unarmed Palestinians have died from the effect of tear gas used by Israeli troops, who have killed nearly 300 other Palestinians in recent months. No one on Capital Hill, however, proposes that US aid to Israel be halted, that trade sanctions be imposed, or that the US government ban further purchases of American tear gas by the Israeli army.

[58] Former US Congressman Paul Findley, "The US Stake in Good Relations With Baghdad," *Washington Report on Middle East Affairs* (December 1988), 15.

government repression to stifle dissent permanently. The international community's failure to act in defense of the victims, combined with their utter inability to withstand such awesome repression from a state so well armed, left few options for Iraqi Kurds. Although grievance framings were not lacking within the population, not even the most brilliant of mobilization strategies could succeed in the face of such grim opportunity structures. The people could no longer believe that any challenger movement stood any chance of opposing such a regime. Unlike Turkey, Iraq had no democratic pretensions to prevent it from instituting its version of a "final solution" to the Kurdish problem. In Iraq, like in Turkey, repression and conflict over the years did heighten Kurdish private and politicized ethnic identity. After 1988, however, many more would likely have come to the conclusion that politicized Kurdish ethnicity in Iraq was folly at best and suicide at worst. A gradual shift to private ethnic identification and perhaps assimilation would not have been unlikely in the face of hopeless prospects for Kurdish nationalism in Iraq.[59]

The 1991 Gulf War – radical changes in Iraqi Kurdish opportunity structures

Other states' public and private attitudes towards Iraq changed on August 2, 1990, when Saddam ordered the invasion of Kuwait and thereby threatened to control much of the world's oil supply. According to Western framings, the people of Kuwait now had to be liberated from Iraq – the injustice of Baghdad's aggression would not be tolerated. The international system demonstrated once again that it placed greater value upon the sovereignty of states than the physical safety of nations. During the pre-war propaganda offensive, reports of how Iraq had used chemical weapons on the Iranians and the Kurds were fetched from the shelves where they had lain since 1988, and no longer questioned for their veracity. An international coalition of states mobilized troops and expelled Baghdad's forces from Kuwait in February of 1991.

At the same time that the ground war against Iraq was being conducted, George Bush publicly called for the people of Iraq to rise up and overthrow Saddam. His message was carried on virtually every television and radio station in the world, including the CIA-run Voice of Free Iraq,

---

[59] I do not feel that this observation contradicts conclusions made in ch. 4, however, regarding the slim chances of politicized Kurdish ethnicity in Turkey receding. Ted Robert Gurr and Barbara Harff, *Ethnic Conflict in World Politic* (Boulder: Westview Press, 1994) make the argument, for instance, that repression generally invokes an ethnic nationalist backlash, except in those rare cases of absolutely brutal genocidal repression, after which no dissent can survive.

broadcasting out of Jedda, Saudi Arabia.[60] Perhaps the Kurds should be forgiven for thinking that this time, unlike in 1975, the Americans would actually back them up for such an action. They were certainly encouraged to believe this, if not given any explicit promises.[61] The Kurds had in fact been careful not to side with the West before Saddam's defeat appeared certain – a Ba'th official in the north had even explicitly warned them: "If you have forgotten Halabja, I would like to remind you that we are ready to repeat the operation."[62] Although the economic language of rational choice appears quite inappropriate in such a context, one might refer to the Ba'th official's threat as a selective disincentive more powerful than even Turkish generals were able to brandish, and against which Kurdish nationalists could not compete. When the Kurds in the north and the Shiites in the south did nonetheless rise up in March, hoping to take advantage of Saddam's crushing February defeat, they succeeded in immediately capturing many cities throughout both regions.[63] Given widespread Kurdish and Shiite hatred for Saddam's rule and the belief that the Allies had incapacitated him, mobilization occurred spontaneously in the south and with only the slightest organized encouragement in the north. The US administration, suddenly worried that a mass uprising in Iraq could lead to unexpected and difficult to control outcomes, backtracked on its earlier statements.[64] Turkey was deeply

---

[60] Entessar, *Kurdish Ethnonationalism*, p. 146.

[61] On February 15, 1991, George Bush had stated: "And there's another way for the bloodshed to stop. And that is for the Iraqi military and the Iraqi people to take matters into their own hands and force Saddam Hussein, the dictator, to step aside and then comply with the United Nations' resolution." (Quoted in "The CIA's Secret War in Iraq – ABC News Report" [February 7, 1998]; transcript available at http:www.payk.net/communicationRecord/mailingList/Iran-news-1998/msg00321.html.)

[62] *International Herald Tribune* (January 25, 1991); cited in McDowall, *A Modern History of the Kurds*, p. 370.

[63] US Intelligence reported that the rebellion had spread to "14 of Iraq's 18 provinces," and former Iraqi General Wafik Samarli stated that, "The uprising almost succeeded. I will tell you a secret. At the very end, we had only two days of Kalishnakov bullets left over in the warehouses of the Iraqi army. The situation was very, very dangerous" ("The CIA's secret war in Iraq – ABC News Report"). Many Iraqi army units defected *en masse* to the rebels' side, showing no great love for "the Butcher of Baghdad."

[64] Peter Jennings, addressing General Brent Scowcroft I, stated: "The United States did want Saddam Hussein to go, they just didn't want the Iraqi people to take over. And what did you think of it at the time?" Scowcroft: "I, frankly, wished it hadn't happened. I envisioned a postwar government being a military government" ("The CIA's secret war in Iraq – ABC News Report"). The US administration felt, as usual, that a military government would be easier to deal with and do business with than a more popular government. Another Bush administration official stated: "It probably sounds callous, but we did the best thing not to get near [the Kurdish revolt]. They're nice people, and they're cute, but they're really just bandits. They're losers" (*Newsweek*, April 15, 1991: 27; cited in Entessar, *Kurdish Ethnonationalism*, p. 155).

worried that such an uprising could lead to a Kurdish state in the north, and the West also feared that if Iraq's majority Shiite population came to control the country, it would ally itself with Shiite Iran. George Bush qualified his earlier statements, insisting that he had not meant that Iraqis should revolt at that particular moment in time. One of the Kurdish leaders, while conceding that the Americans had never explicitly promised military assistance for the uprising, expressed his bitterness towards US public statements at the time:

... when they said openly and officially that they are not supporting this revolt and this is not co-ordination with the United States of America, it harmed us too much, this statement. Because many officers in the army who are promising to co-operate with us and thinking that America is behind us, when they heard that America is not with us, they changed. I am always blaming American friends, that they are not taking into consideration the impact of this inside the army, inside the Iraqi people. For example General Zinni [Commander of the US Southern Command, in charge of the Gulf region], when he is talking about humiliating the Iraqi opposition, he is indirectly supporting Saddam. People of Iraq will think this American's telling us that the opposition are nothing and why should we go with them. It is discouraging people to side with us; it is making the regime strong and saying to people, yes, there is no opposition ...[65]

Talabani essentially stresses the impact that US statements had on the credibility of opposition resource mobilization strategies, dissuading people from attaching their fate to that of a movement whose success seemed doubtful.

As soon as it became apparent to Saddam that outside assistance for the Kurdish and Shiite rebels who had heeded Bush's call was not forthcoming, Baghdad's counter-attack was swift and unrelenting. Saddam mobilized his best Republican Guard units (which were left intact far from the front lines of Desert Storm) to first quell the Shiites in the south.[66]

---

[65] PBS *Frontline* interview with Jalal Talabani, http://www.pbs.org/wgbh/pa ... tline/shows/saddam/interviews/talabani.html.

[66] The rebellion in the south began in the city of Basra. Iraqi troops defected *en masse*, and many army officers who refused their orders to bomb restive Iraqi civilian areas in the southern marshes were later executed by Baghdad (FBIS, "Voice of the Iraqi Opposition," in Arabic [13:00 GM4, July 8, 1991]). The situation described at the outset of this chapter, when the army is no longer willing to repress ordinary citizens, had in effect come into being. Saddam's Republican Guards, however, were not the regular army. Whereas "normal" Iraqi army units had been devastated by the Allied bombing campaign and brief land war, the Republican Guards had been kept safe near Baghdad. Hence the defecting army could not stop these specially trained and indoctrinated troops, who were willing to kill any number of people to protect the regime that had created them and continued to provide them with all manner of perks and rewards. The southern rebels and ordinary army units were left to their fate – no safe haven was established and tens of thousands were killed by the Republican Guards.

Then the brutal repression was moved north, precipitating a massive run of around 2 million Kurdish refugees towards the Turkish and Iranian borders. Kurdish and Shiite rebels had perceived a political opportunity that did not in fact exist – Bush's implied assistance was not a promise, and Saddam still had the most significant elements of his repressive apparatus intact. Speculation about elite divisions within Saddam's regime that might lead to a coup d'état were also mistaken.

Columns of refugees were bombarded by Iraqi helicopter gun ships, which the US had permitted to fly. Live international television coverage of these events, along with images of panicking refugees denied entry at the Turkish border, deeply embarrassed the Allied coalition:

Two million Kurds ... attempted to reach the [Turkish and Iranian] borders ahead of the Iraqi army. These images traveled across the world, in newspapers and on television screens, in April 1991: On narrow, snow-covered mountain roads, an incredible array of vehicles – private cars, but also buses, taxis, bulldozers, tractors, and even garbage trucks! – rolled along at a snail's pace. It was the traffic jam of the century. Some vehicles took twenty-four hours to travel twenty kilometers. Others would never arrive: strafed by the helicopters of the Iraqi air force, they never reached the border ... Children and the old, exhausted after walking for days, died of hunger and exposure. Upon reaching the Turkish border, there was no one to welcome them, apart from Turkish soldiers with guard dogs. Posted in groups every ten meters along the border, they would not hesitate to fire on any Kurdish refugees wanting to cross. These images, and others that one could hardly bear ... caused a somewhat shocked international public opinion to discover the Kurds' existence.[67]

An international public outcry demanded that something be done, and the US, Britain, and France began exploring options with their Turkish allies. Turkey, under significant pressure to admit the refugees, submitted the idea of a temporary, allied-protected safe haven in northern Iraq.[68] Only when they were assured of protection from Saddam would the Kurdish refugees return to northern Iraq, and Turkey certainly did not want them to stay in its territory, where its own Kurdish population was

---

[67] Just a few miles south of the refugees at the Turkish border, a small band of 150 KDP *peshmerga* desperately held back advancing Iraqi armoured columns, skillfully giving the impression of being more numerous than they were (McDowall, *A Modern History of the Kurds*, p. 375). McDowall adds that, "Had Baghdad realized how weak the resistance to their advance really was, it would undoubtedly have pressed its attack" (ibid.). Regarding Turkish troops who "would not hesitate to fire on refugees crossing the border," I have been unable to find any accounts of the refugees actually being fired upon. Rather, the norm seems to have involved physically beating them back. Embarrassed by such scenes captured on live television broadcasts, Turkey soon began letting some of the refugees in (Chris Kutschera, *Le Défi kurde* [Paris: Bayard Editions, 1997], p. 100; my translation from the original French).

[68] McDowall, *A Modern History of the Kurds*, p. 375.

waging an intense guerrilla war against the government.[69] The US in particular reevaluated its policy towards the Iraqi Kurds when it became apparent that the influx of refugees could weaken Ankara's ability to suppress Kurdish rebels in Turkey.

Britain cited the 1948 Genocide Convention as one of the legal justifications for the creation of the safe haven, and the US referred to the recent precedent already set by UN safe havens for Indochinese refugees around the borders of Cambodia and Thailand.[70] With Turkish cooperation and under the juridical cover of UNSCR 688, Operations Poised Hammer and Provide Comfort put in place Allied forces to deny Baghdad the capacity to repress the Kurds in the north. A "no-fly" zone for Iraqi air forces was declared north of the thirty-sixth parallel. Kurdish Front negotiations with Baghdad were unsuccessful at settling the status of the Kurdish safe haven.[71] In October of 1991, facing continual ambushes from Kurdish *peshmergas*, and unable to use its air forces to assist in suppressing the guerrillas, Iraqi forces and government personnel withdrew from an area roughly the size of Switzerland, which became the *de facto* state of Iraqi Kurdistan.[72] The oil producing areas of Kirkuk and Mosul, long claimed by the Kurds, remained in government hands however.

Kurdish self-rule, a long-held goal of Kurdish nationalist movements, thus emerged in part of northern Iraq in 1991. Although the inhabitants of the Autonomous Zone generally aspired to their own state and a greater Kurdistan that incorporates neighboring Kurdish regions, the leaders of the KDP and PUK were more concerned with the precarious nature of their safe haven. In an effort to frame their autonomy as a case of an oppressed people having finally achieved freedom, and to demonstrate their capacity to run their own affairs, the KDP and PUK in 1992 held elections throughout the KRG. Although the elections set an inordinately high threshold for smaller parties (7% of the vote to win a seat), the London-based Electoral Reform Society pronounced the process "free and fair," with "no evidence of substantial fraud that would have significantly affected the results."[73] Perhaps the biggest indicator that the

---

[69] Iran, to its credit, opened its borders to 1.5 million Kurdish refugees, spending up to 10 million dollars a day (with relatively little outside help) to care for them and exhorting Iranian citizens to welcome the refugees into their homes (Entessar, *Kurdish Ethnonationalism*, pp. 155–157).

[70] Entessar, *Kurdish Ethnonationalism*, p. 153.

[71] The extreme lack of trust on both sides combined with the Allied offer of a safe haven made the negotiations' failure not too surprising.

[72] For more regarding the geographical area left under Kurdish control, as well as particulars concerning the withdrawal, see Kutschera, *Le Défi kurde*, pp. 110–117.

[73] Cited in Michael M. Gunter, "Transnational Sources of Support for the Kurdish Insurgency in Turkey," *Conflict Quarterly* (Spring 1991), 229.

Kurds had pursued a relatively legitimate and fair exercise in electoral politics was PUK leader Talibani's remarks that "everyone ended up dissatisfied with the results."[74] The KDP and PUK respectively won 50.22% and 49.78% of the vote, and decided to evenly split the 50 seats in the Kurdish National Council while leaving 5 seats for the Christian minority.[75] No overall leader was chosen, after the final vote left Masoud Barzani and Jalal Talabani too close in standing (466,819 votes to 441,057 respectively). Although Baghdad had pronounced the election "high treason," the PUK leader stated that he "personally believe[d] that the elections proved that the Kurdish people are worthy of freedom and capable of engaging in democracy and the electoral process, despite the lack of experience ... this people can exercise the right to self-determination within a unified democratic Iraq." When he framed the issue in this manner, Talabani was of course very aware that the Iraqi Kurds' autonomy owed a great deal to the international community, and would continue to depend on outside protection and support. Although there had been "dissent and objections" during the elections, the result was one "which all Kurdish parties accepted, albeit reluctantly, in order to safeguard the unity of Kurdish ranks and to portray the Kurds as civilized people before the world."[76]

For two years the parliament seemed to be functioning, and there was talk of merging the various structures of the KDP and PUK parties. In the summer of 1994, however, disagreements over the sharing of limited resources in the Zone, together with the spark of a land-dispute skirmish between groups allied to the two different parties, ignited armed clashes between the KDP and PUK.[77] Essentially, the elected parliament had been carrying out decisions made at the party headquarters of the KDP and PUK, rather than in the KRG legislature. Both parties' administrations were based on clientelism, and controlling the finances that were supposed to be run by the KRG government. Because the KDP enjoyed a higher income from its control of the border trade with Turkey, the PUK felt itself being gradually squeezed out of power and starved of finances. Hence the PUK was probably the party that initiated the 1994 civil war,

---

[74] Ibid.

[75] For a detailed discussion of the electoral process, the results, and the structure of the resulting government, see Falaq al-Din Kakai, "The Kurdish Parliament," in Fran Hazelton (ed.), *Iraq after the Gulf War* (London: Zed Books Ltd., 1994). Each cabinet position was assigned to one party or the other (or one of the Christian parties), with a deputy cabinet minister from the opposing party (ibid.).

[76] Cited in Gunter, "Transnational Sources of Support," 300.

[77] For more details on the elections and resulting administration, see Gareth R. V. Stansfield, *Iraqi Kurdistan: Political Development and Emergent Democracy* (London: Routledge Curzon, 2003), pp. 129–144.

in an attempt to redress the worsening balance of power in Iraqi Kurdistan.

In a June 1994 visit to Arbil, the scene of many of these clashes at the time, the author spoke with many average Kurds (shopkeepers, labourers, traders) who expressed deep worry that such infighting could create an opening for outside powers (especially Baghdad) to assert control of the Kurdish area. Some expressed the wish that their own leadership would pay greater heed to the interests of the Kurdish people as a whole. Officials of the KDP also expressed embarrassment about the events, seeking to minimize the importance of the fighting and stressing that such disagreements were temporary.[78] Although the Kurdish population at large perceived the overarching need to unite in the face of the threat from Baghdad, KDP and PUK party elites were unable to put aside their differences. The fairly even balance of power between the two groups prevented one from eliminating the other and truly uniting the Kurdish administration, while the KRG administration's failure to take control of the region's meager financial income, in a context where party politics were largely based on patronage, gave the KDP and PUK too much (or too little) to fight over.

By the late summer of 1996, the fighting between the KDP and PUK led to one of the worst incidences in the Kurdish nationalist collective memory. Just as divisions between the governing elite of a state can facilitate a challenger movement's opposition, so too can the state take advantage of divisions amongst its challengers. In a move that cost it great credibility amongst the population, the KDP invited in Saddam's forces to temporarily help it against the PUK. Saddam Hussein's forces took advantage of the opportunity to enter the Kurdish Autonomous Zone, and in addition to assisting the KDP against the PUK, Saddam's troops destroyed CIA bases and their supporters in the area. After the Iraqi army withdrew a few days later (staying would have invited too much Allied pressure), the PUK recaptured most of the areas that formed its support base (a little less than half of the KRG territory), however.

Fighting endured on and off until September 1998, when the two parties signed a cease-fire agreement in Washington. The agreement divided the Kurdish Autonomous Zone into two areas, with the KDP administration centered in Arbil, and the PUK in Sulaymaniya.[79] The KDP, the PUK, and the Kurdish population in general, however,

---

[78] Discussions were held with various KDP officials during the week of June 21, 1994. Due to active fighting in the area, no attempt was made to cross over to PUK areas at the time.

[79] Hiwa Osman, "Iraqi Kurds – Waiting for What the Future Holds," BBC (August 11, 2001), http://members.home.net/kurdistanobserver/11-8-01-report-hiwa-osman-bbc.html.

continued to view Iraqi Kurdistan as one single political entity. Nonetheless, this period of internecine warfare cost Iraqi Kurds dearly, as framing their Kurdish nationalist movement as a unified force capable of running its own affairs remains essential to garnering outside support and mobilizing Kurdish nationalists in the region. Opponents of Kurdish autonomy in turn never fail to frame the Kurdish movement in Iraq as pre-modern, divided, tribal, and hence incapable of representing Iraqi Kurdistan in any kind of institutionally enshrined autonomy or political self-determination.

The attacks of their critics notwithstanding, Iraqi Kurds in 1991 nonetheless found themselves closer to independence than any other Kurdish groups in modern history. The most unlikely of circumstances had conspired to fulfill the bulk of Kurdish nationalist aspirations for self-determination in Iraq. Although it might be tempting to credit international support alone for this event, other factors did play a role. After the events of 1988, Kurdish framings in general cast Saddam as the most unimaginably ruthless tyrant, a modern-day Nebuchadnezer intent on genocide. Creating such a perception of his willingness and capacity to repress was no doubt part of Saddam's original intent – hence the warning his government made to the Kurds in 1991 about repeating Halabja. It was this same fear of Saddam that caused millions of Kurds to flee his advancing troops in March of that same year. Were it not for the refugees, the international community would not have been propelled to act in the defense of the Kurds. The Western pre-war campaign to demonize Saddam also provided a powerful context in which his victimization of the refugees would be viewed. The role of the media in this case succeeded in attracting a huge amount of international sympathy for the Kurds' plight, an awareness that would also extend to the situation of Kurds in Turkey and Iran. Such sympathy in turn led the US and Britain to support and protect the Iraqi Kurds as never before. The events that led to the creation of the Iraqi Kurdish safe haven are indicative of the increasing importance of international influences as a structural opportunity variable. In addition to states, the global public, civil society actors, NGOs, and supranational bodies such as the Court of Human Rights in The Hague are now taking a more active interest in the fate of groups such as the Kurds. This interest, and the growing legitimacy of humanitarian interventions (or interventions justified in humanitarian terms) in the affairs of repressive states, can therefore emerge as an increasingly important resource for movements challenging repressive governments. Such movements will in turn have more incentives to moderate their tactics and avoid the unacceptable targeting of civilians, a conclusion that even the PKK came to by the mid-1990s.

The 2003 invasion of Iraq – new opportunities, new risks, and a cautious strategy

The American invasion of Iraq in the spring of 2003 serves as an additional example of the increasing importance of the fifth opportunity structures variable discussed in Chapter 2 – international and foreign influences supportive of the state or its opponents. The United States and Britain justified their attack on Saddam Hussein's regime by referring to both the threat Saddam posed to the world, particularly due to his continuing pursuit of weapons of mass destruction, and his record of inflicting fearful human rights abuses on his own population, particularly the Kurds and Shiites of Iraq. Although the events surrounding September 11, largely unrelated to Saddam and Iraq, put the United States in a position to pursue a more interventionist foreign policy, the human rights violations of Saddam (and the Taliban in Afghanistan, for that matter) played a crucial role in garnering internal and external support for the war in Iraq.

Well-organized and mobilized KDP and PUK fighting forces in the Kurdish Autonomous Zone in turn took advantage of the new, more aggressive US foreign policy stance. First they carefully framed their movements as Iraqi movements, desirous of freeing Iraq as a whole from Saddam's tyranny, rather than Kurdish movements wanting to separate from Iraq. In this manner they assisted American framings that justified the war, and avoided intervention from neighboring states such as Turkey and Iran. When in March 2003 the Turkish Parliament refused the Americans permission to move troops through Turkey to Iraq, Iraqi Kurds again took advantage of the souring relationship between the US and Turkey, to present themselves as the only significant and dependable ally of the US in the Iraqi theater. With roughly 80,000 armed *peshmerga*, the KDP and PUK welcomed the 101st US Airborne division as well as US Special Forces units into the areas they controlled. The KDP and PUK also agreed to function under American command.

Before moving south against Iraqi army positions, the PUK used American assistance to smash Ansar al-Islam, a Kurdish Islamist group based near the Iranian border. Baghdad, and possibly Tehran, had for two years been assisting the Ansar group, as a proxy to weaken the PUK and destabilize the Kurdish Autonomous Zone.[80] Unable to rout out the

---

[80] Throughout 2002 and winter of 2003, Ansar militants staged a number of attacks on PUK positions, including an assassination attempt on Barham Salih, the PUK Prime Minister. Ansar militants also assassinated or bombed the homes of prominent Christians in the KDP and PUK areas.

group on its own, the war on Iraq suddenly gave the PUK the outside assistance, particularly in the form of air strikes, necessary to overpower Ansar. Alternately, the PUK may have intentionally avoided destroying the Ansar militants after September 2001, in order to align themselves with the United States' war on terrorism and receive American support. In any case, PUK control of its part of Iraqi Kurdistan improved as a result of American assistance during the winter and spring of 2003.

In April 2003, as US troops moved on Baghdad, KDP and PUK forces advanced into the key oil cities of Mosul and Kirkuk ahead of their American commanders and allies. As the Iraqi army disintegrated, the KDP and PUK suddenly became the most organized and best armed Iraqi groups left in the country. They brought police officers, administrators, and engineers with them as they asserted control over Kirkuk and Mosul. Because its Arab Sunni population was largely hostile to them, the KDP, after establishing and fortifying a party headquarters in the city, quickly ceded Mosul to American administrators. In the case of Kirkuk however, the Kurds framed their entry into the city as the long-awaited repossession of a traditionally Kurdish city long oppressed by Saddam's regime.[81] With the opportunity given them by the war, the justification provided by their framing of Kirkuk as the traditional capital of Iraqi Kurdistan, and the means available to them as the largest organized fighting force in the north of Iraq, the KDP and PUK moved quickly to consolidate their hold on the city. To the north, however, Turkey threatened to intervene militarily if the KDP and PUK did not leave Kirkuk. Ankara cast the city as a traditionally Turkmen city, with a majority Turkmen population. Due to their affinity to Turkey, Ankara claimed the right to act in defense of the Turkmen minority.[82] Ankara also refused to allow the oil fields around Kirkuk or Mosul to fall under Kurdish control, lest the Iraqi Kurds thereby gain possession of an economic base from which to declare statehood in the future. In light of Turkish threats and American pressure, the KDP and PUK therefore agreed to remove the bulk of their armed forces from Kirkuk a few days after they captured it. Kurdish police personnel, administrators, and engineers, as

---

[81] While the outlying areas of Mosul are largely Kurdish, the city itself has a majority Arab Sunni population, largely hostile to Kurdish nationalists. For both Kirkuk and Mosul, however, the unavailability of recent census data (the last credible census in the area took place in 1956) makes any discussion of population distribution difficult.

[82] The Turkish "stewardship" of the Iraqi Turkmen was most likely based more on an attempt to justify an intervention by Turkey, rather than genuine concern for the Turkmen, however. Otherwise one must wonder why Turkey did not even protest in mild terms when Saddam Hussein's regime was busily engaged in evicting Turkmen (along with Kurds) from Kirkuk throughout his Arabization drives of the 1980s and 1990s.

well as a smaller KDP and PUK armed contingent tasked with guarding Kurdish political offices, remained, however. Municipal elections soon after the city was liberated also put in place a Kurdish mayor. Hence the position of Kurdish nationalists improved significantly in the area, although the potential for KDP–PUK rivalry over control of Kirkuk looms in the background.

The United States installed Paul Bremer and his Coalition Provisional Authority (CPA) to govern Iraq from the summer of 2003 until June 28, 2004. The CPA ordered all militia groups to disband and turn in their weapons, except those groups that functioned under American command during the war. In effect, this meant all groups except the KDP and PUK armed forces. Given that the KDP and PUK also received arms from the Americans at the outset of the war, and then captured large amounts of heavy weaponry from retreating Iraqi army forces, the position of Kurdish nationalists in Iraq improved dramatically.[83] When Iraq's *Transitional Administrative Law* (TAL) was negotiated in March 2003, it also included the first tangible guarantee for Kurds in Iraq: if two-thirds of the population of three Iraqi governorates voted against any proposed permanent Iraqi constitution, the proposal would not pass, even if an overall majority of Iraqis voted in favor of it. Because Iraqi Kurds control three governorates (Duhok, Erbil, and Suleimaniya), this came to be referred to as the "Kurdish veto." Although many Iraqi Arabs objected strongly to this provision, the Kurdish parties insisted on it and its adoption was greeted with celebrations in Iraqi, Iranian, Turkish, and Syrian Kurdish regions. When Iraqi Shiite Arabs successfully pressured the UN Security Council not to mention the TAL in Resolution 1546 (on the transfer of sovereignty in Iraq), however, some worried that the new Iraqi government would renege on the promised "Kurdish veto" right.[84] Even after the transfer of sovereignty to Prime Minister Iyad Allawi's caretaker Iraqi government, the KDP and PUK nevertheless continued to improve their positions – especially by sending large numbers of their *peshmerga* into the new Iraqi Army forces being formed by the Americans and NATO, Iraqi Kurds got access to cutting edge military equipment and training. Especially because central and southern Iraq may descend into complete anarchy with a continuing insurgency against Coalition Forces and the

---

[83] On October 26, the author visited a PUK base near Halabja that contained roughly 40 Soviet T-67 tanks taken from Saddam's armed forces. The tanks did not appear to be regularly maintained and used, however, so the extent to which they can be considered field-ready is questionable.

[84] For more on the TAL and its importance, see David Romano, "Alice Through the Looking Glass? Reflections on an Iraqi sojourn," *Policy Options Magazine*, Institute for Research on Public Policy, 25: 11, 62–65.

new Iraqi government, Iraqi Kurds plan on keeping their *peshmerga*. The *peshmerga* act as the guardians of the relatively stable and prosperous Kurdish Autonomous Region.

At the same time, the Iraqi Kurdish leaders remain aware that declaring themselves a state would be seen as a *casus belli* by Turkey[85] and create huge problems with the United States, neighboring states, and the international community. The KDP and PUK leadership therefore still treads carefully, and avoids making any statements that might upset their recent gains. Although regional actors and the world community may be willing to accept new states in less strategic areas such as Eritrea, such does not appear to be the case in the Middle East. Since Saddam's fall, Iraqi Kurdish groups have therefore stressed that they wish to be a part of the new Iraq and that they must play an important role in Baghdad as well as Iraqi Kurdistan. To this effect, Hoshyar Zibari of the KDP now serves as Iraq's foreign minister and Barham Salih of the PUK serves as one of Iraq's deputy prime ministers, while Jalal Talibani and Massoud Barzani both took seats on Iraq's Interim Governing Council. With a lot to lose should they fail, the KDP and PUK now pursue a strategy of securing their present gains within the larger Iraqi state framework. In a testament to this strategy, since Saddam's fall they have added the Iraqi national flag beside the Kurdish one on many public buildings in Iraqi Kurdistan. They also removed signs at border crossings into northern Iraq, which since 1991 read "Welcome to Kurdistan," and replaced them with new signs that state "Welcome to Kurdistan Region of Iraq."

Kurdish nationalists in Iraq remain adamant, however, in their refusal to be re-incorporated under the tight control of an Iraqi central government based in Baghdad. In their mind, Halabja and the Anfal campaigns removed what little claim non-Kurds in Baghdad had to rule over them. Grudgingly mindful of Turkey, Iran, Syria, and the international community's unwillingness to accept a Kurdish state in the region, however, their slogan remains "autonomy for Kurdistan in a democratic Iraq." When Iraq's permanent constitution is drawn up, Iraqi Kurds will point to loose federal models from Canada, Belgium, and the Basque region of Spain as possible models to emulate. They will also attempt to have the oil-rich region of Kirkuk re-incorporated into a Kurdish administrative region. International factors do appear to have given the Kurds an unprecedented opportunity to at least achieve autonomy within Iraq, perhaps best exemplified by George W. Bush's March 6 pronouncement on the

---

[85] Lale Sariibrahimoglu, "Though Controlled, Business Flourishes in Northern Iraq," *Turkish Daily News*, August 15 (2001).

issue, when he stated that "Iraq will become a place where people will see that Shiites, Sunnis and Kurds can coexist within a federal structure."[86] The challenge ahead for Iraqi Kurds will center around defining what kind of federal structure the country should adopt.

Conclusion: the synthesis of opportunity, mobilization, and framing in Iraqi Kurdistan

Chapters 2–4 on Kurds in Turkey showed how even in a more "natural" state, meaning one not created by a colonial power, state building that relied on only Turkish national identity garnered great opposition from people who valued, or later came to identify with, a competing Kurdish nationalist identity. In the new Iraq, an approach relying on Arab nationalist state ideology was doomed from the start. Crucially, the 1922 Anglo-Iraqi statement and the League of Nations provisions had explicitly recognized the Kurds in Iraq and their claim to special rights *as a group*. The result of this promise was enduring Kurdish nationalist attempts to see their rights fulfilled. When the practice of Iraqi state Arab nationalist cultural framings so patently contradicted the promise of a bi-national (or multi-cultural) state, the grievance framing task of Kurdish nationalist mobilizers was mostly completed from the beginning. While eighty-some years of living under one state may have eventually inculcated an Iraqi nationalist ethic in many Arab Iraqis, the large majority of Iraqi Kurds have never to this day adopted Iraqi nationalism. In the spring of 2004, a Kurdish civil society movement even garnered 1.7 million signatures in support of a referendum on self-determination (i.e. separation) for Kurdistan, including Kirkuk.

While Kurdish mobilization strategies hence relied heavily on Kurdish nationalist framings throughout Iraqi history, the limited opportunity structures context in which Iraqi Kurds operate usually encouraged movements to downgrade their demands from Kurdish statehood to Kurdish autonomy, however. The fifth component of the opportunity structures concept, "International and foreign influences supportive of the state or its opponents," simply limited their perceived room for maneuver. Whereas the Slovenians, Croatians, and Eritreans enjoyed either support or at least disinterest from neighboring states and the international community, the Kurdish nationalists face intense scrutiny and virtually unanimous international pressure against Kurdish

---

[86] "Les Kurdes n'ont d'autres amis que les montagnes," *Courrier International* 677 (October 23, 2003) (my translation from the source's French text).

separatism. In the case of Iraqi Kurds, Turkey, Iran, and Syria could well intervene forcefully to prevent the emergence of a Kurdish state from the remnants of Iraq. In an attempt to lessen the chances of outside state intervention against them, and in some cases in an effort to attract non-Kurdish sympathizers, Iraqi Kurdish movements therefore avoided the "S" word (separation) in the grievance framings they produced.

Foreign support for Iraqi Kurds was at times more substantial than that enjoyed by Turkish Kurds but, as the events of 1975 demonstrated, unreliable at critical moments in the struggle. The oil revenue and military aid that the Iraqi state received from 1972 to 1991 also greatly outstripped the capacity of Kurdish insurgents to mobilize resources, creating a repressive state whose power could no longer be matched the way it was before 1975. When the most extreme levels of imaginable repression were brandished in 1988, it appeared that opportunity structures could not get any worse for Iraqi Kurds – in the face of such repression from a unified and totalitarian Ba'thist state, with no elite allies elsewhere in Iraq, and left to their fate by the bulk of the international community, it seems unlikely that they could have maintained a challenge to the state, no matter what their mobilization strategies. The Iraqi state's complete control of media in the country also limited the Kurds' ability to win support from non-Kurds in Iraq, as the state's grievance frames depicting Kurdish separatist subversion and cooperation with Iraq's enemies (Iran, Israel, and the United States) remained the only message available to most Iraqis. Only through informal tribal and community word-of-mouth networks, or underground newspapers, were Kurdish nationalists able to disseminate their own dissenting cultural framings to fellow Kurds. Kurdish grievance frames that cast light on the crimes of Saddam's regime would prove very useful a few years later, however, and form a kind of synergy with rapidly shifting opportunity structures.

The event that completely changed Iraqi Kurdish opportunity structures was Iraq's invasion of Kuwait. It is difficult to imagine Turkey or Iran making a mistake similar to what the invasion of Kuwait amounted to for Iraq's government (perhaps attacking Greece would qualify in Turkey's case, or launching a blatant strike on Israel in Iran's case). The Iraqi Kurds benefited greatly from the Gulf War's demonizing of Saddam Hussein, as the international community adopted large elements of their grievance frames' depiction of the regime in Baghdad. The genocide of 1988 emerged at this time as a powerful grievance frame for non-Kurds as well as Kurds, much like the Holocaust convinced important segments of the international community (as well as Jews of course) of the need for a Jewish state. The attention Iraqi Kurds gained spilled over somewhat to Kurds in Turkey and Iran as well, raising international awareness of the Kurds as a whole.[87] If Saddam's invasion of Kuwait had not initiated the world's attitudinal shift towards perceiving his regime as a pariah, however, it seems likely that most of the world would have continued brushing over his campaigns of genocide against Iraqi Kurds. Also important by 1991, however, was an Iraqi Kurdish strategy of steering clear of the acts of terrorism that still haunt the PKK's international image. These factors helped attract the kind of international outcry and support that led to the creation of the Kurdish safe haven in 1991, a fine example of the interplay of Kurdish strategy, grievance framings, and new opportunity structures.

Although pragmatism may continue to prevent the KDP and PUK from declaring statehood in the future, virtually all Kurds feel they have such a right, however: "In spite of our right to our own state, we don't raise this slogan ... We only seek federation within a democratic Iraq."[88] Saidi Barzingi, president of Irbil University, adds the following view: "It's time to correct the injustices of the post-World War One settlement. We are not Arabs, Turks or Iranians. Why shouldn't we have the same rights as a string of Gulf tribes who declared themselves states?"[89] In the case of Iraqi Kurdistan, such views do not have to imply "radicalism," however: "'We could be a model for all other areas of Kurdistan,' said Barham Salih, the KRG's other prime minister, contrasting its moderate, democratic approach to self-determination with the all-or-nothing violence of Abdullah Ocalan and his Kurdistan Workers' Party's (PKK) failed bid to win independence for the Kurds in Turkey."[90]

Nonetheless, it should be remembered that while the explicit inclusion of Kurdish group rights in the founding principles of the Iraqi state guaranteed politicized Kurdish framings from early on (e.g. they became established parts of the Iraqi Kurdish 'cultural tool-kits' from the start), resource mobilization based on Barzani's and other tribal forces hindered the development of a more modern, mass-based Kurdish nationalism (such as the PKK in Turkey). Although politicized ethnicity probably also held sway over most Kurdish peasants and urban workers in Iraq, these groups for the most part did not become part of the KDP and PUK

---

[87] Contrary to Iraq, however, Turkey maintains the institutions of a democracy, albeit one with many evident limits regarding Kurdish minority rights.

[88] Massoud Barzani, quoted in David Hirst, "Liberated and Safe, But Not Yet Free to Fly Their Flag," *Guardian Weekly*, August 16, 2001.

[89] Quoted in Hirst, "Liberated and Safe ..."

[90] Unfortunately, it is precisely this example for "all other areas of Kurdistan" that so worries Turkey, Iran, and (to a lesser extent) Syria, as successful Kurdish self-determination in Iraq impacts the cultural frames of their Kurdish minorities (Hirst, "Liberated and Safe ...").

Kurdish nationalist organizations combatting Baghdad, at least not until after the creation of the KAZ. The closed political system in Baghdad also engendered Kurdish "subversiveness" (via adherence to illegal Kurdish organizations or leftist parties such as the ICP) and a long series of armed Kurdish revolts, which erupted every time an opportunity seemed to present itself. These uprisings only subsided when elite divisions in the government necessitated looking for Kurdish allies to prop up weak leaders (the brief opening of 1958–1961 in particular), or when the state's capacity to repress the Kurds became so uncertain that a search for a political agreement with the Kurds became necessary (1922–1926, 1966, and 1970). When Baghdad offered the Kurds a political solution comprising real measures of autonomy (1966 and 1970), the Kurds were willing to agree – constant warfare in the Kurdish region was taking a heavy toll on the communities there. Disagreements on the implementation of such agreements, particularly regarding the territorial delineation of Kurdish autonomy and Kurdish control of oil producing areas, led to a return to the battlefield after the brief respite that the negotiations had afforded both parties. In effect, Kurdish nationalists were powerful enough to occasionally make or break governments in Baghdad, but not strong enough to secede from Iraq.

In 2003, Iraqi Kurdish grievance framings again helped them attract the most international support ever received by any Kurdish movements – Saddam's human rights abuses, and especially the gassing of Halabja in 1988, helped the United States to justify its March invasion of Iraq. When the fall of Saddam's regime opened the political system to all manner of possible changes, Iraqi Kurds strategically chose to pursue their goals peacefully and within the newly transformed political system. Instead of retreating to their mountains in the north, they reclaimed the Iraqi flag as also belonging to them, and eagerly jumped into the political maneuvering taking shape in Baghdad. Astute movement strategies in the new Iraq are in turn putting Iraqi Kurds in an excellent position to take advantage of opportunities provided by the 2003 American invasion of Iraq. While they improve their material position and the military training of their *peshmerga*, Iraqi Kurdish parties continue to frame themselves as reasonable actors trying to make a go of it in post-Saddam Iraq, rather than separatist "spoilers." The new Iraq has missed several symbolic opportunities to make the Kurds feel that the Iraqi state belongs to them as well, however. Their demand for a new flag for Iraq, one that is not associated with the years of repression and mass executions they suffered during the past eighty years, was acceded to and then ignored. The old Iraqi flag still flies, with its three stars and stripes symbolizing Arab unity, and the new flag, with symbols meant to connote Arab, Kurdish, and Turkmen brotherhood, remains nowhere to be seen.[91] Also, the post-Saddam Iraqi dinar and other symbols of state could have been produced in both Arabic and Kurdish, rather than maintaining the old practice of only using Arabic. Failing to adopt such symbolic, bi-national cultural frames will only convince the Kurdish population of Iraq that Iraqi Arabs plan on returning to the old ways of doing things and suppressing Kurdish as soon as possible. The window of opportunity to change the basic character of the Iraqi state and society gradually closes as symbolic opportunities such as these are missed. An additional opportunity structure that may keep the window open a bit longer concerns the stability of elite alignments in the rest of Iraq – as long as the risk of Shiite Arab and Sunni Arab disagreement and strife exists, moderate Shiite Arab parties will likely turn to the Kurds in search of allies. At the time of this writing, Kurdish and moderate Shiite parties were even discussing entering the January 2005 elections on joint party lists. Hence, disunity amongst Iraqi Arabs could facilitate Kurdish bargaining for core demands such as loose federalism and incorporation of Kirkuk into the KAZ. If Sunni and Shiite Arabs arrive at some broad agreement concerning the future of Iraq, however, the stability of the elite alignments component of opportunity structures will turn negative for Iraqi Kurds, necessitating more effective resource mobilization strategies on their part. Effective Kurdish framing strategies in the short term could, however, play an important role in keeping Shiite Arabs favorably disposed towards Kurdish demands – meaning that Iraqi Kurds may want to carefully avoid appearing too separation minded and alienating the Shiite parties. In the meantime, much of the younger generation of Iraqi Kurds in the Kurdish Autonomous Zone do not know Arabic, and have never been to the Arab part of Iraq. The "Green Line" delimitating the borders of the KAZ from the rest of Iraq has also continued to function as a real border in most senses of the word, guarded by *peshmerga* manning checkpoints, and marking one's passage into a part of Iraq different in ways ranging from language and administration to stability and geography.

Furthermore, If Iraq descends into civil war and chaos, Iraqi Kurdish parties could then turn to the international community, and most importantly, the United States, and present themselves as having done the best they could to stay in Iraq, but now deserving to be set free from this failed state. They could present a strong appeal to American leaders and the American population, that as their allies in the war against Saddam, the

---

[91] The new flag, however, drew criticism from many quarters due to its lack of symmetry – a blue crescent above bands of blue, yellow and blue. Lack of aesthetic appeal probably did not help convince Iraqis to adopt it.

US now has a responsibility to protect the Iraqi Kurds from the anarchy and terror emerging in Arab Iraq and, more importantly, from Turkish, Iranian, or Syrian intervention to quash their autonomy or emerging statehood. Should such a sequence of events lead to the emergence of a Kurdish state, it will have been born of the most unlikely and surprising confluence and interplay of structural opportunities, movement strategies, and cultural framings. Even presently, the degree of self-determination practiced in Iraqi Kurdistan stands out as the most significant modern Kurdish nationalist achievement. The Kurdish Regional Government in Iraq continues to powerfully affect Kurdish nationalist cultural frames, as Kurds elsewhere witness (and perhaps aspire to) what self-determination can involve. If Iraqi Kurds continue to consolidate their gains or achieve statehood, they might soon also be in a position to materially assist Kurdish movements in neighboring countries – which is precisely the fear in Ankara, Tehran, and Damascus.[92] From the Kurdish nationalist perspective, as soon as one portion of Kurdistan gains statehood or real autonomy, it can defend neighboring Kurds and bring the Kurdish question to international forums when all other state actors remain silent. Hence the fate of Iraqi Kurds will have a crucial impact for Kurds in neighboring countries and Kurdish nationalism as a whole. Iraqi Kurdish ascendance would have tremendous ramifications particularly due to the improved opportunities this could provide neighboring Kurdish groups, as well as the example it would give to Turkish, Iranian, and Syrian Kurds.

[92] In March 2004, large Kurdish riots erupted in Syrian Kurdistan. As the Syrian government arrested thousands of Kurds across the country and shot scores of protestors, Syrian Kurds wondered if their brethren in Iraq might come to their assistance. Although many demonstrations protesting the Syrian government's repression occurred in Iraqi Kurdistan, virtually all the Kurdish intellectuals this author spoke to at the time agreed that "it was too early" for Iraqi Kurds to intervene on the behalf of neighboring Kurds – "but perhaps one day" (author's interviews, March 2004, Suleimaniya, Iraq).

7 Kurdish nationalist challenges to the Iranian state

The early Iranian state and the Simko revolt

The events surrounding World War One did not witness a disintegration of lands held by the Iranian monarchy in the way they did for the Ottoman empire. Nonetheless, the Iranian state at the time did not effectively control much of the countryside. Parts of Iranian Kurdistan which had been tenuously ruled by Iran since 1639 (when an Ottoman–Safavid treaty ceded some of the Kurdish regions to the Ottomans), rose up in rebellion. Around the same time as the Kuchgiri, Sheikh Said, and Barzinji revolts in Turkey and Iraq, Ismail Agha Simko led the most major Kurdish revolt in Iran at the time. A feudal tribal agha with a villainous reputation for being more of a warlord than a genuine nationalist, Simko first subdued and plundered the Kurdish, Azeri, and Assyrian groups in his region around Lake Uromiyah. These groups and their leaders might otherwise have emerged as competitors to Simko. In an attempt to take advantage of what he saw as Iranian state weakness (lack of coercive capacity and divisions amongst the capital's elites), Simko then declared an independent Kurdish state in the area under his control, proclaiming his actions to be a prelude to independence for all of Kurdistan. Simko held the area against the Iranian army for four years, and even met in 1923 with fellow Kurdish sheikh Mahmoud Barzinji (described in Chapter 6 on Iraqi Kurdistan, Barzinji and Simko had some similarities in style and followings) to coordinate strategies.[1] Cooperation between the two never materialized, however.

Like his contemporary counterparts in Turkey and Iraq, however, Simko failed to raise even a loosely united front:

... in reality, however, many of the larger tribes were fraught with internal rivalries, let alone quarrels between one tribe and another. In the northern reaches of Kurdistan the main tribal groups, the Shikak, the Zarza, Mamash and Mangur

---

[1] Ghasemlou, cited in Gerard Chaliand (ed.), *People Without a Country: The Kurds and Kurdistan* (New York: Interlink Publishing, 1993), p. 105.

were all riven. Most contestants sought external sponsors, one brother seeking help from the Turks, another from the Russians, and the occasional one from the Iranian government or its local officials. The Shikak, the most important group during this period, was divided into three rival main sections: the Abdui led by Simqu, the Mamadi and the Kardar. All three had experienced a high turnover of leaders as a result of the violence that accompanies the life of a chief. Even within the Abdui, Simqu was threatened by several challengers, of whom the most formidable was Amr Khan.[2]

Although Simko stated early on that "only a fool" could not see the need for British support of Kurdish nationalist aspirations,[3] the lack of a more credible and unified movement once again failed to attract their assistance. Nonetheless, Simko did manage to elicit some support from Kemalist troops in Turkey as well as the Bolsheviks. Before he could sufficiently arm himself and expand the rebellion, however, Simko's revolt was put down in 1924 by an Iranian army that had been reorganized and modernized. The Iranians also enjoyed the aid of more allies than Simko had, mainly opposing Kurdish tribes, as well as Azeris and Assyrians who had no desire to be part of Simko's Kurdish state.[4] Once again, a tribal leader such as Simko or even a leader with religious credentials, could not unite and mobilize a Kurdish population with many competing and different identities, despite the use of nationalist rhetoric.[5] Koohi-Kamali characterizes Simko as mainly a predatory warlord:

The tribal relationships and organization dominant in Simko's uprising prevented nationalist mobilization. In a tribal structure, unity is based on more immediate and materially rewarding goals. For a nationalist mobilization, a more defined and disciplined political organization is needed. What Simko did was to employ a modern means (demand for a Kurdish nation-state as was happening with other ethnic groups at the time) to try and obtain an older, traditional goal.[6]

Simko essentially failed to behave or adequately frame himself as a truly Kurdish nationalist leader for a population whose ethnicity had not yet

---

[2] David McDowall, *A Modern History of the Kurds* (London: I. B. Taurus, 1997), p. 215.

[3] Cited in Farideh Koohi-Kamali, *The Political Development of the Kurds in Iran* (New York: Palgrave Macmillan, 2003), p. 78.

[4] Nader Entessar, *Kurdish Ethnonationalism* (London: Lynne Rienner Publishers, Inc., 1992), p. 12.

[5] None of the sources consulted by me and listed in this work's bibliography found that Simko devoted much effort to Kurdish nationalist rhetoric. Unlike the traditional leaders of the Kuchgiri, Sheikh Said, or Mount Ararat uprisings in Turkey, Simko had no Kurdish political organization involved in his revolt. He did, however, publish a Kurdish newspaper in Urumiyah and print Kurdish administrative forms such as customs bills (Amir Hassanpour, personal communication, December 4, 2001).

[6] Koohi-Kamali, *Political Development of the Kurds*, p. 88.

been very politicized. After another attempted uprising together with a few other tribal leaders in 1929, Simko was killed by the Iranians.

The following years saw many more minor rebellions and skirmishes between the government and Kurdish tribes. Reza Khan (Reza Shah after 1925), who had taken power in Tehran in 1921, was in the process of pursuing modernizing and state building policies very similar to those of Ataturk. The changes that Reza Shah instituted, especially the extension of government authority and the disarming and forced settlement of Kurdish, Baluchi, and Lorr tribes, sparked many violent but isolated reactions. Lacking common cultural and grievance frames disseminated broadly by an organized opposition, the uprisings suffered the same fate as Kurdish dissidence of the 1920s and 1930s in Turkey.

Also like in Turkey, the Iranian state's cultural framings presented the fiction of an Iranian identity (based solely on Persian ethnic markers) for all the myriad ethnic groups in the country, and the building of a unified, modern nation-state on that basis:

The use of Kurdish dialects in education, publication, and public speech were forbidden. Many Kurdish schools were forced to close down as their education was disrupted and their funding frozen. A European-style dress code was imposed on Kurds and on other Iranians. Following Ataturk's example in Turkey, Reza Shah even stressed the use of the term "mountain Iranians" to refer to the Kurdish population of the country, although public use of the term "Kurd" was never banned, as was the case in Turkey.[7]

Also similar to Turkey and Iraq, the Kurdish regions of Iran were left an undeveloped economic backwater.

The Mahabad Republic of Kurdistan

During World War Two, however, an unparalleled political opportunity fleetingly embraced Iranian Kurdistan. In 1941, British, American, and Soviet troops occupied Iran and forced the pro-Axis Shah to resign. He was replaced by his son, Mohammed Reza Shah. For the next several years, the new Shah was little more than the mayor of Tehran, and the ability of the Iranian state to repress opposition became extremely limited for a brief period of time. Kurds centered around the city of Mahabad used the occasion to organize and make a push for self-rule. The first political party formed was Komala Jiyanewey Kurdistan (Committee for the Rebirth of Kurdistan), a leftist Kurdish nationalist party composed mainly of urban intellectuals and petty bourgeoisie. With its highly

[7] Entessar, *Kurdish Ethnonationalism*, p. 13.

critical stance towards feudal landlords (excepting "patriotic" ones, the same way the PKK excepted those willing to support the struggle) and tribalism, the party rapidly expanded among the urban and peasant masses. In March of 1945 Komala members

> ... staged a dramatic performance that was unprecedented in form and influence. This was the "opera" called *Daik I Nishtiman* (Motherland). Its message was in the Kurdish language of Mahabad, and the message was Kurdish nationalism. The motherland was in danger, and tears filled the eyes of the audience; the motherland was in chains, and the onlookers groaned; and finally the motherland was rescued by her sons to the applause of all ... The atmosphere became heavy with nationalism, for *Daik I Nishtiman* caused a profound impression among Kurds who for the first time witnessed their anguish in dramatic form. Performances took on the character of religious revivalist meetings. Conversions were many. After several months of playing to full houses in Mahabad, the opera went on the road.[8]

This play, produced and performed by Komala party members, provides an excellent example of nationalist cultural framings – the politicization of ethnicity. It reminded its audience of their shared identity as children of the motherland, as well as the motherland's abuse by outsiders. With the issue framed in this manner, the natural duty of all children is to rise to the defense of their mother. In this way, Komala increased first the ethnic politicization and then its mobilization of Kurds in the area.

Newly mobilized party members notwithstanding, however, Komala still lacked much of a military force. Additionally, the Soviet Union was crucial to the Kurds (Mahabad was just on the edge of the Soviet zone of occupation), but the USSR preferred that a new party be organized to succeed Komala. Hence for a variety of reasons, but particularly due to Soviet pressure, a second party was formed in 1945 to absorb and replace Komala – the Kurdistan Democratic Party [of Iran]. The KDPI, under Soviet influence, presented the following demands.[9]

(1) The Kurdish people in Iran must manage their own local affairs and be granted autonomy within Iran's frontiers.

(2) They must be allowed to study in their mother tongue. The official administrative language in the Kurdish territories must be Kurdish.

(3) The country's Constitution should guarantee that district councilors for Kurdistan be elected to take charge of all social and administrative matters.

(4) State officials must be chosen from the local population.

---

[8] William Eagleton Jr., *The Kurdish Republic of 1946* (London: Oxford University Press, 1963), p. 40.

[9] Quoted from Ghassemlou, in Chaliand (ed.), *People Without a Country*, p. 106.

(5) A general law should provide the basis for agreements between peasants and landowners so as to safeguard both sides' future.

(6) The KDP struggles for complete fraternity and unity with the Azerbaijani people and with the minorities resident in Azerbaijan (Assyrians, Armenians, etc.).

(7) The KDP is committed to progress in agriculture and trade; to developing education and sanitation; to furthering the spiritual and material well-being of the Kurdish people and to the best use of the natural resources of Kurdistan.

(8) The KDP demands freedom of political action for all the people of Iran so that the whole country may rejoice in progress.

An additional demand was also made that all taxes collected in the Kurdish region be spent there as well.[10]

The political activity and publicity that surrounded the KDPI's statement politicized the identity of many Kurds, as the possibility of Kurdish self-rule was demonstrated to them by the manifesto. Also, although the KDPI's declaration only went so far as to demand autonomy within Iran, the Soviet-sponsored declaration of an Azeri republic immediately to the north of Mahabad encouraged the Kurds to do likewise and also declare themselves somewhat more than an autonomous region. They did so formally on January 22, 1946, calling themselves the "Republic of Kurdistan." Although the Mahabad Republic contained only a limited portion of Iranian Kurdistan, its creation was greeted by a great deal of enthusiasm from most Kurds, including those in Iraq and Turkey. Tribal groupings attached themselves to the Republic and provided most of its military force, the most important of which came from Mustafa Barzani's *peshmerga*, who had recently arrived in Mahabad after their failed uprising in Iraq. The president of the republic was Qazi Mohammad, a well-respected, educated religious notable of the city. Perhaps most importantly, the Mahabad Republic was the first modern example of a Kurdish state, demonstrating such possibilities to the Kurdish population of neighboring countries as well. One of the verses of the Republic's national anthem, composed by the poet Hazhar, indicated the ambition for an eventual greater Kurdistan:

> Our oil is water of life
> From Sert [Turkey] to Kermanshah,
> Baba Gurgur [Kirkuk] knows,
> In Mosul we also have it.[11]

---

[10] Entessar, *Kurdish Ethnonationalism*, p. 20.
[11] Cited in Eagleton, *Kurdish Republic of 1946*, p. 75.

Qazi Mohammad had also purchased a printing press from the Azeris in the north, which allowed the fledgling Republic to begin diffusing its Kurdish nationalist framings:[12]

> In spite of the fact that the Mahabad republic exercised authority over less than one-third of Iranian Kurds and lasted less than a year, it has remained the point of reference for Kurdish movements throughout the Middle East. During the republic's existence, many of the Kurds' aspirations came to fruition. Kurdish became the official language, and Kurdish-language periodicals and literary publications flourished. Kurdish *peshmerga* replaced Iranian police units, and a Kurdish government bureaucracy was set up ... No Kurdish movement has succeeded in duplicating the modest achievements of the Mahabad republic.[13]

The atmosphere in the incipient Kurdish state was celebratory, and the population enjoyed previously unheard-of personal freedoms.[14] Qazi Mohammad also enjoyed wide popularity and support during the Republic's brief lifetime. He began forming and training the beginnings of a regular, professional Kurdish army, and a Soviet official in Baku "... promised that military equipment including tanks, cannon, machine guns, and rifles would be sent to Mahabad. He also alluded to the possibility of financial support, and promised places in the Baku Military College for as many students as the Kurds could send."[15] Although modest financial support, a few thousand rifles, and the places in the military college were indeed provided, the promised tanks and cannon never materialized.

The incipient Kurdish state did not have enough time to organize and mobilize resources and a larger army, before a crippling turn of events. In May 1946, Tehran convinced the Soviets to withdraw from Iran in return for an oil concession.[16] The Soviets had employed the Azeris and Kurds in Iran as a tool to pursue their own strategic interests, and if they could attain their goals more readily in negotiations with Tehran, they proved willing to do so. Britain, the US, and the United Nations also applied pressure for the Soviets to withdraw, not wanting to see them gain Azeri and Kurdish puppet states in Iran. Lacking foreign support, the situation of the Mahabad Republic quickly became very tenuous. None of the tribes on

---

[12] Amir Hassanpour, personal communication, January 8, 2002, Toronto. McDowall *A Modern History of the Kurds*, p. 242 and Eagleton, *Kurdish Republic of 1946*, p. 44 claim that the printing press was a gift from the Soviet Union.

[13] Entessar, *Kurdish Ethnonationalism*, p. 23.

[14] Eagleton, *Kurdish Republic of 1946*, p. 101.   [15] Ibid., p. 45.

[16] The Anglo–Soviet–Iranian Treaty of Alliance also obligated all the Allied countries to withdraw from Iran six months after the end of World War Two. The Soviets did not look as if they were going to respect the treaty's provisions, however, until Tehran conceded to them the oil concession they wanted.

whom the Republic's military strength rested wanted to be caught backing the wrong horse, or bearing the full brunt of an Iranian army campaign. Tribal rivalries again resurfaced in the uncertain climate, and the need to supply Barzani's Iraqi Kurdish forces also engendered resentment.[17] Although urban Kurds of the Republic were strongly supportive of it, they were not organized into a large enough fighting force to defend it. Essentially, the Republic's dependence on a military that was still more tribal in identity than nationalist, although unavoidable in the face of no alternate sources of armed support at the time, was fatal.[18] The Republic included barely one-third of Iran's Kurds, and those outside its boundaries did not rally to its defense.[19] The broad front established under the KDPI was also mercurial, and Qazi Mohammad had to devote considerable efforts to preventing tribal chiefs in his orbit from attacking others, or raiding Christian and Azeri communities to the north, or moving against leftists in the Kurdish and Azeri areas. The suspicion that many of these chiefs would turn out to be only "fair weather allies" also existed.

The Republic lacked dependable elite allies and international support, as well as sufficient time to pursue resource mobilization strategies that could eventually attract more dependable allies and support. Its main achievement, however, was the successful framing of a politicized Kurdish ethnicity, exemplified by a decent and well-liked Kurdish government: "Tehran recognized that the very orderliness of the Mahabad Republic and the new Kurdish nationalism were infinitely more dangerous to its authority than tribal rebellion. The Qazi trio [the leaders of the Mahabad Republic, executed by the Shah in 1947] perished because they personified the nationalist ideal. Other members of the Republic's administration were executed . . . [but] most of the tribal chiefs got off scot free . . ."[20] Hence the Shah saw the Mahabad Republic in the same way that the Iraqi Kurdish experiment in self-rule is viewed by Ankara, Damascus, and Tehran today – a dangerous cultural framing that proclaims the right and ability of Kurds to run their own affairs.[21]

---

[17] Entessar, *Kurdish Ethnonationalism*, p. 23.

[18] Given more time, the Mahabad Republic's leaders might have been able to build a regular and more loyal army. Such an army would have been less susceptible to the political calculations and shifting alliance tendencies of tribal forces.

[19] David McDowall, "The Kurdish Question: A Historical Review," in Philip G. Kreyenbroek and Stefan Sperl (eds.), *The Kurds: A Contemporary Overview* (London and New York: Routledge,1992), p. 22.

[20] Ibid.

[21] The PKK attempted to pursue similar framings with the establishment of liberated zones at the height of its insurgency. From a rational choice perspective, PKK-established courts, welfare, schools, and civil works also sought to show local Kurds that Kurdish autonomy under the PKK served their interests better than rule by Ankara (ch. 3).

If such an entity were to receive recognition from the community of states (in 1946 in Mahabad or today in Iraqi Kurdistan), it could also use its new-found voice and relations in the international system to assist irredentist Kurdish claims throughout the region.

After the Azerbaijan National Government to the north (which had also lost its Soviet protection) negotiated a deal with Tehran and reverted back to Iranian rule, the Shah felt less obliged to deal amicably with the Kurds. Delegates of the Mahabad Republic were turned away in Tehran, and the Iranian army retook the Mahabad region in December of 1946. With the Azeri statelet to the north gone, Soviet support cut off, British hostility to the notion of Kurdish independence, and tribal chiefs beginning to defect to Tehran's side, the Mahabad leadership decided to avoid bloodshed and submit to advancing Iranian military. Many people, including Mustafa Barzani (who was still weighing his choices between fighting, retreating to Iraq, or negotiating with Tehran) beseeched Qazi Mohammad to flee the area, but to no avail. Qazi Mohammad insisted that his people had placed their trust in him, and he would not abandon them for exile.[22] Along with some of the other principal leaders of Mahabad, he was tried by an Iranian military court and summarily hung in the center of town at 3 a.m. on March 31, 1947.[23] The Republic had existed for only about a year after its founding.

Under the Shah

After the crushing of Mahabad, the Shah's coercive rule continued, although Kurdish identity (as long as it was not politicized) was accepted more openly in Iran than in Turkey.[24] The Turkish strategy of assimilating the Kurds, of pretending that everyone in the country shared Turkish ethnicity, could not work as easily in Iran, a country composed of six large ethnic groups (Persian, Azeri, Kurdish, Baluchi, Lur, and Arab).[25]

In the early 1950s, however, Kurds in Iran enthusiastically supported an apparent opening in the political system, in the personage of

---

[22] Eagleton, *Kurdish Republic of 1946*, p. 113.

[23] As has been the case with the graves of some PKK fighters, Qazi Mohammad's grave became a shrine to which a great many Kurds traveled. The Shah's men eventually removed his remains to a secret location.

[24] The Shah also by the 1950s allowed very limited radio broadcasts in Kurdish. This concession was largely motivated as a response to Kurdish language broadcasts from the USSR and Egypt aimed at inciting Iranian Kurds, however (Amir Hassanpour, personal communication, December 5, 2001).

[25] Author's interview with KDPI central committee and bureau members Hassan Sharafi, Baba Ali, Mustafa Hijri, Hassan Rastgar, Hadi Khdija, and Ma'azoor, April 29, 2004, Iraqi Kurdistan.

Dr. Mohammad Mossadeq. A liberal pro-democratic Iranian nationalist, Mossadeq led the National Front in the Iranian Parliament. In addition to seeking a reduction of the Shah's role from monarch to constitutional monarch, Mossadeq's National Front "called for the establishment of a strong central government that guaranteed basic freedoms to all Iranians, irrespective of their ethnic or linguistic background."[26] Mossadeq's growing power in Parliament as well as his prestige amongst the population left the Shah no choice but to appoint him Prime Minister. Although Mossadeq's platform did not include an endorsement of Kurdish nationalist aims, it was at least a significant improvement over what the rule of Mohammad Reza Shah held out for the Kurds: "Kurdish rank-and-file support for Dr. Mossadeq's government alienated the Shah and convinced him that the Kurds had to be contained at all costs. For example, in a massive display of support for Mossadeq's campaign to force the Shah to reign and not rule, as stipulated in the Iranian Constitution, Iranian Kurds on August 13, 1953, overwhelmingly voted to limit the Shah's power and make him into a constitutional monarch. According to Abdul Rahman Ghassemlou, in the city of Mahabad, the Shah received only two votes."[27] Support for Mossadeq seems to indicate that, as appeared to be the case in Turkey during the 1960s, nationalist Kurds were happy to pursue their goals from within the system when it appeared somewhat open to them. That Iranian Kurds were amongst Mossadeq's most important supporters also highlights the democratizing role that Kurdish demands can play in certain contexts (Chapter 8 addresses this issue further).

Unfortunately for all the people of Iran, however, Mossadeq's program for a democratic state ran into the opposition of Western business interests, since it included Iranian nationalization of the oil companies. On August 19, 1953, British and American agents engineered a coup that deposed Mossadeq and handed the Shah absolute power. Kurdish aspirations of advancing their position with the help of a liberal reforming leader in Tehran were dashed, and all of Iran found itself under strict dictatorship once again. The Shah's imposition (or rather, the Shah's and American and British imposition) of absolute authoritarian rule in Iran witnessed another Kurdish uprising in 1956 near Kermanshah, which was suppressed. The Shah continued to pursue many of the same strategies as Ankara, eliminating rebellious Kurdish chiefs but co-opting the remaining important traditional Kurdish elites and appointing them to high positions in his government.[28] During his 1960–1963 land reform

---

[26] Entessar, *Kurdish Ethnonationalism*, p. 25.   [27] Ibid., p. 27.   [28] Ibid., p. 25.

program, he made it clear that the estates of cooperative Kurdish leaders would be left untouched.[29] The key difference at this time between semi-democratic Turkey and authoritarian Iran, however, was the absence of civil society in Iran through which any left-wing or non-traditional Kurdish opposition movement could mobilize.[30] There existed no Iranian equivalent to the Turkish Workers' Party in Turkey, or the myriad labor unions, intellectual circles, and cultural associations that provided the initial mobilizing networks of groups such as Dev Genc or the PKK. Tudeh, a broad-based Iranian communist opposition movement, was largely crushed and exiled in 1953. Also, because they only constituted around 10 to 15 percent of Iran's population (compared to 20 percent in Turkey and 25 percent in Iraq), and in light of the very substantial Western military and financial support that the Shah enjoyed, Kurdish opposition faced additional obstacles in Iran. If some innovative, very astute resource mobilization strategies could have countered such a situation, they nonetheless failed to emerge. It seems more likely, however, that although Kurdish nationalist framings and discontent in Iran appear to have been substantial, inauspicious political opportunity structures and the relative size of the Kurdish population left less room for effective resource mobilization methods. Although groups such as the KDPI did pursue organizing and mobilizing efforts during this period, mass arrests, imprisonment, torture, and executions stunted such efforts. As was the case in Turkey and Iraq, such repression also greatly facilitated grievance framing against the state and the maintenance of politicized Kurdish identities, but this was insufficient to counterbalance unfavorable opportunity structures. Opposition to the Shah would have to be organized along broader lines than ethnicity, if at all. SAVAK (the Shah's secret police) was perhaps at the time the most ruthlessly effective such force in the world. It helped insure that people would at least perceive opposition to be futile, whether or not that was actually the case.

The KDPI did, nonetheless, succeed until 1966 in providing significant aid and manpower to Barzani's KDP revolt in Iraq.[31] The Shah might have even tolerated such assistance, since it weakened his enemies in Baghdad. By 1966, however, he shrewdly decided to provide more aid to Barzani than that offered by the KDPI. By doing this, the Shah made

---

[29] Ibid.

[30] The crucial exception to the suppression of civil society in Iran were the mosques, however, which were the one meeting place and public venue that the Shah's secret police left relatively untouched. As a result, religious organizers came to play a role in the events of 1978 disproportionate to their actual level of support in the population, since they were the most organized opposition movement.

[31] Ghassemlou, cited in Chaliand (ed.), *People Without a Country*, p. 112.

the Iraqi Kurds more dependent upon him than the KDPI, after which he convinced Barzani to help him suppress the KDPI as the price for his support. Opportunistically, Barzani complied by demanding that Iranian Kurds cease opposition to the Shah and give priority to the Kurdish rebellion in Iraq, adding that failing to do so would constitute a betrayal of the "Kurdish revolution."[32] Although Iranian Kurds were already giving Barzani's rebellion priority by sending supplies and men to Iraq, such a ridiculous framing of the issue led many to end their support of Barzani and return home to fight the Shah. In 1967 a dissident group within the KDPI (among those who had been forced out of Iraqi Kurdistan by Barzani) launched a guerrilla offensive in Iran, supporting spontaneous peasant uprisings around Mahabad, Baneh, and Sardasht.[33] After eighteen months of mountain fighting, they were surrounded by the Iranian army and cut off from retreat by Barzani's KDP, which executed forty of the Kurdish guerrillas who fell into its hands.[34] It was not a bright moment for pan-Kurdish solidarity. Given the subsequent 1975 betrayal of Barzani by the Shah, it may have also been a huge error on Barzani's part.

Abd al Rahman Ghassemlou, an Iranian Kurdish intellectual who had studied in Prague and lived in Paris, became the leader of the remaining skeleton KDPI in 1971, adopting the party slogan of "Democracy for Iran, autonomy for Kurdistan."[35] Such a slogan, like that of the Iraqi KDP and the PKK after 1995, seemed to represent an attempt to frame Kurdish demands in a light acceptable to Iranians in general, as well as the international community of states. Working together with Iranian Marxists and Islamists, the KDPI continued to oppose the regime, but with little success.[36] However, due to either the KDPI's non-revolutionary political stance or its defeats of the late 1960s, a group of mostly young urban Kurdish intellectuals founded in 1969 a new secret organization called the Society of Revolutionary Toilers of Iranian Kurdistan,

---

[32] Entessar, *Kurdish Ethnonationalism*, p. 28.
[33] Ibid; also Ghassemlou, in Chaliand (ed.), *People Without a Country*, p. 112.
[34] McDowall, *A Modern History of the Kurds*, p. 253.
[35] Koohi-Kamali, *Political Development of the Kurds*, p. 176.
[36] For a discussion on modernization's effect of changing Kurdish socio-economic structures and placing larger portions of the Kurdish population in a position more amenable to the politicization of ethnic identity (akin to the process in Turkey described in previous chapters), see McDowall, *A Modern History of the Kurds*, pp. 254–259. Due to the patently closed nature of the Shah's regime, the KDPI decided to continue armed struggle, despite its extremely weakened state. Its leader, Dr. Ghassemlou, gives the following explanation: "This form of struggle was imposed by the Shah's dictatorial regime. No alternative could bring about revolutionary change, and under the Shah there was no room for democracy or for the national rights of oppressed people" (in Chaliand [ed.], *People Without a Country*, p. 120).

commonly known as Komala ("society" or "committee").[37] Like the KDPI, Komala advocated autonomy for Kurdistan within a democratic Iran. Unlike the KDPI, however, Komala adopted an outlook similar to that of the PKK in Turkey, targeting feudal society in Kurdistan and tribalism as obstacles to the Kurds' quest for self-determination. The group also put forth a more progressive platform regarding the role of Kurdish women, advocating their emancipation from patriarchy together with the emancipation of the Kurdish people. Whereas the KDPI's mobilization strategies relied heavily on tribal elites and their resource networks, Komala's strategy of Maoist mobilization of the peasantry and lower urban classes found its most receptive audience in southern Iranian Kurdistan, which was less tribalized and more sedentary than the KDPI's more northern strongholds.[38] Komala would later cooperate with the KDPI at times, and on other occasions found itself in armed conflict with its more conservative rival.

The Iranian revolution and the Iran–Iraq war – fleeting opportunities

Popular grievances against the Shah within wide segments of Iran's population were becoming evident by the 1970s. This stands in significant contrast to the Turkish case, where the state (personified by the technocrats and the military, *not* the elected politicians) maintained legitimacy among the majority of the Turkish population. Like all modernizing authoritarian states, the Shah's only possible ideological justification for his absolutist rule was the promise of development, of more wealth and a better life for the people. Economic difficulties in the 1970s, exacerbated by the Shah's huge weapons purchases and bloated security apparatus, had left the promise of development unfulfilled, however. Opposition movements had no trouble framing grievances against the regime, which seemed to offer the masses only poverty, authoritarianism, and harsh limitations to civil liberties.[39] Crucially,

---

[37] "Komala" means "society" or "committee," and the Komala founded in 1969 is a different organization than the Komala out of which the KDPI was created in 1945.

[38] For a more extensive discussion of the different support bases of the KDPI and Komala, based on an analysis of Iranian Kurdistan's socio-economic structures, see Koohi-Kamali, *Political Development of the Kurds*. By the 1980s and 1990s, the two organizations boasted similar levels of support and strength, with the KDPI more solidly entrenched in the north of Iranian Kurdistan near the Turkish border and Mahabad, and Komala more popular in the south, around Sanandaj and Saqqiz.

[39] For more on the grievance frames advanced and the role of media in the revolution, see Ali Mohammadi and Annabelle Sreberny-Mohammadi, *Small Media, Big Revolution* (Minneapolis: University of Minnesota Press, 1994).

Kurdish opposition movements were able to find common cause with other insurgents, such as the Islamists and non-Kurdish opponents of the regime. Nonetheless, the revolution that suddenly deposed the Shah in 1979 caught a great many people by surprise. The revolution did not occur through armed struggle led by insurgent organizations. Instead, mass demonstrations against the Shah, loosely organized by various opposition groups but for the most part spontaneous grass-roots affairs wherein each rally led to a bigger one following it, eventually created a situation wherein the Shah would have had to massacre huge numbers of unarmed civilians to maintain order. Some of his generals were ready to do so,[40] but most soldiers and army commanders began to waver on the issue. The civilians in question were viewed as Iranian citizens from every walk of life[41] – i.e. "the people." If the demonstrations had been confined to a non-Persian ethnic segment of the population, such as the Kurds or the Azeris, the Shah's army would have no doubt mowed the out-group down with its machine guns.

After the Shah's overthrow and hasty departure, the most organized group of dissidents able to put themselves at the head of the revolution were the Islamists. Khomeini and his clerics did not consolidate their power immediately, however, and the Kurds who had supported the revolution hoped it would bring them some measure of autonomy in a new democratic Iran. Kurdish support both in the Kurdish regions and amongst Kurds in Tehran and other major cities had made a large contribution to the anti-Shah unrest. Once again, the Kurds sought to take advantage of the political opportunity they all perceived. After the fall of the Shah, they sought to assure themselves that the new government in Tehran would respect Kurdish self-determination within Iran's borders, and agitated for such. Especially because most Kurds in Iran are Sunni Muslims, they wanted to be sure that the newly emerging Shiite state would not discriminate against them or deny them minority ethnic and religious rights. Khomeini, however, had no tolerance for anything that might threaten the unity and territorial integrity of his new and still fragile Islamic state. He rebuffed Kurdish demands for autonomy, framing the issue as one of Muslim unity:

---

[40] See Charles Kurzman, "Structural opportunity and perceived opportunity in social-movement theory: The Iranian revolution of 1979," *American Sociological Review* 61: 1 (February 1996), for an interesting discussion on the issue from a perspective similar to the one employed here.

[41] Entessar points out that the only Kurdish segment of society to not participate in anti-Shah demonstrations were the landed tribal elite such as the Jafs, whom the Shah had co-opted (Entessar, *Kurdish Ethnonationalism*, p. 29).

Sometimes the word minorities is used to refer to people such as Kurds, Lurs, Turks, Persians, Baluchis, and such. These people should not be called minorities, because this term assumes there is a difference between these brothers. In Islam, such a difference has no place at all. There is no difference between Muslims who speak different languages, for instance, the Arabs or the Persians. It is very probably that such problems have been created by those who do not wish the Muslim countries to be united ... They create the issues of nationalism, of pan-Iranism, pan-Turkism, and such-isms which are contrary to Islamic doctrines. Their plan is to destroy Islam and Islamic philosophy.[42]

Khomeini's framing of the issue was largely accepted by the Shiite Kurds around the area of Kermanshah, but the majority Sunni Kurds refused such arguments.[43] Sheikh Izz al Din, a well known Sunni Kurdish religious leader, responded that "Islam does not require that all Muslims should be governed by a single group of people. It recognizes that people are divided into different groups, nations and tribes. There is no reason within Islam why these groups should not order their own affairs."[44] Later, his anti-Khomeini statements would go even further:

Many governments in the past have claimed to act in the name of Islam, but in reality they were not Islamic. The Safavid and Ottoman governments were cases in point; more recently we have the case of Khomeini in Iran. They are *qeshri* – backward and vulgar – and have ruined Islam in its spirit. What we have is not religious government, but a dictatorship under the name of Islam. They are using the name of religion to oppress the people, and the people know this. In Sunni Islam there is no imam as political leader or na'ib (deputy) imam. The role of the clergy is to be a *morshed*, or guide, in knowing God. You will also find some shi'i [sic] clergy who reject Khomeini's concept of the *faqih* [government of a just jurisconsult]. It is not an Islamic regime.[45]

Hence both Khomeini and Sheikh Izz al Din relied on the same set of Islamic cultural tool kits, but used them to frame contrary arguments. Sheikh Izz al Din's basic argument revolved around the contention that Ayatollah Khomeini used an Islamic veneer to pursue an Iranian nationalist state policy. Such a policy did not deviate much from the Shah's approach to the Kurds. Just as Turkish nationalism and Arab nationalism

---

[42] Ayatollah Khomeini, Radio Tehran, December 17, 1979, quoted in McDowall, *A Modern History of the Kurds*, p. 271.

[43] McDowall argues that the Shiite Kurds of Kermanshah "had no interest in autonomy. They wanted, initially at any rate, to remain part of the Shi'i republic ..." (McDowall, *A Modern History of the Kurds*, p. 270). In the context of the Islamic Revolution in Iran, these Kurds therefore stressed their Shiite identity more than their Kurdish one. Nonetheless, many young Kurds from Kermanshah and neighboring Shiite areas were active in the KDPI, Komala, and other leftist groups in Kurdistan (Hassanpour, personal communication, December 9, 2001).

[44] Sheikh Izz al Din, quoted in McDowall, *A Modern History of the Kurds*, p. 272.

[45] Quoted in Entessar, *Kurdish Ethnonationalism*, p. 33.

could not come to terms with Kurdish nationalist challenges to the Turkish and Iraqi states, neither could Iranian nationalism tolerate such a competing force within the territory it controlled.

In 1979, however, Kurdish people were still deciding whether or not the emerging so-called "Islamic" government would be oppressive towards them. The new system was still divided and seemed somewhat open to Kurdish group demands, and a series of negotiations and peaceful jockeying for position occurred within the government.[46] Before it became clear that Khomeini would assume supreme power, several contenders in Tehran voiced conciliatory policy preferences to fulfill Kurdish aspirations. The stability of elite alignments in Tehran was very much in a state of flux, and allies for the Kurds seemed available on several fronts. By March 21, 1979, however, Khomeini had a more solid grip on the reigns of power, and sent his air force and *pasdaran* revolutionary guards to attack the major Kurdish city of Sanandaj, in order to secure it for the revolution and help settle questions regarding the Kurds' future role in the new republic. This attack on the eve of the Kurdish new year (Newroz) proved to many Kurds that the new regime might well be even worse than the Shah.[47] Eighty-five to ninety percent of Kurds then boycotted a national referendum concerning the future of Iran's government.[48]

In the negotiations between the Kurdish representatives and the government, the offers made by the government were virtually all later vetoed by Khomeini, who was rapidly becoming the only real locus of power.[49] Negotiations mainly continued as long as they did because the coercive capacity of the new Islamic Republic and its disorganized army (what was left of it after the Shah's overthrow and various purges) was uncertain. As in both the Turkish and Iraqi cases, when the political system held out the possibility of openness towards the Kurds' basic group demands, the Kurds were happy to pursue the issue within accepted channels. This would also assist Kurdish nationalist framings later on, since they could then point out that they had tried to resolve things peacefully. Komala and the KDPI were also reasonably popular in

---

[46] See Entessar, *Kurdish Ethnonationalism*, pp. 29–41 or McDowall, *A Modern History of the Kurds*, pp. 261–275 for detailed examinations of the negotiations and their eventual decline into armed conflict.

[47] Hassanpour, personal communication, December 9, 2001.

[48] Chaliand (ed.), *People Without a Country*, p. 212. The referendum question was "Islamic Republic – yes or no?" Hence many of those who boycotted the referendum argued that such a question left the future nature of the Islamic Republic very unclear (Hassanpour, personal communication, February 15, 2002).

[49] While the KDPI carried out negotiations with Tehran, Komala as well as a few other leftist and Islamist groups were already engaging *pasdaran* (Revolutionary Guards) troops in skirmishes in Kurdistan.

Iranian Kurdistan. After the setbacks of the 1960s, both parties had quietly pursued grass-roots work within the Kurdish population, which gave them a solid base of support by 1979. When parliamentary elections were held there in March of 1980, Kurdish candidates won eighty percent of the vote.[50]

As it became increasingly clear that the Kurds and Khomeini would not come to any agreement, however, active fighting between the army and various Kurdish forces increased throughout the Kurdish regions. "Ayatollah Khomeini declared a holy war against the Kurds, banned all Kurdish political organizations, canceled the membership of Ghassemlou in the Assembly of Experts and denounced Ghassemlou and Shaikh Izziddin Husseini as enemies of the Islamic Republic. The KDPI was denounced as 'the party of Satan.'"[51] Massive government repression followed, with the Iranian *pasdaran* attacking villages and executing thousands of people. The Kurdish *peshmerga* in turn continued to hold onto large areas, decimating Iranian forces in continuous attacks. Negotiations following major periods of fighting failed to provide the Kurds with any substantial concessions – the final Constitution of the Islamic Republic (ratified in November 1979) even omitted earlier drafts' mention of ethnic minority rights, the equality of various ethnic groups in Iran, guarantees of Sunni religious rights, and the Kurds' right to give the Kurdish language priority in predominantly Kurdish areas.[52] While the Iranian political system increasingly closed itself to Kurdish group demands, Kurdish forces controlled the Kurdish countryside and government forces held the major Kurdish towns when Saddam Hussein invaded in September of 1980.

Not too surprisingly, the Kurdish parties viewed the Iraqi invasion as the perfect opportunity to make Iranian Kurdistan's independence a reality and redress the political losses they had suffered during the preceding year. The KDPI initially offered to help Tehran fight the invading Iraqis in return for recognition of limited Kurdish autonomy in Iran, but was refused.[53] Although the KDPI and Komala never cooperated directly with Iraqi forces, both groups did end up receiving supplies and weapons from Baghdad, which they used to help them fight Iranian troops out of Iranian Kurdistan. As Baghdad had viewed Iraqi Kurds who cooperated with Iran, Tehran now viewed its own Kurds. As in Iraq, the Iranian government pursued major military operations against Iranian Kurdish

[50] James Ciment, *The Kurds: State and Minority in Turkey, Iraq and Iran* (New York: Facts on File, Inc., 1996), p. 70.
[51] Koohi-Kamali, *Political Development of the Kurds*, p. 185.   [52] Ibid., p. 188.
[53] Ibid., p. 190.

groups during the war. Most of the Iranian people probably shared Tehran's framing of the Kurds as traitors in the country's most dire moment, and Kurds who supported the Islamic Revolution (especially Shiite ones) were unhappy with Ghassemlou's stance. At the same time, Khomeini's harsh treatment of the Kurds had by this time become apparent to all. The same way repression after the 1980 military coup in Turkey eliminated legal organizations and swelled PKK ranks, Komala and the KDPI in Iran enjoyed renewed popularity amongst Iranian Kurds as the mullahs in Tehran displayed their authoritarian colors.

To the surprise of many, Iranian troops eventually held back the Iraqi invasion (which occurred mostly south of the Kurdish region, in the mainly Sunni Arab Iranian province of Khuzistan) and began to counter-attack. Baghdad's attack had in effect rallied the Iranian people and army around Khomeini's rule, which was by no means secure before September 1980. By 1982, a re-organized and much larger Iranian army was ready to recapture Iranian Kurdistan, with the assistance of some Shiite Kurds who identified with the regime (ethnicity is not the only possible primary identification people may choose, of course, and Shiite Kurds shared the same religion as the majority of Iranians).

Ideological differences within the KDPI and Komala had in the meantime caused some infighting between the Kurdish groups, further weakening them before the Iranian assault. After a harsh campaign of two years, and with the assistance of Barzani's KDP forces from Iraq, Tehran reasserted its control over the Kurdish region. Although beleaguered KDPI forces received some help from Talabani's PUK forces, with which they enjoyed good relations, it was not enough.[54] Just as Tehran consolidated its control over the Kurdish areas, the KDPI and Komala disagreements caused the two groups to degenerate into active fighting against one another in the fall of 1985. Much like the later KDP–PUK intra-fighting in Iraq from 1994 to 1998, the struggle was mainly over political power and territory, and saw the KDPI generally more successful than Komala.[55]

That Kurdish nationalists were unable to refrain from fighting each other or prevent the reassertion of government control in their areas, even while Tehran was at war with Iraq, also indicated a major weakness on their part and struck a powerful blow to their movement. It likewise pointed to the fact that territory-based warfare is a dead-end for Kurdish movements in Iran, in much the same way it was for Iraqi Kurds in Iraq after 1975. For the remainder of the Iran–Iraq war, Iranian Kurds were limited to night-time guerrilla strikes against the Iranian army.

[54] Ibid., p. 191.   [55] Ibid., p. 183.

Ghassemlou's decision that the KDPI had to negotiate with Tehran rather than continue an indefinite guerrilla war caused further splits in his movement, as those who felt that armed struggle must continue broke away to found groups such as the KDPI-RL (Revolutionary Leadership).[56] Just as Ismail Agha Simko had been assassinated by the Iranian government during negotiations in 1929, the original KDPI's Dr. Ghassemlou and two of his associates were assassinated by the Iranians during negotiations held in Vienna in 1989. Three years later, KDPI's new leader, Sadik Sharafkindi, was likewise lured to negotiations with Iranian government representatives in a restaurant in Berlin, which also resulted in his assassination.

Perhaps somewhat wiser *vis-à-vis* Iranian government pretenses at parley, Komala refused negotiations with Khomeini's government and continued its armed struggle. Komala still suffered changes, however. In 1983, Komala united with the Union of Communist Militants to form the Communist Party of Iran, functioning as the Kurdistan Organization of the CPI. In 1991, a group of mainly non-Kurdish members who were no longer willing to accept the nationalist program of the Kurds in the party split off from the CPI to form the Worker-Communist Party of Iran (WPI). In 2000, another group broke off from Komala-CPI to revive the old 1969–1984 Komala party and platform.[57] When one considers this together with the splits that occurred in the KDPI around the same period, the state of Kurdish nationalist movements in Iran became quite fragmented from the mid-1980s onwards.

The 1990s: limited guerrilla warfare and waiting for opportunities

Since the end of the war with Iraq, some Kurdish guerrilla activity against the government continued in Iran. McDowall provides the following evaluation of the situation in the 1990s:

The KDPI repeatedly and explicitly stated that it harboured no belief or expectation that it could win a guerrilla war, and that there was no alternative to a negotiated settlement. Yet within its ranks some spoke with a new stridency of

---

[56] McDowall, *A Modern History of the Kurds*, p. 278.

[57] In order to differentiate themselves, the section of Komala that remained a part of the CPI now spells its name "Komalah," while the breakaway group that sought to restore "the old Komala" omits the "h." The two groups are also sometimes referred to as "Marxist Komalah" and "Nationalist Komala" respectively.

secession if the Islamic regime proved obdurate to the demand for autonomy. As in Turkey, an adamant refusal to brook the idea of autonomy was beginning to show signs of generating genuine separatism.

Tehran's response to the insurgency ignored two crucial facets of the Kurdish challenge. The first of these was that most guerrilla action was nowhere near the Iraqi border, operating out of the homes of sympathizers the length and breadth of Kurdistan. As one KDPI politburo member remarked, "They [Tehran] are much better equipped; they have all the advantages of a state. But they have no political base. Their only base is a fort on top of each hilltop." The militarization of Kurdistan provided more potential targets for the guerrillas and deepened nationalist sentiment among the civil population.

Guerrilla freedom to live among the Kurdish population was a key indication of the progress of the national movement since the revolution . . . Finally, nationalist sentiment has seeped southwards into the predominantly Shi'i area, partly because of disgust with government savagery against Kurds further north and partly because of the unpopularity and human cost of supporting an ideological regime in its war against Iraq in the 1980s.[58]

While McDowall's observations about popular sentiment in Iranian Kurdistan and the increasing movement of Shiite Kurds towards Kurdish nationalism may be true, my own visits to Iranian Kurdistan in the summer of 1999 and the fall of 2000 failed to uncover much evidence of an active guerrilla insurgency in the area. When questioned in 2004 about their operations against the Iranian government, leaders of the KDPI and both Komala factions all insisted that they were avoiding guerrilla actions at this time.[59] While all three organizations continue political education amongst the people and recruitment, they feel that guerrilla warfare and the resultant government backlash would only bring suffering to their communities in Iranian Kurdistan. They also admit that their forces were not strong enough to face the Iranian army in a sustained manner – throughout most of the 1990s, Iran controlled its Kurdish regions with a force of more than 200,000 soldiers.[60]

Although the resource mobilization efforts of the KDPI, Komala, and other Kurdish groups were not successful in achieving lasting autonomy

---

[58] McDowall, *A Modern History of the Kurds*, p. 278.

[59] Author's interview with KDP Leadership Bureau and Central Committee members Hassan Sharafi, Baba Ali, Mustafa Hijri, Hassan Rastgar, Hadi Khdija, and Ma'azoor, April 29, 2004, Iraqi Kurdistan; author's interview with "Marxist Komalah" Central Committee members Hassan, Ibrahim, Rahman, Rasheed, Karim, and Sirwa, April 19, 2004, Iraqi Kurdistan; author's interview with "Nationalist Komala" Head of Politburo Abdullah Mohtadi and Central Committee member Anwar Mohammadi, April 25, 2004, Iraqi Kurdistan.

[60] McDowall, *A Modern History of the Kurds*, p. 277.

for Iranian Kurds, these efforts along with government repression seem to have significantly heightened politicization of Kurdish ethnicity over the years. The greater sense of Kurdish nationalism among Iranian Kurds was also evident after Abdullah Ocalan's capture by Turkey. Tehran had decided to allow Kurdish protests on the issue, expecting the Kurds to chant anti-Turkish, anti-Israeli, and anti-American slogans. Iranian security forces were then caught by surprise when large, hostile Kurdish crowds throughout Iranian Kurdistan went on to recite chants against the Islamic Republic: "While impossible for independent journalists to verify figures due to restricted access, it seems clear that major disturbances took place. That pro-Ocalan demonstrations erupted into protests against the Islamic regime points to both the transnational volatility of Kurdish issues and underlying dissatisfaction of Iranian Kurds with the regime."[61] As in Turkey, changes wrought by modernization have placed more of the Kurdish population in a position that allows for and encourages the adoption of a Kurdish nationalist identity. The Islamic Revolution's promises of equality are also contradicted by the military's actions and presence, as well as the continuing relative poverty of Iranian Kurdistan. Also importantly, Kurdish nationalists' dependence on traditional Kurdish elites, mainly tribal aghas and chiefs, has become much less significant in Iran than in Iraq (the KDPI includes such traditional elites more than Komala, from which they are generally absent). Movements such as the KDPI and particularly Komala are today composed more of the same social classes that the PKK draws its support from, mainly intellectuals, professionals, peasants, workers, and marginalized individuals. Although they stand no more chance of defeating the central government via guerrilla warfare than did the Iraqi Kurds through conventional warfare, nationalist Kurds appear ready to continue as a thorn in Tehran's side, should it persist in ignoring Kurdish demands for group rights.

Disenchantment with the government in Tehran also appears to be growing throughout Iran, as the student demonstrations of July 1999 in many of Iran's major cities indicate. As the student demonstrations were put down with the threat of extreme force, the regime appeared to be in a very precarious position. Reformers such as Rafsanjani and Khatami likely felt that the only chance of avoiding an explosion similar to that which ousted the Shah was by opening up the political space somewhat and liberalizing laws regarding personal and collective freedoms in the country. Kurdish publications that openly discussed Kurdish national

---

[61] WKI Press Release (March 3, 1999), www.clark.net/kurd/prIranViolence.html.

aspirations, Kurdish history, and similar issues began appearing in the late 1990s, and the regime either decided to allow them or was afraid to overextend its repressive reach and provoke more unrest. Other media sources in Iran also experienced, for a time, greater freedom to discuss issues relating to criticism of the government and the future of the country. The government in Tehran seemed to be considering granting more extensive freedoms and minority rights to the Kurds and other groups, thereby turning them into more willing citizens of the Republic. The old cultural framings of everyone being Muslim and equal in the country appeared insufficient for many Kurds, or even for Persian young people interested in pursuing lifestyles that are not centered on Islamic piety.

At the same time, however, hard-line clerics in the country viewed Iranian reforms with deep suspicion. They opposed many of Khatami's initiatives, and saw themselves as the "guardians of the Islamic Revolution." Although briefly on the defensive after reformist Mohammad Khatami's 1997 electoral victory, the hard-line clerics after 1999 moved to prevent reform and close the system again. The Islamic Council of Guardians closed several pro-reformist media outlets in that year, and arrested many journalists as well.[62] From 1997 to 2002, some 90 newspapers, journals and other publications were banned, and even members of parliament were jailed.[63] In 2001, the Council conducted its usual practice of barring large numbers of candidates from running in the elections, although Khatami was allowed to run and won a second term in government. In 2003, the Guardian Council ruled Khatami's efforts to reduce their power in government as unconstitutional, and continued blocking or vetoing scores of legislative bills passed by the *Majlis* (parliament). In June of that same year, Iranian students frustrated with the lack of reforms again took to the streets of Tehran, this time to demand the resignations of both government hard-liners *and* Mohammad Khatami.[64]

Hence, by 2003 it seemed that the popular enthusiasm behind Khatami, based on many Iranians' hopes for reform and change, waned significantly. One observer cast the mood of the younger generation of Iranians in the following way:

They despise the fundamentalist dinosaurs who want to turn the clock back. They also mistrust most of the born-again democrats who now spearhead the

---

[62] "Profile: Mohammad Khatami," BBC News (June 30, 2003), http://news.bbc.co.uk/2/hi/middle_east/3027382.stm.

[63] Jahangir Amuzegar, "Iran's theocracy under siege," *Middle East Policy*, Washington (Spring 2003), 141.

[64] "Profile: Mohammad Khatami", BBC News.

cause of the free press and the rule of law; they remember them as old revolutionaries who in their heyday (1981–1989) showed no qualms about wholesale executions of their opponents, torture of political dissidents, muzzling of their enemies, seizure and confiscation of private property without due process, and violation of minorities' rights. The freedom these insider reformists now seek is their own liberty to govern and not necessarily the freedom of others to dissent.[65]

Roughly the same argument can be used to describe the attitude of Kurdish nationalists towards the reformers. Kurdish hopes of finding allies amongst the reformists, and essentially taking advantage of reformist–conservative elite divisions in the country, also diminished as the reformists' advances hit the walls that the Council of Guardians erected.[66] In September 2001 the Iranian parliamentarians from Kurdistan Province even resigned *en masse*, "to protest discrimination against the Kurdish and Sunni minority, according to press reports."[67] The parliamentarians complained that "80 percent of the province's residents live below the poverty line and the state universities grant very few places to students from Kurdistan ... the Interior Ministry has never responded to requests that it send a delegation to the province, it rarely replies to any communications, and when it does reply, the response is usually unsatisfactory."[68] The resignations stated symbolically that Kurds willing to try to work within the system were now abandoning their hope that such engagement could produce substantive results.

It also seems clear that the Kurdish minority will not emerge as the principle agent of change in Iran, given its size (around ten percent of the population, compared to roughly twenty percent of Turkey and Iraq's population) and lack of strength *vis-à-vis* the government. Given the precarious situation in Iran as a whole, however, Kurdish nationalist leaders are keeping a close eye on events. They are no doubt attempting to maintain effective organizational structures within their nationalist movements, remaining in touch with their popular base and ready to act decisively at the right opportunity. Should an explosive confrontation flare up between reformists, conservatives, and other groups in Iran, Kurdish movements will move to take advantage of elite divisions in the government. They will likely offer to provide important support to

---

[65] Amuzegar, "Iran's theocracy under siege," 150.
[66] For a more detailed discussion of elite divisions within Iran, see Amuzegar, "Iran's theocracy under siege."
[67] "Ethnicity Affects Parliament," *RFE/RL Iran Report* 4: 39, (October 15, 2001), http:// www.globalsecurity.org/wmd/library/news/iran/2001/.
[68] Ibid.

whichever allies seem likely to reciprocate by recognizing Kurdish aspirations for autonomy.

Conclusion

Due to space limitations, my treatment of the Kurdish situation in Iraq and Iran has unfortunately been much more perfunctory than that of the Kurdish issue in Turkey. Nonetheless, a summary analysis of the Iranian Kurdish case employing the theoretical synthesis of this book can now help us compare the issue to that of Kurds in Iraq and Turkey. What stands out the most in the Iranian case is the degree to which Iranian Kurds have relied on the appearance of auspicious opportunities, even more so than Turkish and Iraqi Kurds. Whereas the PKK in Turkey mounted a severe challenge to the state at a time when opportunity structures appeared quite unfavorable, and Iraqi Kurds challenged Baghdad almost continuously since Iraq's founding, Iranian Kurdish challenges only emerged in significant form at times when the Iranian state was in dire straits – the 1920s, 1945–1946, 1979, and the early 1980s. These were all instances when the state's willingness and capacity to repress were severely weakened, when significant external assistance was available, and the institutionalized political system appeared closed. In the immediate aftermath of the 1979 Revolution, when the political system appeared more open to Kurdish demands and non-Kurdish elite allies emerged in Tehran (various liberals competing for power after the Shah's departure), Iranian Kurds formed a united front (including the KDPI, Komala, and smaller groups) and pursued negotiation rather than armed opposition. When negotiations broke down, the Kurdish groups felt relatively strong enough *vis-à-vis* the fledgling revolutionary government in Tehran to take to the battlefield. Failing to mobilize especially Shiite Kurds, to attract substantial non-Kurdish support in Iran or sufficient international assistance, the confrontation on the battlefield went badly for the Kurds. Had Iraq not invaded in September of 1980, perhaps the internal divisions within the emerging government in Tehran would have produced results more favorable to the Kurds. After Iranians rallied behind Khomeini's new rule in order to fight off the Iraqi invaders, however, sympathy for Kurdish dissenters was no longer possible. As in Turkey and Iraq, Iranian Kurds were framed by their government opponents as the tools of outsiders, bent on breaking the country apart. In 1979, Iranian Prime Minister Banisadr "... characterized the Kurdish leaders as leaders of subversive minorities who wanted to impose violence on the Iranian people, and insisted that brotherly Islamic cooperation could only begin when these elements stopped their actions. He told

Kurdish leaders: 'We accept autonomy, but what you want is separation, otherwise you would not be fighting.'"[69] Even as recently as 2001, the Speaker of the Majlis Mehdi Karrubi "told members of the Kurdistan branch of the Islamic Iran Participation Party on 20 September that Sunni and Shia Iranians enjoy equal rights. Past unrest in Kurdistan, according to Karrubi, was not sectarian and was the result of 'plots of the Iranian nation's enemies who seek sowing the seeds of discord among, based on any type of baseless excuses,' IRNA reported."[70]

Although the Kurds were contributors to the movement that deposed the Shah and a key factor weakening the new Islamic government in Tehran, they do not appear after the 1930s to have pursued resource mobilization strategies that effectively altered the opportunity context in which they function. By taking advantage of the Soviet presence and offer of support (however brief) in 1945, Kurdish nationalists did nonetheless achieve a major coup for the cultural frames of Kurds both inside Iran and outside. The Mahabad Republic crystallized in the minds of Kurds their right to self-determination, as well as their ability to run their own affairs. In this sense, the mobilizing act of establishing the Republic in 1945, even if it survived only a short time, had a powerful, lasting impact on the cultural frames of Kurds in Iran and elsewhere. Such nationalist framings as well as attempts after the Islamic revolution to force Tehran to grant the Kurds more autonomy, appear more vibrant than ever.

Significantly, the KDPI and Komala have never advocated a separate Kurdish state or greater Kurdistan, as did the PKK in its early years. Kurdish nationalists in Iran hope for sympathy from a broad swath of the population, especially other minorities such as the Azeris, Arabs, Lor, and Baluchis, many of whom would also like to see autonomous status for their regions. To date, it does not seem that alliances with other ethnic groups in Iran have developed to any significant extent, however. In the Azeri case, disagreements about where the borders of an autonomous Azeri region would end and where those of autonomous Kurdistan would begin have also bedeviled relations between the groups for generations. Given the very multi-ethnic make-up of the country, however, the possibility of finding other minority elite allies stands out as a potentially important option available to Iranian Kurds more than Iraqi and Turkish Kurds. In the meantime, some form of accommodation between reformists in Tehran and Kurdish nationalists does not appear out of the question if the ruling body in Tehran breaks down into a crisis. But

---

[69] Koohi-Kamali, *Political Development of the Kurds*, p. 186; cites *The New York Times*, August 29, 1979.
[70] "Ethnicity Affects Parliament," *RFE/RL Iran Report*.

particularly if other non-Kurdish elements in Iran heighten their agitation for change and confront conservative members of the regime, Iranian Kurds will attempt to capitalize on such an opportunity and challenge the regime in tandem with such groups. Likewise, the degree of self-government attained by Kurds in Iraq may serve as reference point for Iranian Kurds, encouraging them to demand more from Tehran.

In the meantime, KDPI, Komala, and Komalah leaders refrain from mobilization strategies involving guerrilla attacks on Iranian government forces. In April 2004, the leadership of the KDPI offered the following rationale:

Yes, we have guerrillas but now we have no military action. We are organizing politically within Iranian Kurdistan. We are not allowed by the Iraqi Kurdish organizations to establish an army here and have them act. We believe that in time that organizing people inside Iranian Kurdistan is more effective than military action. The Iranian government is very weak economically and politically right now. They are under the pressure of the US and the EU. The regime is hated by the people and has lost its initial supporters but has every instrument for repression (army, money, religious ideology to organize alliance around them). We can go inside Iran with active military now but it is clear that the Iranian government cannot last forever ... It would not be difficult for us to use armed forces but usually the Iranian forces don't just fight peshmerga but kill innocents and destroy villages and cities; force these people off their lands. We don't want to cause this kind of suffering for the people. Besides we are optimistic about the Iranian future because inside Iran there is a strong resistance of the people. All around Iran there is a process towards democracy. American intervention in the area in Iran and their allies – can be useful for progressing this democratic process in Iran. Also, the Iranian regime has lost its own followers and is a regime that is unable to change and make democracy. Democracy is all around and is coming through Iraq.[71]

The KDPI and Komala would very much like to see an American intervention in Iran aimed at regime change, in the hope that they can benefit from such action in a manner similar to how Kurds in Iraq benefited from international action against Saddam.[72] Awaiting the opportunity of such outside intervention or an implosion of the political system in

---

[71] Author's interview with KDP Leadership Bureau and Central Committee members Hassan Sharafi, Baba Ali, Mustafa Hijri, Hassan Rastgar, Hadi Khdija, and Ma'azoor, April 29, 2004, Iraqi Kurdistan.

[72] Komalah (the Kurdistan Organization of the Communist Party of Iran, as opposed to Komala – the Revolutionary Organization of Toilers of Kurdistan), however, opposes American intervention in Iraq and Iran. Their position stems from their socialist ideology, which sees American actions as always predicated on the interests of capitalism and opposed to workers and peasants. Komala, which split off from Komalah in 2000, places Kurdish nationalism ahead of socialism, and claims that Komalah's obsession with a tired Marxist discourse has marginalized them *vis-à-vis* the Kurdish population in Iran (author's interview with "Marxist Komalah" Central Committee members Hassan,

Iran, Kurdish nationalists continue underground organization and mobilization of cadres, and base their headquarters in neighboring Iraqi Kurdistan, whose autonomous government provides them with sanctuary. They also conduct radio broadcasts and publish underground newspapers aimed at the population of Iranian Kurdistan, in an attempt to keep Kurdish nationalist dissident perspectives alive in Iran.[73]

Ibrahim, Rahman, Rasheed, Karim, and Sirwa, April 19, 2004, Iraqi Kurdistan; and author's interview with "Nationalist Komala" Head of Politburo Abdullah Mohtadi and Central Committee member Anwar Mohammadi, April 25, 2004, Iraqi Kurdistan).

[73] The KDPI, Komala, and Komalah leadership interviewed by this author all stressed one surprising point in common concerning their strategy against the Iranian government: they claimed that Tehran has been encouraging drug use amongst minority groups in Iran, and especially amongst Kurdish youth. They stated that this policy was aimed at denying Kurdish (or other non-Persian) nationalists their recruitment base necessary for a dynamic, strong movement. The KDPI, Komala, and Komalah leaders added that a large proportion of their organizations' efforts in Iranian Kurdistan centered on countering this nefarious government tactic, by having their cadres reach Kurdish youth and convince them not to turn to drugs.

8   Conclusion

As was stated in the introduction to this study, the synthesis of opportunity structures, resource mobilization, and identity-framing is not intended to serve as a falsifiable paradigm or theory (if such a thing even exists in the social sciences). Rather, its intent is to focus analysis of social movements on the most important factors, serving as a theoretical framework of explanation. The Kurdish case has been examined here as a sort of heuristic application of these theories and their synthesis. In this sense, readers must judge for themselves the utility of the approach. Hopefully this study provides a sufficiently interesting employment of social movement theories to aid in such judgment.

The application of individual theoretical approaches to understanding social movements in Chapters 2–4 relied on the case of Kurdish ethnic nationalist movements in Turkey. Chapter 2 found that political opportunity structures (a version of structural approaches in general) were particularly useful for explaining the form that emergent challenger movements take. To a lesser extent, a greater understanding of the likely timing of movement emergence was also arrived at. In the case of resource mobilization and rational choice approaches, Chapter 3 arrived at a better understanding of how a movement that has emerged may build itself up. For movements such as the PKK that start with few or no resources, the RM-RC approach was particularly useful for illuminating the mobilization process. In the case of Kurdish movements based on an alliance of tribes and nationalists, there existed less of a theoretical puzzle for RM-RC theory to address, since the movements in question already possessed a resource base, mobilization network and source of manpower. The issue instead became a question of examining general strategies, interests, alliances with other actors, and tactical moves pursued by the movement. Regarding cultural framing and identity, Chapter 4 placed the values, goals, perceptions, and non-material interests of movements and their constituents at the front and center of the explanatory framework. Although these are the most difficult issues for social scientists to analyze, they proved crucial to understanding both the "why" and the "how" of social movement formation and development. Also, questions relating to future trends and possibilities for resolving the challenges posed by social movements heavily depend on understanding cultural framings and identity. By examining social movements from all three of the above-named theoretical perspectives, a more complete yet hopefully still cognitively manageable picture emerged. Finally, a synthesis of the perspectives helped to further fill in the picture that was drawn, allowing us to arrive at more nuanced conclusions regarding Kurdish social movements in Turkey.

By presenting a brief examination of the Kurdish situation in neighboring Iraq and Iran, additional comparisons based on our theoretical synthesis were offered. In all three of the cases examined (Turkey, Iraq, and Iran), opportunity structures emerged as crucial determinants of the form Kurdish challenges would take and, to a lesser extent, the timing of these challenges. It was perhaps the Iranian Kurdish case that emerged as the strongest example of this, with the most major Kurdish uprisings occurring when the Iranian state was weakened by occupation (1945 and 1980–1986) or internal upheavals (1978–1979). The cooperation of Iranian Kurds with the Soviets and then the Iraqis should not be too surprising, since as Qazi Mohammad explained, weak nations will grasp any helping hand offered them: "Not only will we shake it, we will also kiss it."[1]

The availability of elite allies and the closed nature of the political systems under which Kurds lived affected the form Kurdish nationalist movements took in two major ways: first, closed systems in all three states led to armed uprisings operating very much outside legal frameworks; and second, the reliance of Kurdish nationalists on traditional elites and their mobilizing networks (when these allies were available) acted as a short-term, useful resource, but a long-term Achilles' heel. Apart from encouraging a more conservative form of nationalist discourse, revolts headed by landowning tribal leaders were sure to garner opposition from traditionally hostile and competing tribes, as well as peasant tenants. This greatly hampered the formation of unified fronts. In the case of Turkey by the 1960s, the unavailability of traditional Kurdish elite allies forced the PKK to pursue RM strategies that would eventually form more of a mass, unified movement, although tribal leaders allied with the government

---

[1] Quoted in William Eagleton, *The Kurdish Republic of 1946* (London: Oxford University Press, 1963), pp. 44–45; cited by Hossein A. Shahbazi, "Domestic and International Factors Precipitating Kurdish Ethnopolitical Conflict: A Comparative Analysis of Episodes of Rebellion in Iran, Iraq and Turkey," Ph.D. dissertation, University of Maryland, (1998), p. 122.

(such as the Bucak clan in Turkey) would still oppose the movement. Meanwhile, Iraqi Kurdistan is still fractionalized along mainly tribal lines. Traditional Kurdish elites in Iraq were not successfully co-opted or eliminated by Baghdad, and given their more readily available resource mobilizing bases, they became the leaders of Kurdish nationalism in that country. In this sense, the political arms of both the KDP and PUK became subservient to tribal and traditional elites, which caused an impoverishment of Kurdish nationalist appeal *vis-à-vis* the broader Kurdish masses. If we compare this development to the anti-colonialist struggle in places such as Vietnam, however, it becomes evident that traditional elites can be included in the nationalist movement without necessarily sacrificing the movement to their interests.[2]

In Iran, a process of modernization similar to that in Turkey, yet less advanced, seems to have led Komala (and to a much lesser extent the KDPI) to base its movement on non-tribal elements of the population. In doing so, the organization will be able to remain true to its leftist Kurdish nationalist framings, unlike the Iraqi KDP – which compromised the interests of Kurdish workers and peasants when it integrated Barzani's tribal forces into its leadership. Nonetheless, the passing away of tribal social structures and loyalties has been under way since the 1950s in all three countries (although less so in Iraq):

As "pan-Kurdish" nationalism begins to grow, so one also senses the recession of the tribal loyalties which still dominated much of the Kurdish scene as late as the 1960s. Tribalism has not yet disappeared, as Baghdad's ability to call on Kurdish tribal auxiliaries indicates. But it does currently seem to be in retreat since its social function is so greatly diminished. Ironically the forced relocation of Kurdish villages may well accelerate that process and advance a more proletarian form of nationalism which will prove harder for government to contain.[3]

Of course, "pan-Kurdish" nationalism and Kurdish nationalism are essentially the same thing, as long as Kurds in one country see those in

---

[2] The Vietnamese communists managed to place themselves as the only movement representing the nationalist struggle, and they succeeded to a remarkable degree in including the non-revolutionary classes into their broad front *in a manner subservient to the communist party*. For more on this, see Samual L. Popkin, *The Rational Peasant* (Berkeley: University of California Press, 1979).

[3] In the case of framings that wed Kurdish nationalism to Islam, the strategy was also divisive in the uprisings of the 1920s and 1930s. Sunni sheikhs alienated Shiites and Alevis. In any case, the importance of Islam as a political force in Kurdish society is no longer very significant (Martin van Bruinessen, "Kurdish Society, Ethnicity, Nationality and Refugee Problems," in Philip G. Kreyenbroek and Stefan Sperl [eds.], *The Kurds: A Contemporary Overview* [London and New York: Routledge, 1992], p. 54), and an Islamic identity does not necessarily negate a politicized Kurdish one. David McDowall, "The Kurdish question: A historical review," in Kreyenbroek and Sperl (eds.), *A Contemporary Overview*, pp. 30–31.

a neighboring state as Kurds. Kurds with a politicized ethnicity would generally prefer to unify with the Kurds of neighboring states. If Kurds deserve self-determination because of their status as a nation, then all the members of the nation should ideally be under the same political entity. As a part of the Kurdish cultural tool kit, Kurdish nationalist poetry was pan-Kurdish from the beginning (witness Ehmed-e Xani's poetry cited in Chapter 1). In more recent years, many physical signs of pan-Kurdish solidarity have also emerged. The Iraqi PUK and Iranian KDPI have often assisted each other, and roughly 5,000 Kurdish volunteers from Turkey went to Iran to help the KDPI fight Khomeini's government forces in 1979. In 1988 and 1991, Iraqi Kurdish refugees received a great deal of assistance from Turkish and Iranian Kurds. Finally, the PKK had many militants in its ranks who were from Iraqi, Iranian, and Syrian Kurdistan.[4] Other signs of pan-Kurdish solidarity, which transcend the calculations of various party leaders, include the growth of civil society, publishing, and media in Iraqi Kurdistan and the diaspora, as well as increased traffic between all parts of Kurdistan since the creation of the Autonomous Zone in 1991.[5]

Ankara, Tehran, Damascus, and non-Kurdish Iraqis are of course increasingly weary of growing pan-Kurdish sentiment, which accounts for their hostility to any Kurdish state in the region. While many Kurds would like to see pan-Kurdish sentiment produce a situation wherein their leaders refuse to be made the pawns of these powers and played off against each other (Barzani's actions against the KDPI, for instance), all the states of the region are determined to keep the Kurds divided. Few options for mobilizing outside assistance existed as long as all the Kurdish regions were circumscribed by the Turkish, Iraqi, Iranian, and Syrian states. Until 2003, Iraqi Kurds, if they were to have access to the outside world, had no choice but to pass through either Saddam's Iraq, Turkey, Syria, or Iran. As a result, when Turkey or Iran demanded that they act against the PKK or the KDPI, they were hard pressed not to refuse. Although recent events in Iraq may lead to substantive changes, for the moment the lack of practical opportunities to pursue pan-Kurdish solidarity continues to harm Kurdish nationalism, as Kurdish parties are continually pushed against each other. Even more depressingly for Kurdish nationalists, when a movement in one state (such as Iraq)

---

[4] If a Kurdish nationalist organization in one country (in this case the PKK in Turkey) is able to attract members and support from Kurdish populations in neighboring countries, the implications for pan-Kurdish nationalism are clear.

[5] The increased contact between Iraqi and Iranian Kurds helps to counteract their division between two different states (and before the First World War, two different empires), as they interact and regain familiarity with each other's views, customs, and concerns.

somehow manages to approach success, one can expect vigorous action from neighboring states to prevent Kurdish secession. Since the 1920s, the only thing that Iraq, Iran, Syria, and Turkey all agreed on was the undesirability of a Kurdish state in the region. The foreign ministers of these countries meet regularly to discuss the Kurdish issue, and have committed themselves to preventing Kurdish secessionism in various treaties such as the Sa'dabad Pact and the Baghdad Pact.[6] Hence pragmatism and "realist" appraisals of their political opportunities push most Kurdish leaders to opt for autonomy only within the state in which they reside. It is in fact striking that the five most important Kurdish parties today – the PKK, KDPI, Komala, KDP, and PUK – all advocate autonomy within state borders, and not secession. Of course, their opponents generally view this as a mere ploy, an interim step on their true eventual goal of secession and the formation of a Kurdish state in all of Kurdistan. Hence the vigorous efforts of states such as Turkey to stymie even the more limited goal of Kurdish autonomy, within their own borders as well as that of their neighbors.

Such a view may in fact be correct, but it should not serve as an excuse for the continued refusal to grant the Kurds cultural, linguistic, and group rights, including some degree of self-government. At the same time, Kurdish nationalists must be sensitive to the rights of minorities living within their own midst, such as Turkmen, Assyrians, Azeris, Arabs, Chaldeans, and others. The Kurdish nationalist cause might also be better served by a less patriarchal approach towards Kurdish women. In 1994, when the KDP and PUK broke into armed conflict in autonomous Iraqi Kurdistan, "One group of 200 women trekked for four days and five nights to the Iraqi Kurdish parliament in Arbil, occupied by Talabani's guerrillas early in the fighting. They sang songs asking for a return to sanity. 'We don't want brother to fight against brother. It is very sad. It is killing all of us,' said Nazira Sayfullah. 'Men are making the fire, we are trying to extinguish it . . .' "[7] Kurdish women may have the ability to inject a necessary spirit of peaceful accommodation and cooperation amongst Kurdish nationalists and elites, if they are better integrated into the structures of political power in Kurdish society. In the theoretical language of this study, women can contribute to more innovative resource mobilization strategies as well as grievance framings that place more

---

[6] For more on this issue, see Michael Gunter, "Transnational Sources of Support for the Kurdish Insurgency in Turkey," *Conflict Quarterly* 11: 2 (Spring 1991), 7–29.

[7] Mirella Galletti, "Western Images of the Woman's Role in Kurdish Society," in Shahrzad Mojab (ed.), *Women of a Non-State Nation: The Kurds* (Costa Mesa: Mazda Publishers, 2001), p. 219.

emphasis on cooperation between Kurdish groups. Although some may view such an assertion as a romantic vision coming out of the "woman as mother and nurturer" brand of feminist discourse, observations during time spent in the Kurdish regions lead this author to firmly believe that Kurdish women may add more creative problem-solving approaches to their male counterparts' political process. Some Kurdish movements (particularly the PKK and Komala) have recognized the empowerment of women in Kurdish society as a worthy goal, and Abdullah Ocalan has "repeatedly compared the oppression of women in Kurdish society to the national oppression of the Kurds and called for a double liberation."[8] Also, linkage between Kurdish women and women's movements in the rest of Turkish, Iraqi, and Iranian society may contribute to more accommodating policies regarding the Kurdish issue in these countries.[9]

From the perspective of all three of the theoretical approaches examined here, it also seems clear that a variety of contexts and state strategies have failed to prevent significant Kurdish unrest and challenges. Simon Mayall's observation regarding Turkey's Kurdish problem can be just as true for Iran and Iraq: "The Kurdish issue, initially viewed by the army as a straightforward domestic security matter, became the focus of all Turkey's internal and external concerns. It challenged the roots of Turkish identity and security, the role of the state in society, the nature of its democracy, the economic health and development of Turkey, its relations with the West from a human rights angle, and the rest of the region from a security perspective."[10]

Non-Kurdish citizens of Turkey, Iraq, and Iran have also suffered from the conflict with the Kurds. Apart from the common problems of war,

---

[8] Susan McDonald argues from an international law perspective that groups seeking self-determination or secession justify their struggle in part as a reaction and remedy to their subjugation and oppression by others. Therefore, "A group seeking secession must be willing and able to protect the individual rights of its members after receiving independence. A claim could fail for the reason that the new state would deny its members their fundamental human rights ... The realization of self-determination should not result in the replacement of one oppressive regime for another" (cited in Shahrzad Mojab, "Women and Nationalism in the Kurdish Republic of 1946" in Mojab [ed.], *Women of a Non-State Nation*, p. 143). Essentially, a struggle against national oppression should not omit the struggle against gender oppression (Martin van Bruinessen, "From Adela Khanum to Layla Zena: Women as Political Leaders", in Mojab [ed.], *Women of a Non-State Nation*, p. 105).

[9] Unfortunately, the women's movement in Turkey appears even more subservient to a Turkish nationalist discourse that rejects Kurdish claims than the Turkish Left was. For more on the issue, as well as the subjugated position of Kurdish women in general, see Mojab (ed.), *Women of a Non-State Nation*.

[10] Simon V. Mayall, "Turkey: Thwarted Ambition," McNair Paper 56, Institute for National Strategic Studies, National Defense University, Washington, DC, January 1997, p. 84.

these people have been denied the increased economic and democratic development that would have occurred in the absence of the conflict. The following 1999 observation regarding Turkey further elaborates Mayall's argument:

Considered a strategic NATO ally, Turkey has benefitted from a U.S. policy that is long on military assistance and short on constructive criticism. U.S. arms sales actually undermine many U.S. foreign policy goals by providing physical and political support to the Turkish military at the expense of democratically elected leaders and civil society. The Turkish military's 15-year war against the rebel Kurdistan Workers' Party (PKK) ... has served as an excuse to repress political leaders, journalists, and human rights activists ... Turkey spends about $7 billion a year on the war with the PKK, which contributed to a 99% inflation rate for 1998 and a national debt equal to half the government's revenue. War-related political and financial instability has discouraged foreign investment ... An end to the war and improvements in human rights are also necessary preconditions for Turkey's entry into the European Union (EU), which the U.S. believes would draw Turkey closer to the West ... The conflict has also created entrenched governmental corruption, touching all central political actors in Ankara.[11]

Turkish citizens concerned with democratizing their country should be particularly leery of the United States' post-September 11 foreign policy stance. As the US focuses more on its "war against terrorism," we might witness an American *carte blanche* for Turkish military policies and anti-democratic measures that repress Kurdish groups and Islamists. Uncritical American support will postpone reforms in Ankara, as the sustainability of current policies is maintained.[12] In this sense, the demands of Kurdish and other minority groups for national and religious rights are actually a possible source of democratization for Turkey, Iran, and Iraq, since freedoms granted to one group presumably extend to

---

[11] Tamar Gabelnick, "Turkey: Arms and Human Rights," *Foreign Policy in Focus* 4: 16 (May 1999), http://www.foreignpolicy-infocus.org/briefs/vol4/v4n16turk.html.

[12] Gabelnick's pre-September 11 hopes regarding US foreign policy now seem less likely to be fulfilled than ever:

The December 1997 State Department agreement to link an export license to human rights improvements would signal – if implemented – respect for international human rights law. It would also bring U.S. policy in line with Section 502B of the Foreign Assistance Act, which states that weapons may not be provided to any country "the government of which engages in a consistent pattern of gross violations of internationally recognized human rights." The State Department's annual human rights reports have documented Turkey's flagrant human rights abuses year after year in a pattern that is clearly gross and consistent. Arms exports to Turkey also contravene President Clinton's Presidential Decision Directive (PDD) 34, issued in February 1995, which directs the State Department to factor into arms export decisions the impact of an export on regional stability and on human rights and democracy in the recipient state. (Gabelnick, "Turkey: Arms and Human Rights")

every member of society. Likewise, Turkey's efforts to join the European Union and the reforms demanded of it by the EU offer the possibility of great changes. Many historic and significant reforms have begun emerging from Ankara as a result of EU pressure, and if these reforms lead to genuine, substantive, and enduring changes in practice towards Kurds in Turkey, the conditions for violent ethno-national dissent in the country may well fade away.

In the absence of basic democratic reforms to address the non-material grievances of an increasingly politicized Kurdish ethnicity, however, Turkey and Iran can expect an indefinite continuation of Kurdish challenges to their rule. By the same logic, a new Iraq that fails to accommodate Kurdish aspirations for significant measures of autonomy will necessarily be undemocratic. A return to the authoritarian kind of central rule that Iraq experienced for so long under the Ba'th party would make a travesty of what all Iraqis suffered during the last thirty-five years. On a general level, reliance on repressive measures to solve "the Kurdish issue" by all states in the region has only increased Kurdish nationalism in the long term. If we rule out genocide (and one can only hope that it will be ruled out), repression cannot serve as a long-, or even medium-term, solution. In his analysis of the denial of basic individual and group needs, Burton concludes that, "Where there are important values at issue, as distinct from negotiable interests, the use of coercion or pressure in any form, to force an opponent party to compromise is likely to be dysfunctional in that it will tend to promote protracted conflict, even after a settlement."[13]

It remains questionable, however, whether Kurdish actors and the states involved with the Kurdish issue can even pursue viable long-term, or even medium-term, strategies. These actors must function within an exceedingly complex milieu, including states and the different power-blocks within them, various non-state actors, and external actors as well. In such a complicated and dynamic environment, most decision-makers fall back to a very short-term strategic logic, dealing with the most pressing immediate issues first and avoiding, whenever and for as long as possible, difficult choices that could impact the more long-term dynamic between the states in the region and the Kurds.

This study should make clear that human ingenuity can find ways to mobilize challenges in even less than auspicious circumstances, however.

---

[13] J. W. Burton, "The Means to Agreement: Power or Values?" (Washington DC: mimeo, March 1985), p. 23, cites A. J. R Groom, "Paradigms in Conflict: The Strategist, the Conflict Researcher, and the Peace Researcher," *Review of International Studies* 14 (1988), 71–98.

In the early 1980s, the PKK effectively mobilized dissent even in the absence of very favorable opportunity structures. As the history of the KDPI, Komala, KDP, and PUK also shows, Kurdish nationalists can be extremely tenacious, continuously renewing armed struggle, defeat after defeat. Each defeat (as well as brief victories) in turn contributed to an increasingly politicized Kurdish ethnicity. At every emergence of what they perceived as a political opportunity, in most cases a moment of weakness in the capital, Kurdish movements rose up to challenge the state. Elites in Ankara, Baghdad, and Tehran would therefore be well advised to reformulate their relationships with the Kurds, for their own well-being as well as that of others. Turkey in particular should be anxious to arrive at a longer-term solution to Kurdish disaffection, since Kurdish population growth is occurring at a much faster rate than that of ethnic Turks in the country.[14] Increasing globalization and larger Kurdish diaspora communities also lessen the ability of states in the region to quietly repress the Kurds, whose increasing levels of politicization in turn mitigate against states' ability to ignore them.

As became evident in Chapter 4, a solution to the issue must address Kurdish non-material as well as material needs. The former is probably even more important than the latter. If we accept that recognition of one's identity is a basic need, and that large numbers of Kurds have rejected the identities framed for them by the states in which they live, then Kurdish identity must be accepted and valued by the states in question. While interests are negotiable, basic needs and values are not: "Protracted social conflicts universally are situations which arise out of attempts to combat conditions of perceived victimization stemming from: (1) a denial of separate identity of parties involved in the political process; (2) an absence of security of culture and valued relationships; and (3) an absence of effective political participation through which victimization can be remedied."[15] If we follow Azar and Burton's arguments regarding protracted social conflicts to the next logical step, significant measures of self-government for the Kurds must be the solution:

Societies which have undergone decades of violence and hate retain very little trust for any sort of government – local or central and distant. They become cynical. They transform even benign systems into deformed political and economic entities and they show very little inclination to participatory politics.

---

[14] For an analysis of data on relative family sizes and other demographic indicators of Turks and Kurds in Turkey, see Ahmed Icduygu, David Romano, and Ibrahim Sirkeci, "The Ethnic Question in an Environment of Insecurity: The Kurds in Turkey," *Ethnic and Racial Studies* 22: 6 (November, 1999), 991–1010.

[15] E. Azar and J. Burton (eds.), *International Conflict Resolution: Theory and Practice* (Boulder: Lynne Rienner Publishers, Inc., 1986), p. 147.

Decentralized political structures promise to provide the sort of environment which permits groups to satisfy better their identity and political needs. They promote local participation and self-reliance. They give the groups involved the sense of control over their affairs.[16]

Such an argument convincingly explains why Iraqi Kurdistan today stands out as the most stable, secure part of Iraq – still governed by the Kurdish parties that took control of the area in 1991. American troops are currently able to walk the streets of Erbil, Suleimaniya, Dohuk, and Zakho without their Kevlar armor and heavy caliber machine guns, while troops and Iraqi civilians in the rest of Iraq live under continual fear of attacks and banditry.

The implications of a solution based on Kurdish self-determination thus does not necessarily include secession of the Kurdish regions. In a more democratic milieu, where one can express one's identity freely, exert more control over one's own life, enjoy basic rights of freedom and cultural practice, and have a greater say in government, people may forego secessionist programs. The Basque and Welsh examples are a case in point. Once truly significant powers of self-government were given to these regions, the majority of the population was satisfied and expressed a willingness to remain within the larger state framework. In the case of the Basques, however, a small and more radical hold-out group continued to demand separation from Spain. Significantly, the majority of Basques today reject and ostracize the separatists, whose campaign has now been reduced to occasional bombings and assassinations. To Madrid's benefit, the Basque population itself is now working to eliminate the remaining radical fringe.[17]

Of course, given the history of repression, the promises of the Treaty of Sèvres and other factors, a scenario similar to that of the Basques and Welsh might not emerge if the Kurds are granted autonomy. The majority of the Kurdish population might still desire outright secession from the states in which they are presently located. If Kurds in these states are given real measures of autonomy, however, they are very likely to settle for less than statehood. Both Kurdish political parties as well as the population in general are not willing to pay any price for their own state, but they are willing to risk a great deal for their minimum basic needs of recognition and freedom.

---

[16] Ibid., p. 151.

[17] A contrary example to the Basque and Welsh cases appears to be that of Quebec, however. Nonetheless, after a high point in Quebec separatist sentiment in 1995, the Québécois population's appetite for separation from Canada appears to be receding.

The international system: frozen state boundaries?

Those Kurdish nationalists who are nonetheless determined to achieve Kurdish statehood obviously face a daunting task. Although recent events in Iraqi Kurdistan are the most promising developments yet for Kurdish statehood, Kurdish nationalism still suffers from its late development in the world arena. After World War One, the changes in state boundaries were apparently a one-time rearrangement from the point of view of the international community, which thereafter became loath to contemplate any changes in territorial borders. According to Robert Jackson, self-determination as an international norm has now lost the meaning Woodrow Wilson implied in his Fourteen Points, and today applies to states rather than nations or peoples:

The new doctrine explicitly denies self-determination to ethnonationalities since if it were granted most existing ex-colonial states would be broken up just as the Austro-Hungarian empire was broken up by granting self-determination to the nationalities of Central Europe ... Consequently, ethnonational self-determination is now illegitimate and the prospects of independence for the numerous ethno-nationalities of the Third World are bleak. And since most of the new states also do not provide minority rights and internal autonomies to compensate ethno-nationalities and indeed often deliberately withhold them, they tend to provoke civil discord along ethnic lines as did the old multinational empires of Europe.[18]

In this sense, the international aid component of opportunity struc-tures has remained largely unfavorable for the Kurds. The migration of large numbers of Kurds to other parts of Turkey, Iraq, Iran, and the rest of the world also presents some problems for the territorialization of Kurdish claims for autonomy. However, recent trends witnessed in places such as Yugoslavia, Eritrea, and East Timor are encouraging signs for Kurdish nationalists – the sanctity of state borders is no longer as solid as during the Cold War. In any case, from an ethical and moral perspective, the possibility of Kurdish statehood should be a function of the preferences of the populations in question and the degree to which the governments currently ruling them have exercised their authority in a responsible fashion.[19] The sanctity of state sovereignty and "geo-strategic interests" (of existing states, of course) should not be

---

[18] Robert Jackson, *Quasi-states: Sovereignty, International Relations, and the Third World* (Cambridge: Cambridge University Press, 1990), p. 78.
[19] I should note that my own identity as a Canadian and a Québécois no doubt influences this point of view. Quebec, with the acquiescence of the Canadian federal government, has held two referendums (in 1980 and 1995) to determine if it should remain a part of Canada.

perpetually respected over all other possible considerations. According to K. J. Holsti,

Today, some observers believe while the state remains the basis of international action, the state's legitimacy comes not from the nature of the international system but from its people. If a ruler mistreats his population, other states have the right – perhaps even the duty – to intervene to correct inhumane treatment. Sovereignty cannot mean that states are free to indiscriminately slaughter ethnic, religious, or racial minorities within their borders. Quite the contrary: the view that clearly was the basis for UN action in Iraq is that sovereignty includes a dimension of responsibility. If a state does not live up to its responsibility, international intervention is permissible.[20]

Nonetheless, a Kurdish project for statehood at this time seems both plagued with incredible obstacles as well as ill-advised. Turkey, Syria, and Iran could all be expected to continue collaborating in order to prevent such a development, and the chances of other states coming to the aid of repressed Kurds in Turkey, Iraq, or Iran appear extremely small.[21] In an international system where states remain the most powerful actors, the Kurds' only enduring allies remain civil society groups and non-governmental organizations. As long as even very astute Kurdish nationalist movements mount challenges that are perceived as coming from a group outside the general populations of Turkey, Iran, or Iraq, they can also expect to be countered with unflinching state repression.[22] Hence Kurdish leaders and their people need to carefully consider the possibilities for extremely destructive conflicts that could accompany a sustained push for a Kurdish state. Perhaps this is what Abdullah Ocalan had in mind when he stated that "There's no question of separating from Turkey. My people need Turkey: we can't split for at least 40 years ... unity will bring strength."[23] Ocalan probably meant that only after

---

[20] K. J. Holsti, *International Politics* (Englewood Cliffs, NJ: Prentice-Hall, 1992), pp. 45–46.

[21] The reader will recall from ch. 5 that even during Iraq's genocide of 1988, the international system made no move to threaten Iraq's sovereignty. Only after Saddam Hussein's poorly considered invasion of Kuwait (another sovereign member of the international system) was Iraq branded a pariah of the system, setting the stage for international intervention on the Kurds' behalf (and in defence of Turkey, lest it be overrun by Kurdish refugees). In 2004, Canadian Prime Minister Paul Martin presented a plan to avoid such international paralysis in the face of gross human rights abuses or genocide, entitled *The Responsibility to Protect*. At the time of this writing, the response of other state leaders appears lukewarm.

[22] One of the arguments presented in ch. 5 pointed out how states find it more difficult to repress a challenge that seems to come from the population in general, rather than an ethnically differentiated "out-group."

[23] *Hurriyet*, April 1, 1993, quoted in Paul White, *Primitive Rebels or Revolutionary Modernizers? The Kurdish National Movement in Turkey* (London: Zed Books, 2000), p. 163.

conditions in Turkey begin to resemble those of states such as Canada, Belgium, or Czechoslovakia could Kurdish separation be considered a viable option. In countries such as these, many people have opposing views on the possible division of the state, but more importantly, they do not accept the need to take up arms to accomplish or prevent such an eventuality.

Kurdish nationalists might also want to consider being careful of what they wish for. The realization of a greater Kurdistan would unite disparate Kurdish groups that have spent the last eighty-some years living in very different Turkish, Iraqi, Iranian, and Syrian state contexts. The cultural frames and mobilizing strategies of Kurdish groups in these four states include very significant differences, and the potential for civil strife in a future Kurdistan seems high. One need only recall how the PKK destroyed rival Kurdish groups in Turkish Kurdistan, the KDP and PUK fought each other in Iraqi Kurdistan, and the KDPI and Komala came to blows in Iranian Kurdistan. While no nation should have its legitimate rights and aspirations dismissed and cast aside, Kurdish nationalists should remain cautious about the desirability and feasability of pursuing maximalist demands for statehood. They will no doubt attempt to further develop Kurdish nationalism to the point that such intra-group conflict becomes less likely. At the same time, neighboring states and other opponents of the Kurdish nationalist project will continue to try and foment divisions amongst the Kurds, divisions that have been their historic Achilles' heel.

Bibliography

"A Brief History of the Kurdistan Workers Party," undated ERNK document, courtesy of Toronto Kurdish Information Centre.

Ahmad, Feroz, *The Making of Modern Turkey*, London: Routledge, 1993.

Ala'adeen, Dlawer (ed.), *Death Clouds: Saddam Hussein's Chemical Attack Against the Kurds*, London: Kurdish Scientific and Medical Association, 1991.

Alkan, Turker, "Yatak Odasi Savaslari," *Radikal*, September 27, 2000, http://www.radikal.com.tr/2000/09/27/yazarlar/turalk.shtml.

Allison, Christine and Philip G. Kreyenbroek (eds.), *Kurdish Culture and Identity*, London: Zed Books, Ltd., 1996.

Alpay, Sahin, "After Ocalan," *View* (Spring, 2000).

Amit-Talai, Vered and Caroline Knowles (eds.), *Re-Situating Identities*, Peterborough: Broadview Press, 1996.

Amnesty International, *Turkey: Walls of Glass*, November 1992 (AI Index: EUR 44/75/92).

Amuzegar, Jahangir, "Iran's Theocracy Under Siege," *Middle East Policy* 10: 1 (Spring, 2003), 135–153.

Anderson, Benedict, *Imagined Communities*, London: Verso, 1983.

Anonymous, "Desert Shame," *The New Republic* 204: 17 (April 29, 1991), 7–9.

Asprey, Robert B., *War in the Shadows: The Guerrilla in History*, New York: William Morrow and Company, Inc., 1994.

Azar, E. and J. Burton (eds.), *International Conflict Resolution: Theory and Practice*, Boulder: Lynne Rienner Publishers, Inc., 1986.

Barkey, Henri J. and Graham Fuller, *Turkey's Kurdish Question*, New York: Rowman & Littlefield Publishers, Inc., 1998.

Barth, Fredrik, *Ethnic Groups and Boundaries: The Social Organization of Cultural Difference*, Boston: Little, Brown, 1969.

Besikci, Ismail, *Kurdistan and Turkish Colonialism*, London: Kurdistan Solidarity Committee and Kurdistan Information Centre, 1991.

Billig, Michael. *Social Psychology and Intergroup Relations*, London: Academic Press, 1976.

Billig, Michael and Henri Tajfel, "Social Categorization and Similarity in Intergroup Behavior," *European Journal of Social Psychology* 3 (1973), 27–52.

Boulanger, Philippe, *Le Destin des Kurdes*, Paris: L'Harmattan, 1998.

Brass, Paul, *Ethnicity and Nationalism*, London: Sage Publications, 1991.

Brinton, Crane, *The Anatomy of Revolution*, New York: Vintage, 1965.

Brown, David, "Ethnic Revival: Perspectives on State and Society," *Third World Quarterly* 11: 4 (1989), 1–16.

Bruinessen, Martin van, *Agha, Shaikh and State*, London: Zed Books Ltd., 1992.
  "Kurds, Turks and the Alevi Revival in Turkey," *Middle East Report* (July–September, 1996), 7–10.

Bulloch, John and Harvey Morris, *No Friends But the Mountains*, London: Penguin Books Ltd., 1992.

Burton, J. W., *Deviance, Terrorism and War*, New York: St. Martin's Press, 1979.
  "The Means to Agreement: Power or Values?" *Perspectives on Negotiation; Four Case Studies and Interpretation*, Washington: Center for the Study of Foreign Affairs (1986), 229–241.

Byman, Daniel, "The Logic of Ethnic Terrorism," *Conflict and Terrorism* 21: 2 (April–June, 1998), 49–69.

Calhoun, Craig, "The Problem of Identity in Collective Action," in J. Huber (ed.), *Macro–Micro Linkages in Sociology*, Newbury Park: Sage Publications Inc., 1991, 51–75.

Carment, David and Patrick James, "Escalation of Ethnic Conflict," *International Politics* 35: 1 (March, 1998), 65–82.

Center for Kurdish Political Studies, Public Relations Office, "Abdullah Ocalan Proposes 7-Point Peace Plan," November 26–27, 1998.

Central Committee of the Kurdistan Workers Party (PKK), "5th Congress of the PKK is the Guarantee of Success and Victory!" February 1995, courtesy of Toronto Kurdish Information Center.

Chaliand, Gerard (ed.), *Les Kurdes et le Kurdistan*, Paris: François Maspero, 1978.
  People Without a Country: The Kurds and Kurdistan, London: Zed Press, 1980.
  Guerrilla Strategies, Berkeley: University of California Press, 1982.
  People Without a Country: The Kurds and Kurdistan, New York: Interlink Publishing, 1993.

Christie, Kenneth, *Ethnic Conflict, Tribal Politics*, Surrey: Curzon Press, 1998.

Cigerli, Sabri, *Les Kurdes et leur histoire*, Paris and Montreal: L'Harmattan, 1999.

Ciment, James, *The Kurds: State and Minority in Turkey, Iraq and Iran (Conflict and Crisis in the Post-Cold War World)*, New York: Facts on File Inc., 1996.

Cohen, Jean L., "Strategy or Identity: New Theoretical Paradigms and Contemporary Social Movements," *Social Research* 52: 4 (1985), 663–716.

Cohn, Edwin J., *Turkish Economic, Social, and Political Change*, New York: Praeger Publishers, 1970.

Cottrell, Ann B., Robert St. Cry, Phillip Rawkins, and Jeffrey A. Ross, *Mobilization of Collective Identity*, Lanham, MD: Rowman & Littlefield, 1980.

Criss, Nur Bilge, "The Nature of PKK Terrorism in Turkey," *Studies in Conflict and Terrorism* 18: 1 (1995), 17–37.

Criss, Nur Bilge, and Yavuz Turan Cetiner, "Terrorism and the Issue of International Cooperation," *The Journal of Conflict Studies* 2 (Spring, 2000), 127–139.

Davies, James C., "Toward a Theory of Revolution," *American Sociological Review* 6: 1 (1962), 5–19.

Debray, Régis, *Revolution in the Revolution?* New York: Grove Press, 1967.

DeNardo, James, *Power in Numbers*, Princeton: Princeton University Press, 1985.

Deutsch, Karl, *Nationalism and Social Communication*, Cambridge: MIT Press, 1953.

Dodd, C. H., *The Crisis of Turkish Democracy*, Huntingdon: Eothen Press, 1990.

Eagleton, William, *The Kurdish Republic of 1946*, London: Oxford University Press, 1963.

Economist, The, "Democracy at Gunpoint: Turkey Survey," Parliamentary Human Rights Group, June 8–14, 1996.

Elahi, Maryam, "Clinton, Ankara and Kurdish Human Rights," *Middle East Report* 189 (July–August, 1994), 22–23.

Enloe, Cynthia, *Ethnic Conflict and Political Development*, Boston: Little, Brown and Company, 1973.

Entessar, Nader, "The Kurdish Mosaic of Discord," *Third World Quarterly* 11: 4 (1989), 83–100.

"Kurdish Identity in the Middle East," *Current World Leaders* 34: 2 (April, 1992), 270–282.

Kurdish Ethnonationalism, London: Lynne Rienner Publishers, Inc., 1992.

Ergil, Dogu, *Dogu Sorunu: Teshisler ve Tespitler*, Ozel Arastirma Raporu, Ankara, 1995.

"Suicide Terrorism in Turkey," *Civil Wars* 3: 1 (Spring, 2000), 37–54.

Esman, Milton J., *Ethnic Politics*, Ithaca: Cornell University Press, 1994.

Fall, Bernard B. (ed.), *Ho Chi Minh on Revolution*, Toronto: Signet Books, 1967.

Fanon, Francis, *The Wretched of the Earth*, New York: Grove Press, 1963.

Findley, Paul, "The US Stake in Good Relations With Baghdad," *Washington Review on Middle East Affairs* (December 1988), 15.

Finkel Andrew and Nukhet Sirman (eds.), *Turkish State, Turkish Society*, London: Routledge, 1990.

Fuller, Graham, "The Fate of the Kurds," *Foreign Affairs* 72: 2 (Spring, 1993), 101–121.

Gabelnick, Tamar, "Turkey: Arms and Human Rights," *Foreign Policy in Focus* 4: 16 (May, 1999), http://www.foreignpolicy-infocus.org/briefs/vol4/v4n16turk.html.

Geertz, Clifford, *The Interpretation of Cultures*, New York: Basic Books, 1973.

Gellner, Ernest, *Nations and Nationalism*, Oxford: Blackwell, 1983.

Nationalism, London: Weidenfeld & Nicolson, 1997.

Gershoni, Isreal and James Jankowski, (eds.), *Rethinking Nationalism in the Arab Middle East*, New York: Columbia University Press, 1997.

Gokalp, Ziya, *The Principles of Turkism*, Ankara: Leiden, 1920.

Goldstone, Jack, *Revolutions: Theoretical, Comparative, and Historical Studies*, San Diego: Harcourt Brace Jovanovich, 1986.

Revolution and Rebellion in the Early Modern World, Berkeley: University of California Press, 1991.

Greene, Thomas, *Comparative Revolutionary Movements*, Englewood Cliffs, NJ: Prentice-Hall, 1974.

Griffith, Samuel B. (ed.), *Mao Tse-Tung on Guerrilla Warfare*, Washington DC: Praeger Publishers, 1961.

Groom, A. J. R., "Paradigms in Conflict: The Strategist, the Conflict Researcher, and the Peace Researcher," *Review of International Studies* 14 (1988), 71–98.

Gunter, Michael, "The Kurdish Problem in Turkey," *The Middle East Journal* 42: 3 (1988), 389–406.

"Transnational Sources of Support for the Kurdish Insurgency in Turkey," *Conflict Quarterly* 11: 2 (Spring 1991), 7–29.

"A *de Facto* Kurdish State in Northern Iraq," *Third World Quarterly* 14: 2 (December 1993), 7–24.

"Mulla Mustafa Barzani and the Kurdish Rebellion in Iraq: The Intelligence Factor," *International Journal of Intelligence and Counterintelligence* 7: 4 (Winter, 1994), 465–474.

The Changing Kurdish Problem in Turkey, London: Research Institute for the Study of Conflict and Terrorism, 1994.

"The Iraqi National Congress (INC) and the Future of the Iraqi Opposition," *Journal of South Asian and Middle Eastern Studies* 19 (Spring, 1996), 1–20.

The Kurds and the Future of Turkey, New York: St. Martin's Press, 1997.

"The Foreign Policy of the Iraqi Kurds," *Journal of South Asian and Middle Eastern Studies* 20 (Spring, 1997), 1–19.

"The Iraqi Opposition and the Failure of US Intelligence," *International Journal of Intelligence and Counterintelligence* 12: 2 (Summer, 1999), 135–167.

The Kurdish Predicament in Iraq, New York: St Martin's Press, 1999.

Gurr, Ted Robert, *Why Men Rebel*, Princeton: Princeton University Press, 1969.

Gurr, Ted Robert and Barbara Harff, *Ethnic Conflict in World Politics*, Boulder: Westview Press, 1994.

Hakim, Halkawt (ed.), *Les Kurdes par delà l'exode*, Paris: L'Harmattan, 1992.

Hassanpour, Amir, "The Pen and the Sword: Literacy, Education and Revolution in Kurdistan," in Peter Freebody and Anthony R. Welch (eds.), *Knowledge, Culture and Power: International Perspectives on Literacy as Policy and Practice*, London: Falmer Press, 1993.

"MED-TV, Britain, and the Turkish State: A Stateless Nation's Quest for Sovereignty in the Sky," paper presented at the Freie Universität Berlin, November 7, 1995.

"Satellite Footprints as National Borders: MED-TV and the Extraterritoriality of State Sovereignty," *Journal of Muslim Minority Affairs* 18: 1 (April, 1998), 53–72.

"Language Rights in the Emerging World Linguistic Order: The State, the Market and Communication Technologies," in Miklos Kontra (ed.), *Language: A Right and a Resource*, Budapest: CEU Press, 1998.

"The Identity of Hewrami Speakers: Reflections on the Theory and Ideology of Comparative Philology," Research paper prepared at the Department of Near and Middle Eastern Civilizations, University of Toronto (undated).

Hazelton, Fran, *Iraq Since the Gulf War*, London: Zed Books Ltd., 1994.

Hechter, Michael, *Internal Colonialism*, London: Routledge & Kegan Paul, 1975.

Principles of Group Solidarity, Berkeley: University of California Press, 1987.

Heper, Metin (ed.), *Strong State and Economic Interest Groups*, Berlin: Walter de Gruyter, 1991.

Hitchens, Christopher, "Struggle of the Kurds," *National Geographic* 182: 2 (August 1992), 32–63.

Holsti, K. J., *International Politics*, Englewood Cliffs, NJ: Prentice-Hall, 1992.

Homer-Dixon, Thomas F., "They and We: An Empirical and Philosophical Study of a Theory of Social Conflict," Ph.D. Dissertation, Massachusetts Institute of Technology, 1989.

Horowitz, Donald, *Ethnic Groups in Conflict*, Berkeley: University of California Press, 1985.

Howell, David, *Roots of Rural Ethnic Mobilization*, New York: New York University Press, 1993.

Hughey, Michael W. (ed.), *New Tribalisms: The Resurgence of Race and Ethnicity*, London: Macmillan Press Ltd., 1998.

Human Rights Watch, Helsinki, various reports 1985–2000.

Hutchinson, John, "Ethnicity and Modern Nations," *Ethnic and Racial Studies* 23: 4 (July, 2000), 651–669.

Hutchinson, John and Anthony D. Smith (eds.), *Ethnicity*, New York: Oxford University Press, 1996.

Icduygu, Ahmet, David Romano, and Ibrahim Sirkeci, "The Ethnic Question in an Environment of Insecurity: The Kurds in Turkey," *Ethnic and Racial Studies* 22: 6 (November, 1999), 991–1010.

Ignatieff, Michael, *Blood and Belonging: The Road to Nowhere*, Video Documentary, BBC Wales, 1995.

The Warrior's Honor: Ethnic War and the Modern Conscience, Toronto: Viking Press, 1998.

Imset, Ismet G., *The PKK*, Ankara: Turkish Daily News Publications,1992.

Inal, Celal (ed.) *Demokrasi diye diye: "demokrasi radyosu" programlari*, Ankara: Toplum Sorunlari Arastirma Vakfi, undated.

Insan Halklari Dernegi (IHD), "Evaluation by Mr. Akin Birdal, President of the Human Rights Association, on the Human Rights Practices in 1997 in Turkey," Ankara, January, 1998.

International Human Rights Law Group, "Criminalizing Parliamentary Speech in Turkey," Washington DC, May, 1994.

Izady, Mehrdad, *The Kurds: A Concise Handbook*, Washington DC: Taylor and Francis, 1992.

Jackson, Robert, *Quasi-States: Sovereignty, International Relations, and the Third World*, Cambridge: Cambridge University Press, 1990.

Johnson, Chalmers, *Revolutionary Change*, Stanford: Stanford University Press, 1966.

Journal of Kurdish Studies, The, Volume 1, Louvain: Peters Press, 1995.

Kahraman, Ahmet, "Icte Teror, Dista da," *Ozgur Politika*, September 16, 2001 (http://www.ozgurpolitika.org/2001/10/16/hab41.html).

Karadaghi, Mustafa, *Kurdistan Times 3*, Fairfax: Kurdish Human Rights Watch, December, 1993.

Kedourie, Elie, *Nationalism*, London: Hutchinson & Co. Ltd., 1966.

Kedourie, Sylvia (ed.), *Turkey Before and After Ataturk*, London: Frank Cass, 1999.

Khalil, Samir al, *Republic of Fear: The Politics of Modern Iraq*, Los Angeles: University of California Press, 1989.

Kingston, Paul and Ian S. Spears (eds.), *States Within States: Incipient Political Entities in the Post-Cold War Era*, New York: Palgrave Macmillan, 2004.

Kirisci, Kemal and Gareth M. Winrow, *The Kurdish Question and Turkey*, London: Frank Cass, 1997.

Klandermans, Bert, *The Social Psychology of Protest*, Cambridge: Blackwell Publishers, Inc., 1997.

Klandermans, Bert, Hanspeter Kriesi, and Sidney Tarrow (eds.), *From Structure to Action: Comparing Social Movement Research Across Cultures*, International Social Movement Research 1, Greenwich: JAI Press, 1988.

Koohi-Kamali, Farideh, *The Political Development of the Kurds in Iran*, New York: Palgrave Macmillan, 2003.

Korn, David, "The Last Years of Mustafa Barzani," *Middle East Quarterly* (June, 1994), 13–24.

    "Interview with PKK Leader Abdullah Ocalan," http://www.etext.org/Politics/Arm.The.Spirit/Kurdistan/Articles/apo-korn-interview.txt, 1995.

Kramer, Heinz, *A Changing Turkey*, Washington DC: Brookings Institution Press, 2000.

Kreyenbroek, Philip G., and Stefan Sperl (eds.), *The Kurds: A Contemporary Overview*, London: Routledge, 1992.

Kurdish Information Center Toronto, "Information About the Kurdistan Workers Party PKK: Kurdistan a History of Oppression," ERNK undated document.

Kurdish Institute of Paris, "The New Turkish 'Anti-Terrorism' Law," *Information and Liason Bulletin*, 74–75 (May–June, 1991).

Kurzman, Charles, "Structural Opportunity and Perceived Opportunity in Social-Movement Theory: The Iranian Revolution of 1979," *American Sociological Review* 61: 1 (February 1996) 153–170.

Kut, Gün, "Burning Waters: The Hydropolitics of the Euphrates and Tigris," *New Perspectives on Turkey* 9 (Fall 1993), 1–17.

Kutschera, Chris, *Le Mouvement national kurde*, Paris: Flammarion, 1979.

    Le Défi kurde, Paris: Bayard Editions, 1997.

Lawrence, David Aquila, "A Shaky De Facto Kurdistan," *Middle East Report* 215:30:2 (Summer 2000), 24–27.

Leezenberg, Michiel, "The Kurds and the City," *The Journal of Kurdish Studies* 2 (1997), 57–62.

Lichbach, Mark Irving, "An Evaluation of 'Does Economic Inequality Breed Political Conflict?' Studies," *World Politics* 41: 4 (July, 1989), 431–470.

Lichbach, Mark Irving, and Alan S. Zuckerman, (eds.), *Comparative Politics: Rationality, Culture and Structure*, Cambridge: Cambridge University Press, 1997.

Makarenko, Vadim, "The Non-Existent State and the Unknown War ..." *New Times* (November, 1995), 50–53.

Makiya, Kanan, "The Anfal: Uncovering an Iraqi Campaign to Exterminate the Kurds," *Harper's Magazine* (May 1992), 53–61.

    Cruelty and Silence, New York: W. W. Norton and Company, 1993.

Mango, Andrew, "Turks and Kurds," *Middle Eastern Studies* 30: 4 (October, 1994), 1–25.

Marcus, Aliza, "City in the War Zone," *Middle East Report* 189 (July–August, 1994) 16–19.

"With the Kurdish Guerrillas," *Dissent* 41 (Spring, 1994), 178–181.

Mayall, Simon V., "Turkey: Thwarted Ambition," McNair Paper 56, Institute for National Strategic Studies, National Defense University, Washington DC, January 1997.

McAdam, Doug, John D. McCarthy, and Mayer N. Zald (eds.), *Comparative Perspectives on Social Movements: Political Opportunities, Mobilizing Structures, and Cultural Framings*, New York: Cambridge University Press, 1996.

McCready, William (ed.), *Culture, Ethnicity, and Identity*, New York: Academic Press, 1983.

McDowall, David. *A Modern History of the Kurds*, London: I. B. Taurus, 1997.

Medico International Germany and the Kurdish Human Rights Project, *The Destruction of Villages in South-East Turkey*, London, 1996.

Melson, Robert and Howard Wolpe, "Modernization and the Politics of Communalism: A Theoretical Perspective," *American Political Science Review* 64 (December 1970), 1112–1130.

Melucci, Alberto, "Getting Involved: Identity and Mobilization in Social Movements," *International Social Movement Research* 1, (Greenwich: JAI Press), 1988, pp. 329–348.

Middle East Report: The Kurdish Experience 189, July–August, 1994.

Migdal, Joel S., *Peasants, Politics, and Revolution: Pressures Towards Political and Social Change in the Third World*, Princeton: Princeton University Press, 1975.

Miller, Judith, and Laurie Mylroie, *Saddam Hussein and the Crisis in the Gulf*, New York: Times Books, 1990.

Minh, Ho Chi, *Ho Chi Minh on Revolution: Selected Writings*, Bernard B. Fall edition, New York: Frederick A. Praeger, Inc., 1967.

Mohammadi, Ali and Annabelle Sreberny-Mohammadi, *Small Media, Big Revolution*, Minneapolis: University of Minnesota Press, 1994.

Mojab, Shahrzad (ed.), *Women of a Non-State Nation: The Kurds*, Costa Mesa: Mazda Publishers, 2001.

Moore, Barrington Jr., *Social Origins of Dictatorship and Democracy: Lord and Peasant in the Making of the Modern World*, Boston: Beacon Press, 1967.

More, Christiane, *Les Kurdes aujourd'hui*, Paris: L'Harmattan, 1984.

Moris, Aldon and Carol M. Mueller (eds.), *Frontiers in Social Movement Theory*, New Haven: Yale University Press, 1992.

Munck, G., "Social Movements and Democracy in Latin America: Theoretical Debates and Comparative Perspectives," mimeo, 1991.

Nagel, Joan, "Conditions of Ethnic Separatism: The Kurds in Turkey, Iran, and Iraq," *Ethnicity* 7: 3 (September, 1980), 279–297.

Nash, Kate, *Contemporary Political Sociology: Globalization, Politics, and Power*, Oxford: Blackwell Publishers, Inc., 2000.

Nielsen, François, "Towards a Theory of Ethnic Solidarity in Modern Societies," *American Sociological Review* 50: 2 (1985), 133–149.

Nisan, Mordechai, *Minorities in the Middle East*, Jefferson, NC: McFarland, 1991.

Nouri Pasha, General Ihsan, *La Révolte de l'Agri-dagh*, Geneva: Editions Kurdes, 1986.

O'Ballance, Edgar, *The Kurdish Struggle: 1920–94*, London: Macmillan Press, Ltd., 1996.

Oberschall, Anthony, *Social Conflict and Social Movements*, Englewood Cliffs: Prentice-Hall, Inc., 1973.

Olson, Mancur, *The Logic of Collective Action*, Boston: Harvard University Press, 1965.

Olson, Robert, *The Emergence of Kurdish Nationalism and the Sheikh Said Rebellion, 1880–1925*, Austin: University of Texas Press, 1989.

Olson, Robert (ed.), *The Kurdish Nationalist Movement in the 1990s*, Lexington: The University Press of Kentucky, 1996.

Olzak, Susan, *The Dynamics of Ethnic Competition and Conflict*, Stanford: Stanford University Press, 1992.

Olzak, Susan and Joane Nagel (eds.), *Competitive Ethnic Relations*, New York: Academic Press, Inc., 1986.

Opp, Karl-Dieter, *The Rationality of Political Protest*, Boulder: Westview Press, Inc., 1989.

Ozbudun, Ergun, *Social Change and Political Participation in Turkey*, Princeton, NJ: Princeton University Press, 1976.

Ozoglu, Hakan, "'Nationalism' and Kurdish Notables in the Late Ottoman – Early Republican Era," *International Journal of Middle East Studies* 33 (2001), 383–409.

Permanent Mission of Turkey, Geneva, "Information Note," undated secret document.

Peuples Méditerranées, *Les Kurdes et les états*, no. 68–69, juillet–decembre 1994.

Popkin, Samuel L., *The Rational Peasant*, Berkeley: University of California Press, 1979.

Radu, Michael, "Is the PKK on the Ropes," E-Notes, Foreign Policy Research Institute, September 28, 1999.

Randal, Jonathan C., *After Such Knowledge, What Forgiveness? My Encounters with Kurdistan*, Oxford: Westview Press, 1999.

Romano, David, "Refugees and IDPs into the Maelstrom: Return Problems in Iraq," *Forced Migration Review*, Refugee Studies Center, University of Oxford (forthcoming in 2005).

"Alice Through the Looking Glass? Reflections on an Iraqi Sojourn," *Policy Options* Magazine, Institute for Research on Public Policy, 25: 11 (November 2004), 62–65.

"From Dictatorship to Democracy: Uniting Diversity in the Tent of Federalism," *Policy Options* Magazine, Institute for Research on Public Policy, 25: 02 (2004).

"Turmoil in Post-Saddam Iraq: Speed Bumps or Roadblocks?" *Policy Options* Magazine, Institute for Research on Public Policy, 25: 05 (2004).

"Modern Communications Technology in Ethnic Nationalist Hands: The Case of the Kurds," *Canadian Journal of Political Science*, 2002, 35: 1.

Ron, James, *Weapons Transfers and Violations of the Laws of War in Turkey*, Human Rights Watch, November 1995.

Rothschild, Joseph, *Ethnopolitics*, New York: Columbia University Press, 1981.

Rubin, Michael, "Interview: Barham Salih, Prime Minister, Kurdistan Regional Government (northern Iraq)," *Middle East Intelligence Bulletin* 3: 9 (September 2001), http://www.meib.org/issues/0109.htm.

Ryan, Nick, "Television Nation," *Wired Magazine* (March 1997), http://wired.com/wired/archive/5.12/scans.html.

Salih, Khaled, "Anfal: The Kurdish Genocide in Iraq," *Digest of Middle East Studies* 4: 2 (Spring, 1995), 24–39.

Samii, Bill, "Ethnicity Affects Parliament," *Iran Report* (October 15, 2001), Volume 4: 39, http://mywebpage.netscape.com/kurdistanobserve/15-10-01-rfe-kurdish-parliamentarians-resign.html.

Sammali, Jacqueline, *Etre Kurde, un délit?* Paris: L'Harmattan, 1995.

Scott, James C., *The Moral Economy of the Peasant*, New Haven: Yale University Press, 1976.

Serxwebun, "Interview with PKK leader Abdullah Ocalan," April 1995, translation by American Kurdish Information Network.

Shabazi, Hossein A., "Domestic and International Factors Precipitating Kurdish Ethnopolitical Conflict: A Comparative Analysis of Episodes of Rebellion in Iran, Iraq and Turkey," Ph.D. dissertation, University of Maryland: 1998.

Sim, Richard, "Kurdistan: The Search for Recognition," *Conflict Studies* 124 (November 1980), 1–9.

Skocpol, Theda, *States and Social Revolutions*, London: Cambridge University Press, 1979.

Smith, Anthony, *National Identity*, London: Penguin Books, 1991.

Snow, David, B. Rochford, S. Worden, and R. Benford, "Frame Alignment Processes, Micromobilization, and Movement Participation," *American Sociological Review* 51: 4 (July 1986), 464–481.

Spears, Ian S., "States Within States: Incipient Political Entities in the Post-Cold War Era," Paper presented at the University of Toronto, Munk Centre Conference on States Within States, October 20, 2001.

Stack, John F. (ed.), *Ethnic Identities in a Transnational World*, Westport: Greenwood Press, 1981.

The Primordial Challenge, New York: Greenwood Press, 1986.

Stansfield, Gareth R. V., *Iraqi Kurdistan: Political Development and Emergent Democracy*, London: Routledge Curzon, 2003.

Steinitz, Mark, "Insurgents, Terrorists and the Drug Trade," *The Washington Quarterly* (Fall 1985), 145–150.

Stephen, Chris, "When the Allies Leave," *New Statesman and Society* (June 7, 1991), 54–56.

Swidler, Ann, "Culture in Action: Symbols and Strategies," *American Sociological Review* 51: 2 (1986), 273–286.

Tajfel, Henri, "Experiments in Intergroup Discrimination," *Scientific American* 223 (November 1970), 96–102.

"Intergroup Behaviour, Social Comparison and Social Change," Katz-Newcomb Lectures, University of Michigan, Ann Arbor, mimeo, 1974.

Talabani, Nouri, *The Kurdish View on the Constitutional Future of Iraq*, London: Nouri Talabani (privately published), 1999.

"Ethnic Cleansing in Iraqi-Kurdistan," Kirkuk Trust for Research and Study (KTRS), 2000.

Taylor, Michael, *Rationality and Revolution*, New York: Cambridge University Press, 1988.

Thompson, Dennis L. and Dov Ronen (eds.), *Ethnicity, Politics, and Development* Boulder: Lynne Rienner Publishers, 1986.

Tilly, Charles, *From Mobilization to Revolution*, Reading: Addison-Wesley Publishing Company, 1978.

Tocqueville, Alexis de, *Democracy in America*, New York: Vintage, 1954.

Toprak, Binnaz, *Islam and Political Development in Turkey*, Leiden: E. J. Brill, 1981.

Touraine, Alain, *The Voice and the Eye: An Analysis of Social Movements*, New York: Cambridge University Press, 1981.

Treaties of Peace 1919–1923, The, Vol. II, Carnegie Endowment for International Peace, New York, 1924; via The World War I Document Archive, Brigham Young University, Harold B. Lee Library, Provo, Utah.

Tucker, Robert C. (ed.), *The Marx-Engels Reader*, London: W.W. Norton & Company, 1978.

Turkish Democracy Foundation, *Fact Book on Turkey: Kurds and the PKK Terrorism*, Ankara, May 1996.

Turkish Republic, Ministry of the Interior, "Secret T. C. Interior Ministry, Public Relations Office Chairmanship", Number: B050HID0000073/472 03/01/1997, Matter: Measures to be taken against PKK activities in 1997, Regarding: Prime Ministerial orders dated 12.11.1993," obtained from Kurdistan Informatie Centrum Nederland.

Turner, John C., "Social Comparison and Social Identity: Some Prospects for Intergroup Behaviour," *European Journal of Social Psychology* 5 (1975), 5–34.

Uclu, M. S., "Kurdistan'da Yeni Insan," *Serxwebun* (March 21–23, 1996).

United Nations, "Report of the Second Panel Established Pursuant to the Note by the President of the Security Council of 30 January 1999 (S/1999/100), Concerning the Current Humanitarian Situation in Iraq," March 30, 1999.

"Report of the Secretary-General Pursuant to Paragraph 5 of Resolution 1360 (2001)," Sept. 28, 2001.

United States Department of State, "Saddam Hussein's Iraq," Sept.13, 1999.

Human Rights Report: Turkey, 1992–2000.

US Congress, *Situation of Kurds in Turkey, Iraq and Iran: Briefing by the Commission on Security and Cooperation in Europe*, Washington DC: Government Printing Office, 1993.

Vali, Abbas, "Nationalism and Kurdish Historical Writing," *New Perspectives on Turkey* 14 (Spring 1996), 23–51.

"The Kurds and Their 'Others': Fragmented Identity and Fragmented Politics," *Comparative Studies of South Asia, Africa and the Middle East* 18: 2 (1998), 82–95.

Vanly, Ismet Chériff, *Le Kurdistan irakien: entité nationale*, Neuchatel: Les Editions de la Baconnière, 1970.

Vanly, Ismet Serif, *Survey of the National Question of Turkish Kurdistan*, Europe: Hevra, Organization of the Revolutionary Kurds of Turkey in Europe, 1971.

"Kurdistan, the Kurds and the Kurdish National Question: Historical Background and Perspective," background paper prepared for the Preparatory Commission for Parliament of Kurdistan in Exile, 1993.

Wahlbeck, Osten, *Kurdish Diasporas*, New York: St. Martin's Press, Inc., 1999.

Waldner, David, *State Building and Late Development*, Ithaca: Cornell University Press, 1999.

Warreport, Special Feature: The Crushing of Kurdish Civil Society, November/ December, 1996.

Weber, Eugen, *Peasants into Frenchmen*, Stanford: Stanford University Press, 1976.

Weber, Max, *From Max Weber: Essays in Sociology*, New York: Oxford University Press, 1958.

Weiner, Myron, "Peoples and States in a New Ethnic Order?" *Third World Quarterly* 13: 4 (1992), 317–333.

Weir, Stuart, "In Iraqi Kurdistan: Living Short, with Dignity," *New Statesman* 4: 2 (Winter 1993), 63–65.

White, Paul, *Primitive Rebels or Revolutionary Modernizers? The Kurdish National Movement in Turkey*, London: Zed Books, 2000.

Wolf, Eric, *Peasant Wars of the Twentieth Century*, New York: Harper and Row, 1969.

Yalcin-Heckmann, Lale, *Tribe and Kinship among the Kurds*, Frankfurt: Peter Lang, 1991.

Yassin, Borhanedin A., *Vision or Reality? The Kurds in the Policy of the Great Powers, 1941–1947*, Lund: Lund University Press, 1995.

Yavuz, Hakan (ed.), *Journal of Muslim Minority Affairs* 18: 1 (April 1998).

Yegen, Mesut, "The Turkish State Discourse and the Exclusion of Kurdish Identity", *Middle Eastern Studies* 32: 2 (April 1996), 216–229.

Young, Crawford, *The Politics of Cultural Pluralism*, London: The University of Wisconsin Press, 1976.

"Patterns of Social Conflict: State, Class and Ethnicity," *Daedalus* 111: 2 (Spring 1982), 71–98.

Index